Dr Burney at Calis in the Year 1770

CHARLES BURNEY, MUS.D.

MUSIC,
MEN, AND MANNERS
IN FRANCE AND
ITALY
1770

Being the Journal written by
CHARLES BURNEY, Mus.D.

during a Tour through those Countries
undertaken to collect material for

A General History of Music

Transcribed from the Original Manuscript
in the British Museum
Additional Manuscript 35122
and Edited with an Introduction by

H. EDMUND POOLE

EULENBURG BOOKS
LONDON

Originally published by the Folio Society in 1969

This edition first published in 1974 by
Ernst Eulenburg Ltd
48 Great Marlborough Street, London WIV 2BN

Reprinted 1977, 1980

Add. MS. 35122 is printed by courtesy of the
Trustees of the British Museum

Introduction, and Notes
© The Folio Society Ltd 1969

ISBN 0 903873 03 6 paperback
0 903873 16 8 hardback

Printed and bound in Great Britain by
Page Bros (Norwich) Ltd

CONTENTS

Contents

ILLUSTRATIONS

Permission to reproduce originals is gratefully acknowledged to Mr. James
Osborn (Frontispiece); The Trustees of the British Museum (1, 2, 3, 5, 9,
10, 12, 14); Mr. Edward Croft-Murray (4); The Trustees of the National
Gallery (6); The National Gallery of Victoria, Melbourne, Australia (7);
The Harry R. Beard Theatre Collection (8); The Victoria and Albert
Museum (11); The Labatorio Photographico della Soprintendenza alle
Gallerie, Napoli (13).

MAPS

The map on pages 32 and 33 is reproduced from *Guida per il viaggio
d'Italia in posta*. Nuova editione. Genoa, 1786. The rest are reproduced
from C. Barbieri, *Direzione pe' viaggiatoria in Italia*, Bologna, 1771. The
books from which the maps were taken are in the collection of Mr. Edward
Croft-Murray.

ACKNOWLEDGEMENTS

THIS edition of the Journal which Dr. Charles Burney kept during his visit to France and Italy in 1770 was prepared in twelve months to meet a fixed publication date. The text of the manuscript was transcribed, studied, annotated and otherwise worked over at home at the end of days taken up with very different pursuits. Under this pressure I importuned friends–and strangers–beyond the limits accepted by tradition as decent in editors, and I am grateful for the generous way in which they responded to what may well have seemed peremptory and unreasonable demands for information in fields where they had special knowledge and I had little or none.

To two friends I am particularly grateful, as without their support the enterprise would have foundered. Mr. Edward Croft-Murray, C.B.E. not only helped with the collection of illustrations, but laid his wide knowledge of Italy and the arts of the period unreservedly at my disposal, and opened many doors.

Dr. C. E. Wright, the Deputy Keeper of Manuscripts in the British Museum, directed me along many short cuts through the Burney collections, provided details about the accession of the Journal to the Museum and assisted me in clearing up doubtful readings.

Although the amount of Burney material in the British Museum is substantial there is much more in America, notably in the Osborn Collection at Yale. Mr. James Marshall Osborn was kind enough to allow me to study and quote from a micro-film of a manuscript version of those parts of the Journal, which Charles Burney did not publish in the printed editions of 1771 and 1773 but late in life prepared for inclusion in his memoirs. In addition he offered from his collection an hitherto unknown portrait of Charles Burney for reproduction as a frontispiece to this book. For these kindnesses and for his sustained interest in the project I am most grateful.

To Professor Joyce Hemlow, whose biography *Fanny Burney* first introduced me to the rich complexity of the family affairs of the Burneys, I owe much: she pushed me on with good advice and was kind enough to dredge up some facts for me during her own researches at Somerset House in the spring of 1968.

I am much indebted to Dr. Roger Lonsdale's splendid book *Dr. Charles Burney, a Literary Biography* (1965). As well as dealing with Burney's literary activities in their setting more fully than has ever been attempted before, Dr. Lonsdale has sketched in much new

Acknowledgements

biographical material based upon primary manuscript sources of which I have taken advantage.

The written transcript of the Journal reproducing as it does all Burney's variants, contractions, corrections and alterations is a daunting sight, and I am full of admiration for the skill, and gratitude for the speed and accuracy, with which Elizabeth Marshall found her way through my editorial indications and at first intention typed an all but perfect setting copy for the printer.

For help with special problems I am indebted to Dr. Ursula Hoff, Curator of Prints and Drawings at the National Gallery of Victoria, Melbourne, Australia; Alec King, Superintendent of the Music Room at the British Museum; Miss Helen Wallis, Superintendent of the Map Room at the British Museum; A. Graham Reynolds, Keeper, and Jonathan Mayne, Assistant Keeper, of Prints and Drawings, Victoria and Albert Museum; The Director the Photographic Services at the British Museum; F. H. W. Sheppard, General Editor, the Survey of London; Dr. S. R. Parks, the Librarian the James Marshall and Marie-Louise Osborn Collection, Yale University Library; D. G. C. Allan, Curator-Librarian, Royal Society of Arts; R. J. D. Smith, Past Master and Clerk The Worshipful Company of Coach-makers and Coach Harness Makers; J. O. H. Norris of Joseph Cockshoot and Company Ltd, an authority on coach building; Miss Jean M. Kennedy, City and County Archivist, Norfolk and Norwich Record Office; Noel Coward; R. H. Hubbard, Chief Curator, the National Gallery of Canada; The Librarian, City of Westminster Public Libraries; R. C. Kenedy, Assistant Keeper the Library the Victoria and Albert Museum; The Librarian, The Guildhall Library, Corporation of London; Mrs. Walter Emery; James C. Fraser and Harry R. Beard.

To my wife–who created the domestic atmosphere which made it seem the most natural thing in the world that for months on end I should spend night after night, week-end after week-end, in un-sociable isolation pursuing Burney and his doings, and who concerned herself with arduous preparatory work on the index–I owe most of all.

H. E. P.

INTRODUCTION

IN his *Instructions and directions for Forraine Travell* (1650) James Howell laid it down that any man who undertook a *Peregrination*

> must alwayes have a *Diary* about him, when he is in motion of Iourneys to set down what either his eares heare, or his *Eyes* meetes with most remarquable in the day time, out of which he may raise matter of discours at night, and let him take it for a rule, that *Hee offend lesse who writes many toyes, than he, who omits one serious thing*. For *the* Penne *maketh the deepest furrowes, and doth fertilize, and enrich the memory more than any thing else,*
> *Littera* scripta *manet*, sed *manant* lubrica *verba*.

Many such diaries have survived: the majority dull and compounded from second-hand material, a few lively with original observation and containing new and valuable information. Among this minority is the Journal which Charles Burney kept during a tour of France and Italy in 1770. At this time Burney was a successful professional musician, a doctor of music (Oxford), a bookish man well known in the world of letters, with influential friends in fashionable society. He was laying the foundations of his *History of Music* which was to bring him fame; a man of substance in fact; but he had known many vicissitudes.

Charles Burney was the son of James Macburney, the third of that name. This James was born at Great Hanwood, Shropshire, in 1678 and later moved to London where he was a day scholar at Westminster School. He was well grounded in school learning, and his son Charles later recalled some of his many other accomplishments: 'he danced remarkably well, performed well on the violin, and was a portrait painter of no mean talents': in this last art he had been trained by Michael Dahl, a celebrated Swedish portraitist settled in London. In 1697 James eloped with a young actress, Rebecca Ellis, 'then in her sixteenth year', was disinherited by his father, and cast on his own resources. He had to exploit his musical and artistic talents to support his rapidly growing family and he seems to have had a very up and down existence, often on the move, 'unsteady' in his conduct. He was at Shrewsbury in 1720 when his wife died: he married again within a year. His second wife was Anne Cooper, daughter to a 'herald painter'; she had a small fortune. She bore James Macburney five children: the last two born on 7 April (old style) 1726 were twins, Charles and Susanna. Although the twins appear in the parish register as 'Mackburny', the prefix was dropped about this time and the boy was always known as Charles Burney.

[ix]

In early childhood he was sent with his elder brother Richard to Condover where they were under the care of a Nurse Ball, and by about 1737 Charles was attending the Free School at Shrewsbury. In 1739 he joined his family–now in Chester–and entered Chester Free School as a King's Scholar. Charles seems to have received his first formal music lessons from Edmund Baker, the organist of Chester Cathedral. He tired of Chester in 1742 and ran away to Shrewsbury where he joined his half brother James who was organist at St Mary's Church. As James's assistant, he was kept hard at work, but he found that his brother could teach him little; he worked at his musical education alone. Encouragement from eminent visiting organists stimulated him to make great efforts to extend his knowledge in many fields:

> ... besides writing, teaching, tuning and playing for my Brother, at my *momens perdus*, I was educating myself in every way I was able ... I tried at least to keep up the little Latin I had learned. Practiced both the spinet and violin many hours a day, which with reading, transcribing music and poetry, attempts at Composition, and my brother's affairs filled up every hour of the longest day.

He had lessons in dancing, the violin and French, too. He was no prig, however: he had a passion for angling and enjoyed playing with other boys.

Disappointed in his brother and warmly entreated by his father, Charles returned to Chester in 1743 and devoted himself relentlessly to his music, composing , practising on the keyboard and playing with professional musicians in the town. Chester was a busy port for travellers taking passage to and from Ireland: Charles had seen Handel making his way to Dublin for the first public performance of *Messiah* in 1741; two years later he met and played with the master of the King's Band in Ireland, a famous violinist Matthew Dubourg who was a friend of James Macburney. In 1744 Charles was introduced by his teacher Edmund Baker to Thomas Augustine Arne, the leading English composer of the day, who broke his journey at Chester on his way from Dublin to London where he was to take up an appointment as composer to Drury Lane Theatre. Arne was impressed by young Burney's powers and after negotiation offered to take him to London as his apprentice for seven years without premium. Burney, aged eighteen, reached London in September 1744 and was plunged into an endless round of routine work. He was expected to transcribe Arne's music for Drury Lane, teach it to the singers as required, attend rehearsals, play in orchestras and pass any earnings on to his master. His drudgery was relieved by his meetings with eminent musicians of the day and by the welcome he received at the home of

Introduction

Arne's sister, Mrs Susannah Maria Cibber where, among wits, poets, actors, authors and men of letters, Burney's own considerable social gifts, inherited from his father, were called into play and developed. Arne was a slave driver and had many other unpleasant characteristics which Burney recorded, but did not publish, and his apprentice's life would have been harsh indeed but for the kindness of Mrs Arne who watched over the young man's welfare with an almost parental solicitude.

In the summer of 1746 Fulke Greville, while trying a harpsichord in the house of Kirkman the maker, asked his host if he knew any young musician 'who had a mind and cultivation, as well as finger and ear' and who was fit company for a gentleman. Kirkman suggested Burney and arranged for him to attend, ostensibly to demonstrate the qualities of several instruments for the benefit of Greville. Greville was impressed by Burney's musical knowledge and technical skill, and at a later interview was taken no less by the young man's conversation. Greville was eager to appoint Burney as his domestic musician, but Arne was unwilling to cancel his apprentice's indentures; however he did give Burney leave (at a price which Greville paid) to go with Greville to his country house at Wilbury, near Andover. Here and at Bath Burney played for Greville and his friends. On due date Burney returned to his servitude with Arne, but his life in London was made more rewarding by the attention of Lord Holdernesse who had met Burney at Wilbury and who now invited the young man freely to visit his house and encouraged him in his career. Nor did Greville on his visits to London forget his young musician.

In the autumn of 1747 Burney again visited Wilbury where he met Samuel Crisp, a man of wide culture with a passion for Italian music. Greville and Crisp, says Dr Lonsdale, 'won him from his "ancient worship" of Handel Geminiani, and Corelli ("the divinities of my youth") to a taste for such composers as Scarlatti, Hasse, and Pergolesi, which was to orientate his musical thought for the next forty years'.

In 1748 Fulke Greville married and in the same year he paid £300 to Arne to transfer Burney's apprenticeship to him. Burney's association with Greville, his wife and his friends was of the highest importance to his development. His run of the mill work for Arne made him only too well aware of the position of social inferiority to which the majority of musicians had to accommodate themselves in the eighteenth century. (The social ease and familiarity with good company which Dubourg had shown during his visit to James Macburney at Chester in 1743 was matter for remark to the young Charles Burney.) In the Greville household he was given a position which he could respect; it was carefully established and safeguarded: he was never relegated to the position of servant. He lived a familiar among people of wealth, cultivated in literature, music and all the arts. In this atmosphere the range of his interests and information widened, his mind was formed along wide perspectives, he won the esteem and friendship of men and women of rank and influence who were later to come to his aid in time of need; most important, perhaps, his aspirations were lifted: never would he be content henceforth to be a 'mere musician'.

He had other aspirations also: with Greville's consent Burney married on 25 June 1749. His wife was Esther Sleepe, a gifted and elegant girl, who had already borne him a daughter–Esther too–in May 1749. Burney, now released by Greville, entered upon a busy professional life as organist, solo performer on the harpsichord, teacher and later as a composer of music for theatrical pieces under Garrick's management (*Robin Hood*, December 1750, *Queen Mab*, a pantomime, 26 December 1750, *The Masque of Alfred*, 23 February 1751).

In the spring of 1751 Burney was taken seriously ill. Dr John Armstrong, an eminent physician (poet and essayist too), was called in but he could not diagnose the condition. The patient was moved to Canonbury House, Islington, away from the smoke and grime of London: but without much improvement. Then, through the influence of friends, Burney was offered the appointment of organist at St Margaret's Church, King's Lynn. This he accepted and travelled to Norfolk in September 1751 leaving his wife and three children in London.They followed him in 1752 probably in the spring. Burney had thought little of the attractions of society in King's Lynn when he arrived, but his opinion changed as he found himself warmly received by the professional and other cultivated inhabitants of the town. His charm and intellectual powers commended him to the local nobility–most notably the third Earl of Orford who invited him to Houghton, encouraged his pursuits, and gave him free run of the magnificent collection of pictures there. In 1754 a superb new organ built by John Snetzler replaced the 'execrably bad' instrument which Burney found at St Margaret's when he arrived. He and his wife read together in an amazing range of subjects which covered as he said 'history, voyages, poetry, and science, as far as Chambers's Dictionary, the French Encyclopédie, and the Philosophical Transactions could carry us'. He was busy in French, Latin and Italian as well as English. He entered into correspondence with Samuel Johnson (February 1755) on the subject of the *Dictionary* for which Burney collected six subscribers. His reputation was growing, his interests were varied, his social life was full and rewarding in every way, but friends in London urged him to leave provincial fame and to resume his career in the capital. It was not until 1760 however that he heeded their advice.

In London he was soon as busy as he wished: his success as a teacher hardly left him 'an hour unappropriated to some fair disciple'. His prosperity seemed assured, but his happiness received a cruel blow with the death of his wife in September 1762. Disconsolate, he forced himself to keep going and in 1763 occupied himself in new theatre projects with David Garrick which were not rewarding. At Garrick's suggestion he adapted Rousseau's opera *Le Devin du Village* for presentation in English. It was put on at Drury Lane as *The Cunning Man* on 21 November 1766, but met with only qualified success. In 1767 a misunderstanding with Garrick over a commission to write some music for a burletta called *Orpheus* so upset Burney that he decided never again to write music for the stage. The same year brought pleasure too. He was appointed 'Extra Musician' in the King's Band which gave him a little honour and a small supplement to his income, and on 2 October he married Mrs Allen, the widow of Stephen Allen, a friend of the Burneys from their days at Lynn. This marriage, providing as it did a step-mother's care for Burney's own children and family stability for Mrs Allen's three, enabled Burney to pursue his career with more assurance.

His next step, however, was not successful. He proposed himself as composer of the music for the Ode that was to commemorate the installation of the Duke of Grafton as Chancellor of the University of Cambridge in July 1769. His offer was accepted but the project misfired. This was doubly unfortunate, for Burney had hoped that his music would not only install the Chancellor but would lead to his own election as a doctor of music by the university.

Frustrated at Cambridge he decided to try his luck at Oxford: he matriculated from University College on 20 June 1769, his exercise was 'performed with singular applause' two days later and he took the degrees of Mus.B. and Mus.D. on 23 June. The importance of this achievement is stressed by Dr Lonsdale: 'The Oxford doctorate . . . marks the turning-point in his life, the moment at which he made his last bid for fame, no longer as a "mere musician", but as a scholar and a man of letters.'

He pursued this road to the end of his life. His published works cover a variety of subjects, but his fame and importance rest upon his *General History of Music* and on two curtain raisers, the accounts of his journeys to France and Italy, and to Germany, the Netherlands and the United Provinces, both of which he undertook in order to collect material for his major work. There is no evidence to say when exactly Burney developed his plan for writing a history of music. He often referred to his days at Lynn as the period of its germination: as we have seen, he read voraciously there and he was collecting books on music at that time. There is no doubt, however, that in the winter of 1769–70 he began 'seriously to concentrate his meditation, and arrange his schemes' so as to lay down a basis for his history.

The first statement of his intention is preserved in a letter dated 27 May 1770 to the Rev. William Mason, where he says that encouraged by friends he had already spent time meditating upon the task of writing a *History of Music* and collecting materials. After making the point that nobody had ever before attempted a history of music in English he speculates on current theories about ancient music–Greek and Roman and that which followed Guido Aveline–and concludes:

> I have got together and consulted an incredible number of books and tracts on the subject with more disappointment and disgust than satisfaction, for they are, in general, such faithful copies of each other, that by reading two or three, you have the substance of as many hundred. It is far more easy to complete a dull book of bits and scraps from these writers, than to get any one to read it after it is done. I have therefore determined to fly to Italy this summer, and to allay my thirst of knowledge at the pure source, which I am unable to do by such spare draughts as are to be attained from the polluted works through which it is conducted to us here. No one that I know of has gone into Italy merely upon such an errand, though the Italians at present surpass the rest of Europe in no one art so much as in their music.

He travelled through France and Italy in 1770, Germany and the Low Countries in 1772, and, in 1773, he was writing the first volume of his *History* which was published in 1776 (Burney presented a splendidly bound copy to the Queen–to whom at the author's request Johnson had written a dedication–on 25 January). The second volume appeared in 1782, the third and fourth volumes in 1789. The sixteen years covered in this progress were full of chances and changes: his writing was laid aside while he directed his energies to other ventures. In 1774 he was involved in an ill-fated attempt to establish, on the model of the Italian conservatorios, a public music school in the Foundling Hospital in London. In 1784 he was drawn into the preparations for the musical celebrations commemorating the centenary of Handel's birth, and he wrote an account of the performances (with a life of Handel) which appeared–much delayed by the King's intervening enthusiasm–on 17 January 1785. He was handicapped by bouts of crippling rheumatism and by the death of friends who had materially assisted him with the writing and launching of the first two volumes of his *History*. On the other hand, the fame which had come to him as a result of his *History* had brought him the stimulation and comfort of a new circle of friends whose company he enjoyed and to whom he was ever willing to devote his time. In December 1776 he was engaged as music teacher to Queeney, the eldest daughter of the Thrales, and it was not long before Burney was in high favour at Streatham, welcome as a visitor and able to enjoy the fellowship and conversation of others in the circle – Johnson (his idol), Garrick, Reynolds, Murphy, and Boswell among others. This happy conclave, providing as it did for Burney the company he most enjoyed, and particularly the long hours of talk with Johnson, broke up in the 1780s after the death of Thrale and the development of Mrs Thrale's passion for Gabriel Piozzi. The survivors, including Burney, consoled themselves at the Essex Head Club which Johnson had formed in 1783. In 1783, as a result of Burke's interest, Burney was appointed Organist at Chelsea College but the organist's appartments were occupied and he was not able to move in until 1787. He remained at Chelsea Hospital, busy with his *History* and with the articles he wrote during 1801–5 for *The Cyclopaedia* (edited by Abraham Rees), with material for his memoirs, and with other projects until his death on 12 April 1814.

The decision to make the journey to France and Italy cannot have been taken lightly: it is true that most of his pupils were out of London for the summer and his loss of earnings would not be great, but the cost of the venture, unsubsidised as it was by loan, gift or subscription, must have been substantial, for not only did he have to meet the normal charges of travel – transportation and sustenance – he had to lay out money to buy books, engravings and music, and fee copyists and artists. He took with him letters of recommendation 'to the several ambassadors and ministers from our Court' in the countries through which he was to travel, and perhaps more valuable still he had letters of introduction to men of learning in Paris and in the provincial cities of Italy, and he accumulated others as he made his scholarly progress.

Burney was not unfamiliar with the dangers and difficulties of travel in Europe. He had already been twice to France and he was familiar with at least some of the most important contemporary accounts of Italy. The dangers and difficulties were very real. At Dover the traveller could look back on his journey from London and congratulate himself that he had survived the passage along the Old Kent Road to New Cross, over Bleak or Black Heath, Shooter's Hill, long the haunt of footpads and highwaymen, Gad's Hill (similarly unsavoury), Rochester and the Medway marshes, Harbledown and Canterbury, where the night was spent, and then on to Dover, a town 'commonly termed a den of thieves: and,' continues Smollett, 'I am afraid it is not altogether without reason, it has acquired this appellation. The people are said to live by piracy in time of war; and by smuggling and fleecing strangers in time of peace: but I will do them the justice to say, they make no distinction between foreigners and natives.' The cross channel service was maintained by packet boats which sailed, weather and other exigencies permitting, three times a week. Those who could afford five guineas could have a boat for their exclusive use: in Burney's day any gentleman could have passage for half a guinea and his servant for five shillings. Before striking a bargain with the ship master for his journey the traveller was advised by all the old hands to stipulate that he was to be carried into the harbour at Calais. Otherwise, on the pretext of low water or other natural mischance, he might be transhipped at sea and rowed ashore, much to his discomfort and cost, and much to the advantage of the ship's captain who so avoided the payment of 28s port duty.

Once on board, the traveller could prepare himself for a crossing that might last four hours or three times four hours, or more, and speculate about the chances of the voyage arising inevitably from the weather, the state of the sea, the quality of the boat and its captain and the characteristics of the other passengers. Never make new acquaintances at Dover, at sea, or at Calais was a maxim of travel. Safely arrived at Calais – either landed in proper form from the packet boat or tumbled from a small boat run up on to the sand – the voyager was taken before an officer and asked his name, occupation and reason for travelling, and his luggage was taken to the custom house for later examination. If he had horses or a coach with him they would be taken to his hotel – the Silver Lion, the post house kept by Grandsire, or the *Hôtel d'Angleterre* the establishment of M. Dessein (or Dessin) who not only kept a good house, but, at a price, could also provide the traveller with an English or reliable French vehicle for his journey onwards. He would also buy it back again, at a discount on the return.

In England at this time there were basically four ways of travelling: to take one's own carriage and horses (which few could afford); to take one's own carriage and hire horses stage by stage; to hire a chaise or some other vehicle and horses stage by stage or to jog along in the public stage coach. This same pattern held in France and Italy too where the roads were divided by 'posts' rather than 'stages'. Burney himself summarises the practice in Italy:

There are several ways of travelling in *Italy*, such as with post-horses; with a vettura or hired chaise or calash in which they do not change horses; with a cambiatura or chaise that changes horses; and finally with a procaccio or stage coach that undertakes to furnish passengers with provisions and necessary accommodation on the road. Of these, the cambiatura was the most convenient.

Although road vehicles existed in great variety, differences in name did not always indicate more than minor differences in type. They were all based essentially on two originals: the two wheel car or chariot, and the four wheel agricultural or timber wagon. Perhaps the most familiar of the two wheel type was the French *chaise de poste*. It had a small body, very little longer than a sedan chair; in front there was a door hinged at the bottom which fell forward on to a dash board. There was a window in each side. According to G. A. Thrupp in *The History of Coaches* (1877) the chaise 'was hung upon two very lofty wheels and long shafts for one horse, and the body was rather in front of the wheels . . . It was suspended at first upon leather braces only, but later upon two upright or whip springs behind, and two elbow springs in front from the body to the cross-bar, which joined the shafts and carried the steps.' A second horse, ridden by the postillion, was usually attached to an outrigger-bar on the side of the shafts.

The four wheel coach was basically a closed vehicle made of wood with a hard top covered with leather and suspended by leather braces and steel springs above the 'carriage' or lower framework to which the wheels were attached. The coach had two seats across its width with accommodation for two or three passengers on each, *vis à vis*. 'The widths usual for the inside of bodies . . . was 3 feet 5 inches for two persons, and 4 feet to 4 feet 2 inches, for three persons on each seat. The height of the seat from the floor was 14 inches, and from the roof 3 feet 6 inches to 3 feet 9 inches.' The French stage coaches or *diligences* had large bodies with three small windows on each side and were hung by leather braces on long perch carriages with tall rear wheels and low front wheels. They were fitted with large baskets back and front for passengers or baggage. There was no driving box; they were drawn by five horses and driven by a postillion on the off wheeler. The fastest diligence, Paris–Lyons, had springs and travelled at between five and six miles an hour.

The coachmaker's art could produce superb vehicles, matched by wonderful harness and furnishings: the average was much less than splendid:

In the shafts of our chaise [wrote the Rev. W. Jones in his *Observations in a Journey to Paris* (1777)] they place a horse of the cart-breed, but below the size of our drawing horses, harnessed with ropes and a great wooden collar. By the sides of the shaft-horse are two ponies, on one of which the postillion rides, with boots, literally as big as two oyster-barrels, and armed with hoops of iron, to save his legs in case of accidents. The horses used for this work are generally stallions and therefore vicious and quarrelsome.

The French roads were the best in Europe in the eighteenth century: they had a stone pavement in the middle, called the *pavé*, wide enough for two carriages to pass and on either side a road of natural earth, the *parterre* which was comfortable to ride on in the summer but not passable in wet weather or winter. The roads in Italy were generally inferior to the French. Their quality varied from state to state: some stretches were excellent, others were so bad that the vibration set up by the inequalities and surface conditions of the road was intense enough to damage the luggage and seriously to shake up the travellers.

Of two things the traveller was absolutely certain: that the postillions in France and the vetturini in Italy were in league with inn keepers to fleece the helpless traveller, and that French and Italian inns were dirty and the food they offered poor. Let Smollett summarise many longer tales of woe and vexation:

> The house was dismal and dirty beyond all description; the bed-cloaths filthy enough to turn the stomach of a muleteer; and the victuals cooked in such a manner, that even a Hottentot could not have beheld them without loathing. We had sheets of our own, which were spread upon a mattress, and here I took my repose wrapped in a great coat if that could be called repose which was interrupted by the innumerable stings of vermin.

Travellers in Italy were advised by Thomas Nugent in *The Grand Tour*, one of the most widely used guides to European travel, to carry a complete bed with them or failing this 'to make provision of a light quilt, a pillow, a coverlet, and two very fine bed cloths'. The minimum requirement was that the traveller should take sheets 'and upon coming to an indifferent inn, where the bed may happen to look suspicious, you may call for fresh straw and lay a clean sheet over it'.

The roads were infested with highwaymen ready to pounce on treasure unwisely exhibited by a traveller: and according to Nugent there were many villains

> ready to murder or assassinate a stranger in private houses, when they happen to have a prospect of some considerable prey. For this reason a traveller should always be furnished with some iron machine to shut his door on the inside, which may be easily contrived, and made of several sorts; for it frequently happens that the doors of the lodging-rooms have neither locks nor bolts, and *opportunity*, according to the old proverb, *makes the thief*. 'Tis proper also to travel with arms, such as a sword and

pair of pistols, and likewise with a tinder-box in order to strike a fire in case of any accident in the night.

Accidents were to be expected on the road too: wheels could fly off, the axle tree or some other part of the carriage might fail. For these emergencies hammer and nails, spare iron pins, knives and other tools and a bladder of grease were the minimum required.

Difficulties, if not dangers, arose among passengers out of the very physical conditions under which they travelled. It was often necessary to find somebody to share a chaise or carriage at very short notice. There was no opportunity to take up references or judge his character before you committed yourself to his company perhaps for days or weeks. To commit yourself to share a small vehicle with a stranger must have been bad enough: to share a bedroom, or bed even, must have been penance. Some strangers no doubt made delightful companions, others were less desirable: apart from the vicious and dishonest there were the bores, the contentious, noisy and quarrelsome; there were those who argued about every bill, were disagreeable with the vetturini, complained in a hectoring way about food and accommodation and were the centre of perpetual ill-feeling wherever they went. To the quiet and ruminative traveller such companions were dear at any price, but they had to be endured. So had other inconveniences: the inevitable early start (1.30 a.m., 4.30 a.m., and so on), the rudimentary protection against the weather in some chaises, the manhandling of heavy luggage at post houses and state boundaries, the gross discomfort of the diligences, where passengers in their heavy travelling clothes were so tight packed as to be in danger of suffocating, the dizziness and travel sickness caused by the swaying of the vehicle on its straps and rudimentary springs.

Slight indispositions arising from infection or from the local diet were common, but unless the traveller came from home prepared with tried palliatives he would be at a loss to know what to obtain abroad: nor were doctors easy to find except in the large towns. A serious illness threw the sufferer upon the good nature of his fellows to see him safe with a roof over his head, summon medical aid and warn his family and friends by post or messenger.

To travel fully equipped to study the country and its antiquities called for a great deal of luggage. Apart from a bed and linen, clothes (fine and rough), food, weapons of defence and the other gear mentioned above, the voyager bent upon the pursuit of information required a measuring rod to take dimensions of things, a mariner's compass and quadrant and 'prospective glasses'. Not many travellers were so completely fitted out: most wayfarers travelled light and put up with the discomforts and inconveniences of the road as they found them; but however they travelled–in comfort or rough–maps and guide books were essential to the stranger. Guide books were of two main kinds: the accounts of other travellers who had passed over the ground before him, and guide books proper issued locally and dealing exhaustively with the history and antiquities of the region. The early accounts of travellers in Italy (George Sandys, for example, 1615) were very general and were concerned with what the author saw and did, but later books such as Joseph Addison's *Remarks on Italy* (1705) and Thomas Nugent's *The Grand Tour* (1749) set out to give the traveller detailed information about how to travel–cost, means, state of the roads, posting regulations, the quality of the inns, currency, etc–and books of this kind became the model for later and fuller guides containing systematised travel information. Detail was particularly important in Italy where the peninsula was divided in 1770 between nine major states all with frontier regulations, different customs formalities, different currencies and different laws.

Another essential aide in large towns was the *valet de place* and his Italian equivalent, who for a stated fee would escort his temporary master about to show him the way around the sights or to particular addresses for appointments.

Burney left Dover on 7 June 1770, was in Paris by 11 June and into Italy (Turin) on 12 July. As he explained in a letter to David Garrick, written on 17 October 1770 from Naples, he had two objects in view when he left England

> the one to get, from the libraries to the viva voce conversation of the learned, what information I could relative to the music of the ancients; and the other was to judge with my own eyes of the *present state* of modern music in the places through which I should pass, from the performance and conversation of the first musicians in Italy.

He was systematic in his researches. He mentions tablets for his notes, he had a memorandum book, he had at least one blank book for the extracts which he copied from books and manuscripts, he had a music journal. He had his general travel journal in which he kept a day by day record of musical and non-musical information and anecdote. This has been preserved and is now printed entire for the first time. He wrote his journal from notes and recollection when occasion offered; during a halt on the road in the discomfort of a post house with hands cramped with cold or rheumatism; or at his ease in the comfort of a good inn, when his elegant and flowing hand reflects the pleasure with which he recalls and gives form to his impressions of the day–the sights on the road, the people he had met, the antiquities, the events musical and social. As the material he collected grew under his hand it acquired a life of its own: 'As my general history must be a work of time,' Burney says in his letter of 17 October 1770 to Garrick, 'I intend publishing, as soon as I get home, in a pamphlet, or small volume, an account of the present state of music in France and Italy, in which I shall describe, according to my judgment and feelings the merits of the several compositions and performances I have heard in travelling through those countries.'

When he reached home, and while the books, music and other material he had collected for his *History* in France and Italy was being assembled in one place, he returned to the idea of separate publication of his French and Italian tour, and in 1771 consulted those of his friends whose judgement he most valued – David Garrick, Mr Mason, the Earl of Holdernesse and John Hawkesworth. At their suggestion he agreed to omit from his published journal 'all that was miscellaneous of observation or of anecdote' on the grounds that France and Italy had been so written over by travellers that there was nothing left to be said. On the other hand Burney's information about music, unfamiliar, up to the minute, would meet a ready demand in its own right, and blaze a trail for the *History* too. He was rather shaken in his resolution when his old and valued friend Samuel Crisp found the whole journal entertaining and urged that it be published in full. Burney persisted in his earlier decision however: he worked up the musical substance of his journal, supplemented from other sources deriving from his tour, and excluded the miscellaneous, non-musical aspects of his journey. *The Present State of Music in France and Italy: or The Journal of a Tour through those Countries undertaken to collect Materials for a General History of Music* was published on 3 May 1771. The first edition was sold out and a second, corrected, appeared in 1773. In 1773 he published *The Present State of Music in Germany, the Netherlands, and United Provinces, or, the Journal of a Tour through those countries, undertaken to collect Materials for a General History of Music*. A second edition, corrected, appeared in 1775. The books were well received by the cultivated reader of the day. It was particularly gratifying to Burney that David Garrick, Oliver Goldsmith, Sir Joshua Reynolds, and Dr Johnson all expressed their admiration of his works. Indeed Dr Johnson went so far as to say that he had his friend Dr Burney's 'elegant and entertaining travels... in his eye, when writing his "Journey to the Western Islands of Scotland" ' (1775). This was praise from the source Burney most respected, but the welcome which his 'Travels' received at the hands of the 'blue stocking ladies' Mrs Vesey and Mrs Montague, who collected in their drawing rooms for enlightened conversation the cream of intellectual London society, was of more importance to his standing as an author. As he recalls, he was 'constantly invited and regarded as a member': his status as a man of letters was established. Fanny made the point in her *Memoirs of Dr Burney* (1832): 'From this period', she wrote, 'the profession of Dr Burney, however highly he was raised in it, seemed but of secondary consideration for him in the world; where, now, the higher rank was assigned him of a man of letters, from the general admiration accorded to his Tours . . .'

The *Tours* are valuable for the information they contain and for the light they throw upon Burney as a person. The published version of his German *Tour* contains a full account of his travels; musical incident and information, and the miscellaneous kind of material that he had excluded from the Italian *Tour*. For a rounded account of the Italian *Tour*, the Journal is essential.

Burney was travelling in stirring days. The foundations of the traditional autocracy of absolute monarchy and feudal landlordism which still survived in so much of Europe were being eroded by forces of change–economic, social, political and intellectual. The general drive for innovation developed its energy from the ideas released by the scientific achievements of the late seventeenth and early eighteenth centuries. The work of Newton particularly, with its demonstration that a human mind could understand, and demonstrate–re-order–the mechanism of the universe itself, had encouraged men to appraise every aspect of human and social activity according to criteria derived from the rigorous application of human reason. This searching appraisal of the human condition was carried on with tenacity and brilliance in France: its greatest single monument was the *Encyclopédie* 1751–72 (80) which enshrined the thoughts of the revolutionary enlightenment–Voltaire, Montesquieu, Rousseau (on music), d'Alembert, Diderot, Holbach, Condillac, Necker, Boulanger, Marmontel, and others–on scientific, social, philosophical, political, economic and technological questions. Their ideas spread throughout Europe particularly where French influence was strong, as in the German states for example, and in Austria too.

The ideas of the Encyclopédistes had a direct influence upon the development of music: its theoretical basis was re-examined, its 'subject matter' or content re-assessed. Naturalness and simplicity were qualities to be striven for. The serious opera, reflecting the ethos of the autocratic court, based upon mythical subjects and constructed according to artificial and rigid musical formulae was discredited. Opera buffa, comic, critical of social customs and institutions, dealing with situations such as would arise out of normal human relationships was preferred. In France the battle was joined in polemics centred principally on the nature of opera.

Introduction

In the German states the spread of the enlightenment gave impetus to movements of economic and social transformation which saw the gradual emergence of a middle class unsympathetic to the cultural aims and outlook of the autocratic princelings. This new, substantial and enlightened social class established its own cultural ethos, and, through patronage of a kind quite different from that of the courts, encouraged the development of music which found expression in new forms. The growth in importance of instrumental music rather than opera, the evolution of the sonata form, the development of the symphony are all characteristic of this movement.

Burney had subscribed to the *Encyclopédie* at its first appearance, and he thought highly of the musical writings of d'Alembert and Rousseau (whose censorious *Lettre sur la musique Françoise*, 1753, Burney considered the 'best piece of criticism on the art, perhaps, that has ever been written'). He maintained this interest in French music and French critical writing and took the trouble to keep himself supplied over twenty years with the best music and the best writings on the subject of music produced in France. This background enabled him to talk readily and effectively with the French savants he met in Paris: it also predisposed him to adopt the vehemently critical view of French music expressed by Rousseau and others, and to indulge his own partiality for the Italian.

The printed *Tour* was drawn from the Journal and from other records which Burney kept as he travelled, and it shows him everywhere eager to find new music and new musicians. To use one of his own favourite words he ferretted out information and people in a dauntingly persistent way: so much so that his mention of a composer or a performer is often the only record and is quoted as such in subsequent works of reference. He found much to please him musically in Italy. Galuppi, Jomelli, Latilla, Paesiello and others he approved of were writing attractive music, the conservatorios of Venice were still training good musicians, there were still good instrumentalists to be met with, amateur music was flourishing; but he harks back constantly to the days of the greater past. The conservatorios of Naples were at a low ebb, their teaching methods were crude, their instrumentalists and singers but indifferent; the music of the church was disappointing, even at the opera the singing was not up to the high standards which the Italians had set in London thirty or forty years before. Some of the renowned male sopranos were still singing occasionally, but for the most part they were old and their voices were rough, uneven or worn out: the high day of the castrato was past, though boys were still mutilated to supply a declining demand. The keyboard instruments Burney played and heard were poor and he could not find a decent piece of new music for the harpsichord anywhere. He fared much better in Germany later.

The air of disenchantment is stronger in the Journal than in the printed *Tour*: perhaps fuller information gathered but not digested in Italy and a perspective view from England of what he had met with helped to balance the account.

Apart from the musical material however the Journal has a great deal to offer any reader interested in the reactions of an active mind to events in the France and Italy of 1770. Burney was a true son of the enlightenment. He showed lively interest in every aspect of the world around him: he was ready to speculate about geology, botany, astronomy, meteorology or any other science, he knew a deal about farming practice and could make informed comparisons between crops, the seasons, methods of cultivation and harvesting at home and in the countries through which he passed. Nor did the state of the peasants escape him; he noted with disapproval the extremes of wealth and poverty which he saw to exist side by side, and he was fearful of the consequences of the disregard which men of substance showed towards the labouring poor.

He responded to the charm of roadside flowers and evoked the atmosphere and characteristic detail of the countryside through which he jogged: but he was sufficiently of his age to see the landscape as a whole as something prepared for the setting of an opera. Nor did the gothick in architecture please him.

His curiosity was never sated, his desire to know and discover was never quenched by fatigue, accidents, danger, illness or discomfort. Almost insensible at the end of a long journey in a 'villainous' chaise over 'fiendish' roads, sometimes without protection against the weather, he was ever ready to rally himself, to rush off to a theatre, or a concert, or a festival and later to comment upon the qualities and shortcomings of what he saw and heard. He was ever ready to pop into churches and palaces to note down what he saw–statues, paintings, monuments. The lists of pictures and artists which fill pages of his Journal may not be the most stimulating fare to the reader, but they form an invaluable record–too little studied perhaps–of the collections as they existed in 1770. He carried with him M. de la Lande's *Voyage en Italie*, the contemporary account of Italy and its antiquities most favoured by travellers for its description of Italian painting, sculpture and architecture, but he was no mere copyist. He observed for himself: he draws attention to the inaccuracies and omissions of his guide. He recalls where he has seen other versions of some of the pictures, he breaks off to mention engraved copies in his parlour: he was alive to what he saw.

Introduction

The wide range of his general reading in English, French and Italian, his informed appreciation of the arts, his charming social manner commended him to polite society wherever he went. In some fields, astronomy for example, he was able to hold his own with professionals. His special knowledge of music commanded the respect of theoreticians, composers and performers alike.

He wrote in a direct and colloquial English and though his narrative is full of contractions and sometimes in almost note form, his language has real power and flexibility. He throws in at appropriate places evocative dialect words, explicit and forceful; some of them unrecorded in the standard reference books. His judgements are as direct as his language, though for publication he sometimes softens or removes asperities. He sometimes smothers original terseness by subsequent writing up for conventional reasons and from a desire to please the person mentioned – 'he called on me' could well become 'he did me the great honour of waiting upon me at my inn'.

He deleted passages which represented his own conduct in a good light, or which reported the opinions of others favourable to himself. He showed himself – but usually not for publication – pre-occupied with the details of his profession: he noted the rates of pay of music teachers, was eager to demonstrate the correct way of fingering his own harpsichord music; he was pleased when his playing met with applause but he disclaimed any pretentions to mastery as a performer on the keyboard – he had put that aside years ago, as he said. His judgements of performers and music were always professional, never complaisant.

He enjoyed the patronage of the great, but he would not be put upon. He was wary of entering into relationships with strangers, but without hesitation he did his Christian duty by a fellow traveller stricken down with a serious illness. He confessed to being under the sway of the 'foul fiend hypochondria' yet he described the discomforts, accidents and dangers through which he passed without self pity. He was generally patient and good humoured but he could be fussed and splenetic. He was perhaps a little vain, but he was ashamed of his vanity. He was full of general and specific anxiety: about expected news from home which did not arrive, about the state of Europe and the likelihood of war for example, but he managed his journey admirably according to a strict timetable, and handled his business in a determined and unhurried manner.

These apparent contradictions are aspects of the character of a fascinating man who for six months directed his well informed observation upon the countryside and towns, the people, institutions and antiquities, the arts and sciences of large tracts of France and

Italy and wrote down what he saw in his Journal now before us. The art historian, the musician and other specialists will find much of value still unworked in this unvarnished tale. The general reader open to the variety of human experience will find profit, and it is to be hoped, pleasure, in Burney's delineation of the commonplaces of his daily life in France and Italy in 1770–and much to speculate upon too.

H. Edmund Poole

NOTE ON THE TEXT

Burney clearly regretted that he had mangled his original Journal when preparing the text of his printed *Tour*, for he transcribed a great part (but not all) of the omitted non-musical material for publication in his 'Memoirs'. This part of the memoirs survived in manuscript and passed eventually into the hands of Dr Percy Scholes who with his *The Great Doctor Burney* (1948) and other writings did much to arouse interest in Burney and the Burney family. Dr Scholes felt that it would be useful to produce an edition of the *Tour* which would conflate the printed text and the manuscript of the omitted portions. This he published in 1959 as *An Eighteenth-Century Musical Tour in France and Italy* and expressed the hope that it would be definitive. It was assembled from the two English editions (1771 and 1773), 'the two manuscript copies of the omitted portions' and the footnotes to Ebeling's German translation (Hamburg, 1772). In fact close examination of the text shows it to be less authoritative than he had intended. The most unsatisfactory features rise from Dr Scholes's ambivalent attitude towards the original Journal (British Museum Add. MS: 35122–Journal B) which, he infers, was no more than another copy of the same unpublished material as was contained in his version (now in the Osborn Collection, 73.1–Journal O).

In the bibliography of Burney's published books (*The Great Doctor Burney*, 1948, vol. 2, page 331) he writes:

> The incidents of travel which Burney omitted from his book as published he nevertheless preserved, copying them twice, once in a set of note-books now in the British Museum (Add. MS. 35122) and once in another set in the possession of the present author. These two sets have been roughly collated for the sake of the present work; they are found to be sub-stantially the same but occasionally vary slightly in the wording; each of them also contains a little matter not found in the other one and the British Museum copy repeats a little matter to be found in the published volume which the copy in the possession of the writer does not. (Com-plete collation has not been undertaken . . .)

He repeats the substance of this description in the preface to *An Eighteenth-Century Musical Tour in France and Italy* (page ix). Journal B is mentioned: 'Another copy in Burney's own hand is to be found in the British Museum.'

In fact Journal B is a single quarto volume of 185 leaves, which measure 7·8 inches deep by 6·3 inches wide. Some leaves have survived in pairs without separation but most of them are single, guarded, and bound in half morocco boards. Before the text is an incomplete manuscript index (Ci–Z) and a leaf bearing an inscription 'Edward Francisco Burney, the gift of his Sister-in-Law Mrs Burney'. The manuscript was bought by the Trustees of the British Museum on 11 October 1897, folioed in November 1897 and was at the binders between 14 January 1899 and March 1899.

Nothing is known of the physical form of the Journal before it reached the Museum. In view of these facts it is difficult to understand how Dr Scholes came to describe the manuscript so inaccurately.

Journal B supplies very considerable portions of the printed *Tour* as well as forming the basis of Journal O, and for this reason alone it is to be regretted that Dr Scholes did not make fuller use of it while preparing his conflation. Neglect to do so led him to make mis-statements of fact and to pass over material of real interest otherwise not recorded. Perhaps the worst of the errors appears in the pages dealing with Burney's stay in Paris at the beginning of the tour. The miscellaneous events which are recorded for Wednesday 13 June are described in much the same words in Journal B and Journal O but at the end of one passage (erased in Journal O) there is a broken sentence 'This was succeeded . . .' Scholes working from Journal O made a footnote here which reads 'BM also is incomplete at this point, its pages, indeed, for part of Wednesday, the whole of Thursday, and part of Friday being cut away. Possibly Burney found that he had merely duplicated at this point the narrative as it appears in the printed book—which is what we shall now read.' In fact Journal B is intact, continuous and complete throughout Wednesday 13 to Friday 15 June. The narrative 'in the printed book' to which Scholes refers is based upon Journal B (verbatim in part, edited in part) and upon some other source. None of the matter relating to Thursday 14 June occurs in Journal O.

Far from their being 'identical' as Scholes suggests, the texts of Journal B, Journal O and the printed *Tour*, bristle with dissimilarities many of them merely verbal, some substantial and important. For example the account of Burney's visit in Paris to Madame Brillon, a famous keyboard player, varies fundamentally as between the three sources, yet the contribution of Journal B which demonstrates Burney the teacher, the professional musician in action, is passed over where the information it offers is unique. There are other cases too. The interrelationship of the two Journals and the printed *Tour* can be demonstrated only by the comparison of long extracts for which unfortunately there is no room here, but the interested reader would certainly find the study of this edition of Journal B against the printed *Tour* rewarding.

The text of Journal B is on the whole clearly written, though Burney's hand varies considerably, sometimes from page to page. It is tight with contractions–s^d, Sep., w^{ch}, and so on–and the punctuation is erratic, sometimes little more than dot and dash, sometimes carefully worked out in the conventional gradations of comma to full stop. Capital letters seldom appear. There are corrections and alterations on almost every page, some of them merely affecting single words, others calling for the re-writing of extensive passages. Editorial marks abound: brackets and vertical lines mark out sections selected for the printed *Tour*, signs of all kinds and figures are used to indicate the order of scattered passages. Some of these pointers mark out a connected narrative, others lead nowhere at all.

In view of all these factors it was decided to publish a version of the text as close as possible to Burney's first draft, ignoring his editorial marks, expanding contractions, but preserving the spelling and, as far as possible, the punctuation. Common names were given capital letters.

The passages with little or no correction were straightforward, but the passages black with alterations and corrections presented real difficulties. It was clear that some of the revisions were made as he wrote, discarding one word or phrase for another; others were made editorially after drafting, but in a hand similar to that which wrote the original words; others again were made in the stiff vertical hand of Burney's later years, probably in 1805. In establishing the version of the manuscript printed here, corrections made as the writing proceeded have been adopted, so have editorial corrections in a local 'journal' hand, but late (1805) corrections have been excluded except where they clear up obscurities in the first draft or offer new material of special value. The 'late' corrections appear in the text between half square brackets ⌊ ⌋.

No attempt has been made to produce a typographical facsimile of the manuscript, or to present a text supported by elaborate apparatus, but footnotes have been used to give alternative readings where additions and other changes materially affect the original draft, and to offer a certain amount of explanatory and illustrative material which, it is hoped, will usefully supplement the narrative. The 'Explication of some musical terms and foreign words, which occur in the following Journal' which Burney printed in *Tour* (1773) has been slightly extended into a glossary and should be consulted for definitions of musical terms as current in the eighteenth century. A biographical index gives the minimum of information about the major figures mentioned by Burney.

In addition to the ⌊ ⌋ mentioned above, three other editorial marks have been used. Words appearing within square brackets [Mengs] correct, translate or explain the term which they follow or, very occasionally, complete the text. Gaps in the manuscript are indicated by angle brackets 〈 〉. Words appearing within angle brackets 〈noted〉 are editorial conjectures for matter illegible in the manuscript.

Footnotes which end with B are Burney's own and are taken from the printed *Tour*, 1773.

Clearly the soundness of the text here offered is determined by the accuracy and the consistency with which I have recognised Burney's first intentions. Errors there will be. Further work may well improve the text and interpret the many, and sometimes baffling and conflicting, editorial indications which are scattered through the original manuscript. It is to be hoped however that systematic reading, or skipping, or dipping, in the narrative as here offered will confirm to the candid mind Dr Johnson's opinion that Dr Burney was 'one of the first writers of the age for travels'.

H.E.P.

TUESDAY JUNE 5th 1770. Arrived at Dover in order to embark for France but was detained there by a foolish accident which happened on the road, for having left my sword, that necessary passport for a gentleman on the continent, I thought it of consequence enough to remain at Dover till I recovered it which was not till Wednesday night. However this delay gave me an opportunity of seeing the Castle and of lounging about the town with a person very dear to me who had accompanied me thither: and the situation of Dover is such as must strike every one who sees it as unique. It is wonderfully bold and sublime; but Shakespeare's description is so much more wonderful than the thing itself, that this famous cliff is always diminution in my eyes, compared with his poetical picture of it.*

On THURSDAY the 7th I embarked with a fair wind and arrived at Calais without any other accident than the very common one of being intolerably ill during the whole passage. This ever deprives me of the pleasure which others enjoy in observing the two shores when equidistant from both. The doing this with a good glass in a fair day would enable one to form some judgment concerning the supposition England having been once part of the continent, whence it was divided by an earthquake or some violent concussion. Indeed as far as I have been able to observe there is great probability in the conjecture: the rocks, soils, plants, general face of the country in both have a very great resemblance. But having other objects constantly in view, and other thoughts to furnish reflexions I shall wave any further discussion of this point to those to whom it in a more particular manner belongs—namely the naturalists and philosophers who have leisure and depth of intelligence sufficient to investigate so dark and curious a question.

Tho' this was my third voyage to France,† yet the different appearance, costume, manners, and language of these people from those of England, from whom they are separated but by so few leagues, was still very striking. The difference of complexion in the people is not the least circumstance which on this occasion occasions surprise. The English at Dover are as fair as in any other part of the Kingdom, for

* *King Lear*, Act IV, scenes 1 and 6.

† Charles Burney's first voyage to France was in 1764 (June?) when he took his daughters Esther and Susan to Paris to establish them in a school or family where they could learn French. His second journey was in the summer of 1765 when he travelled to Paris to escort Esther back to England. On this same occasion he pushed south as far as Lyons. See below, p. 25.

[1]

anything that I have been able to remark to the contrary; but the French at Calais are at least as swarthy of skin and have as black hair as those of Provence or any of the southern parts of that extensive country. Then the slovenliness of the better sort on one side* and the courtliness of the other with respect to dress–the cleanliness of the English common people and the dirtiness of the French are at once striking and unaccountable. But I travel not only too fast to write but even to make *general* reflexions. Indeed they can never be made with fairness by persons who like meer birds of passage only fly over a kingdom without stopping to consider its constituent parts. I shall therefore, in the course of this journey only remark such particular circumstances and incidents as can be fairly seen and accounted for ⌊in my flight⌋.

At Calais the ceremonial at the custom house† gives a specimen at once of pride and meanness. The chief *commis*, or clerk there, was sitting in a velvet suit of clothes with every other appurtinence of the dress and appearance of a gentleman or indeed rather of a man of fashion and quality; who when he had signed my passport being asked what there was to pay–ah Monsieur c'est que la politesse–a mere compliment sir: and upon giving him a piece de 24 sous, his eyes sparkled and he seemed as pleased as a man of equal appearance in England would be with a place at court or a regiment.

Not being able to find at Grandsire's,‡ the principal inn, a partner in a post chaise to Paris I hired one to myself as far as Lisle [Lille] and went as far as St Omer with the same horses that night; 'tis near 30 English miles. On arriving at the gates of the town, I found them

* Other writers commented upon what seem to have been national characteristics of the time: '. . . the Frenchman is always attentive to his own person, and scarce ever appears but clean and well dressed; while his house and private apartments are perhaps covered with litter and dirt, and in the utmost confusion;–the Englishman, on the other hand, often neglects his external dress; but his house is always exquisitely clean, and every thing in it kept in the nicest order; and who shall say, which of the two judge the best for their own ease and happiness? I am sure the Frenchman will not give up his powdered hair, and laced coat for a clean house; nor do I believe those fineries would sit quietly upon the back of an Englishman, in a dirty one'. Philip Thicknesse (1719–92) in *A Year's Journey Through France and Part of Spain* (2 vols) Dublin, 1777. (Vol. 1, p. 6.)

† 'After being examined immediately on landing, before an officer, (to whom you are carried by a couple of soldiers), who only requires your name, business in France and occupation, you are dismissed, and may go where you please; only the baggage is sent to the Custom House, with your servant and porters, to be searched for contraband goods.' The Rev. William Cole, *A Journal of My Journey to Paris in the Year 1765*. Edited by F. G. Stokes, 1931, p. 6.

‡ Grandsire was the landlord of the *Lion d'Argent*, the Posthouse and one of the two great inns of Calais at this time. Pre-eminent during the first half of the century, it later lost ground to the *Hôtel d'Angleterre*, the establishment of Monsieur Dessin. Some idea of the services that Dessin offered (and something of his character, too) is given by Sterne in *A Sentimental Journey through France and Italy* (1768).

[2]

No. 3

Our Host at Abberville July 1754.
1878—2—7—10

No. 2

CALAIS.

1878—2—9—109

No. 5

Black Veils worn by all the women of AMIENS.

THREE FLEMISH CHARACTERS

LYONS

shut,* and was forced to put up at a miserable house in the suburbs, where I could get nothing to eat after my sea sickness and total depletion, but stinking maquerel; a sallad with stinking oil; and an omelet made of stinking eggs. No meat of any kind or sort could be found. The room and bed were of a piece with the supper. The wine sour and the whole uncomfortable. However the poor people were civil and I was disposed to be satisfied, so we agreed very well together. I was afraid to undress for fear of bugs and damp bedclothes for there was a very dirty appearance throughout every part of the house I saw. Cross people in general are cleanly and housifely but these were good humoured.

The gates of St Omer were opened at 4 o'clock. I passed through very soon after and found a very large and tolerably well built city. The *grande place* or great square, very spacious, and many of the streets wider than is usual for Flemish and French ⌐provincial⌐ towns. While the postilion stopt in the grande place to get a *permission* [pass], an old beggar woman told me she would *prier Dieu* for me, and immediately began a pater noster. And a great crowd of people were coming from matins at one of the churches thus early, who had been there to pray for themselves.

All the road from Calais to St Omer is very much à l'angloise, being made of excellent gravel, which is far more agreeable than the *pavé* one meets with in most of the other French roads. Not a single carriage, horse or foot traveller did I yesterday meet from Calais to St Omer. The country in general of French Flanders is flat and rich, like the Lincolnshire Fens, but well cultivated, with excellent roads and canals from one great town to another. The land is chiefly arable, as I don't remember seeing a bit of hay cut, or grass or meadow ground in my journey of yesterday or today. The only fences in this country are dykes like those of marshland.†

The pavement of Calais streets, that of St Omer and of all the towns in French Flanders are of large flat stones like the new Scots pavement in London,‡ with this difference that the kennel is in the

---

* The gates of cities were shut at a stated hour in the evening and those travellers who were locked out had to find what accommodation they could outside the walls until the gates were opened on the following morning. This mischance was often fraught with danger as well as discomfort.

† Editorial revision made this more explicit later: '. . . ⌐opposite to Lynn in⌐ Norfolk'.

‡ In the first half of the eighteenth century the streets of London were in a scandalous state: they were filthy, uneven and rugged. As a result of a series of Acts of Parliament passed in the four year period following 1762, 'the streets were either raised or lowered to bring them nearer to a level, the footways on each side were elevated, defined by kerb stones, and paved as smooth as the floor of a room; the carriage way was paved with squared Scots granite, closely laid in gravel, arched

middle and there is no place at the side for foot passengers as in London; but as the sides are made higher than the middle, the water runs off and leaves them dry very soon after rain.

From *St Omer* to *Aire*, 4 leagues distant, I travelled before breakfast, and found this town very large but not so well built as the former. The streets were extreamly crowded, it being market day, women innumerable without hats and without beauty; not merely on account of their almost copper colour but in feature. On the road beyond the town I met a great number of them riding on horse back ready to *split themselves* not with laughing, tho' *ridere* is to laugh in Italian, but all *en cavaliers.**

At Aire I got some poor coffee and milk with bad bread and worse butter; but I shall soon cease to be dainty and forget to mention these sensual trifles. From thence to Bethune the distance is 5 leagues, the country much the same as that of yesterday but better the further one is off Calais, that is to say the sea, which has formerly without doubt inundated the greatest part of it. But whether the country is rich or otherwise, there is always an appearance of great poverty and wretchedness in the inhabitants, more indeed in their garb than countenance, though they have not quite the gaity there which is to be met with in other parts of France. The Flamands were always a heavy people and perhaps they have not quite lost that gravity which they acquired when under the Spanish yoke.† The inn here is by far the best I have met with since my landing. The French Ambassador M. du Chatelet is expected here to night or tomorrow morning from England and that will make this route a la mode. The fat landlady endeavoured to persuade me that it was the nearest, tho' at least 30 miles about. However 'tis by far the best road and it is but justice to my landlady here to say that she gave me an excellent chicken and asparagus for my dinner and a bottle of the only good wine I had tasted since my landing. 'Tis somewhat extraordinary that the best inn is *out* of the town and at St Omer and elsewhere the worst. There is so great a sameness in the face of this country that it leaves nothing to describe after one has said that it is flat, rich in corn and poor in inhabitants.

* Riding astride, not on side-saddle. Smollett *Travels*, Letter xxxv describing a journey in the region of St Remo mentions that 'in this country even the ladies sit astride'.

† For centuries this part of Flanders had been the cockpit of wars in which the interests of Spain, France, Burgundy and Austria, as well as of the powerful Flemish towns, were in conflict. In 1633 Flanders was under Spanish rule, but from 1659 to 1713 a series of treaties assigned certain regions in the southern part of Flanders to France: it was through this French Flanders that Burney was now passing.

in the middle, with proper channels on each side'. (J. Noorthouck, *A New History of London, including Westminster and Southwark*, 1773, pp. 414–15.)

FRIDAY JUNE 8. Bethune. 11 o'clock. While dinner was preparing I ran over the town. Between Bethune and Lisle there are several towns, but none of note except Lilliers [Lillers]* and the most singular thing there seems the numbering the houses in large figures over the tops of the doors.† It seems newly done whether in imitation of London or no I cannot tell, but I have seen it nowhere else on the continent. Bethune tho' a poor town seems more thoroughly fortified and guarded than any one in French Flanders. I left it before 1 and arrived at Lille by 6 o'clock.

LILLE

I was a day too late for the diligence, which set out yesterday, and does not go out again for Paris till Sunday the 10th. I was likewise too late for the play which begins at 5 o'clock. Harlequin Sauvage, and le Tableau parlant‡ were the pieces of to night which I wished much to see, as the former is an excellent comedy with a speaking Harlequin, which part is written with great wit and satyr; and the other is a kind of comic opera which is new and has been received at Paris with great applause. It will not be entertaining for any one to read, but may be a useful memorandum to myself if I mention as I go on the expense of travelling. The chaise, horses and man from Calais to this place, Lille, cost me just 4 guineas–'tis near 80 miles 50 of which they performed to day. The diligence to Paris, from hence is, I find, near 3 guineas; 'tis two days on the road and you are boarded all the way.

Lille is a very fine town, the great square very spacious and uniform. The garrison at present is less numerous than usual, as a considerable part of it is drawn off to work at the new canal at St Omer. I expected at 9 o'clock to hear some good music, which I remembered to have done 5 years ago at the time of beating *la retraite* or tatoo but was disappointed, there being only a few side drums and 2 miserable trumpets.§ I shall visit the churches tomorrow. Their best organist here it seems is blind, but a man of gallantry, for tho' he has a very

---

* Lillers is in fact west of Bethune.

† An attempt to number houses in Paris had been made as early as 1512, but it was not until 1787 that numbering had become all but universal throughout France, and it was not enforced by police regulations until 1805. In London some houses were numbered as early as 1735, but after the removal of hanging signs as a result of a proclamation in 1762, numbering was essential, and by 1770 had been widely adopted.

‡ *Le Tableau Parlant*, a very comic and original opera by André Ernest Modeste Grétry, first produced in Paris, in 1769.

§ '⌊I here began my musical enquiries etc. See Mus. Journal p. 5.⌋'

pretty wife and several children, he keeps a mistress which is publickly known.* Music seems ever to favour *la belle passion*. An abominable head-ache will let me write no more tonight. I never travelled at my ease with so little delight, I think, as now; being in want of one with whom to communicate, and participate such things as are worthy of notice. I dread any one coming into the room, lest I should be forced to talk to 'em. This is half John Bull's sulky pride and half ignorance what to say for want of practice. This will wear out in a few days.† I gave away my ham–'My dear Ham': as Lord Orrery says–to the steward of the ship I came over in who nursed me in my sickness, and since, I would have given the world for it as I have met with nothing so good since. It is *jour maigre*, toujours maigre!

FRIDAY. I have walked till my feet can no longer wag in seeing churches. I was in hopes of hearing music better than ordinary as 'tis tems de Jubilée‡ with 'em; but was disappointed.

There are several very handsome churches here and organs in 'em all, yet none are played except on Sundays and great festivals, but of this in another place. I visited the arsenal, citadel, and hospital, not only *des Enfans Trouvées* but also *des vielles et viellards trouvé*§–for there seem to be as many of these two last as of the former. I suppose they are well fed and lodged but they are made to work too hard. The children are confined in rows, the girls at making lace–the boys as shoe makers, taylers etc, but I find their task masters allow them very little respit from 7 o'clock in the morning to 8 at night. The room where the girls were so confined was very much crowded and too hot to be wholesome, if one may judge by the smell of stagnant and putrid air which was intolerable. The number which this hospital contains of every age and sex is 2500. I am tired to death of the King of Prussia's March which is played by the chimes every half hour.∥

I never saw streets better laid out than in this town. *La ville est très bien percée* as they say here. 'Tis I think an improvement on Sir Christopher Wren's for rebuilding London after the Fire. He proposed the whole city to form a star, St. Paul's to be the nucleus and each street a ray of it, terminated by a church. But here the street is

---

* This sentence does not appear in *Tour* 1773, where (p. 12) Burney refers to a 'M. Anneuse, organist of the church of St. Maurice in this town', who was blind.

† '⌊I gave away some ham which I had brought from England . . .⌋'

‡ A term given to 'an ecclesiastical solemnity . . . performed in order to gain a plenary indulgence from the Pope'. It was also applied to celebrations held in certain towns to mark the concurrence of particular festivals, as when the feast of St John the Baptist happened on Corpus Christi Day, for example.

§ The foundlings' hospital, and the home for the aged (men and women).

∥ Frederick the Great composed two military marches, one for the king's regiment of dragoons (1745) and the second for insertion in a play by Lessing, *Minna von Barnhelm* (1767).

straight (*tirée au cordeau*) and the town cut into several stars of 4 rays each only, which terminate at both ends with a view of the country. It has a very pleasing effect, and must have a useful one in letting in fresh air. The most spacious and regular street here is *la rue Royale*. The houses are not so high as at Lyons or Paris. Out of all the churches I saw to day there was only one, that of the Recollets,* without pillars and it is amazing what a noble effect it has with respect to that grandeur which uninterrupted space can afford. It seemed larger though less than many other churches here. The eye is instantly filled by the entire view of the whole building at one single glance. 'Tis observed that it rains more in and about this town than anywhere else in France. But it seems a kindness rather than a hardship to the inhabitants: as they themselves say if a drouth of a month or two happens it is so unwholesome as to occasion great sickness and mortality among them. I question whether I shall be able to write another word till I arrive at Paris for which place I set out at 4 o'clock tomorrow morning.

The road from Lille to Paris offers nothing worth stopping for, except the cities of Douay, Cambray and Senlis. Indeed Peronne *has* been much better than it is now; for a great part of it is in ruin. Before the conquest of the Low Countries it was fortified with great art and strength, being the frontier and boundary between the French and Spanish territories. At present its only garrison is custom house officers; for at the entrance into this town all travellers and even the inhabitants, are visited and very narrowly searched, and this to prevent the bringing into France the productions of Flanders, which are subject to a very high duty: such as the laces of Valencienne, Lille, Dunkirk, cambricks of St Quinten [Quentin], Arras, Douay and above all Cambray whence this beautiful manufacture had its name. The French never now call it Batiste.† Tobacco, too and snuff are seizable at the gates of Peronne, as they are $\frac{2}{3}$ cheaper without than within them.

In general, the churches of the Flanderhein [Flemish] towns are superb and magnificent, and the people and houses poor and dirty. At Cambray one of the most pleasantly situated of all I passed thro', this is true to a supreme degree, the houses and people here being so dirty as to strike the inhabitants of the neighbouring towns with wonder. The Lille diligence made but a very short stop at Douai so that I was unable to go into the churches. I could only make such remarks on the outside of men and things as were in the power of a meer bird of passage to make.

* The Franciscan Recollects, a reformed branch of the Franciscan Observants.
† Batiste (cambric) derived from Baptiste, its original maker, of Cambrai.

The Lille diligence set out at 4 o'clock with only myself in it. At about a league's distance from the town, a young Strasbourgoise was taken up. She began to be very communicative and to tell her story and adventures before we reached Douay; but upon the entrance of another *female* passenger, she was silenced and remained a mystery all the way. Women are always, and everywhere more afraid of each other than of the men. I could perceive these two taking every opportunity to peruse each other.* And even among the French, if a new female entered among people, before intimate and loquacious, a sudden silence ensued which seemed wholly spent in the contemplation and study of the new object.

The 3rd female passenger which we took up at Douay was rather turned of 30 as handsome as her fat would allow. Upon her entrance into the vehicle which even with my assistance she found to be rather a difficult feat of activity, she cried out with a good natured laugh ah je suis si Flamande! The Flemish women having ever been remarkable for the 'heavy load under which they groan and sweat', this sally seemed to promise well, but the conversation was spoilt till we reached Cambray where we dined.

Here our outside passenger, a poor unfortunate Tar a young man seemingly worn out with labour and adversity—sour and vindictive—with parts, reading and reflection, joined us. He spared no folly in age sex or condition and all this was rather acrid than rude. He said some things at dinner about the English which rather worked me, but before we got up from table my national pride was gratified by his declaring that he thought them the first people in the world for learning and probity, and what made this eloge more palatable was his having been a long while our prisoner during the last war.

At Cambray several officers of the Irish Brigades† who having quitted the service, live, I suppose, for cheapness and the conveniences of being near their countrymen who serve and are usually stationed in Flanders. They still wear the English uniform, red and blue with some difference of button and cuff. These troops and the Swiss Guards, are, I believe, the only corps in the French service who are clothed in red. The rest are white except the French Guards which are in blue with silver trimmings.

---

* The passage to the end of this paragraph was much edited and finally emerged as: 'I was surprised at this among the French who are in general so easy and well-bred—if a new female entered among people that were before, intimate and loquacious, in the provinces a sudden silence ensued, which seemed wholly spent in the contemplation and study of the new object.'

† The Irish Brigade had its origin in the supporters of James II who had fought in his cause in Ireland and who had joined him in exile in France. The Brigade enjoyed a high reputation in the French Army.

There we took up an officer of the Irish Brigade who was going to Corsica, Captain Seagrave a well bred, agreeable man, and by the time we reached *Peronne*, I became very well acquainted. He had been 6 months in England, being related to many of the catholic nobility there, as well as in Ireland. At first I took him and the officers I saw and heard speak English at Cambray to be in the English service, for their uniform had undergone very little change since they quitted it with James the 2nd. At present it is only the officers of these Brigades that are Irish, the common men are *Liegeois*, *Germans* and of all countries, except France but the words of command are still English–though no more intelligible to the men that the beat of drum– 'tis the number of sillables with metrical distinctions of long and short in the one and the strokes of the drum stick in the other which directs their motions.

We passed our time ⌊the 2nd day very chearfully⌋ from *Peronne* where we lay to *Pont St Maixance* (a great market for corn upon the River Oyse, where we dined), as most others so circumstanced usually do; that is to say more in sleep and silence, than in conversation. We had by this time added to our number another internal and external passenger. The dinner revived us all. The conversation became very lively and interesting. There were some religious points discussed by my fellow travellers with more freedom than is usual in mixed companies wholly strangers to each other, even in England. On this occasion I was totally silent, and a mere by-stander which was not the case with the seaman, who showed himself to be a man of great reading and a profound thinker. The new inside female passenger was an agreeable woman with certain marks of having lived in the world with good company. She was ill all the morning as if at sea in a storm, but at dinner and afterwards bore a very intelligent part in the conversation. She was the wife of an officer in Champagne to whom she was going. She was a little *passée* but had an extream fine skin and great delicacy of features not in the least overloaded in the Flemish way, her muscles being hardly enough covered.

The only tolerable town which we passed through between dinner and our arrival at Paris was Senlis a place famous for *bonne Biere de Mars* or good March beer. There are many fine churches and convents here and a few good houses.

PARIS

By 7 we arrived at the Barrière, took in a Custom House officer who attended us to the *Bureau de la Diligence*, where our baggage underwent another scrutiny, but it was *a la parisienne*, that is to say more politely performed than in the provincial towns. Captain Seagrave and I did not care to separate, so one fiacre carried us both to the *Hotel d'Espagne* rue *Guinegaud* [Guénégaud], *Fauxbourg St Germain* where we got appartments on the same floor. In the morning the tayler and friseur were the 1st to be called upon, as no respect or consequence here can be obtained without them, as Dorat tells us 'Grace à mon habit etc.'* My first visit was to Mr. Lumisden whom I found to be all I expected, and more, as to intelligence, good breeding, good nature etc. With him I had a long conference on the object of my Italian Journey, and he kindly undertook to make out a *route* for me—and gave me much information as to customs, manners, books etc. I found him to be a man of taste and learning, and though no musician he was able to give me satisfaction on several subjects relative to my chief errand, such as the libraries, Popes Chapel, conservatories etc. He has a very pretty and well-chosen collection of books made at Rome during 19 years residence there where he had been secretary to the Chevalier St George [the Old Pretender]. He showed me several tracts on music necessary for me to consult and to get when in Italy and lent me others. After a correspondence was settled between us and a promise of being neighbourly during my stay at Paris, I found out several of my old friends. Lady Clifford with whom a long conversation—then met my captain at the Hotel de Grenelle where we dined extreamly well on 2 courses, a dessert and a pint of good Burgundy for 16 pence. From thence we went to the Place de Louis

* The Osborn MS. has: 'In the morning the tayler and friseur were to be summond. Dress, at Paris, is at its height of sumptuosity and importance. Sédaine describes its influence in an Epistle of some length (Elite de Poésie To. II) from which I shall extract some of the ideas:

> Thanks to the gay, the well-made suit,
> Whose charms can render censure mute;
> Can gain the Cerberus porter o'er
> To open wide his Lordship's door;
> And prove at court sufficient omen
> To gain protection from the yeomen.
> Full well I know myself, and feel
> The Tayler's power from head to heel;
> He with embroidery and lace
> Can give each awkward action grace,
> Can shrewd discernment soon beguile
> And metamorphose frown to smile;
> The idiot phrase can make a joke;
> And turn to wit each word that's spoke.
> The secret magic of his shears
> Can hide deformity and years,
> Can captivate the world's opinion
> And gain o'er head and heart dominion:
> For 'tis not me—but 'tis my Dress
> The proud, the vain, the Great caress.'

15 to visit the late scene of so much blood. The account of the killed and wounded there at the playing off the fireworks for the marriage of the Dauphin increase every day: it is now said to surpass 1000.* There being no temptations at the theatres, after coming home to write letters we went to see the humours of the Boulevard where was much company. *Comus,*† still there, to whom we sacrificed. He has several new and surprising tricks.

WEDNESDAY 13. Being disappointed by my tailer I could not go out till near noon which enabled me to read and write. At noon I got in to the Library of the *College des Quatre nations* founded by Cardinal Mazarin–'tis a noble one–I consulted the catalogues and found several of the books I wanted. It was not a day when people are allowed to make extracts it is only done on Thursdays and Mondays– tomorrow *Fete Dieu* and no business is done or public place opened except the *concert spirituel.*‡ I found my banker this morning, who had been advised of my coming, so I settled some business with him again. In that quarter lives Madame de Sinmar [St. Mart] who had the care of my girls. I called on her, she screamed out with joy and could not talk of *her children* without tears. It is a good and tender hearted being. Went to Arthur's the English watchmaker's here who is a thoroughly sensible and philosophic man. Then I met several English Scots and Irish–dined again with my captain, who had an Irish gentleman and his son who is going a cadet with him into Corsica.

* Among the elaborate and costly entertainments arranged to celebrate the marriage of Marie-Antoinette of Austria and Louis-Auguste, Dauphin of France, Grandson of Louis XV, was a fête in Paris. It took place on 30 May, 1770. The general merry-making went forward as planned but the fireworks, designed as a great climax to the day, were not a success: a misdirected rocket set off the centre-piece before time and the great effects did not materialise. There are different accounts of what followed, but it is agreed that enormous crowds (300,000) started to move from the Place Louis XV (now Place de la Concorde), and from other points round about, towards the boulevards and a crowd of similar magnitude moved from the boulevards to the Place. These two movements in opposite directions crammed into the Rue royale. To add to the confusion the reserve store of fireworks and the scaffolding round the King's statue were accidentally ignited and the firemen with their appliances and the stampeding crowd were mingled in a wild confusion. Men, women and children were thrust into pits left open in the road by workmen who had been laying water pipes where they were crushed and suffocated: 132 were killed, four or six times as many were injured.

† Le Sieur Comus was a famous magician, who attracted large crowds wherever he went. Burney may have seen Comus on one (or both) of his earlier visits to Paris. He may well have seen him perform in London because Comus was there in 1766 and is said to have acquired by his dexterity no less than £5,000.

‡ The Concert Spirituel was founded by Anne Danican Philidor to offer performances on the days of the great religious festivals when the Académie Royale de Musique (the official name of the Paris Opéra) was closed. The first concert was held on Sunday in Passion week, 18 March, 1725. At first neither French nor opera music could be performed, but this restriction was later withdrawn.

Paris 13 June

At night the Comedie Italienne* where there was a Harlequin piece, in which 2 thirds of the characters spoke Italian which I was glad to find I understood full as well as the French. Carlin the Harlequin wonderfully comic and entertaining – the rest, who sung now and then, but too French for me, Italian airs I could not much relish. This was succeeded by a new piece called 〈   〉 One of these pieces was new and meant as a comic opera in all its modern French form of Italian music (that is music composed in the Italian Stile) to French words: no recitative, all the dialogue and narrative part being spoken, and this piece was as thoroughly d—d as ever piece was here. I used to imagine that a French audience durst not hiss to the degree I found they did tonight, indeed quite as much mixt with horse laughs as ever I heard at Drury Lane or Convent Garden. In short it was condemned in all the English terms except breaking the forms and the actors heads – instead of hissssssss – hishshsh. The author of the words, luckily for him or rather judiciously by him, lay concealed, but the composer M. de St Amant, is very much to be pitied, for a great deal of real good music was thrown away upon bad words and upon an audience not at all disposed, especially in the two last acts (there were 3,) to hear anything fairly. I never saw a house filled with better dressed people.

But this music though I thought it very much superior to the poetry which it accompanied was not without its defects. The modulation was *trop recherchée*, too studied, so much so as to be unnatural and always to disappoint the ear. The overture was real good music full of good harmony, elegant and pleasing melody, with many passages of effect. The hautbois at this theatre 〈   〉 is admirable, I hardly ever heard a more pleasing tone or manner of playing except from Fischer. Several of the songs would have been admirable too, if they had been sung with the true Italian expression, but the French voice never comes further that from the throat. There is no *voce di petto* no true *portamento* or direction of the voice on any one of their stages. And though several of the performers in this theatre are Italian, they are so degenerated since they came thither that if I had not been assured of it their performance would never have given birth to the least suspicion of that sort. The new piece had several movements in it so like what one has heard at the Serious Opera† (it must be re-

* Companies of Italian actors, known as the Comédie Italienne since 1680, had been very popular in France since the 16th century. Their art became less characteristically Italian, however, and developed a strong French element. In 1723 they were given the title of Comédiens ordinaires du roi with an annual grant from public funds – from this time they were Italian only in name.

† The serious opera was an art form developed in Italy during the 17th and early 18th centuries and copied in almost every other European country. Its subjects

membered that the whole was in verse and extreamely serious except some attempt at humour in Calliot's part)* that it was what all the audience prounced it to be–*detestable*.

THURSDAY. 14 JUNE. My adventures of this day were so musical that they will have place elsewhere. In the morning after a visit made with Captain Seagrave to Lady Clifford, who it seems is his relation, though I was the 1st that made them acquainted, I went to Notre Dame to hear high Mass. I had great difficulty to get there–coaches are not allowed, till all the processions with which the streets swarm, are over. The streets through which they are to pass in the way to the churches are all lined with tapestery, or, for want of that, with bed curtains and old peticoats. I find the *Gens comme il faut* all go out of town on these days to avoid the *embarras* of going to Mass, or the *ennui* of staying at home. Whenever the Host stops which is frequent for the priests to sing a psalm, all the people fall on their knees in the middle of the street, be it dirty or clean. I readily complied with this ceremony rather than give offence or become remarkable. At length I reached Notre Dame, where I likewise was a conformist, though here I walked about frequently as I saw others do round the quire and in the great isle. I made my remarks on the organ, organist, plainchant, motets etc. saw the Arch Bishop of Paris who performed in the Mass and several other Bishops, and then went to see St. Julien des Menestriers said to have been founded in 1331 by 2 of Philip de valois, King of France's 24 Fiddlers,† but of this likewise elsewhere. Though by the way of memorandum I must observe that the people told me the King's musicians performed here on the Feast of Dedication and have done so for time immemorable. On one of the painted glass windows is a date so late as 1591, but the church seems much older. Perhaps it may have been founded by 2 minstrels-musicians, which *menestrier* means, as it was one of the titles given to the ancient bards with us and to the *troubadours* of Provence, but as to these founders being 2 of the 24 violins in the service of Philip de Valois credat Judæus.

Dined with my captain and the young abbé, who had accompanied me all the morning and was an excellent guide and expositor, at the Hotel de Grenelle, where there is always good company and a good

---

* 'M. Calliot is deservedly the favourite actor and singer of the comic opera at Paris. His voice which he can made [*sic*] a bass or a tenor at pleasure, is admirable, and he is in all respects a most interesting and entertaining performer.' B. *Tour* 1773.

† ⌊See other journal⌋.

---

were drawn from mythology or from classical history: convention imposed a rigid formality upon the author; and upon the composer too, for the lay-out of the music was no less rigidly predetermined than the dramatic action.

^s ^d
dinner of two courses for about 1. 6 English including a pint of
Burgundy. I separated from *Church Military* after dinner in order to
make calls and deliver letters. The only person I found at home was
Garrick's banker who was ill, the rest all gone into the country and
doors locked up. After this trapes* I went to my lodging to write for
about an hour. 'Tis not easy to do it at night while I am connected
with these messieurs—every desirable thing seems to have its opposite inconvenience!—and at 5 o'clock went to the concert spirituel,
the only public amusement allowed of on these great festivals. It is a
great concert where the vocal consists of detached pieces of church
music in Latin. The French have never yet had either a serious Italian
opera or regular oratorio of any sort performed in their country. I
suppose Messieurs les Intendants des menus plaisirs† of Paris know
too well the taste of the people to attempt them, tho' every other
species of novelty is tried and they even suffer Italian to be *spoken* by
several of the characters in the Harlequin pieces. Of the performance
I shall not speak here. It is in the grande sale du Louvre—where the
serious opera used to be from the time the opera house at the Palais
Royal was burnt down,‡ to the building of a new one, that is to say
till this summer—so that at the going out if the weather be good all
the company goes full dressed in to the Tuilleries at this time of the
year it being over by 8 o'clock.

FRIDAY, 15. I went to the King's Library§ and found the collection
immense, full of people, both readers and writers. My first enquiry
was after the catalogue of MSS. They reached me one in folio which
I found to be the 3rd volume! I was lost in it, I found, however the
numbers of many things to my purpose which I ⟨noted⟩ down in a
blank book I carried with me—called for a 2nd volume and was there
still more fortunate and just on the point of asking for the books themselves, when behold, to my great mortification the clock struck 12 and
a signal was given for everybody to go out. It is only two days in a
week that the public is admitted into this library and then only from
8 or 9 o'clock to 12. This has greatly lowered my expectations from
this resource—all I can do in the few days I shall be here, will be to
consult catalogues, to read indexes and to dig out treasures for other
people.

* Tiresome or disagreeable walk.
† Master of the Revels, 'managers of public diversions' (B).
‡ In 1763.
§ The King's Library had its origins in the 14th century and its ups and downs
through the ages reflected very much the interests and personality of the reigning
monarch and the fortunes of war. At the end of the reign of Louis XIV the library
contained 70,000 volumes, printed and in manuscript. It had many homes but in
1720 the collections were settled in the Hotel Mazarin.

All this time I have not delivered one of Garrick's letters of which I have 4, and 2 of them full of commissions for him and Mrs G. which hang upon my mind and plague me more than all I have to do for myself. I have not been able after many hours spent in vain every day almost, to find M. Monnet who was the 1st I wished to see, as from him I was to have an address to the rest. I begin to think I shall leave this place without delivering those letters which are written merely in my favour, as I shall not have time to avail myself of any civilities his friends may offer.

This evening I went to the serious opera, but of that in another place.*

†SATURDAY 16 morning. Spent all in visits and enquiries after people I could not find. Every one here tells me it will be absolutely necessary to get a passport for my leaving the kingdom. This is a new regulation since I was last in Paris, supposed to have had its rise from the great number of bankrupts etc who have gone off with great sums of public and private money. If so the regulation is wisely intended for the benfit of the *whole*, tho' inconvenient to me, a part of it. I have been consulting Lady Clifford about it and she has promised to enquire by a note to Mr Walpole, who *was* secretary to Lord Harcourt, but now, in his absence, is Minister Plenipotentiary for our Court. He is I believe brother to the Lynn member.

I had another very comfortable and agreeable conference this morning with Mr Lumisden—found 2 sensible Scotsmen with him, obtained many satisfactory informations relative to Italy. He had likewise ferreted out 2 or 3 choir books for my purpose. I have settled Wednesday for my last visit and enquiries, when he has promised me a route in writing. My captain and young Abbé are impatient to be gone and fight hard for Wednesday, but I hope they'll stay till Friday as I cannot get into the Library of the Quatre Nations till Monday nor the King's till Tuesday—and it will hurry me terribly. From Mr. Lumisden's I went a book hunting till dinner—have picked up so many offices, graduals, missals, rituals etc in order to get a thorough knowledge of their plain-chant and church music that I shall be taken for a Jesuite at Dover on my return to England, come over to propagate the Roman Catholic Religion.

I met with Molini this morning who is attending the great sale of scarce and *dear* books for the King of England and other persons. His brother who is a bookseller here likewise had undertaken to get me the work I so much wanted in England concerning ancient MSS,

---

* Burney gives an account of his evening, and of the speculations to which it gave rise, on pages 29–36 of *Tour* 1773.

† ⌐'Saturday chiefly spent in delivering letters and in book hunting and I . . .'⌐

but as it is two vols. folio I cannot travel with it, so I have begged it may be sent to England.

I met my friends at dinner as usual, enquiring 1st after famous organs and organists for tomorrow. In the afternoon it rained and as no temptations were thrown out at the theatre I stayed at my lodgings the whole evening to write.

SUNDAY 17 JUNE. A very busy day. At last–tho' the first, thing this morning, I met with Lacombe, Garrick's bookseller, did his business there and some for myself. 'Tis the author of Christina Queen of Sweden. As he is more intelligent that the rest of the booksellers with whom I have conversed I gave him a list of books and pamphlets to get for me which Nourse's correspondent could not–and he has promised me to procure most of 'em during my absence in Italy. Some of 'em he furnished me bound up together out of his own books for his private use and 1 or 2 more.

From hence to St Gervais at the Greve to hear [Armand Louis] Couperin one of the most famous organists here–then to Monnet's, who had at last been discovered to me by La Combe–by the way this last tells me Rousseau is now in Paris–I must see him. Monnet had been apprised of my journey by G. I had a very long and not useless confab with him about my work, but 1st I did Mr and Mrs G.'s business. He has promised wonders as to the King's Library. He says he can be of great use to me either by meeting me there, or even by getting any particular books out for me: is to meet me on Tuesday there. He's an old hand: knows every body and thing connected with the theatres and public exhibitions, is an author too– brought over the French players to England four years ago, about which there was made a riot,* and was the first to introduce comic operas at Paris and is now one of the entrepreneurs of the new Vaux Hall† here.

From hence to Lady Clifford's (to-day a remise for the first time) and it was like going from the City to St James's and from thence back again over and over again all this day; so awkwardly did things lie and happen. Her ladyship was ready for me, had received a note to

---

* In 1755 Jean Monnet, at this time director of the Opéra Comique in Paris, was invited by David Garrick to take to Drury Lane a French company to perform *Les Fêtes chinoises* 'a grand pantomime entertainment of dancing composed by Mr. Noverre, in which above an hundred persons were employed'. Anti-French popular feeling in one part of the house, and sympathy with the players in another, split the audiences into factions and on the sixth night battle was joined and a great deal of damage was done.

† Vauxhall Gardens, or Spring Gardens, Vauxhall, as they were originally known, were one of the most celebrated centres of entertainment in London for almost two centuries. They were imitated in Paris and elsewhere but the attractions of the foreign imitations often fell short of those offered by the London prototype.

Mr. Walpole to confirm the necessity of a passport and to say if her
friend would send his servant, a passport from him to be sent to the
D. de Choiseul to be signed.* I thought it would be more civil to go
myself than send, as I was so well known to the minister's family. I
went and had a long audience: told him my design in travelling. It is
Robert Walpole—of a very cold and grave appearance; but he seemed
to grow a little warmed and animated during our conversation: the
subject being my own, that is music and musicians, I bore the greatest
part. Mr. W. informed me that by going through Lyons I should
meet with Rousseau who was there and had written and composed a
little opera called Pigmalion† which was acted there but of which not
a word or note was to be obtained from the actors. Upon taking my
leave Mr. W. very civilly assured me that if he could be of any use
during my stay on this side the water he would be always ready. From
hence I went to Arthur's to dinner but hurried away before the 2nd
course appeared to St. Rocque to hear the famous Balbastre play the
organ. We were too soon, but at length he came and as I had the day
before let him know an English Lover of Music was very desirous to
hear him play he took great pains and I heard him both in the organ
loft and below. After church I went home with him to hear and see a
fine Rucker‡ harpsichord which is in all respects a bijou. 'Tis painted
and varnished like a snuff box. He had likewise a very large organ in
his house, which was full of company: 12 or 14 ladies and 10 or a
dozen gentlemen en verite says one of the ladies who had been at
church M. Balbastre vous etes ravissans. He played a great deal and
soon found out by my talk, and approbation that I was a performer
he pressed me very much to play and as he had been so obliging himself I sat down at the harpsichord with as little fuss as my great want
of practice required. French politeness was not wanting, tho' I had
not much partiality for myself. However this was a useful and agreeable visit.

From hence to the Tuilleries where I found everybody in mourning. At first I feared it was on account of the numbers killed at the
fireworks but on enquiry was informed that one of the Dowager
Queens of Denmark was dead. The Tuilleries seem hurt by the
removal of the Opera House, at the emptying of which in 64 and 65

* This confused sentence is amended in the Osborn MS. to read (p. 47) 'From
Monnet's I went to Lady Cliffords. Her Ladyship was ready for me; had received
a note from Mr. Walpole to confirm the necessity for a passport and to say that if
her friend would send his servant for a passport from him to be signed at the Duc
de Choiseul's office, one should be ready.'

† Rousseau's *Pygmalion* was first produced in Paris on 30 October, 1775.

‡ Hans Ruckers (*c*.1550–*c*.1620) and his sons Jan (1578–1643) and Andries
(1579–*c*.1645) were a family of instrument makers settled in Antwerp. Their keyboard instruments were prized for their sweet tone and robust construction.

there used to be a very great crowd of well dressed people. Went home to finish dinner with Mr and Mrs Arthur and to talk Shropshire. He was born in the same village there as my father and grand-father. She is the daughter of a French refugé—and an obliging, soft and agreeable character. When I came to my hotel, I was informed that all the places in the Lyons diligence were taken for Wednesday—glad of that—and for Friday only one left—sorry for that—as it will keep me here longer than I wish. The abbé goes in the morning to take place for this Day 7 Night—we want 4.

MONDAY 18. No entry into the Mazarine Library today on account of the octave of the Fete Dieu not being over! This is vexatious, as I was prepared for this Library by having already found in the catalogues etc the books I wanted. However I shall go to that of the great abbey St. Germain.* This morning I delivered one of Garrick's letters to M. Suard at the Bureau de la Gazette de France. I was very politely received and presented to Madame who is a pretty, and pretty sort of, woman. Had a long conversation with him on the subject of my voyage. He told me of the new memoires of the music of the ancients by the Abbé Roussier of which the French make grand cas. I had purchased the book since my arrival. He proposed my dining there on Thursday and meeting l'abbé Arnaud one of the members of the Academy of Incriptions who has written a dissertation upon Greek accents which M. Suard recommended and lent me 32 vol of the Memoires of the Academy of Sciences† in which it is printed to read at my lodgings.

This morning M. Monnet called and proposed me meeting several men of letters and talents at his house on Saturday to dinner. I have given him commissions for my work and Arthur is to get me an account of the salaries given here to first rate organists which it seems are much greater than in England.

TUESDAY 19. From 8 to 12 o'clock at the King's Library where with some difficulty I saw a MSS. catalogue of the books on music which I copied as far as the beginning of this century. The oldest book among those that are printed in this collection is an edition of Boethius, de Arithmetica, Gramatica et Musica Venet, 1492. The appendix to the catalogue of MSS on music I could not see.

From the library to Madame Sinmare who was removed—saw Madame and Mademoiselle de la Veau—heard the latter play on the harpsichord and played in turn. She is much improved, went to

---

* The library was 'decimated' by fire in 1794 and a great many of the books which survived were taken into the collections of the Bibliothèque Nationale.

† The Académie Royale des Sciences was formed in Paris by Jean Baptiste Colbert in 1666.

Rougemont Freres and made some dispositions for my journey – dined at the Hotel de Grenelle with my Captain and Cadet and then came home to write, and to read the new book Lexicon Diplomaticum, which Molini had got for me. If it was not so large it seems the best book in the world for my purpose, being a complete dictionary of old letters and abbreviations from the eighth to the fifteenth century when printing was invented. At 9 walked out and chatted a couple of hours with Arthur. He undertook to get my *plan* translated into French by noon next day.

WEDNESDAY 20. This morning I went after the translation of my plan and from thence to Mr Lumisden, who gave and explained to me my routes for Italy. Then to M. Monnet's with whom I went to Passy to dine at M. Brillon's – Lady of Le Receveur des Consignations a very lucrative place, and he's reckoned very rich. Madame Brillon in person is rather pretty, but in her manner charming – polite, easy, and always naturally chearful. There was a good deal of company at dinner which was excellent and *bien servi*. After coffee we went into the music room where I found an English pianoforte* which Mr. Bach had sent her. She played a great deal and I found she had not acquired her reputation in music without meriting it. She plays with great ease, taste and feeling – is an excellent sightswoman, of which I was convinced by her executing some of my own music. She likewise composes and she was so obliging as to play several of her own pieces both on the harpsichord and piano forte accompanied with the violin by M. *Pagin*, who is reckoned in France the best scholar of Tartini ever made. He accompanied very judiciously, and with great expression, the compositions of Madame Brillon, which I suppose he had often seen before; but I did not find him so correct in my own – especially a slow movement in my second sonata† in the time of which though he played it twice over with me and twice with Madame B. he was constantly mistaken. However upon the whole he is a good player. His manner is easy, his coup d'archet admirable and his execution great; but whether he did not exert himself as the room was not large, or from whatever cause it proceeded I know not, his tone was not powerful, not so much so as that of Traversa and *his* was many

* The pianoforte was effectively introduced into England by Johannes Zumpe, a German, who came over in about 1760. He made his instruments rectangular rather than wing-shaped as the harpsichord and grand piano, and these 'square' pianos met with great success not only in England but France also. Johann Christian Bach who came to England in 1762 gave the first public performance of a solo on the pianoforte in London on 2 June, 1768 and was largely responsible for popularising the instrument in England. The pianoforte, accompanying, first appeared in London in 1767.

† One of the *Two Sonatas for the Harpsichord and Forte Piano with Accompanyments for a Violin and Violoncello* (c.1770).

many degrees short of Giardini's. I could not persuade Madame B. to play the piano forte with the stops on*—*c'est sec*, she said—but with them off unless in arpeggios, nothing is distinct—'tis like the sound of bells, continual and confluent. This Lady has many accomplishments besides her music, such as drawing and engraving etc. Her husband seems to be nearly twice her age, but she is very attentive to him and they behave extreamly well and properly to each other. She is a pretty, short, little fat woman, with the most constant, agreeable and natural smile on her face in the world. She has two little daughters, which seem well brought up. M. Pagin no longer makes music his profession: he has a place under the Comp de Clermont and has 250 Louis a year appointment. The abbé Robert of the French Academie Royale of painting† was there, who I found had lived 2 years in Italy, about which country we had a good deal of talk. He puts great contempt upon the mal-aria of the Campagnia of Rome. He is a pretty sort of man and passionately fond of music. I presented Madame Brillon my harpsichord sonatas and lessons which she sat down to play with great avidity. I showed her my manner of fingering the capriccio in the 3rd lesson, which she otherwise I found would have done in the common way with *one finger* instead of two.‡ She played the second of my sonatas very well at sight on the pianoforte accompanied by M. Pagin—and for want of a violoncello I played that part on the harpsichord.§ I stayed till eight o'clock, and then came home to write.

THURSDAY 21. I had destined this morning to the making of visits and had bespoke a remise, but I reckoned without my host, for it being the octave of the Fete Dieu or petite Fete—when the streets are full of processions, I could not stir; as neither remise [hired carriage] or hack are allowed to stir in the streets, till after twelve o'clock, so I stayed at home and sulked—it was the last day I had to spare—Friday at the King's Library and Saturday would be given to packing and paying: *pazzienza*! il faut de la patience. It rains eternally!

I got a coach at last and made visits. The Baron d'Holbach had been lately ill and was out of town, the Abbé Morellet not to be found, and afterwards I was told that he likewise was out of town, which I was not

* The stops were usually two levers placed to the left of the pianoforte keyboard by which the player could raise the dampers from the strings (bass and treble separately) and restore them at will. The stops were later superseded by pedals.

† The Académie Royale de Peinture et Sculpture was founded in 1648.

‡ Madame Brillon is here playing the third of Burney's *Six Sonatas for the Harpsichord* which he published at his own expense in 1761. The capriccio in the third sonata is marked Presto and has as its principal figure a repetition of semiquavers in groups. It is easier to play this, and the result is more effective musically, if two adjacent fingers are used one after the other to strike the same key rather than to strike repeatedly with the same finger.

§ See note † on page 19.

sorry for, having so little time to spend here. I found out, however, my old Lyons acquaintance M. Rigaud de Terre Basse. He sets out next week for that place so that there is a chance for my seeing him there yet. His lady I shall find on my arrival, as she had not been at Paris. The dinner at M. Suard's was very agreeable. There was rather a large company of both sexes but the conversation rational and charming. M. l'abbé Arnauld suits me very much. We had so much *larned** talk on the subject of ancient and modern music that I was quite ashamed of it. After dinner all was very lively and joyous, without drinking or ribaldry. M. Suard who reads every English book that comes out without being able to speak a word is very clever and sensible, of rather more grave turn than is common to his country-men. From hence I went to the play–La Surprise d'amour and George Dandin† both of which were admirably acted. Preville truly comic in the clowns of both! And in order to wind up the libertinism of the day I went to one of the Vaux Halls (they have 3 or 4 here) paid half a crown for my admission and had my eyes put out by the quantity of lights and my ears stunned by the number of fiddles etc for the dancing. When I have described this Vaux Hall it will be easy–no it will not be easy–to find the resemblance. It is on the Boulevard. At the first entrance is a rotund–not very large–with galleries round it well light up and decorated. Then you pass through a quadrangle in the open air well illuminated and the galleries continued on each side to another square room still larger with a row of Corinthian pillars on each side with festoons and illuminations. This is a very elegant room. In this and in the 1st room minuets, allemands, cotillons and contre dances, when the weather is cold, which was now the case, in the extream. There was a great number of people all at present in mourning for a Queen of Denmark and this was all the change that was given for my half crown. Not a morsel of garden.

FRIDAY 22. At the King's Library all the morning making extracts from Salinas,‡ a scarce book in England, and as I had so little time and they made such difficulty to show the MSS even the catalogue of them, I would not ask again nor trouble my friends to make interest for me to see them. At my return if I can spare a few days they shall be dedicated to that purpose. I called at de la Chevardieres, a great

* Learned. Burney often uses provincial, dialect, and colloquial words in situations of happy self-depreciation, or when thoroughly put out. It was a characteristic which he revealed in his speech and letters also.

† *La Surprise de l'amour* (1722) by Pierre Carlet de Chamblain Marrivaux (1688–1763). *Georges Dandin, ou le mari confondu* (1668) by Jean-Baptiste Poquelin [Moliere] (1622–73).

‡ Francisco de Salinas (1513–90) a Spanish musician and writer on music published *De Musica libri septem* in 1577.

music seller here in correspondence with Bremner,* to get a copy of my sonatas which I wished to present to Mrs Hamilton at Naples. I brought over 2 sets but have given them to Madame Brillon and Mademoiselle de la Veau. He had none left of what I wanted here. I met with the Abbé Roussier ⌊at la Chevardieres music shop⌋. We were soon made acquainted and had a great deal of musical talk. We *took* much to each other and promised at my return to improve the acquaintance. This abbé has a great collection of books. I showed him my catalogue at which I found his mouth watered–Oh! Monsieur vous etes bien riche!–I was glad to meet with him as the Abbé Arnauld spoke highly of his ability. I dined at Monnet's and there met the Abbé Arnauld again, who improves very much upon acquaintance. He has rather a sour look but brightens up in conversation, when his eyes sparkle and he has one of the most animated countenance imaginable. With him were the famous Geneva painter Leotard and Mr Grettry the best and at present most fashionable composer of the comic opera. He is a thin delicate gentlemanlike young man, very well bred and proper. I must not forget Madame Monnet, who is a very pretty woman and about half the age of monsieur. A great many good stories were told at table and afterwards by the abbé, who has as much wit as learning. He has a *justesse d'esprit* in speaking upon the arts that is irresistible–clear in his conceptions, and expressions. In short I like him as much as any man of genius I ever saw upon so short an acquaintance.

SATURDAY 23. To pack and to pay were the chief employments of this day. I began to be so well laid in at Paris that I left it with regret– but I believe I forgot to mention that last night for the first time I went to the Comedy Françoise which is now removed to the Tuilleries. I there saw two comedies admirably acted La Surprise d'amour and George Dandin. Preville was admirable in both. His humour is truly simple and natural and the applause he gains is as incessant as the laughter he occasions. It is such as Garrick receives in Abel Drugger.†

This morning while I was waiting at home for my banker's letters and making dispositions for packing up, I was favoured with a visit from the Abbé Roussier. Our conversation was of course very musical and we parted great friends with a promise to see one another again at my return and to write when I got to England. The good Mr. Lumisden came himself with his letters for Rome; when I shewed him my *Plan* and received his compliments–but the Abbé Rousseau

---

* One of the leading music publishers in London. He published much of Burney's music.

† A character in Ben Jonson's comedy *The Alchemist*.

cried out every moment ma foi, c'est vaste! I told them both that I did not promise all this to the public it was only what I had promised *myself*.

Being detained by a milliner's breach of promise I did not go to the inn with my companions, but order⟨ed my case⟩ to remain in the same part of the town where I had some ruffles etc making, and went in my travelling dress to the Theatre Italien where I saw on ne s'avise jamais de tout and The Huron, an opera taken from Voltaire's Ingenu,* the music by Gretry which gave me an opportunity of judging of the talents of that favourite composer. This afternoon Mr Bullock found me out, so that as the business of the French theatres is all over by eight o'clock, I went to Arthur's and wrote a couple of letters ere I set off for the Quay des Celestins which is quite on the opposite side of Paris. At ten I joined Captain Seagrave and his two cadets—Messieurs Fitzgerald and Keating. The father of this last was there and we supped comfortably enough.

At four next morning the 24th JUNE I left Paris in the diligence after Mass—it being Sunday. Unluckily once a week the vehicle of that name which goes to Lyons has ten passengers (a late Regulation—it used to have but eight) and this it was my lot to go in. Such a pack of legs etc squeezed together, made it very fatiguing and disagreeable, and made all our legs swell terribly. Our company consisted of my friend the Captain and two cadets under his care, a *Chevalier de St Louis*, a gentleman of *Provence*, a young officer, an old wine merchant, a merchant of Amsterdam native of Milan, the Duke of Parma's surgeon and your Humble. We dined at *Fontainebleau* about 42 miles from Paris. By this time we were all acquainted and though there were no females, the conversation never slept if either the Chevalier or provençale gentleman were awake; for such eternal talkers and prosers the whole fair sex has never yet been able to boast. 1st night at Pont sur Yonne at a miserable village and Inn—but, compared with the English, the Inns throughout France are all miserable—and as to dirtiness one need only say once for all that the French are intolerable. The eating and drinking all the way was good enough for me though my countrymen would find fault with it, had it been better. Monday morning we set out at 4 and between 5 and 6 were at Sens, a large but ill built City, where we only stopped to change horses—dined at Joigny, passed through Auxerre another large old City, and at night lay at Vermonton—where I remembered with regret the company and evening I spent 4 years before. Dined on Tuesday at Rouvray by the waterside—where we saw the first pretty girl we had met with since we

* The libretto was by Marmontel. The opera was first performed in 20 August, 1768.

[23]

left Paris and the whole company was so struck with the novelty of the sight, that they all at the same instant applauded her by clapping hands violently. To say the truth as one goes towards the south the complexions are not only worse and worse but even the features. We got pretty soon into *Arnay le Duc* a small old fortified town–terribly mauled and tired. However after supper the company rallied their spirits and sung and danced till near 11 o'clock tho' we had been called up that morning at ½ an hour past 2 and were to set off at the same time next day. Wednesday we dined at *Chalon sur Soane* a large city, where we left the diligence and went on board a *Coche d'eau*, ⌞or passage boat⌟, which was more agreeable to us all, we as had more room for our feet and frame, and could see more of the fine country through which we went and enjoy the air when the weather would let us, as it was cold and wet great part of the way. Here we read, slept, played at cards, told stories etc as is so usual in the like situation that it is hardly worth mentioning. We did not get into *Macon* where we were only allowed 3 hours to sup, sleep and breakfast, till 11 at night. However to cut matters short by 5 o'clock we arrived at Lyon thro' a most beautiful country and in fine weather, which we could perceive grow better and warmer as we past the Mountains of Burgundy.

LYONS

There was a disagreeable ceremony at the Custom House, but 2 Italians who were going on to Italy and with whom I had agreed to travel had a friend of Lyons to meet 'em and matters were shortened. We took up our lodging at the *Parc* near the Place de Terreaux. Here we parted from the rest of our fellow travellers, and though not of the 1st or most entertaining sort, such *animaux d'habitude* are we, that all appeared very sorry to be separated--*embrassades sans fin*–and my military friends who were going to *Corsica* seemed extreamly sorry to part. My legs here were so swelled that I thought I should be laid up. However as it was too late for the play we* walked about and at last blundered upon a Coffee House where 2 Italian girls were singing a duo accompanied by 2 violins and a base. The customers were of both sexes.† In the same Coffee House upstairs where we had heard singing, M. *Pelletin* performed most of Comus's tricks and afterwards all the illuminations of Paris for the marriage of the Dauphin. They were I believe extreamly pretty and exact, except in the consequences of

* ⌞'hobbled about in order to see the humours of the town. See other journal to end of Lyons'⌟.

† ⌞'in other journal'⌟.

those at the Place de Louis 15, but so tired and sleepy I was that I could not possibly keep my eyes open. These illuminations represented in miniature those at the palais de Bourbon d'Orleans–du Louvre–de la place de Louis 15 & de Versailles.

Next morning having had about 5 hours sleep I found myself a new man. After unpacking, dressing etc we went to the Cathedral of St Jean to hear the Mass a la Romaine. We dined at our Hotel and after dinner played at cards, *one and twenty*, with some Italian merchants of my companions acquaintance at a pretty house on one of the hills which commands almost the whole city of Lyons with a view of the *Soane* and *Rhone*. This was a good lesson for me in Italian. It rained *à verse* all the evening so that it was our only recourse. At night to the play–Phedre and Nanette et Lucas. After supper at our Hotel, to the Coffee House. Next morning book hunting etc.

There are many English people in this town and while I am writing this somebody is playing 'Through the wood Laddie'* on the German flute in the next room till they are ready to die. It is not at all certain now whether we shall get away tomorrow or no for the Dutch merchant who fights all our money battles seems to have overshot the mark. He has Dutcheconomy joined to Italian cunning, which makes him very fit for such work, but he's too suspicious and too passionate– from such squabbles as he has from morning to night Good Lord deliver me! The *vitturini* have offered us two chaises (they were to find the 4th passenger) for 14 guineas to carry us first to Geneva–to stop there 2 or 3 days, then to go to Turin–to board us on the road and to pay all the expenses of our being carried over Mount Cenis. Moiana offered 12–then 13–but now they won't go under 16. I would rather pay a guinea or two more than lose my time and hear all this noise, but I dare not say so, lest the Dutch-man should think my money not worth saving, or should chuse to think me worth fleecing by himself. In short suspicions beget suspicions and he says he'll trust nobody not even his own brother. He won't stir out of our common room without locking up every bit of paper that is not good enough even to wipe one with, and taking with him the key. I never saw stronger marks of misanthropy–composed of cunning, avarice and an utter distrust of his own species.

Whether it proceeds from my not being so young as five years ago– that I am more difficult to please than then by having more judgement and less appetite or both–or that things are really dearer and worse than they were at that time I know not; but I neither relish their cookery so well as formerly, nor do things appear so cheap. The soups

* A well-known Scottish tune. The German flute was the side-blown wood-wind instrument, precursor of the modern orchestral flute.

at the *Tables d'Hote* seem made of boiled dish-clouts, and neither their boiled or rost-meats have any taste but of pepper, salt and garlick. I am sorry to say this, as I always supposed these complaints in others proceeded from ill humour, sensuality, and want of experience—but at present, such are *my* feelings. Perhaps the novelty may be wanting, which in my former journey to this city kept my attention alive, and gilded everything I saw. But this will be proved as I advance further, for every step I take beyond Lyons will be as new to me as every part of France was in my first landing in that kingdom in 1764.

SATURDAY evening-JUNE 30th. It is now agreed that we set out for Geneva in our way to Turin at 6 o'clock tomorrow morning at 15 guineas the 3. By we I mean the Italian Dutch merchant, the Gentleman from Parma and myself. With the second I usually travelled in the same chaise. He was a man of letters and we hit it off very well together. The 1st, who would neither think nor speak of anything but his own concerns seemed to like the opportunity a chaise to himself gave him of meditating on them.

SUNDAY 1 JULY. The road from Lyons to Geneva at first setting out is charming. The Rhone on the right side and the *Collines* or chain of fertile and beautiful hills on the left—and this lasts for upwards of 20 miles with scarce a single link of the chain broken. We dined at *Monthuel* a very old fortified Town. The Citadel is on the summit of the hill, where there is a high round tower which we tried to ascend but could find no steps. Near this is a very old church built in 1250 which we entered and found very clean and decent. Here, as we were attended by 2 little boys, I had an opportunity of examining the large Church *Graduals** which I was always afraid of doing elsewhere, and found them printed on 4 red lines and black Gregorian notes. The prospect from this hill covered with vines, is the most beautiful imaginable. Here we saw the Rhone winding through a rich country, Burgundy on one side, Dauphiny on the other, with high mountain like clouds at a distance. There is a large bleaching ground here—and the houses on the whole road we travelled today have frightful large pent-houses hanging above an ell [45 inches] in length over the streets. About 4 it grew intolerably cold, and at 5 began to rain furiously. We stopped at *St Jean le vieux*, a most miserable inn and scarcity of even *bad* beds. I chose to sit up in an easy chair as there was a most promising appearance of bugs from the dirt and beggary around us.

MONDAY. Set out about 6 the rain continuing still. I did not find myself much the worse for sitting up all night, having slept more and

---

* 'Gradual' is here taken to mean the book containing all the Gregorian music of the Mass.

sounder in the chaise than the bugs would have suffered me to do in bed, unless it had been on the floor, but it was too cold for that expedient. We had a fire lighted and kept in all night in Lat 46° ½* July 2nd! Between St Jean le vieux and Cerdon a high ridge of hills on one hand, a rapid river with a fertile plain and *collines* covered with trees on the other, and 2 or 3 villages and monastrys prettily placed in view. Here the 2 chains of hills meet and form a *corona*. The outlet is a narrow fissure or crack in a huge rock, just sufficient for the river and a narrow road. Afterwards between *Cerdon* and *St Martin du Frene*–a mixture of rocks with clouds hanging on the top and sides–trees– shrubs, among which a great deal of wild box–vines–pasture–tours and monasteries on the point of the highest of all these crags, composed, tho' a vile wet day, one of the most amazing and pleasing scenes imaginable. A botanist and lover of fossils would surely find great amusement here, and it is somewhat wonderful that no one has hitherto travelled into the mountainous countries of Savoy, Piedmont, Swisserland and the Alps, merely to collect and examine the stones and plants with which they abound. I, who am neither one nor the other could have spent a month very delightfully in this journey only from Lyons to Geneva which is chiefly through Bresse only, a part of Lower Burgundy. M. Rousseau is at present much attached to the study of botany, and it is to be hoped, he who has so long been an inhabitant of these countries will supply the deficiency of other botanists. When we arrived at what had long seemed to be the summit of these mountains, we discovered groves of trees on others still higher and literally *in the clouds*. To the botanist and fossil-monger I would join the painter in this tour, for such beautiful, such stupendous views as he would find would fill his mind with such images as he could never forget, and with such a variety of them as would last him his whole life. On the plains at the top of the highest of these mountains I found daisies, king-cups and all the flowers of Spring with us, though the 2nd of July. After travelling several leagues between two mountains we came to an opening truly theatrical–I never saw so beautiful an opera scene.

After dinner at *Pont Maillard* [Maillat] the weather was fine, and we continued to travel between 2 chains of mountains, some of them wholly covered with box, which the poor people were cutting for firing. Hitherto we were still in that part of Burgundy called Bresse and passed by a *green* lake above 2 miles long and 2 or 3 of the most beautiful cascades I ever saw. One gushed out of the solid rock and turned 2 mills. One ran strait down from the summit of a very high rock. In another place on the left hand of this lake a shower from

* Actually Burney was somewhat south of this reckoning.

[27]

dripping rocks of a great height, which the people here say is eternally raining in the same manner. It has made holes in the rock on which it falls. Here quote Horace.*

We lay this night at Chatillon [Châtillon de Michaille]–still between 2 chains of high mountains. The mountains of Bresse are not only higher and more fertile than those of the Peak in Derbyshire but of much longer continuance. From Lyon to the place where we lodged last night is 72 miles, and this double chain continued still to Coulanges [Collonge], 18 miles further, where we dine at 10 o'clock. About 2 miles before we arrived here we were asked for our passports at a fortress called *Ecluses*† belonging to the King of France, and had no other interruptions till we reached Geneva. After dinner the chain on the right hand was broken and another appeared at a distance, which were the mountains of Savoy. Those on the right hand, now in the Country of Gex had the snow on them in patches, and at Geneva they say these mountains are never without. We did not see Geneva till we were just upon it. The level country we passed through was for 3 or 4 miles like many parts of England. We had no interruption at the gates but just had to write our names and to take a Billet to the inn where we were to lodge. The most striking objects we met in our way thither were the piazzas‡ at the sides of the houses for the people to walk under, the covering to which was as high as the roof of the houses and therefore did not darken the under rooms. The pillars are wood. The Rhone which runs with great rapidity out of the Leman Lake close to the city is absolutely of a light blue colour bordering a little on green. I never saw a river of such a colour before. The Rhone itself at Lyons is white.

GENEVA

WEDNESDAY morning 4th JULY. The weather is fine and I am in love with this place. I have eat drank and slept more comfortably than since I left England. Cleanliness, industry and plenty appear wherever one turns one's eyes. All the way from Lyons the common people were all mendicants dechaussées§–withered–hungry, and wretched–but here no beggars, no barefooted people are seen in the streets, and

---

* In the Osborn MS. he enters *Gutta cavat lapidem* (The drop hollows the stone) from Ovid.

† The fortress was in a gorge with a passage so deep and narrow that a carriage had difficulty in making way.

‡ By piazza is usually meant a public square or market place. Burney, here, and elsewhere, applies the word incorrectly to indicate a colonnade or covered gallery surrounding an open square, or even a single colonnade in front of a building.

§ Altered to '. . . were all half naked, withered . . .'

if they knew it, they have it in their power to be the happiest state upon Earth. Liberty in Religion a mild government and an almost equality of condition one would think might content them, if it were possible to content mankind; but, alas! the ambition of some, the want of parts in others, and that restlessness which is inherent in human nature, makes it impossible for any government where men are much left to their own guidance, and to the gratification of fickleness to last long. One perturbed spirit of great abilities is sufficient to overset any mild Government that was ever invented, or at least to disturb it, and to sow the seeds of sedition and total subversion.

THURSDAY. mem. François–an excellent servant here.

I have not time to write down half I see or half I think. This has been a busy day. The Lake, the library, churches, and fortifications I visited yesterday, and today walked quite round the town. Its situation is truly charming, surrounded with neat country houses which it seems the fashion to sleep in all the summer. I went on the lake in a boat, it was very calm and pleasant: the water is the clearest I ever saw. The town is surrounded with mountains. In going into it from France those of Gex are at your back–facing you are those of Swisserland; on the left hand–with a peep at the glaciers 54 miles off, in eternal frost; and on the right those of Savoy. The Lake on the left hand to the East, and the Rhone on the right to the west. There are 4 wooden bridges over the two parts of the Rhone which form a small island covered with houses. The Town is well built, chiefly of white stone: the streets not very regular but clean, paved with pebbles. The trout in the lake are famous and we had some every day both at dinner and supper.

The people here are as little sensible of their happiness as their neighbours. Eternal quarrels and parties rage here with great fury–they have lately come to blows. It hurts the trade as well as peace of the town. The great number of young foreign strangers sent here from the protestant countries of Europe, but chiefly English, is much diminished and it now becomes a fashion to prefer Lausanne.*

WEDNESDAY. I visited the ingenious M. Serre, a famous miniature painter here who has written 2 very clever musical pamphlets, and is thought very deep in the science of sound. He was formerly many years in England, speaks English–and seemed much pleased with my visit. He returned it the same night. I communicated to him my plan and talked it over with him and he entered very heartily into my views and seemed solicitous that I should pursue it.

Next day I visited M. Fritz, a famous performer on the violin here

* ⌊'Gen. other journal'⌋.

and a good composer whom I have many years wished to hear. He has taught several of my friends and acquaintances – among whom was Lord Brook and Lord Orford when in Swisserland. It was rather awkward to go to him, but I sent a message over night and he appointed two o'clock the next day. He was at a house about a mile out of Town. We soon grew very well acquainted. I let him know that many of his English scholars were my particular friends and that his name and his music were well known in England. I enquired after his new compositions, and he told me he was about publishing a set of overtures by subscription. This I rejoiced to hear, and immediately subscribed for 2 sets, at ½ Guinea each – and tho' there was no instrument of any kind in the room where we sate, ere we parted I prevailed on him to go into another and play me a solo, which he did most admirably, tho' I am certain he must be near 70 – a thin sensible looking old man – but I never heard more spirit in a young man of 20, and his solo was good.

The going to M. Fritz at the time above mentioned broke into a plan I had formed of visiting M. de Voltaire at the same hour with some other strangers that were then going to Fernay [Ferney]; but to say the truth, besides the visit to Fritz being more *my business*, I did not much like going with these people, who had only a bookseller to introduce them – and I had heard that some English had lately met with a rebuff from Voltaire by going without any letter or recommendation, or anything to recommend themselves. They were asked by him what they wanted. Upon their replying they wished only to see so extraordinary a man he said, well, Gentlemen, you now see me; and did you take me to be a Wild Beast or a Monster that was fit only to be stared at, as a show? – This story very much frightened me, for not having any intention of going to Geneva when I left London, or even Paris, I was quite unprovided with a passport. However I was determined to see his place which I took to be cette Maison d'Aristippe ces Jardins d'Epicure to which he retired in 1755, but was mistaken. I drove to it alone after I left Fritz. His house is 3 or 4 miles from Geneva – but near the Lake – and I approached it with reverence and a curiosity of the most minute kind. – I enquired *when* I first trod on his domain – I had an intelligent and talkative coachman who answered all my questions very satisfactorily.

His estate is very large here – and he is building pretty farm houses upon it. He has a quadrangular *Justice* [gallows] upon it to show that he is the *Seigneur*. One of his farms or rather manufacturing houses (for he is establishing a manufacture upon his Estate) was so handsome that I thought it was his *Chateau*. But we drove to Ferney through a charming country covered with corn and vines and a view of the Lake and mountains above described. On the left hand approaching the house is a neat chapel with this inscription.

Deo

Erexit

Voltaire

MDCCLXI

This seems a little ostentatious in one who has as little religion of any sort perhaps as ever fell to the share of a thinking man. I wanted to write two lines of Pope under the Inscription

Who Builds a Church to God and not to Fame

Ne'er mars the Building with the Donor's Name

I sent in to enquire whether a stranger might be allowed to see the house and was answered in the affirmative. The servant soon came and conducted me into the cabinet or closet where his master had just been writing, which is never shewn when he is at home, but being walked out, I was allowed that privilege. From thence to the library, not a very large room but well filled. Here I found a whole-length figure in marble of himself recumbent in one of the windows and many curiosities. In another room a bust of himself not 2 years since, his mother's picture, that of his niece Madame Denis, her Brother M. Dupuis, the Calas Family etc. etc; it is a very neat and elegant house not large, or affectedly decorated. I should have said that close to the chapel, between that and the house, is the theatre he built some years ago to treat his friends with some of his own tragedies.* It is now only used as a receptacle for wood and lumber, there having been no play acted in it these 4 years. The servant told me his master was 78 –but very well–il travaille pendant writes constantly without spectacles and walks out with only a servant, very often, a mile or 2–et le voila, là bas. He was going to his workmen. My heart leaped at the sight of so extraordinary man——⊙ here I am interrupted by the Company and supper–I write this in a wretched Inn between Geneva and Chamberry among the mountains of Savoy, not yet upon 'em but always mounting.⊙ This servant's words were these: il travaille pendant dix heures chaque jour–he studies ten hours every day.

⊙ These signs relate sentences as they appear in the Journal.

* Voltaire was passionately interested in the theatre and much of his contemporary fame rested upon his verse tragedies. He built private theatres in which his plays were performed for himself and his friends. The last and best of the theatres was at Ferney. Originally it held only about 50 people, but was later enlarged to seat 200.

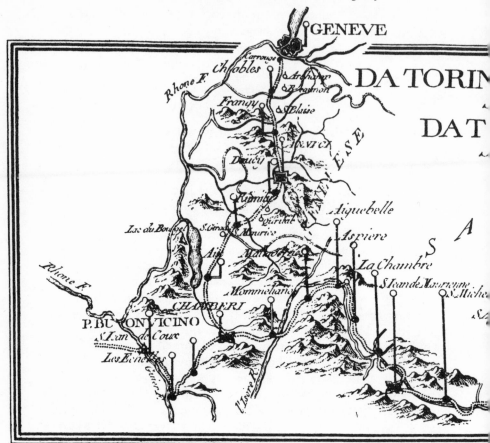

SATURDAY Night. Montmellian. There now only a river between us and the mountains covered with snow which tomorrow I suppose we must ascend. But I am very much in arrears. FRIDAY morning. The weather set in fine, and at 6 o'clock when we quitted Geneva, the Mountains of Gex were very beautifully covered with white clouds lying close one to the other as I have seen 'em only before in an opera scene. They remained still several hours and at length their highnesses got up with great state and mounted the sky very slowly on their aerial journey. Today I saw several of these clouds begin to form themselves on the sides of the hills I passed, and found that what I took for snow was often these thin clouds, but tonight there is no doubt left of the snow in our neighbourhood.

But to go back to Geneva I must just make a remark or two concerning hasty conclusions in a strange country. At the *Ballance* in

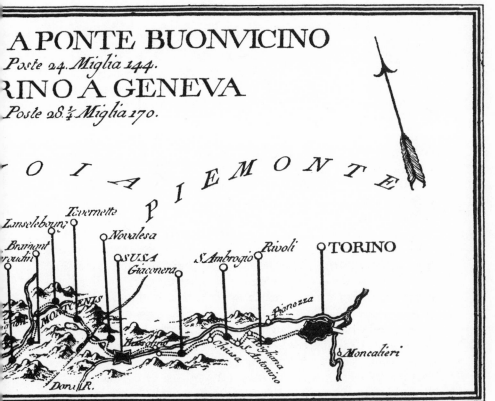

A PONTE BUONVICINO
Poste 24. Miglia 144.

...INO A GENEVA
Poste 28¼ Miglia 170.

O I A — PIEMONTE —

Lanslebourg
Tavernette
Brarmont
roullin
Novalesa
SUSA
Giaconera
S. Ambrogio
Rivoli
○ TORINO
MONTCENIS
Pianezza
Ressogne
Chiusa
S. Antonino
S. Moncalieri
Doru. R.

Geneva where we lodged and boarded and were very well entertained, an excellent table, good company, good wine and cleanliness, which we all agreed was comparatively better than anything we had met with since Paris and indeed superior to the general entertainment in that place. But I find there is no judging of the provisions of a country or the manner of serving it, by what entertainment one meets with at inns or hotels—for all these good things we had met with at the Ballance in Geneva were so much surpassed by those of what was looked on as a *plain* supper in a private family to which I was invited with my companions, that it set me a reflecting that at Passy chez M. Billon, at Paris with M. Suard and at Lyons with M. Rigaud etc the same thing had happened. The soup so much better, the boullie, better meat and better dressed—the ragouts, fricandeaux, entremets etc etc all so much better than at the best inns or hotels, that it is the highest injustice to say how the French families in general live from what these tables afford. But basta—I shall now quit Geneva without staying to relate what passed between M. Voltaire and me as I shall never forget it. My cabriole overtook me on the road walking to his workmen.*

Suppose me now in Savoy on the other side the Rhone in the Territories of the King of Sardinia. I expected here to meet at every step with Savoyard musicians, such as abound in London and Paris—but not one musician of any sort have I met hitherto except a miserable blind fiddler and a dulcimer—dreary. Barren mountains on each side the road, which is full of beggars more than half naked. But this is not so wonderful or so hateful as in France, where the country is rich and abounding with all the luxuries and comforts of life, to see its cultivators in beggary and rags, makes one regard England in a very favourable light.

In Savoy, near Geneva, I found it was the custom for the gentlemen to wear high crowned straw hats. All kinds of husbandry are performed both here and in *Bresse* by oxen—no horses in the teams, and but few mules on the road. They have but just begun here to cut their hay (of which but a poor crop as well as of other things). We dined at a village too mean to excite sufficient curiosity to enquire its name. Here however we found excellent Swiss cheese, good brown bread and the best white wine I had tasted since my arrival on the continent. With these I could have been contented, but my fellow travellers calling about 'em—the landlady cries *faut-il faire travailler la broche?* —*oui—mais c'est bien vendredi*—. We did very well here, *I* thought, but there was sad grumbling. We lay at a wretched old fortified town where we were much worse off. SATURDAY 7th. We went to *Aix* [Aix les Bains] to breakfast—that is to some raw hartichoaks stinking oil, salt and pepper—*a la poivreade*. We visited the famous hot baths here—the water of which seems to me much hotter than that at Bath in England.† I drank 2 glasses of it to facilitate digestion of that nothing I had to eat etc. These baths I believe were built by the Emperor Gratian. There are several Roman inscriptions here, and many other antiquities; but nothing can have a more antique or *ruinous* appearance than the whole town, which however is in summer

---

* This sentence was first written 'my cabriole overtook him on the road walking to his workmen'. In *Tour* 1773 Burney relates what passed between Voltaire and himself. Voltaire asked after English news, and enquired 'what poets we had now'. Burney replied suitably and came away with a quote for posterity: 'Disputes among authors are of use to literature; as the quarrels of the great, and the clamours of the little, in free government, are necessary to liberty. When critics are silent it does not so much prove the age to be correct, as dull' (p. 61).

† The temperature of the hot springs at Bath ranges from 117° to 120° F.

a good deal frequented on account of its waters, in dispight of every inconvenience of bad lodging, provisions, etc. The water is very offensive to the smell –

From Aix to *Chamberry* is a very good road but bad country; always barren hills on each side poor farming and poorer farmers in the narrow valley below. SATURDAY JULY 7. We lay at Montmellian at the foot of very high mountains covered with snow and close to the River Isere into which it runs at Valence after passing by Grenoble. There is an old fortress upon a high rock just by the town, which is a very poor one. But in time of war the bridge over the Isere is a very important pass. At this place we had a very good supper and excellent wine for which it is famous. It had been very hot all the afternoon. It rained hard almost all night, and in the morning ere we set out there was a violent storm of thunder and lightening. The thunder reverberating from mountain to mountain was more awful than any I had heard. Almost all the way from Montmellian to Aiguabelle where we dined it rained, but after stopping a little while, there was immediately after our arrival the most violent rain I ever saw. The mountains we passed by this morning are not so barren as those of yesterday, the highest of them all are covered with trees and the plain or bottom is better cultivated than any part of Savoy I had yet seen. At Aiquabelle, 2 posts from Montmellian the hills are covered with snow. The clouds all this morning had, to me, very extraordinary appearances, sometimes lying in rows on the sides of the mountains: sometimes in patches – sometimes mounting slowly into air – sometimes stationary. In our journey over the Alps there were few things more new and amazing to me that these appearances.

From the miserable town where we lay on Friday night to Chamberry is a very good road, but bad country. We travelled between high and barren mountains, without anything to amuse us or even that kind of interest in the road, when it is bad, which is occasioned by fear of danger. Chambery, the capital of Savoy is a very poor town without trade and consequently full of idleness and beggars. Its inhabitants are said to amount to between 4 and 5000. Rousseau, after he left Geneva, retired here and dates from hence some of his works. It is about 40 miles from Geneva. There are pretty fair women and children in it. An organ in the great church with a brazen frame, upper pipes painted white. The clergy here seem the best off of any of the inhabitants. There is no play-house nor public diversion. It is fortified and has a small garrison, and 4 sub-urbs. In the road from Geneva hither the Rhone was on the right hand with the mountains of Gex to the north, Swisserland behind, and Chamberry in front. The frogs here are I suppose very large, for the noise they make is like that of ducks. The poor people all may truly be said to be of the order of *Méndicants Déchaussés.* *

SUNDAY night, we lay at la Chambre, and it was here so rainy and cold that we had a fire. My companions, tho' old travellers and natives of Italy were for ever quarelling with the landlords about bad wine and poor provisions, but I found both better than I expected. Between Aiquabelle and La Chambre constant rain–and it being Sunday I found that the common people (they are all so here) could find no other amusement than to sit in companies under some rock which kept 'em from the wet. Lyons, Geneva, Chambery etc are called *pots de chambre des montagnes* on account of their having rain more frequently than elsewhere, but here the mountains are so high that no cloud can pass without being broken. From la Chambre to St. Jean de Morienne [–de Maurienne], country still wilder and more barren. About this last place there seem to be coals–the soil is black. From hence to St Michel where we dine Monday. The River, which we are constantly near, is like the Derwent by Matlock in Derbyshire. At the entrance into St Jean de Morienne, a sugar loaf mountain is seen, which it resembles not only by its conic figure, but by its colour being entirely covered with snow. Here the plain grows narrower mountains higher and the country more wild. A rapid muddy river running by the roadside–its fury shows how much we mount. I find the chimneys thro' all these mountainous countries covered at the top with pigeon holes at the sides to let out the smoak–this may be a useful hint to such as live near mountains, trees, or high buildings which cause their chimneys to smoak.

MONDAY 9th JULY. This being the first fair day since Friday I walked on foot from St. Michael to St André about 9 miles, and the river almost all the way was one perpetual cascade and so noisy one could scarce hear any one speak. I wished very much for time and knowledge to make botanical observations, as I saw in my walk many plants, shrubs, and flowers to which my eyes had not been accustomed. Here I first observed the pine-tree to grow wild on the mountains. There were some of every species of fir, with mirtle, laurentinus, wild-gooseberries etc. On the right-hand at the summit of one of the highest moutains is a vast plain on which much cheese is made of goats milk. There is likewise a lake there of several leagues long; and at this time of the year while the snow melts and runs into this lake it discharges itself in an infinite number of cataracts and cascades which fall in torrents down the rocks into the river below whose rapidity and fury are scarce credible.

We lay this night at a town called *Modane*, not a post town but

* Shoeless wanderers, or beggars, seem to have been much on Burney's mind.

between 2 post-towns–St André and Villa Rodin. TUESDAY at 4 o'clock we set out for Mont Cenis, the highest of all the passable Alps, and from Modane to Villa Rodin we mounted the Alps in good earnest, and were obliged to alight 2 or 3 times to walk. Here hanging woods of large pine trees of many leagues–from Villa Rodin to another village a great quantity of little chapels and crucifixes in the road, and in these 2 towns there are more churches and chapels than houses. Fine clear morning, but as cold as February, hills, and what little plain there is very barren. Very near the snow now on all sides. With regard to these chapels etc one might venture to say 'There is more cost than worship', for I saw no use made of them. No strawberries or cherries yet ripe here–nor nothing like a vine to be seen this morning. They weed here the bits of ground they have, very carefully between plowing and sowing, and carry muck on the backs of asses in bags. The people here seem a nation of *Calibans*. One room almost always served the whole family, mules, asses, cows and hogs included, but when they give way to luxury, the quadrupeds have the parlour to themselves–the bipeds, the dining room to which they ascend by steps on the outside of the house–and the hay is lodged in the second floor. All the towns here are equally miserable. Between Bramant and Lanébourg [Lanslebourg] we passed by a considerable town for this country, built at the confluence of 2 rapid rivers, part on one side and part on the other of each. We descended a mountain at the entrance and ascended one still higher at the exit.

At Lanébourg the foot of the great mountains, we were met by a great number of muleteers who offered their services to carry us up, but there was a diabolical tapage [squabble] between them and our vitturini about the price. It is regulated by the King of Sardinia at about half a guinea for the whole in case a passenger is carried on a sort of wooden horse by 2 men from Lanébourg to Noveleze [Novalesa], that is from one foot of Mont-Cenis to the other, and well they would deserve their money. But an evasion has been found out by the vitturini, who undertake to board you and to pay all expenses of passing this mountain. For in summer time, at least, it is much safer to mount this precipice on mules, and much cheaper–so that the *porteurs* have nothing to do with you till you arrive at *La Croce*, the end of the plain on Mount-Cenis, and then a fresh bargain is to be made with them. In short the muleteers and porters who used to impose on travellers are now, in their turn, hardly used by the vitturini. They used to be paid too much and now are not sufficiently paid–and I found at the inns, these vitturini had frequent quarrels about the bills for our board and those at the bottom and top of Mount-Cenis I thought would never end. There are such swarms of these poor people in this miserable country, where there is no other kind of trade, that at the town of Laneburg I counted above 50 that were squabbling about us and our baggage with the vitturini. The being *nourri* certainly saves trouble and money to the traveller, but he is pinched in every particular by the inn-keepers – who are sure to furnish the worst of everything knowing how ill they shall be paid. All the way if we had a bottle of good wine we were obliged to pay for it under the denomination of *vin etranger*. Any one who has once crost the Alps and knows these things and the current coin of the country, had better board himself. And then again the chaises all over the continent, especially those a l'Italien or the *Calessi*, are so very wretched to ride in that the worst I ever entered in England is luxury compared with the best here. A chaise had best be bought in England which is taken to pieces for the mountains and feluccas.

But to return to Lanebourg; from whence I thought we should never get on account of the quarrels above mentioned, we did at last mount our mules. I had neither boots, spurs nor whip or switch – but these creatures are very sure footed and careful, for their own sakes, and will not go a bit faster than they like for yours. Each cavalier has an esquire to carry his arms – sword, pistols, etc and there is a certain hideous noise these people make to which the mules pay some attention, otherwise their obstinacy is invincible. It is reckoned a league from the bottom to the top, but as we winded round and round, I did not find the ascent so craggy or steep as I expected. If you do not look behind you, it is nothing to any one accustomed to Derbyshire or Wales; but if you do, you are in as much danger of losing yourself as the wife of Lot or Orpheus. When we arrived at the top there was a plain 3 miles long with a large lake on it famous for its trout. But I found on each side this plain still high rocks and mountains eternally covered with snow – which is *glacée*. I had great curiosity to ascend one of them and see what was on the top – whether other mountains or only snow, but my curiosity was a good deal repressed by hearing from the muleteers that there were wild bears and wolves in great quantities who retired there in summer. At Gran Croce on the end of the plain next Piemont we descended from our mules, after having run races with them in which they tried who should go slowest, or rather which should get to the wrong end first when I was victorious. We got some excellent trout and goat's-milk cheese and butter – the former were better than those from the Lake of Geneva. Here we were in sight of the Piemontese mountains, but not the plains which cannot be discovered till you come to the end of the mountains at Rivoli. My fellow travellers and myself were each of us carried from hence by 2 men on a kind of field stool fastened to 2 poles, with knobs to hold by. This is 10 times worse than ascending as you constantly see your danger, and besides it is much farther down than up– 'Tis a dreadfully laborious trade for the poor men: they were obliged to rest 5 or 6 times ere we reached Novelese. In short this descent is both terrific and fatiguing. I never was more thoroughly tired in my life. But the rocks, precipices, cataracts and torrents amused as well as frightened us, so that I did not know how much I was tired till all was over. We underwent a custom-house visit, always disagreeable– though here not uncivil. But the squabbles of the porters and vitturini I thought would never *be over*: they knocked me up more than the journey.

We are now in Italy, though a very bad part of it: 'tis however something to have Mount Cenis on one's back. WEDNESDAY morning. Clear weather, though very windy. About a mile below Novelese the double chain of mountains ends, and as if nature intended a new and insuperable bar to the entrance into Italy on this side, a new chain appears at the bottom, which runs all along on the right hand as far as Rivoli–obliging us to turn short on the left and to cross the river. There is likewise a new chain of mountains on the left hand, though less high, which runs on to Swisserland. Upon turning the corner and looking up to Mont Cenis the prospect is amazingly dreary, from the height and great quantity of snow upon it. From the lake upon this mountain the 2 greatest rivers of France and Italy, namely the Rhone and Po are fed. Susa is an old battered town, but the Fortress Brunetta, on a hill, just by it, is reckoned one of the strongest fortifications in Europe. I thought at Novelese I could discover the women and children to look more like human creatures than what I had seen in Savoy. At the bottom of Mont Cenis vines begin to appear and I perceive those of Italy are planted in rows–espaliers–and between them corn and fruit trees. In France 'tis different–being mixed with nothing else and only supported by sticks–not in rows–old castles at Fenestrelles and St. Ambroise etc with battlements in the manner of those built before the invention of cannon. The women here have shoes but no stockings. Six children on one bench without either. Corn almost all got in here, tho' quite green in Savoy. Still snow on the tops of the hills on each side. Scarce any corn but rye throughout Savoy and that part of Piemont which I have yet seen.

There was a violent west wind in our backs the whole day which so overwhelmed us with dust that it destroyed the pleasure I should otherwise have had in having that beautiful city and all Italy before me, after having being so long shut up among the Alps. At Rivoli there is a fine palace belonging to the King of Sardinia at the foot of a hanging wood which terminates the Alps on the right hand side, to the south. The other chain, to the north, is continued to Swisserland. From this charming spot or point Hanibal is supposed first to have had a view of Italy, which cannot be seen till one is upon it. From Rivoli to Turin which is 6 miles, is a strait, broad road, planted on each side. The want of gravel here makes the dust at this time of the year intolerable. As one approaches the city, the *collini* on the right hand afford a most beautiful prospect, being covered with villas and vineyards.

TURIN

Upon our entrance into the city the custom house officers visited very gently and with civility. The streets are strait, regular and well built, mostly of white brick which at a distance have the appearance of stone. The grand place (with the King's palace, which entirely fills one side, and the place of *Madame* in the middle, both of white stone) built it is said, after designs of Vignola, are very fine and striking, but amidst all this grandeur I am so devoured by flies, fleas and bugs that I cannot get a wink of sleep. Place St Charles, or the place D'armes is still more regular than that above mentioned. The piazzas here are uniform. There are indeed in the streets of this beautiful city piazzas of all sorts, in some of which there are shops, where you are sheltered from heat and wet, and nothing is wanting, with respect to utility but broad stones to walk on. I visited in great haste the King's palace. Found the appartments very elegant and many good pictures, but no Raphaels, Coreggios, Dominichinis or Titians. Some fine Albanos, Guidos, Rubens, Vandykes (among which Charles the first's children) Claude Lorraine etc. The taste in everything here is half French–except in music–at the comic opera, such a noise and inattention I never heard –but music here is cheap and common, whereas in England it is a costly exotic and more highly prized. Signor Baretti, who is a very handsome gentlemanlike man has 2 or 3 good pictures, among which a Susannah by Rubens, treated like that at Houghton* which is spoilt and thrown aside, but this is perfect. There are 3 fine old men's heads in it–on the left side a fountain and dog–it wants nothing but elegance in the figures and a more delicate beauty in the woman to

* Over the years 1722–35 Sir Robert Walpole, the first Earl of Orford (1742), had built a mansion at Houghton, his family estate in Norfolk. Throughout the house, and in galleries specially prepared for them, he distributed his great collection of pictures, which contained works from the hand of the greatest masters. Burney was familiar with the paintings since, during his residence at King's Lynn, he had been given the run of the galleries by the 3rd Earl of Orford, who eventually sold the collection to the Empress Catherine of Russia for £40,000–£45,000. Most of the pictures now hang in the Hermitage, Leningrad.

make it one of the finest pictures in the world. Signor Baretti has likewise a whole length of our Charles 1st by Vandyke.

In consequence of a very short letter from his brother in London he received me very politely and took great pains to be useful to me while I remained at Turin and in this he succeeded very much by introducing me to Padre Beccaria, for whom at first sight I conceived the highest regard and veneration. He is not above 40–a large and noble figure–he has something so open, natural, intelligent and cosmopolite in his countenance as immediately captivates. We had much conversation on the subject of electricity–Dr Franklyn, Priestly etc. He was pleased to make me a present (finding me an amateur which should be always translated a dabler)* of his last book in Latin,† and the syllabus of the memoire he lately sent to our Royal Society. He likewise in my tablets wrote a recommendatory note to M. Laura Bassi at Bologna–a famous dottoressa and academician there–recommended to me some books and was so kind and with a manner so truely simple that I shall for ever remember this visit with pleasure and gratitude. Mr. Martyn my banker here came after me to Signor Beccaria's; this great mathematician is so new to most worldly concerns and especially money matters that he was quite astonished and pleased at the ingenuity and novelty, to him, of a letter of credit. M. Martin desiring in his presence to look at mine in order to know how he might send my letters after me, the good father could scarce comprehend how this letter should be *argent comptant* ready money throughout Italy. He charged me with compliments to Padre Boscovitch at Milan and Padre Martini at Bologna and I left my new acquaintance impressed with the highest respect and affection. I must just mention one particular more relative to this great and good man, which I had from Signor Baretti; namely that he through choice lives up 6 pair of stairs among his observatories, machines and mathematical instruments–and there does every thing for himself, even to making his bed and dressing his dinner.

At the palace Valentine I first saw the Po, which afforded me great pleasure, I hardly thought myself in Italy till I beheld this renowned river, with which under the ancient name of Eridanus as well as its modern one I had so long been acquainted. The Royal Family here is so numerous as to require a Memoria Tecnica. I saw the King 3 times at chapel where his attendance is very constant. He's a little worn-out old man, a great bigot, but a well-meaning and good prince. Upon the whole tho', from the King's excess of piety (which is affected by all

---

* 'smatterer' offered as a later alternative.

† *Experimenta, atque Observationes, quibus Electricitas vindex late constituitur atque explicatur. Taurin:* 1769 (B).

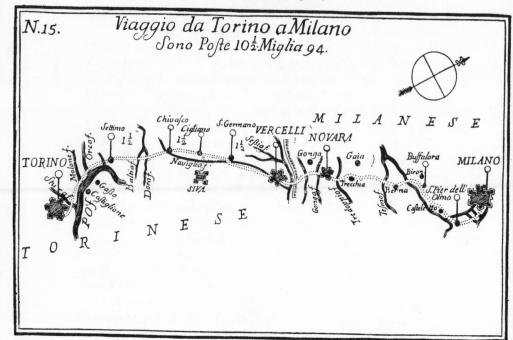

15. Turin to Milan. On this journey the road crossed a number of rivers at seven of which the traveller had to pay: the Stura and Melone, Baltia and Dora, Sessia (the fee here was a half Paul), Gogna (when there was water the fee was one Paul), Tesino (here the crossing was by ferry boat and the fee was fixed according to the amount of water flowing).

who have expectations in this world as well as in the next,) Turin is but a *triste sejour*. The poor Jesuits are still at peace here. There was a horrible execution here the morning before I came away. A wretch who in an ale house quarrel had killed a man by stabbing him in 20 places was not broke on the wheel as in France and other parts of Italy (the people here value themselves upon torture not being practiced) he was only pinched with red hot pincers thro' several streets on his way to the gallows just out of the gates.

I visited the University or Royal Library where there are 50,000 volumes and many MSS of which the catalogue fills 2 volumes in folio. The access to these books is very easy every day before and after dinner, and I was very politely and obligingly treated there on Mr Baretti's account by Signor Grela the distributor of the books, who showed me several of the most ancient MSS. The taste in gardening here is still French – or rather Dutch.

I was sorry I had not more time to spend at Turin, but having so many other places to visit in the few months allowed me to remain in Italy and as I had done all that my plan required there, I left that place with my 2 companions, (who had stayed a day longer than they intended on my account) at 5 o'clock on Saturday evening the 14 JULY and lay at a village called *Civasco* [Chivasso] 10 miles from Turin. There are broad milage stones, upon which the inscript runs thus *da Turino, milia una*. A diabolical chaise we got here put me abominably out of humour. It was *little ease* complete–so ill made in every respect–so out of repair–so small that its flap in front quite crippled me by pressing so constantly on my knees. I wished a 1,000 times I had brought a chaise from England. It would have been as cheap to have travelled post then and so much more expeditious and comfortable.

It was curious upon first entering Piemont on the side of the Alps to observe by what small degrees the French or rather Savoyard language became Italian–on this side Turin, no French is spoken, nor is it hardly understood. The 1st mile or 2 from Turin is barren disagreeable land; then a little better till *Civasco*. We crossed the Po on a bridge of boats about 4 miles from Turin. Scarce anything to be seen in the fields on this road but rye and fermentone, a Turkish wheat. The mountains of Swisserland still to be seen covered with snow, and the collini continued on the right from Turin. Cookery here al l'Italiana, bastoni de pane, pretty good butter and excellent cheese, usually parmesan of which a plate (grated) is brought up to mix with the rice soup.

SUNDAY 15 and MONDAY 16. The country all flat, but grows richer and richer, not entertaining till Novarra [Novara],* after which it is more varied, and is from thence to S. Germano where we dine rather wild. We crossed the Tesino, a rapid and broad river–remarkably clear after passing by a place which has been often fatal to travellers called la Callata di S. Giovanne pomicana, where there are two grills or iron cages fixed on high posts with the skulls of murderers who have been executed there. From thence to the waterside and even to Buffalora is a wood of shrubs and cops very pretty, but dangerous– there being now 24 outlaws in it with a reward on them dead or alive. This morning between Novarra and Buffalora I saw more farming and more cultivation than since my arrival in Italy. Rice by the road side in water–there is a small rivulet here which runs almost all the way from Vercelli, of great value–'tis let out by the hour for the rice grounds. They have here 3 or 4 crops of hay. Bad fences of licino a bitter plant with a white flower to prevent cattle from penetrating into the corn–but it wastes a great deal of land being 3 or 4 yards wide.

* A glance at the map shows that Burney's recollection or note-taking were defective in this part of the journey.

The produce here of the land is wheat, rye, fermentone, flax, etc. The land never seems to lye still, the instant the corn is off 'tis broke up again with hoes by women, for something else—no vines here. From Turin to Milan bad inns, worse carriages and the road often neglected owing to the poverty of the people who mend and use them. The great seldom stir out of the cities, and consequently seldom feel these inconveniences, but it would be worth while for the sake of strangers to attend a little to the comforts of travelling. Italy has at present no commerce as profitable as that of English noblemen and gentlemen of fortune, who never enter it without large sums or quit it with a guinea in their pockets. 'Tis all clear profit to them, but so totally uncomfortable is travelling here and so utterly neglected is every comfort of life that one would think the Italians thought dust, dirt, cobwebs, flees, bugs and all manner of filth were necessary mortifications in this world, in order to entitle us to better usage in the next.

At Buffalora we first saw the famous acqueduct of Vinci* which runs to Milan and from thence to the Po. 'Tis taken out of the Tesino. From hence to the Po 'tis quite a garden, full of vineyards and grain, but the trees and hedges on each side the road are so high as to prevent the seeing much of the country or Milan itself till one is in the fauxbourg.

MILAN

'Tis a very large and populous old city, but not at all striking when one first enters it. The streets are narrow and irregular. The great church or *Domo*, as they call it, is not yet finished tho' begun 400 years ago.† It size was not what I expected. I know not its proportions or measures, but it seems less than many of our Gothic cathedrals— this is Gothic. The pillars very massive, more elegant than those of *Notre Dame* at Paris, but the marble of which they are made not being polished its beauty is thrown away, for if I had not been told it, I should not have discovered of what they were made. It is much ornamented with statues and pictures. There are 2 organs—one on each side of the alter. The famous Ambrosian Library too disappointed me very much; it seems diminutive after the King's Library at Paris, or even after that at *Turin*, only one room and that not large.

The men here all use fans, and the country folks straw hats died black and cocked like our bever hats, which in hot weather on account

* This attribution is later corrected. See p. 61.

† This sentence, or at least its substance, appears almost without exception in the 18th century accounts of travel in Italy. The Duomo was finished over the years 1805–9 under Napoleon's influence. He was crowned King of Italy in it in 1805.

of their lightness seem convenient. An ash coloured linnen gown, with ruffles of the same made like a peignoir is used to travel in by the men: it is called a *polvesino* [spolverina] and is a fine preservative from the dust, which is here 10 times more intolerable than in the roads about London during the hottest months of summer.

TUESDAY 17. Spent in hunting books, unpacking, visiting churches and the Ambrosian Library till near 8 at night–or 24 o'clock here–I shall never understand either how to count time or money in this place:* but now to the Burletta–there is no serious opera here but in Carnaval Time.

L'Amore Artigiano was the opera buffo or dramma giocoso. It began at 8 and was not over till past 12: Compositore della Musica il Signor Floriano Gasman† all' attual Servizio di sua Maesta l'impera-dore. There were 7 characters in it all pretty well done but no one *very*, well, as to singing. There was a very entertaining dance by an infinite number of principals and figuranti with 2 saltatori a man and woman who gained more applause than all the rest. Their activity was wonderful–there were 2 others who danced all'Inglese, and there was a french friseur in the burletta whose singing was to be French, but these imitations here are like ours in London when we take off the Italians–as far from like as a miserable sign post of the King or Queen's Head is to George the Third or Queen Charlotte–we laugh *at* not *with* these mimics. In the dance the stage was illuminated in a most splendid, and to me a new manner–with *Lampioni coloriti*, or coloured lamps which had a very pretty effect. The theatre here is very large and splendid: 5 rows of boxes on each side, 100 each row with a room behind every one for cards and refreshments. In the fourth galery was a pharo table. There was a very large box, bigger than my dining room ⌊in London⌋ for the Duke of Modena, who is Governor of Milan, and the principessina his daughter, who is to be married to

---

* Time-keeping in Italy was an art rather than a science. The perplexities are well described by Samuel Sharp in his *Letters from Italy* (1766): 'They [the Italians] do not reckon as we do, from the moment the sun is in its meridian, or, in other words, from noon, but they begin their account from the time it is almost, and not quite dark; which instant of time varying every day, renders this reckoning very inconvenient, vague and perplexed. For example; if to-day they begin to count from our six o'clock in the evening, it will be one with them, when it is seven with us; but to-morrow at our seven, it will with them exceed one, by as many minutes as the day is lengthened. To obviate, therefore, this error in time, they alter their clocks and watches as often as the error amounts to fifteen minutes, advancing, or putting them back, as the days shorten or lengthen . . .'

As for money, every little state and principality coined its own, and the traveller had to be alert to see that conversion rates were fairly calculated when he was settling his bills. See note * on p. 46.

† *L'Amor artigiano* was by Florian-Léopold Gassmann (1729–74) and had already been performed in an alternative version elsewhere before its Milan production in 1770.

the 2nd brother of the present emperor. There was an abominable noise except during 2 or 3 arias and a duet, with which every body was in raptures. During this last, the applause continued till the performers returned to repeat it. This is the method of *encoring* an air here. The first violin is Signor Lucchi: the band was very numerous and orchestra large in proportion to the house, which is much bigger than the great opera house at Turin. Each box of the 3 first rows contains 6 persons who sit 3 on each side facing each other. Higher up they sit 3 in front and the rest stand behind. There are very wide galleries that run parallel with all the boxes, where people after the first act walk about and change places perpetually. The English are seldom disposed to be satisfied with their present condition or possessions, or else one might be very well contented with such a comic opera as that we had last year; which on the side of singing was greatly superior to this, nor do I expect throughout Italy to meet with such performers as Lovatini, Moriggi, and la Guadagni, at least on the same stage. The opera here is carried on by 30 noblemen who subscribe 60 zechins* each for which each has a box. The rest of the boxes are let by the season. The chance money arises only from the pit and upper row of boxes or piccionas ['the gods']. They perform every night.

WEDNESDAY 18. Went this morning to the Ambrosian Library,† which appears very diminutive after the pompous account given of it in books of travels and after having seen the Bibliotheque du Roi at Paris, which is at least 10 times as big. There is in fact but *one* room of a moderate size filled with books to which one may add 2 small ones, or rather closets of French literature, then a room full of copies only of the best ancient statues at Rome and Florence and lastly the picture room, full indeed of wonderful fine paintings by the first rate masters among which are many of Leonardo da Vinci. I could with pleasure have lived among them for 24 hours, but I tore myself away in order to enquire for the catalogue of MSS in order to find something relative to my mission and in order to facilitate matters, gave to the Cicerone a double fee—when behold he recommended me to another signor—the 1st of 3 librarians for so few books! who told me that I could not see the catalogue as it was not usual to shew it. I might have had a book it seems if I had asked for one by name that was in the collection—but how could I divine its contents. I was in quest of new existences, of new literary beings unpolluted by profane compilers and printers—but to say the truth I begin to suspect they

---

* Zechin = sequin, 'a gold coin, current all over Italy, equal in value to about nine shillings and sixpence English' (B).

† This Library was founded (1609) in memory of St Ambrose by Cardinal Frederick Borromeo, Archbishop of Milan.

are ashamed of the collection and afraid to discover the nakedness of the land. They have long talked of Milan in a *great* style and now try to persuade you by their shoulders and a big tone of voice that everything in it is *Spaventosa, terrible, Maravigliosa, stupenda* etc, etc. I will if possible pace the Duomo about the grandeur of which they make such a fuss. I am sure 'tis less than several churches in France and England, though they tell you 'tis bigger than St. Peter's at Rome.

This morning I heard the whole service after the Ambrosian manner, was introduced to the Maestra di Capella, Signor Jean Andrè Fioroni, who invited me into the orchestra, shewed me the service they were to sing printed on wood in four parts, separate, cantus–altus–tenor–bassus–out of which after the tone was given by the organist Signor Jean Corbeli they *all* sung, namely 1 boy, 3 castrati, 2 tenors and 2 basses, under the direction of the Maestro di Capella, without the organ. He beat the time, though there were no bars: the music by Signor ⟨   ⟩ who was Maestro di Capella in this Church about 150 years ago. I afterwards heard the first organist play a quarter of an hour in a very masterly and grave stile, suited to the place and instrument. From thence I went home with Signor Fiorini, who shewed me all his musical curiosities, and played and sung to me a whole oratorio of his composition, and was so obliging as to promise me a copy of a service of his in 8 parts, with which I begged of him to favour me in order to convince the world that tho' the theatrical style is very different from that of the Church, yet this latter is not wholly lost.

Then I went a book hunting and *denichèd* several curious things, one or 2 more than 200 years old and some modern tracts and treatises I had never heard of, then dined at Signor Moiano's in an Italian family way with a clever young abate who had attended me all the morning. I must not forget to say here that I had the pleasure of seeing Signor Giovanni Battista san Martini and delivered him Giardini's letter, which procured me a very polite reception. I am to see him again and shew him my plan which is now well translated in bon Tossano.–I have just heard that Piccini is here and that one of his comic operas is to be performed here to night.–I have a letter for him too–Jomelli is at Bologna! I always had been told that he was at Stutgard [Stuttgart] and that I had no chance of seeing him in Italy.

THURSDAY 19. I was very much disappointed yesterday. The opera was *not* Piccini's but a pasticcio,* nor is he here. However, there were pretty things and some of them I am sure by him. Before the opera I

---

* Literally a 'pie', a 'species of lyric drama composed of airs, duets and other movements, selected from different operas and grouped together, not in accordance with their original intention, but in such a manner as to provide a mixed audience with the greatest number of favourite airs in succession' (*Grove*).

went to see the Church of St Victor which is immensely rich and full
of fine pictures—the revenue above £10,000 a year for only 25 monks!
From thence to the Convent delle Grazie with one of the padres,
brother to Mr Moiana—2 or 3 fine pictures here, then to the corso—or
boulevard—where was a great deal of company and the Duke of
Modena *painted*, the princepessina etc among them. The carriages
are brilliant, but less so than at Paris. The finest weather thus far in
the world. Mornings and evenings cool, and the heat at noon dry and
sufferable: a true Italian sky, without a cloud for several days, nor does
it rain here for the 3 months of June, July and August. The Millanese
dialect is corrupt—Già—Già for yes, *vech* for vecchio, adess for adesso
etc. The Queen of Hungary is sovereign and the garrison German.
Moiana borrowed the box belonging to the family of Bel Gioioso
where he, his sister, Righi a young *abate* and myself sate—2nd row—
left hand—a complete room belonging to it and to all the boxes crossing the gallery.

This morning I hobbled up to the top of the dome like a fool, by
persuasion of Dr Righi and our abate, to see all the vanities of this
world—against inclination and an abominable, I fear, rheumatic lame-
ness in my hip which at first I attributed to the long confinement in an
uneasy and narrow chaise; but it continues too long to be that. I
mounted in great pain near 600 steps to see nothing that my mind's
eye could not in speculation paint much more beautiful. It was only a
view of the tops of the houses, covered with red tiles and a fine
fertile plain without a hillock in sight except the very distant prospect
of the mountains of Swisserland. All the rest of the horison was as
smooth as if I had been 5 leagues out at sea in a calm. It is astonishing
what an eternal expense they are at in building this gothic church—
has been begun more than 400 years and is not, nor ever will be
finished. They advance so slowly, that the old parts must decay faster
than the new can possibly be constructed: its pouring water in a
sieve. 'Tis built of white marble unpolished which they have from the
Lago Maggiore, near Novarra. They have a fund of more than a
100,000 livres to spend every year. There are fine *parts* of this building, but the *whole* is in bad taste, even as a gothic structure. The pillars are too massive and heavy and there wants space to see it as well
as our St. Paul's. The subterraneous chapel of St Charles is immensely
rich, all of silver gilt: the story of this saint's life is told in basso relievo.
I paced the great isle and found it 150 paces to the quire, 70 to the
end, and 97 broad. My pace is 3 feet.

From hence I went (having a carozza de remissa) to make formal
visits to il marchese Minafoglia and to Signor D. Francesco Carcano—
but both were in the country. All I want of them is to procure me a

sight of the MSS in the Ambrosian Library. The rest of my business here is nearly done. On Saturday they are expected in town. I should have waited on his Excellence Count Firmian with Strange's letter and prints to day, but was told it would be in vain, on account of its being post day, so I went with my friend Righi to the Jesuits College with a letter to Padre Boscovitch from M. Messier giving him an account of a new comet he had discovered the 11th of last month.

The good father received us with great courtesy, and being told I was an Englishman, a lover of the sciences and ambitious of seeing so celebrated a man, he addressed himself to me in a particular manner. He had several young eleves of quality with him and said he expected 3 persons of condition to see his instruments and offered me, if it would be any amusement, to be of the party. I gladly accepted the offer and he immediately began to shew and explain to me several machines and contrivances he had invented for making optical experiments before the arrival of the Signori, who were, a Knight of Malta, a nephew of Pope Benedict 4, and another cavaliere. He then went on, and surprised and delighted us all very much, particularly with his *stet sol*, by which he can fix the sun's rays passing through an apperture or a prism to any point of the opposite wall he pleases. He likewise separates and fixes any of the prismatic colours, or their shades or mixtures in the same manner. He likewise shewed us several experiments to prevent refraction, to invert the colours of the rays—how to form an aquatic prism, the effects of joining together different lenses etc. etc.—all extreamly plain and ingenious. He has published a Latin dissertation on these matters at Vienna. He had but one copy left here or would have given me one. Then we ascended to different observatories, where I found his instruments mounted in so ingenious and convenient a manner as gave me the utmost pleasure. He was so polite as to address himself to me always in French, as I had at first accosted him in that language, and in which I am, as yet much more at my ease than in Italian. M. Messier had told him the comet had very little movement, being almost stationary; but Pere Boscovitch has since found its motion so rapid as to move 50 degrees in a day. Mais la comete, Monsieur lui dis-je, où est elle a present?* Avec le soleil—elle est mariée. Our late Duke of York made him a present of one of Short's 12 inches reflectors of 20 guineas price, but he has an accromatic one by the same maker which cost 100. The expense of his observatory must have been enormous which is defraid by the Society at Pavia where he is professore and spends his winters.† If any new

* Corrected to 'où est elle ⌊actuellement⌋?' later.
† Altered to: '. . . defraid by himself. He is professor at the University of Pavia where he spends his winters.'

discoveries are to be made in astronomy, one has a right to expect 'em from this learned Jesuit–whose ingenuity and intelligence where attention to optical experiments for the improvement of glasses, upon which so much depends, and his great number of admirable instruments of all sorts–joined to the excellence of the climate and the wonderful sagacity he has discovered in the construction of his machines and observatory, make one's expectations from the concurrence of so many favourable circumstances very sanguine. He complains very much of the silence of the English astronomers, who answer none of his letters. He was 7 months in England, and during that time was very much with Mr. Maskyline, Dr Shepherd, Dr Bevis, Dr Maty etc with whom he hoped to keep up a correspondence. He has indeed lately received from Mr. Professor Mascaline the last nautical almanac, with Meyer's lunar tables, who gives him hopes of reviving their literary intercourse. He is a tall strong built man upwards of 50, of a very agreeable address. He was refused admission into the French Academy when at Paris though a member, by the Parliament of Paris on account of his being a Jesuit. But if all Jesuits were like this father, making use only of superior learning and intellects for the advancement of science and the happiness of mankind one would have wished for this society to be as durable as the world. As it is, it seems as if equity requires some discrimination should be made in condemning the Jesuits, for tho' good policy may require a dissolution of their order, yet humanity certainly makes one wish to preserve the old, the infirm and the innocent from the general wreck and destruction due only to the guilty.

After dinner to the corso and then to an academia or private concert, all of dilitanti. Il padrone played the 1st violin, and had a very strong hand. There were 12 or 14 hands, several of the violins good, with 2 German flutes. They executed several of *our* Bach's* symphonies reasonably well, but what I liked the most was the vocal part by La Signora Padrona della Casa: she had an agreeable well-toned voice, a good shake, the right sort of taste and expression, and sang (sitting down, with the paper on the common instrument desk) wholly without affectation, several pretty airs of Traetta. Upon the whole this concert was much of the same kind as our private concerts among gentlemen performers in England–sometimes in and sometimes out. In general the music was rather better chosen, the execution more brilliant and full of fire, and the singing much nearer perfection than we can boast on such occasions: not on the side of voice or execution, for in ⌊these particulars⌋ we are at least equal to our

* Johann Christian Bach.

ST. JEAN DE MAURIENNE

VINES IN LOMBARDY

Car: P.L. Gherzi del: Romæ   *Matth: Oesterreich Sculp: Dresdæ 1782.*

Domenico con Suo Fratello Bresciani

*Il primo, che é di facciá Suona mirabilmente il Calascioncino á
due Corde, l'altro che é di Schiena, l'accompagnava con la Chitarra
Furono nell Mese di Aprile 1765, nell Palazze à Sans-souci, dove Sua Maestá il Ré di
Prussia li intese ambédue à Sonare.*

THE CALASCIONE PLAYER

neighbours; but in the carriage of the voice in expression and decoration.*

FRIDAY 20. This morning to his Excellency Comte Firmian, who was out of town–thence to the Church of ⟨   ⟩ to hear a *messa in musica*, ⌊or a mass in figurative counterpoint⌋† composed and under the direction of Signor Monza, Maestro di Capella. His brother played the violoncello with much facility of execution, but not a very pleasing tone or taste. The first violin, Signor Lucchini, who leads at the Burletta: 2 or 3 castrati sung. There was a paltry little organ erected on the occassion, though there is a large one in the church; but in a gallery too small for a band. The music was pretty. Long and ingenious introductory sinfonias to each *concento* or verse. The whole was in good taste and spirited; but the organ, hautbois and some of the fiddles being bad, destroyed the effect of several things that were well designed. The singing, though better than at our oratorios in general, yet not so perfect as we often hear in England at the Italian opera. As yet I have heard no great singer since my arrival in Italy. Signor Lucchini is about the same speed as a first violin with M. Lahanssay: there is no want of hand, but of high finishing. The 1st soprano was what we should call in England, a pretty good singer, with a pretty good voice; his taste neither original nor superior. The contr'alto, who was the second singer was likewise *pretty* well. His voice pleasing and he never gave offence by the injudicious management of it. But

> "Tis in song as in painting
> Much may be right yet much be wanting.'

However, one should not criticise such a performance as this too severely for one hears it *for nothing*. I speak as a traveller. But the people of Italy who contribute so much to the support of the church, are well entitled to these treats on the Feast of Dedication, which happens but once a year.

I was too soon at the church for the music, but had my curiosity satisfied as to the preaching *nella lingua volgare*. The sermon was begun ere I arrived and continued at least an hour and ½ afterwards. It was a perpetual harangue–a monotonous declamation in a very disagreeable kind of chant or cant, in praise of the saint–which could easily have been reduced to a few musical notes–more like the 2 or 3 used by a hen when by her cackling she declares the *labour* of egg-birth to be over.

* The conclusion of this sentence was altered to '. . . but in the *portamento*, or delivery of the voice, in expression and energy'.

† Florid counterpart was the fifth of the five species into which the rules for combining melodies were codified by the theoreticians. To Burney 'florid' and 'figurative' were interchangeable terms.

Piccini I find *was* here in the carnaval time this year and composed a serious opera called *Didone Abbandonata*–the principal singers were Signor Aprile and la Signora Piccinelli; the 2 principal dancers M. et Madame Piquet; and a comic one called *Il Regno nella Luna* for the performers who are still here, namely Signor Gioachino Garibaldi a good tenor, but inferior to Lovatini, the 3 Baglioni sisters–midling–Signor Francesco Caratoli, a baritone at whom they laugh very much *here*, but his humour is too national to please in England, he is always noisy and blustering in comic character–Signor Domenico Poggi a midling baritone and Signor Filippo Capellani, virtuoso della Capella di S.M. il Rey delle due Sicilie, a very midling tenor.

This afternoon I lost my friend and constant companion Dr Righi who set off for Parma. My other fellow traveller with whom I shall continue to proceed as far as Venice is at his father's house. I made there an acquaintance with 2 young abati–one very musical–who can neither speak a word of English or French, so that in despight of myself I must now blunder out Italian as I can. At Turin, French is sufficient, but no further. Here I cannot help observing that the 2 *sides* I have often observed to belong to every thing in this world, or, in other words, the *good* and *evil* principle are manifest in the connections I have formed during this journey. 'Tis very convenient to have people to fight one's battles on the road, to make bargains, explain customs etc, but by that means my time is often broke into when I want to be alone–I am obliged to stay when I want to go, and the contrary. But it has been said a million of times that there is nothing perfect in this world, and yet we are as out of humour at imperfection as if it was not in the nature of things, but when our choler subsides we are obliged to submit. Little or nothing is to be gained in the scuffle–and therefore with a good grace we had better take things as we find them. My Italian Dutch merchant is in a perpetual fever on the road, he disputes every bill, he abuses every dinner–without gaining any other thing than universal hatred by it, for he is at last obliged to pay the bills and to eat the dinners.

Almost the whole day was spent in church hunting where good music was to be heard. At night to a grand academia. I was again this evening at the *Corso* which is here so constant and uniform ⌐a diversion⌐ that I am already tired of seeing the same faces and the same equipages, the Governor D. of M's painted face and his insipid daughter's pale one. Friday there being no opera is best for musical masses and *academie*.

SATURDAY 21. This morning went with Padre Moiana, an agreeable, chearful young fryer, to hear the famous ecco, about 2 miles from Milan, at the Piazza Simonetta, at which the D of Modena's mother formerly lived, but now 'tis *delabré* and uninhabited.* I now find it will be Wednesday ere I can get away from hence: this vexes me as time is so precious, and where I am going shall have much more occasion for it than here, but pazienza! Coming from the ecco we went into the castle, which is reckoned very strong. The town walls and fortifications are nothing. The whole defence of Milan depends on this castle: there is now a regiment of 3000 Germans in it. After dinner purchased some MS music–a great deal of trach was brought to me, out of which however I have found some good stuff. Then I was carried by one of my young abate's to hear 3 ladies sing who are sisters and scholars of Lampugnani–who I found there and a good violin player, a young man–Pasqualini. Lampugnani has been twice to England–in 1744 and 1757. He speaks a little English and we had a great deal of talk about England. His scholars sing very well and are pretty young women. From hence my young abate carried me to the *Corso* upon which he doats, and thinks the whole universe produces nothing like it, but his universe is Milan and a very few miles round it. After this to the opera where the audience were very much disappointed. The 1st tenor and only good singer in it was ill–all his part was cut out and the baritono, who did a blustering old father's part that was to abuse his son violently in the first scene and song, finding he had no son there, gave a turn to the misfortune which diverted the audience very much and made 'em submit to their disappointment with a far better grace than they would have done in England, for instead of his son, he fell foul on the prompter, who here as at the opera in England pops his head out of a little trap door on the stage. The audience were so pleased with this attack upon the prompter that they encored the song in which it was made. However after the 1st act and the dances I came away, as the lights at the opera house here affect my eyes in a very painful manner and there being no retribution for this suffering to night, I denied myself the rest of the performance.

SUNDAY 22. The 3 great folk to whom I have letters are still out of town and my time begins to hang on my hands. However I shall go to church this morning to hear the ambrosian service in all its perfection. I was too soon for the service at the Duomo so went to a convent

---

* The Palazzo Simonetta was built in the form of an E turned on its side without the cross bar. The echo was 'occasioned by the reflection of the voice between the opposite parallel wings of the building, which are fifty-eight common paces from each other, and without any windows and doors, by which the sound might be dissipated or lost . . . A man's voice is repeated above forty times, and the report of a pistol above sixty by this echo.' J. G. Keysler, *Travels through Germany, Bohemia, Hungary, Switzerland, Italy and Lorrain*. Third edition 1760 (Vol. 1, pp. 428–9).

where I heard a nun sing divinely–dined at Moianas–after dinner went again to the Convent San Maria Madalina–heard the same motet by the same singer with double delight. Then to the Corso, which being Sunday, was in all its pride: their best carriages and best cloathes–they seem so satisfied with themselves and so proud of each other and of their bit of ground, not so long as from High-park Corner* to Knightsbridge–that it is quite ridiculous. The whole town was there: the evening fine and the air and ground so dry, that the adjoining field was covered with people, sitting and lying on it. The D. of Modena as *blooming* as ever, and his daughter as insipid. From hence to the opera house, where there was no opera, the 1st singer being ill, but instead of it an *Academia* in the manner of the annual performance for the benefit of decayed musicians in England†–with this difference, that there were no solos, but dances between the acts. The singers were the same as I had heard at the Burletta: the Baglioni sung better to night than I had heard them. 'It never rains, but it pours!' When I came home from the academia I was told that his Excellence Count Firmian had sent his lackey to inform me he was come to town and could give me *audience* (a big word) at 12 on Monday. The importance which my valet de louage assumed on this occasion was truly diverting. This afternoon too I was honoured with a visit from Signor D. Francesco Carcano, who only stayed in town a few hours, invited me to accompany him to his country seat, and upon being informed that I should not have time to avail myself of his politeness, he said he would recommend me to a friend of his and of Signor Baretti to go with me to the Library of St. Ambrose etc.–

MONDAY 23. This morning I went early with Padre Moian to the Ambrosian Library, and with some difficulty got a sight of 2 or 3 very ancient MSS to my purpose, and of the pompous edition of the services at the Duomo printed in 4 vast volumes in folio 1619 for the use of that church only: the printing very neat upon wood without bars, not in score, but the parts all in sight on opposite pages–soprano and tenor on the 1st and alto and bass on the second page. I shall make several extracts from all these. Signor Oltrocci, the librarian begins to be more communicative than at first. One of the most ancient MSS he showed me is of the ninth century and very well written and preserved. 'Tis a missal, before the time of Guido 200 years, and consequently before the lines used by that monk were invented. The notes are little

* Hyde Park Corner.
† The annual concert arranged by the Royal Society of Musicians of Great Britain, founded in 1738, to raise money to help the poor and needy among professional musicians and their families.

more than accents of different kinds put over the hymns in this manner*

Adoramus te Christe et benedicimus te etc

I met with an old fryer there who had studied these characters and had formed some ingenious conjectures about them. During my conversation with him Signor Carcano's friend came to me: 'twas a very polite abate not above 4 or 5 and 30. I set Padre Moiana to work for me in copying some things I wanted while I conversed. When I left the library to go to his excellence, I took with me the abate who proposed to call upon a friend of his and of Signor Carcano to carry me to Count Firmian who is a sort of King of Milan. We found this friend, who turned out to be Conte Po, a very intelligent and agreeable young man: a bit of an author himself, he has written upon the first of all subjects – agriculture – and has promised to shew me his work. It was too soon for his Excellence, so we went to see the hospital and several other places, but so fast that the impression on the mind is as soon effaced as that of a stone in water. M. Porri† and I are to dine with M. Firmian to morrow. Il Conte Po would have carried me to-night to a conversatione at one of the first lady's houses here, but I excused myself by saying I was engaged, not thinking such an assembly at all necessary to me or my errand here. Besides, my little proficiency in speaking the Italian language was not sufficient to enable me to bear a part in the conversazione or hardly to understand the eloquence and wit of others. So I went 'a book hunting with Padre Moiana, whom I like more and more and my young abate, his relation, whom I like less and less. The copyist I was at first carried to here sticks close to me. He writes, begs and borrows all sorts of things

* At this point in the manuscript Burney enters a series of marks over the words 'Adoramus te Christe et benedicimus te etc'. The signs are so tentative, however, that they would not convey much if they were reproduced; instead part of an extract from 'a MS Missal of the 9th Century in the Ambrosian Library at Milan' which appears as an engraving on page 40 of the second volume of Burney's *A General History of Music* (1782) is shown here as an example of the type of notation he is referring to.

† M. Porri and il Conte Po are written one above the other, and are both deleted with the rest of the sentence.

to tempt me: he succeeds but too well. I have bought more already than I know how to carry. For about a zecchin and ½ – 18s 6d – I have as much *new* music as for meer copying in England would have cost me £3: 10 – without reckoning paper or composition. I am afraid of the carriage or else could get some excellent masses, motets, opera songs, symphonies, trios etc. There are here some very good composers of all these things. However I have bespoke a charming sinfonia of S. Martini – a favourite duo in the 1st opera I heard here – and 2 motets, besides what I've already bought. I hope at Venise to find out a method of sending them by sea to England, but my old devil of ill luck has sent away Mr Richie our Chargé D'affaires there to Vienna just at the instant I wanted him. He lodged in the house where I now am while at Milan, whence he departed but 2 days before my arrival. I am sorry Martinelli's friend *il Marchese Menafoglio* is not here, as he is generally well spoken of – Signor D. Carcano's friends have done the honours for him in his absense in a manner very flattering for me. I could buy some very old MS missals here on vellum very cheap, but know not how to get them home. Those I have bought already are sufficient I believe to make me be taken up for a Jesuit on my arrival in England who is going to propagate popish doctrines and convert his majesties leige subjects to the Roman Catholick religion.

Memorandum. At the Chiesa de Monastero di S. Ambrogio Collegio Brera an ancient idol on a porphyry column – a kind of serpent.* Linea Meridiana Horizon – Verticalis Studiosis rite constructa CIƆIƆCCLVI Pere Boscovich all'Università dei Scolari.†

The streets here are narrow but well enough managed for passengers: the gutter is in the middle, and on each side a row of broad flagstones for the wheels of carriages, which run very easy upon them, and for foot passengers – and on each side are large stones of the same kind, equidistant (about ½ a yard) which in winter serve as a kind of stepping stones for people on foot – the rest is usually small pebbles or brick placed edge ways. Not a lamp to be seen in the whole city – every coach must have a flambeau and every foot passenger a lanthorn – sometimes both. This last is large and of white paper. The carriages of the great calculated for more than one servant behind

---

* Serpent: 'This last by the vulgar is believed to be the serpent which Moses set up in the wilderness, though others more modest judge it to have been only made of some fragments of the former: others again maintain it to be a symbolical image of Æsculapius. This however is certain, that on Easter Tuesday great numbers of sickly children are placed before this pillar from a superstitious expectation of their being restored to health.' Keysler, *Travels*, Vol. 1, pp. 393–4.

† Although the date of erecting the mark for the meridian is given here as 1766, La Lande *Voyage* (3rd edition, 1790, vol. 1, p. 297) says that the meridian was made by 'P. Ferramola who died in 1765'.

have 2 places for them to stand on, one above the other—Chiesa and Monza seem (and are said) to be the 2 best composers here at present. Serbelloni—a contr'alto castrato—who was in England some years ago, has had a dispensation to become a prete and now only sings in the church. Milan, which in the time of its own Dukes, Visconti and Sforza, contained 300,000 inhabitants, has now not more than 80,000. The taste in architecture here is light and elegant, less French than at Turin. The pillars in the front of the public and private buildings are so proportioned as to have an elegant and noble effect. The Grand Quadrangle of the Hospital begun by Duke Sforza, and even the collums of the Lazaretto, next the fields, are in my eyes very beautiful, though this latter next the road seems more like an alms house than any thing else. It was constructed in great haste by St. Charles, when the plague was at Milan 1365 and looks now as fresh as if it had been only built 50 years, so pure is the air of this place!—Language a good deal corrupted here—già, già, yes, yes—miga for mica—nuri, not at all—vecchio, chiesa—as the English would pronounce—nay worse sometimes, *vetch*.*

TUESDAY 24. This morning a solem procession passed through the streets to the church of St. Ambrose *for rain* on which account the public library was not open, which was a great disappointment to me, being the last day I have to stay here—but pazienza is the word here. My worthy friend and father Moiana walked over a great part of the town and into several churches I had not seen before. One I cannot forget—St. Stefano—where the bones and sculls of the Milanese slain in an engagement with the Arians in the 9th century are preserved above ground in frames against the wall curiously piled one on another, forming pictures not very pleasing to humanity. They put me in mind of the pyramid of human heads constructed by order of the Inkerman Shah Nadir in Persia, according to Mr. Hanway's account—The Milanese tell strange stories of the blood of the Christians after this engagement remaining above ground, while that of the Arians sunk into the earth etc. When these hereticks were totally sillenced, the bones in question were dug up and brought in this church or one that stood on the same spot.

Upon presenting myself at the Ambrosian Library, I found the Abbe Bonelli, Signor Carcano's friend waiting for me, and, I believe on his account more than my own the Library was opened to me and indeed for the first time all its treasures—the most curious MSS etc were all displayed, among which several books of Petrarca's and Leonardo da Vinci's own hand writing. One of the former was a Virgil with notes finely written on vellum—and of the latter an

* ⌊Here the article about Ballad Singers, p. 71⌋.

immense unedited book of plans and drawings of machines and mathematical instruments.* All the descriptions of these machines etc is written backwards, or rather with the letters reversed for the engraver to copy, as the art of engraving was then in its infancy. Many machines are to be seen in this book which are supposed to have been invented long since, among which mortars and bumbs etc. 4 lines only of an old Roman missal MS in the 9th century, 873, will cost me 20 soldi to have coppied, but 'tis very curious and earlier by more than 2 centuries than anything of the kind explained in Walter's Lexicon Diplomaticum. I was shewn several very ancient MSS. upon papyrus, well preserved. In short I was made amends this morning for former disappointments, being carried into a room containing nothing but MSS. to the amount of 15000.

From hence the abate carried me to Padre Sacchi a very learned musician here as to theory: he has published 2 very curious books which I had before purchased. He received me very courteously, and we entered so deep into conversation and were so well contented with each other, or at least ourselves and the subject that I was in danger of being too late for his Excellency's dinner. Padre Sacchi got my direction and gave me great encouragement to write to him if on reading his books I met with any doubts.

From hence to Conte Po, who was to go with me to dine at Count Firmian's. However he said we should be [in] time enough if we went to see the library and pictures of Conte Pertusati – which are admirable – the former immense, consisting of 6 large rooms. Among the books of science I found Practica Musica Franchini Gafori Laodensis quatuor libris compræhensa – which is very scarce and in which I found more about the Ambrosian and Gregorian chants than is to be met with, even in the lives of the 2 saints from whom they have their names. A printed missal too, very curious, so early as 1475. Among the pictures which are of the most exquisite choice, are several very remarkable by Leonardo da Vinci – 3 or 4 in a row with cupids and children playing on musical instruments, several resembling viols of different sizes – no bows in the right hand of any but one, which is not very clearly a bow neither, but rather a stick or plectrum. The number of strings are not easily ascertained neither, but there seem more than 4 upon all of them. The children hold them like viol da gambas, the necks in their left hands. A beautiful and speaking picture of Queen Anna Bullen too is here by the same admirable painter.† The garden here is full of

* This is the Codice Atlantico (so called because of its size) a collection of manuscript material of Leonardo da Vinci assembled by the sculptor Pompeo Leoni from other books, which he broke up for this purpose. The volume has 402 sheets and shows more than 1,700 drawings.
† A fanciful attribution.

very large orange trees *out* of pots—and on my asking Count Po if they could stand the winter in this country, he told me they could, but it was by means of an entire covering or a boarded house—thatched.

From hence to Count Firmians where everthing breaths taste and affluence. We were shewn into a drawing room where a great deal of company was waiting for his Excellence. I was introduced by my guide and conductor to 2 reverend fathers, the one a great mathematician who had been in England and France, said he had been much used to the company of the English—the other Padre Venini of Parma—a very able composer and theorist of taste in music. The conversation with these 2 fathers entertained me very much till the arrival of the great man, and indeed without a sneer he seems to me to have all the marks of a truely great man. His person, inclinable to corpulent is full of dignity and his address full of graceful ease. He accosted me in French in a most condescending and engaging manner, thanked me very much for trouble I had taken in bringing M. Strange's charming prints to him—and then spoke for half an hour in their and in his praise—said he was a great admirer of him and his works and then told a story of his patience and good nature when going a way from Milan in unpacking his drawings 3 times to shew them to him and 2 of his friends—said there was an other eminent engraver from Italy he had been told—Yes, I said, Bartolozzi, an able engraver—but Mr Strange had still his admirers.—Oh for my part, says the Count, I am a professed *Strangist*. Dinner was served and we dined in a magnificent hall, full of good pictures and elegant furniture—je me place entre votre nation—says the Count to me in making me sit on one side of him, and a young English officer Mr Fothergal, on the other. A plate of everything at the table was *offered* by a servant to all the guests, and wines of all sorts, and after dinner fruits and coffee in the same manner. There were upwards of 20 at table—all men—the Count had never been married. The conversation was very general and agreeable. Rousseau and his little opera were part of it. His Excellency had received a letter from a friend at Paris who had said that Rousseau was not the misanthrope people took him to be, but on the contrary—soft, polite, and engaging in his manner. I had the honour to tell his Excellency that that was exactly the character Mr. Hume had given me of him but just before their quarrel. That pleases me very much, says the Count, I am glad to find such a character rescued from envy and detraction. Well, continues he, it is necessary to see for one's self.—Yes, I said, chacum a ses lunettes.—Very true, replies the Count—and we never can I fear see without spectacles— meaning prejudice. After dinner the company got up and went into another room to wash their mouths—water being offered in salvers—

and then we were called in to a still different room for conversation–
no drinking. A gentleman who had dined with us, a man of taste in
painting and literature, who I found read English and could speak a
little, was desired by his Excellence to show me his pictures and
books–exquisite–charming paintings by Spagnoletto, Vinci, Guido,
Coreggio, Titian, Paul Veronese, Salvator Rosa, Guercini, Rubens,
Vandyke, Claude Lauraine etc etc. The books chosen and classed with
great taste: theology in one room, law in a second, history in a third,
poetry in a fourth, the beaux art and criticism in a fifth, English books
of which a great quantity, in a sixth etc. I was told that the Count both
reads and speaks English. Upon taking my leave his Excellence told
me that I used them very ill in going away so soon and pressed me
very much to stay longer at Milan. Indeed I wished it very much, as
with such an acquaintance as I now can boast it would be charming. I
took my leave of Count Po, with regret and came home to the old
cursed work of packing and paying–where I found a present of books
with a polite note from the Abbate Bonelli. Could I have spared
more time for Milan it might have been filled in the most agreeable
and profitable manner imaginable–with his Excellence for honour,
good chear and consideration, with il Conte Po for a knowledge of the
country with respect to its productions, cultivation etc as [he] is very
fond of agriculture, and has written something on the subject and is
now engaged in writing a treatise upon farming in the Milanese, of
which he was pleased to shew me a part in MS. He has a cabinet of
books solely on the subject of agriculture in different languages. This
gentleman likewise offered to carry me to the first houses and conversatione of Milan and il Marchese Menafoglia expected in town every
day would have done the same. Pere Boscovich and the 2 fathers I met
at Conte Firmian's for science, Padre Sacchi for the theory and Mart-
tini, Fiorone, Lampugnani etc for the practice, 2 or 3 abbés and
fathers for every-day acquaintances etc etc.

But at 6 o'clock on Wednesday morning 25th JULY I left Milan, with
Signor Moiana in a sedia di posta, the 1st I had entered since I
landed on the continent. The post horses here are in general better
than in England, but such carriages! I would rather go a 100 miles in
English post chaises than one post in these–so small, inconvenient
and uneasy–without any covering from the sun cold or rain. The 1st
post we had a covered chaise all'Italiana–But what an admirable
thing is a procession! How efficacious and irrisistible its power over
the atmosphere and clouds!–but yesterday morning it passed through
the streets to the church of St. Ambrogio and before midnight a
copious and abundant rain refreshed the earth–it continued till we
set out and then the weather became fine and it was very pleasant.

The visit very slight at going out of Milan–an affair of 1 paulo only: but I must not forget to mention that before I had left Count Firmian's an hour, his Excellency's running footman came to wish me a good journey and upon my asking my servant, che vuol dir questa cortesia, he told me that a zechin only would be enough, but that was the lowest, for some English he had served gave 3 zechins. This is worse than England formerly–but the Italians tell you the Count knows nothing of all this: if he did the servant would lose his place.

The country on this side Milan is still flat and in winter must be wet, but 'tis rich and well laid out and cultivated–never suffered to lye idle, but the instant one crop is got in, something else is sown. I had not time to learn the succession. At present the year seems as forward as with us in October–the corn all got in and the land ploughed up. About Milan the lands lye neat and level, are regularly planted –chiefly indeed with willows–but the willow here is a smart tall and spruce tree. There is a great deal of meadow ground, all as smooth as a bowling green. This kind of country continued to Casina bianca, which is a post and ½ from Milan–from thence to Canonica the road is very pleasant for several miles by the side of the Naviglio della Martesana, which is the famous acqueduct begun and finished by Leonardo da Vinci after it had been in vain attempted by several others–and not that I mentioned before too hastily.* At Canonica ends the flat country. It is built on a hill, on the banks of the *Adda* a large rapid river, which here receives the water of several other small rivers and canals. After crossing these and ascending on the other side about ½ a mile further there is a kind of common, which was very much burnt up by the drowths and in the boundary between the Milanese and Venetian State–but before I quit the former I must observe that a great deal of the cheese which goes all over Europe by the name of Parmesan cheese is made in this rich country. From Casina Bianca to Canonica there is a mixture of vines with other trees and the road weather and chaise were so good that I began to exult in the change we had made from a vittorino to a sedia di posta, but the instant we get into the Venetian State the road becomes intolerably rough and stoney. From hence to Bergamo I was racked by 100 pleuricies–the loose stones, joined to the badness of the chaise and fury of the driver filled me so full of stitches that I almost lost my breath.

At Bergamo, which is a large fine town divided into upper and lower we got one still worse. The upper part of Bergamo, which is very like Clifton near Bristol, is on a hill and the country about it abounds in beautiful villas. The Alps or Appenines begin to appear at

* See p. 44.

N.18. *Viaggio da Milano a Venezia*
~ *Sono Poſte* 22 . · *Miglia 194.*

18. Milan to Venice. Between Colombarolo and Canonica the traveller passed over the River Adda by ferry and paid one Paul. The five miles between Fusina and Venice were covered by boat. It was possible to shorten this journey by going direct from Canonica to Cavernago, leaving Bergamo to the north.

Canonica and now we are at the foot of them and shall continue so till Venice. Harlequin in the Italian Comedy at Paris always says he comes from Bergamo. I walked about a little while the horses and chaise were changed. The houses are very high, but there seems in Italian architecture as much taste and harmony of proportion as in the music. Every pillar one sees, every gateway, colonade has something exquisitely light and elegant in it. The windows are spoilt for want of glass or larger panes, but I suppose the climate requires they should be as they are. It is wonderful with what ingenuity the Italians in this country dispose of every little river–the only manure the land here seems to want is *water* and that want is so supplied by art that it entertained me very much in this bad road and carriage to see every rivulet was divided into 100 streams and conducted one can't tell how, into as many different directions. After such a dry time as they have lately had here they throw up a trench with a plow of about 3 feet wide to conduct the first shower that falls where it will be most wanted. The boys and girls I saw in the streets of Bergamo that were not sunburnt were very handsome. Between this and Brescia the country is pleasant and

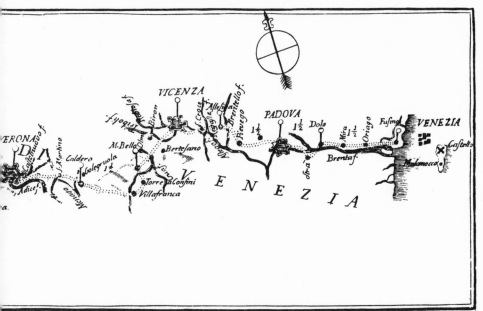

well cultivated, though not so rich as the Milanese. On the left hand a fertile and most beautiful coline, with a convent on the summit which affords a fine prospect. At *Palazzuolo* [Palazzolo] we pop upon a charming valley all at once, covered with vines and quite a garden. The Italians shew taste in planting even their vines in the fields, which they conduct from one fruit tree to another in festoons amongst corn, *formentone* etc. This evening turned out so very bad I was unable to make many remarks. In approaching Brescia we were overtaken by a very heavy shower with the most violent thunder and lightning I had ever been exposed in, and this continued all night.⊕ We had not a dry thread on our arrival at the inn, and were forced to have a fire to dry our things which we found all spoilt by the wet and bad carriages, ⟨top⟩ that with the stony roads which had shook our trunks to pieces, we were so tired and out of humour that we could scarce get a morsel down, tho' we had tasted nothing the whole day save a dish of chocolate at 5 o'clock in the morning at Milan.*⊕ The horses trembling with 'their hair like quills upon the fretful porcupine' seemingly transfixt and could not be prevailed by whip, spur, or kindness to stir till the thunder and lightning had ceased.

⊕ These two marks relate the text as in the manuscript.
* Revised, with deletions, to '. . . so tired and comfortless that nothing the inn afforded could restore our good humour and spirits'.

BRESCIA

THURSDAY MORNING 26. Still a hard rain and there is no stirring out. In the next room to us a company of opera singers are very jolly. They are just come from Russia, as the waiter tells us, where they have been these 12 or 14 years but he knows none of their names. 'Tis a holiday and nothing stirring. Galluppi is just come from thence and Traetta gone there, as I was told at Turin, to replace him. Well–I have been out and seen what is left of this town which was almost wholly destroyed last September by a thunder storm. Had I known this last night I should not perhaps, dare-devil as I am, have slept so sound. The town walls, gates, palaces, houses etc now lye in rubbish without end, tho' many are patched up. The particulars of this terrible calamity I shall try to get authenticated. I remember some mention was made of it in one newspaper last year, tho' yesterday it was quite forgotten.

There are some fine pictures here and beautiful churches: that of la Donna dei Miracoli, is an exquisite piece of architecture, tho' very old. There is a buffo opera here, but for my misfortune only a farce or as 'tis called here a commedia to night. I shall go however if it be only to see the theatre. The price is ⟨. . .⟩ 20 soldi, about 10d. English. But 1st to see some churches. A Dominican to whom I had a letter is out of town. The church and library I have seen however–the former a very fine one, the latter but midling. Some other churches too, whose names I forget are very richly ornamented and have now and then an exquisite picture–that of the Dominicans has one of our Saviour on the Cross in Spagnoletta's manner, which is very striking. The women here all walk the streets in long black silk hoods. The town is well contrived for foot passengers in bad weather. The broad penthouses, which I first observed on this side Lyons continue still–they keep people dry during the very heavy rain which fall here in summer, and the sides of the streets are paved with bricks placed edgeways and some times with broad stones. Immediately after the rain it was very good walking here. One street only and that an old one has a broad piazza like Covent Garden with shops and coffee houses in it, which is in winter the general walking place.

The singer next room to ours is I find the castrate Luini just come home very rich from Russia tho' he lost one night £10,000 of the money he had gained *per la sua virtù*. He is a native of Brescia–was welcomed home by a band of music at the inn, the night of his arrival, and by another the night before his and our departure, consisting of 2 violins, a mandoline, French horn, trumpet and violoncello–and tho' in the dark and by memory they played long concertos with solo

[64]

parts for the mandoline. I was surprised at the memory of these performers–in that it was excellent *street* music and such as we are not accustomed to: but ours is not a climate for serenades. The famous Venetian dancer, la Colonna is likewise just arrived from Russia and in the same house. They are all going to Venice, where I hope both to hear and see them.

The church of St. Afra has many charming pictures in it by Giacomo Palma, Paul Veronese, an altar piece by Tintoret, most admirable for the disposition of the lights–Bassan, rich in a great number of high finished heads. In a picture by Julio Romano's son, the Gloria or figures in the clouds are by his father, among which is an angel playing on the viol with a *bow*, another on the lute etc.

The country from Brescia to Peschiera, an old fortified town which formerly belonged to the Dukes of Mantua, but now is part of the Venetian State, the road is less stoney and more pleasant than on the other side. On the left hand a charming and fertile colline covered with vines and houses for several miles: afterwards at the foot of the Alps, brown and barren, with a small river on the left, which becomes bigger as one advances further, it having been divided and sub-divided into such innumerable little streams near that city. The Palazzo del Conte Mazzuchelli on the right hand seems a fine structure but is remarkable for the little ridiculous figures carved in stone and placed on the parapet wall by the road side resembling the dwarfs painted for children in England: 'rat me, miss, how I adore you.' etc.

From Peschiera to Desenzano* the country, wild, uneven and stony, with however pleasant and fertile bits–Lago Garda in sight, some time before Desenzano upon which lake that town is built. It is upwards of 30 miles long and often 12 or 14 broad losing itself among the Alps but runs as far as Peschiera–the water remarkably clear and of a bluish cast. 'Tis rough and noisy on the shore like the sea. The opposite shore very wild and broken famous for the best eels in Italy–several fishing vessels in sight. The fortress of Peschiera through which we passed is the strongest I have seen in Italy: 'tis built at the end of Lago Guarda but at present has only a few invalids in it.

In travelling through this country it must strike every candid observer that the Italians have greatly the advantage over the other nations of Europe in the article of taste. That is to say in the exteriour of every thing. But the English surely must be allowed to be superiour to them in solidity and generally in the interiour of all things. Tho' an Englishman, I will bow down to them in the beaux arts–in the disposition and neatness of their lands etc–but tho' a professed admirer

* Peschiera is in fact east of Desenzano.

of Italy as the finest country in Europe and of its inhabitants as a most ingenious people I cannot help observing that they are deficient in all the comforts of life–that universal dirtiness prevails in their persons and habitations, which perhaps the heat of the climate may occasion by rendering them listless and lazy, tho' it requires a double attention to cleanliness–and the clumsiness of their vehicles–the maladroitness of their mechanics and artisans–the poverty of the people and want of encouragement in the great, may likewise perhaps account for. I was so pleased with the manner of laying out their grounds that if I were a gentleman farmer the first thing I would do on my arrival in England would be to destroy all the fences of my estate, to level all the grounds and to lay them out all'Italiana–that is to say regularly in oblong squares, by which means not a bit of land would be wasted. It would be much more easily ploughed and cultivated and would look much pleasanter to the eye, which is more pleased with an oblong than a regular square, as it is by an oval than a circular figure and a curve than a straight line. All the road to Verona strait, and tolerably good, the country rich and pleasant.

VERONA

SATURDAY JULY 28. This city covers a great deal of ground–is divided into upper and lower–3 fine bridges over the Adigge [Adige]–has many antiquities and fine churches in it, one St. Anastasia close to the inn, has a very fine toned organ which was playing on my arrival and all dinner time, and was as well heard as if I had been in the church. There are 2 or 3 very fine pictures in this church. This city is remarkable for its ancient amphitheatre, its triumphal arch, old castle, numerous buildings of white marble, for having been the birth place of Vitruvius, Cornelius Nepos, Emilius Macer, Pliny, Fracastorius,– Paul Veronese etc. The ladies here wear black hats cocked as those of the men are in England. The women all affect long black silk hoods and some of them wear at the theatre half masks, up to the mouth. I saw here a comedy in all its buffoon perfection–Harlequin and Brighello, Pantalone and Colombina all in Italian purity. The Cicerone here was cook at the inn–or osteria–"Is Verona populous–hoo ——! and a whistle.–Are there many coaches in it–hoo ——! pish ——" From Verona, which we left on Sunday morning 29 JULY, to Caldier [Caldero] (where there is a hot bath, famous for its prolific virtues) the road good and country charming–excellent farming–ground laid out regularly, and always smooth as a bowling green. We found here the road full of pilgrims going to St. Francesco d'Assisi to obtain pardons and indulgences, granted there on the second of August.

CANAL LOCK
AT DOLO

VENICE

They used to fetch these from Loretto, but are now forbidden to go there for them by the Venetian Senate. They go in companies with each a capellano or abate at their head. Some were singing psalms in canto fermo–At *Monte Bello* (which has not its name for nothing) the colline on the left hand has on its summit a monastery. Here Alps are seen on both sides, but become lower and lower, and ere we reach Vicenza those on the left disappear and the hills on the right are fertile, gentle and too beautiful to be called alps.

VICENZA

Here we dined and walked about for 3 or 4 hours. It is most remarkable for the birth of the famous architect Palladio, for his own house– 2 or 3 beautiful palaces, the town house, a theatre in the style of the ancients–now used for masked balls only–and for a noble triumphal arch at the entrance into the town from Verona on the right hand, being placed near the *Corso* or public walk which is a very beautiful field. The streets are ill paved and houses in general irregular and ruinous–┌however they are chiefly of┘ white marble ┌which┘ is ┌hereabouts┘ very plentiful. There is a very fine picture by Paulo Veronese in the church of the Dominicans. At our inn were the arms and names of great personages who had either dined or lain there– among whom our late D. of York, and the present D. of Marlborough and his brother etc. The ancient theatre is kept in good repair–it was erected in 1584. Lord Bute had been lately at Vicenza and had ordered drawings to be made of all the works of Paladio there. There are 2 large pictures of Tintoret in the cathedral not so well coloured as that I saw at Brescia. In the cool of the finest evening *imaginable* we arrived at

PADUA*

The entrance into this town is very disagreeable, the streets narrow, dark, and diabolically paved, with great rumbling stones of different sizes. At a distance, however, the public buildings afford a fine prospect: I counted near 30 tho' seen from a flat. It is remarkable for its porticos almost thro' the town, which are low and render the ground floors very dark, but yet they are not only convenient in wet weather but I found by experience their use in *hot* weather.

MONDAY 30th JULY. My Moiana went on to Venice, and I am now wholly by myself, in the heart of Italy. I went to see the Town Hall which is Gothic and of the same dimensions as our Westminster Hall. There are several monuments of eminent persons in it–among whom

* 'In signa della stella servo di piazza Francesco.' The Star Hotel.

that of the famous historian Livy who was a native of this town. The church of Santa Giustina is one of the richest and most beautiful in Italy—it is modern. The floor is of fine polished marble in mosaic—the chapels on the sides are richly adorned with sculpture or Corinthian pillars etc in fine marble which serve as frames to the following pictures: 2 by Carletti—ditto Bastian Ricci—ditto Luca Giordano in his best manner—1 by Palma Giovane, Carlo Lotti, Cavalier Liberi etc—but the altar piece which represents the martyrdom of the saint to whom the church is dedicated is the finest picture I ever saw by Paul Veronese. I next carried my letters from Messrs Baretti and Martinelli to Dr Marsili at the Botanical Gardens who received me very courteously, shewed me several books on *my* subject etc and is to introduce me to a learned padre a great musician and particular friend of the late Tartini, who left him his papers. Then book hunting, catalogue reading, writing etc—

The people here speak so Venetian I can scarce understand a word they say: c is always changed into g or s. There was a serious opera here about a month ago composed by Sacchini. The principal singers were the Mattei and Potenza, with a famous tenor cavalier Ettori. The principal dancers M. Pic and Signora Binetti. This is the place for fruit. I saw none hardly till I came here. At Turin the 1st apricots—Milan abounded with figs and pairs—but here peaches, figs, pomgranates, melons etc are in great abundance and cheap.

31st. This morning I went to the College to see the degree of a doctor conferred on a student in the University of Padua. Met there with Dr Marsili who carried me to the Maestro di Capella of San Antonio, Signor F. A. Vallotti who shewed me his books among which a MS treatise on composition by himself and promised me some of his compositions. Many of the churches here being built of brick have but an ordinary appearance but within they are the richest I have yet seen. The air here is reckoned as salubrious as in any part of Italy—the sick Venetians all come here to refit. The wine is good and pleasant, rather strong—piu tosto forte e Galliardo ma assai amabile a bevere says the cameriere at the Stella. Perhaps this may account for the people being more noisy and quarrelsome in the streets than in any Italian town I have yet visited. Fra Vallotti has among his books Keppler's Harmonices Mundi, Salinas—Glareanus's ΔΩΔΕΚΑΧ-ΟΡΔΟΝ, Doni, Bontempi etc, all scarce books. Dr Marsigli lent me a scarce book in which are some curious and satisfactory particulars relative to Turkish music, from whence I made large extracts. This work confirms what Dr Russel has said in his Voyage to Aleppo and totally oversets M. Blainville's assertion that the rebba or rebec is the Turkish instrument from whence we had our first idea of the violin –

the Crusca Dictionary defines Ribeca a κιτασα, chitara, which is played without a bow–and the Turkish violin is not called Ribta but Alla-jee.

WEDNESDAY. AUGUST 1st. This was a rich morning spent at Professor Padre Colombo's with whom Dr Marsigli and I breakfasted, and it was seasoned with a particular account of Tartini from this Padre for whom he had always particular affection: then to Signor Vallotti's–who read to me more of his treatise and showed me his most curious scores. He had 2 large book-cases filled with them. Then to St Anthony's Church to hear the voluntary during the offertorio, which was very solemn and was well played. After this to Dr Marsili's, where I heard his sister taught to sing by a good master who belongs to St Anthony's Chapel. He has but 16 lire: there are 22 lire in a zechin which is little more than 9s English. All the keyed instruments I have yet heard on the continent, except some of the organs are very bad. They have generally little octave spinets to accompany singing with in private houses. The instrument they call a spinetta is made in the shape of our old virginals, of which the keys are so noisy and tone so feeble one hears more wood than wire. This afternoon, I was honoured with a visit from the Cavalier Valcinieri, to whom I had a letter from Dr Righi and with whom Martinelli desired Dr Marsigli to make me acquainted. He is professor of Natural History and Experimental Physics here–he invited me to see the Museum tomorrow morning. At night I met him again and Dr Marsigli at the coffee house and got several particulars cleared up about Tartini and other musicians of this place. The first court at the entrance into the university is a fine piece of architecture: 'tis a square of 2 different orders–the 1st doric with 28 columns, which support as many of the ionic order. It is a disputable point whether Palladio or Sansovino was the architect.

AUGUST 2nd. This morning has been a busy one. Up before 6–as I am every morning; went out at 7 to see a famous picture of St John the Baptist in the desert by Guido Reni. It is at the altar in the sacristy of the *Chiesa Eremitani*–'tis an almost naked figure–admirably painted, with more force than is usually found in the works of Guido. My friend Mr Robertson has the copy of a copy of this picture–but the original is so precious that, tho' as big as the life, there is always a glass over it by way of preservation. In one of the chapels of the same church are some paintings in fresco by Mantegna which are much admired for the perspective. At the Duomo, in the sacristy is a Madonna and Child by Titian, so well preserved that one would almost suspect it to be the work of some more modern artist. However 'tis much in his manner and an admirable picture. On the right hand is a

[69]

S. Girolamo by Giacomo Palma il giovine, and S. Francesco on the left by the same–both well preserved. Over these an old picture of Domenio Campognolo. There are still in this city the remains of an ancient amphi-theatre but the present owners have been so stupid as to destroy the seats and to leave only the walls round it standing. At the end is built a modern and despicable palazzo. The next visit was to the street, the house, the church where poor Tartini lived and is buried. Then I visited his scholar and successor Signor Guglietti. After this went to see the museum which was very obligingly shewn to me by the professor himself Signor Cav. Valciniere. It contains a great number of curiosities, such as animals, vegetables, minerals etc. Here I met with a conte and contessa from Palma, friends of my fellow traveller Dr Righi, who had wrote to them, it seems about me, and they had expressed to the professor Valcinieri a desire to see me. This morning was fixt and I received great civilities from them and many invitations to go to Palma, where many curiosities in the musical way awaited me etc.

From hence al *Santo*, where there was an hour's good church music of il padre Maestra Vallotti's composition–who was there to beat the time*–with solo verses. Tho' it was not a great festival, yet the band was better than ordinary, being the Day of *Pardons*. I wanted much to hear old *Antonio Vandini* the famous violoncello, who they say plays and expresses *a parlare* upon his instrument–and the famous oboe Matteo Bissiote, but neither had solo parts. However I'll give these 2 performers credit for great abilities, as they are highly extolled by their countrymen, who must by the frequent hearing of excellent performers of all kinds be good judges in spite of them-selves. People accustomed to bad music, may be pleased with it, but those on the contrary, long used to good music and performances cannot.–It is remarkable that Antonio and all the other violoncello players here hold the bow in the old fashioned way with the hand under it. The choir is immense. The basses are all placed on one side; the violins, hautbois, French horns and tenors [violas] on the other: the voices half in one organ loft and half in an other. The 4 organs here are all alike–no pannels to the frames–but the pipes seen on 3 sides of a square extreamly bright. After mass I took my leave of the good Father Vallotti, who is a character I grow to very much. He has promised me 2 of his masses in score as fast as they can be transcribed, and wished very much for a copy of my book when in any other

* In churches the conductor, beater of the time, played an essential part from at least the 15th century to when Burney is writing: the rhythmic sublety of poly-phony demanded this kind of control. Elsewhere, in the opera house or concert hall, performances were directed from a keyboard–harpsichord or organ–long before the 18th century.

language than English. He read my plan with great attention and was pleased to say it was a public concern to Italy. He is not at all satisfied with padre Martini's work, which tho' called a history consists of dissertations and matters of doctrine and science more than narrative or historical facts – indeed I never saw this famous book till now, but it does not seem to preclude my plan even in Italy where alone it is known. – There is but one volume yet finished and that, tho' a thick quarto contains only 8 pages of history, but I must read and talk with P. Martini ere I form a judgment. Hitherto I have been unable to get this book all over Italy as far as my travels have extended – and I want to read it ere I converse with the author.

THURSDAY evening – it has thundered and lightened furiously and they have been ringing all the bells in town on this occasion as they had done at Brescia before, and as I find is the custom throughout Italy in thunder storms. It has rained and still rains *à verse*. There is a passage from here to Venice on the Brenta by water but I am dissuaded from going that way. They say here 'tis tedious and the company usually bad – always mixed. I saw some of the boats to day which look very smart. They are painted on the outside and look very inviting.

FRIDAY morning. After a heavy rain, such as this country requires, succeeds a fine morning such as I required, but ere I mount the *Carozzina* to leave this place, in all likelihood, for ever – let me just stop to say that I never saw such a quantity of fragrant and beautiful flowers as there are in the streets here – such as double Spanish jessamine, carnations etc.

At leaving Padua there is much waste ground within the gates, such as seems never to have been built upon. The first 2 or 3 miles are along the Brenta, then a very elegant villa on the left hand with dwarf ridiculous figures on the parapet wall before the garden like those I saw near Brescia, but on the house and gates charming statues. Two or 3 miles further a delightful borgo, or large kind of village called Stra full of fine houses. Then, leaving the banks of the Brenta a little while and turning to the left, pass by another noble house and gardens, on the gate of which is written, Horti Pisani; soon after this the Brenta shews itself again on the right hand. On the left elegant houses with gardens full of temples, statues, orange groves etc. The air is scented with arabian sweets. – I never saw villas till now. – Brenta lost again – and again found with a covered bridge. Here 'tis divided into two, and soon after into more canals. Dolo – post and $\frac{1}{2}$ – for the first time, grapes, not yet ripe, on the high way side within reach. They are planted against other trees which they gently embrace, not with the ivy's sick'ning Cornish hug.

The carozzina is a kind of double open chaise. That part facing the horses has a cover to it – the other none, but is like the sedia or post chaise I travelled in from Milan to Padua. This vehicle would hold 4 and a great deal of baggage. The fare to Fusina is 18 lire. Horses are changed at *Oriago*, 6 miles before Fusina which is the land's end. About a mile before one arrives at it, Venice appears in the sea. The land on the left flat and marshy, but on the right fertile to the very last. At Fusina I got into a very comfortable gondola, a quattro when I was accosted by custom house officers, who were very gentle – only asked for a *Cortesia* for their politeness – and upon giving them about 2 or 3 livres they went away very contented, and left me so, for I had heard terrible things of the severity of these officers at going into Venise. The water was smoother than the Thames at this time of the year – and Venice swelled upon the sight, but one forms such romantic ideas of this city from its singular formation about which one reads so much, that it did not at all answer my expectation. As I approached it, I found it like other towns, composed of houses of different sizes – different colours and of different ages and materials. There was not that symetry I expected, nor the richness of materials. But behold in the midst of my contemplations I am carried to the dogana or custom house, which stands alone in the middle of the sea and am accosted by 10 or 12 officers, who row along side me with the same speeches as the others assuring me *they* were the true servants of the state. I offered them my keys and bid them do their office, but they said they hoped for a buona mano for their civility, which I compiled with, and there it ended.

VENICE

3rd AUGUST. I am now at the *Scudo di Francia*, on the great canal of this city, within 20 yards of the *Ponte di Rialto*. The approach to this *osteria* or *albergo* was thro' a number of different canals and by innumerable bridges over them – the great canal is as busy as the Thames below bridge. The gondolas are all covered with a kind of black crape and look like hearses. This is* [I] suppose on account of the heat – but then I wonder: the Italians where ever I have yet been affect much the opposite colour, white in their houses. All the villas are milk

* The rest of this paragraph is a reconstruction of Burney's first intentions. It was edited to: 'This is on account of a sumptuary law, before the passing of which there were no bounds to the vanity and expence of the Venetians in these boats. The Italians where ever I have yet been affect much the opposit ⌊ion of white and black in their buildings⌋, white, in their houses – all the villas ⌊on the banks of the Brenta⌋ are milk white.'

white. They build much with brick here and then stucco or plaister them over in imitation of stone.

I find this place *molto più allegro* than any place I have yet seen in Italy. The 4 gondolieri who brought me from the continent were difficult to satisfie. Their fare from Fusina is settled at 9 lire ½, but the *buona mana* or *mancia* is always asked, for every two pence or three pence one lays out. I gave 'em about a livre and ½ – but still not enough, and all I had for it, (I could not scold with 'em or understand a word of their lingo) was to make a noise in the few words I could muster. However by an additional livre I got rid of 'em at last. After dinner in my riding dress I went with the 2 people I dined – M. Moiana and a Swiss to see the famous glass manufacture of Briati, which produces very beautiful and cheap things. The proprietor showed us at least 50 different appartments all better and better filled with furniture of their ingenious manufacture. The instant I got to the inn a band of musicians consisting of 2 good fiddles a violoncello and female voice stopt under the windows and performed in such a manner as would have made people stare in England, but here they were as little attended to as coalmen or oyster women are with us.

SATURDAY. Being a little settled in my appartment I dressed and went out with an intention to visit some of the persons to whom I had letters. Mr. Richie whom I wished to see first was out – then I found out my banker and a letter which had lain in his hands some time, the 1st I had received from England since I left Paris. I had sent immediately upon my arrival to enquire for letters, but a scoundrel servant, out of laziness I suppose, told me he had been but non c'è niente – upon which I sent a letter a way to England full of complaints – which I would have given £50 to have had back. I next went to see the famous church of St Marc and the piazza and the square, and tho' neither of which were quite what I expected, yet very rich and gay. The day was cold and unpleasant. It had thundered, lightned and rained very much the night before, but began to brighten up. The church of St Marc is too full of fine things – it seems loaded with ornaments – which tho' inestimable in their intrinsick worth, yet by being jumbled together have less effect than half the number would have if well placed. The people here and all over the Venetian State seem to enjoy more liberty than those of the rest of Italy, as far as I have yet seen. There is a great air of industry and business in every place and countenance. Fruits of all kinds abound here – enormous melons, peaches, nectarines, grapes etc. After dinner I went again the house of our Chargé D'Affaires and found him and his lady at home: had a very polite reception, a comfortable chat and an excellent dish of tea, all a l'angloises. Mr. Richie entered heartily into my plan which I communicated to him and immediately began to form schemes for being useful to me. After this I went to the conservatorio of la Pieta to hear music all performed by girls, then came home to read catalogues of books in which I am in hopes of finding many to my purpose. I rummaged several stalls in the morning.

SUNDAY 5th AUGUST. Went to the Greek Church which is quite as rich and full of ornaments as the Catholic. Then to the island of S. Giorgio Maggiore. The church is by Palladio and one of the finest in Italy. The front is all of marble. In it are many fine pictures particularly of Tintoret, and in the sacristy are admirable pictures of this painter and of old Palma. In the refectory too is a very large picture by Paul Veronese of the Marriage of Cana in which are more than 120 figures. This was the first he ever painted in Venice. In it he has introduced a concert in which he has painted himself on the viola, or tenor–with 6 strings, Titian on the violone (an old man), Tintoret on the violin (with 4 strings and short bow) a young man, and Bassano on the flute. There is likewise a lute but cannot discover the figure that holds it. The Emperor Charles 5 and his Empress, Francis the first and queen, the great Turk and sultana etc are on the left hand side of this admirable picture. This is a convent for noble Venetian monks–as St. Zacchari is for noble ladies. The church of this last is extreamly rich and full of admirable pictures by old Palama. P. Veronese etc. There is a concert by the former over the organ in which is a violin with 4 strings and played by a bow. This afternoon to 2 conservatorios. This evening I saw a truly ridiculous contention of boys on the canal rowing in a kind of kneading tub with 2 trenchers for oars. There were 3 small prizes for the 3 first: it was upon the Grand Canal–roasting hot weather to day. At night I walked on the great Piazza di San Marc, which was crowded with all sorts of people mixed together from nobles and their ladies to tinkers and coblers with ladies of pleasure. I must not forget to mention the having seen at noon all the nobles march up the Scala dei Giganti in order to assemble in councel. Their dress is black, not unlike that of our lawyers, with enormous tye wigs: their number is 1500. They received petitions as they passed along and the petitioner at parting kissed the furbello of the senator's robe. Mr Richie was so kind as to send Signor Giuseppe a famous coppyist to me to day, who has undertaken to furnish me with many curious things.

6th. This is a kind of scarlet day here. The Doge went in procession to the church of *S. Giovanni e Paolo* and was attended by all the nobles who were well and in town. I went to the palace of St. Mark's and saw them assemble–and afterwards saw them on the water in 2 most sumptuous barges. Yesterday they were all in black–to day the robes were a crimson kind of uncut velvet, very rich and over the left shoulder a kind of velvet scarf of the same colour. At the church they were met by prodigious number of secular and regular priests. I thought the procession would never end. Such a quantity of silver supports for the wax candles carried 2 and 2 by the whole fraternity, major and minor! This ceremony over I tried again to meet with some of the gentlemen to whom I had letters to deliver, but found none at home. After dinner I was favoured with a visit from Signor Latilla an eminent composer here, who had been desired to call upon me by Mr. Richie. I found him a sensible man, who had both read and thought a good deal about the music of the ancients as well as that of the moderns to which he has contributed a considerable share for many years past. He's about 60 years of age, and a plain unaffected man. I admired his candour in advising me to go to the Conservatorio degl'Incurabili to hear some music there of Galuppi, which was to be performed by his scholars. He likewise told me if I wished to converse with Signor Galuppi he would gladly carry me to him, and promised to call again upon me himself in 2 or 3 days, in which time he promised to try to think of something or other that would be of use to my plan. After this conversation I went directly to the Incurabili. I found I was too late for the overture and part of the first air which vexed me for the rest pleased me very much, both in the composition and execution. From hence to the piazza, which was again very much crowded and very hot. When I came home I found il Conte Bujovich had honoured me with a visit in return for that I had in vain made him in this morning.

7th. This morning to make visits and to the church of S. Gaetano, where there was a mass in music which did not please me much, and the heat and crowd which made it very difficult to be pleased. I met Signor Latilla at the church door, who promised to call on me on Friday morning. In the afternoon I went to see churches particularly that of S. Giorgio Maggiore by Palladio, the most perfect building in Venice. There is such a noble elegance and simplicity in this structure that it inclines one to prostrate one's self upon entering it, as it has the true appearance of a temple to the Supreme Being; but the pulpit and a rich alter piece placed there, not by Palladio, have a bad effect, breaking the proportions and hiding the most beautiful collumns imaginable. At the front of this church, placed on an island facing the Gran piazza di S. Marco I could not help stepping back 17 or 1800 years in history and supposing myself in view of some ancient Greek city–the number of public buildings had so beautiful an appearance across the water, which was smooth as glass–the sun just setting and there was such a sky as we never see in England except in the landscapes of Claude Lorraine.

8th. WEDNESDAY. This morning Dr Rigghillini called on me. I had letters to him both from Mr Martinelli and Barretti. He is something like Dr. Armstrong – a little younger. He is very tall, and has a gentleman like appearance but plain and sensible in his manner. He went with me to the Abate Martini, who was his friend as well as Dr Marsili's of Padua who had favoured me with a letter to him. We found him at home among books, papers and letters, which afforded not a chair to sit down on. He made some droll excuses, said there was a good deal of philosophy about his room, meaning the dust and litter. He is really a curious man and was much to my taste and purpose – he had travelled into Greece in order to make observations in geography, agriculture, natural history etc. but was unable to satisfy himself as he expected, and his pride was so hurt by it that he would not publish any of his remarks or discoveries. Among many other curious researches he made many about the music of the modern Greeks. He knows, I believe as much as any one else concerning that of the ancients, being a very learned musician and well read in Meibomious, Rameau, Tartini etc. – as well as a good practical musician. He is a great admirer of Marcello and sings by heart all his cantatas and best melodies. He read my plan which, chemin faisant, we discussed article by article; he entered much into my views, shewed me his Grecian and other MS papers, offered me some of them very politely – and we parted good friends and acquaintances. At night I met him again on the piazza, and we had a long peripatetic conversation – I had from him many curious musical anecdotes. Count Taxis left a card this morning – but we always miss each other – I wanted much to see him on account of Tartini's and other papers of which he was in possession.

9th. This morning after visiting Mr. Richie I went a book hunting. After dinner l'Abate Martini called on me with his Grecian papers, which are really curious and very much to my purpose. He staid 2 or 3 hours and I found him deep in every part of music, but more particularly inclined to the ancient. When he left me I went to hear music at the church of St. Laurence. It was composed and under the direction of Sacchini – a great croud and heat. In the former I lost my handkerchief and in the latter my patience. I suffered too much to be easily pleased, and the music seemed more common than that I had before heard of this author. One of my gondolieri, upon my telling him I had had my pocket picked – said this was a fair for thieves and told me a great many stories concerning their dexterity upon such occasions. The weather grows hotter and hotter. However, if it was not for the bugs, mosquitos, gnats and fleas I could bear it well enough, but I am devoured. The canals are crouded with *musical* people at night – bands of music – French horns – duet singers in every gondola.

10th. I had this morning a long visit from Signor Latilla, and got from him several particulars relative to the present as well as past state of music here. He says the conservatorios have been established at Venice about 200 years, as hospitals, that at first the girls were only taught psalmody and canto-fermo (as our parish girls are) that in the process of time they learnt to sing in parts, and at length joined instruments to the voices. He says the expence on account of the music, is very inconsiderable–there being but 5 or 6 masters to each for singing and the several instruments–as the elder girls teach the younger. The maestro di capella only composes and directs, some-times writes down closes,* and attends all the rehearsals and public performances. There has been a constant succession of able masters employed in these schools. Hasse was once Maestro to the Pietà and has left a miserere which is still performed here in Passion Week and is, according to the Abate Martini a wonderful fine composition. Signor Galuppi the present Maestro of St. Mark's church and of the Incurabili hospital was a scholar of the celebrated Lotti and very early noticed as a good harpsichord player and genius in composition. The Venetian is a good school for contra punto as well as for a lively fancy. Signor Latilla, who has been Maestro to the famous Hospital della Pietà, has favoured me with a *Credo* of his composition, and written with his own hand, for that place.

I lament the want of time to see pictures and buildings, as both abound here in great plenty. It is the place to see the works of *Titian*, Paolo *Veronese*, *Tintoretto* and the 2 Palmas, and in architecture, the 1st are Palladio, Sansovino, Scamozzi, Sardi, etc. I have seen the best but have no time to make minutes. The language here is so different from Tuscan that I wished to impress upon my memory the character-istic deviations. They seem to try in pronouncing *good* words to make the language still more soft than it is ⌊in correct pronunciation⌋–for instance–Francesco is Franṣeco–Giorno, Zorno–c'è, x'è pronounced z'è–dico, digo–and the common people use constantly the accusative for the nominative case to verbs–as *mi digo*, mi vengo, mi sento for io dico, io vengo, io sento etc. Calla, a street–as Calla di Fumo, is, I believe peculiar to Venice: eccellenza servirla–the waterman say–as our blackguards–*here*, your *Honour*. If they ask whether you'll stay any time in a place–resterà troppo quì?

The heat here at present is very violent–not a cloud has appeared

* 'Close in music simply means an end or termination to a movement, vocal or instrumental. . . . But since the establishment of the opera, or musical drama, and singers of great abilities, taste and execution, have been employed and frequently left to themselves, *ad libitum*, at a pause, or at the conclusion of an air–by a close or cadenza is understood such an extemporaneous effusion of taste and fancy, termin-ated by a shake, as could be executed in one breath' (A. Rees, *Cyclopædia*, Vol. VIII).

in the sky these 10 days – this renders the vermin and insects innumerable and intolerably voracious. I am obliged, by the heat, to leave my windows open all night, during which time, as it is situated on the water, such a quantity of gnats, come in as both stun and devour me. A purgatory or moderate hell can be no punishment to people so taught to *stand fire* as these Venetians. If the D—l has nothing worse than heat in store for the sinners of this country; they, like Mr. Quin's cook may bid him kiss their a—s, but Dante, an Italian was more enlarged in his notions of hell torments, he makes the last and most terrible pit intensely cold, and punishes with ice more than fire.

11th. SATURDAY. I never suffered so much from heat in my life: and the gnats are still infinitely worse than the heat. This morning I was too bad to go out. My hands and face are like those of one in the small pox, and the itching so painful and violent I am almost distracted with it. There is not a stranger in this house who has not been attacked by myriads of these little dragons, but none have felt their rage so much as my self. I went to the Pietà to night, but there was little company and the girls performed but indifferently. They played a thousand tricks in their closes especially in the duets, where they in sport tried who could go highest, lowest, quickest etc to the utmost exertion of their powers. This hospital has the reputation of being the best, not for what it does *now*, but for what it *has* done heretofore for I think, in point of singing both the Incurabili Hospital and the Mendicanti are before it. In coming home to night I was hemmed in by as many gondolas near the Doge's palace as I should have been by coaches in the Strand on the D. of N[ewcastle]'s night. It was a *pregada*, or great Counsel of State, which happens frequently and is so called on account of the senators being summoned by the Doge. News arrived here this morning that the Turks have been defeated by the Russians which 'tis thought has occasioned this meeting.* This morning I bought of Pasquali, the greatest bookseller here as many new and old books either written expressly on the subject of music, or which speak of it occasionally as cost me 11 zechini or 5 guineas.

Sunday was spent in musical matters related elsewhere. I have only to observe that at an academia to which I was carried at night by Signor Marin Giorgi, al Casa Grimani where I heard Signora Bassa perform, it was a company of the chief of nobility of Venice, the 3 persons I have named being among the first class here. This lady who is now passèe has still de beaux restes – she plays neat and with taste but her fingering as well as that of a professor who played on the

---

* A Russo-Turkish War had broken out in 1768 and, in 1770, the Turks suffered a series of defeats culminating in that of the main Turkish army at Kagul on 12 August.

harpsichord there was miserable. In running up the keys it was always with the 2 or 3 finger tumbling over each other – and in descending 'twas with the 2 and 1st. – She had not the brilliancy now in her playing that many of my own scholars as well as those of other people can boast and yet she's the cream among lady players here, and has long had that station. I was very well received here and *obliged* to sit down twice to the harpsichord which with the heat of the weather almost drowned me. I was invited again for Thursday.

MONDAY 13. I am roasted to death*– the weather grows hotter and hotter and my fellow traveller Moiana was seized last night with a phleurisy, which I fear will be fatal to him. He has been twice blooded, but is delirious and has spit blood. The poor man is in despair – at the immense distance from his family and the confusion of his affairs here, among strangers. I tremble for him and can do him no kind of good, but his case renders me unfit for anything either of business or pleasure. I staid at home the whole day and may well say, *Diem perdidi*, for it has been of no use to any one. I wish to help this poor man, but know not how – and yet he begged of me not to leave him, but without this request I should not have done it. I am now alone with him in this house as a flemish gentleman M. Dierexsens from Antwerp a man of great taste and judgment in painting sculpture and architecture, and a young German, with whom we had made a kind of mess acquaintance by eating together at the inn were just gone. My spirits have not been so much sunk as now, since I left England.

MONDAY night. This poor man *must* die, they say. There has been a consultation of physicians at noon and I believe they have passed sentence on him. I am very miserable about it. I cannot in honour or mental comfort leave him alive or dead till some of his friends arrive from Milan, to which place an express goes off to night; but 'tis 200 miles thither from Venice so that 4 days is the least time in which one can expect any one to arrive from thence in consequence of this express. He was too worldy and anxious. He is a jeweller at Amsterdam and has had a good deal of business to do here. The weather has been uncommonly hot to the Venetians even, who are used to it and never stir but in a gondola night or day, whereas *he* had hurried about the town on foot wherever he is, in order to save a little miserable money for these miserable doctors, who I fear will by their ignorance, shorten his days. The poor man had not one grain of true philosophy, fortitude or religion about him, but gave way to every little accident like a weak woman or a child; add to hurry heat and fretting, the intemperance of which he had been guilty in eating and drinking and

* Edited to: 'I was almost roasted alive and frightened to death – the weather grows hotter and hotter. . . .'

the situation he is in will appear a necessary consequence and result of the whole.

The Italians are esteemed the most temperate people in Europe, and I believe *par force*, as the climate requires it–they seldom have more than one meal a day here: I thought it hard at first to submit to this custom, but I now feel no want of anything more than a moderate dinner.

TUESDAY. This poor man continues very ill. I sent away an express to his friends at Milan. I did not go out till it was late, and then with such a dejection as rendered it impossible for any thing to amuse or fasten on the mind. I went into some churches, but remember nothing I saw except some sarcophagi, which it suited my disposition then to examine. They are in the cloysters of the *Servi*; the dates are 1372 to 77 on which are sculptured in rilievo figures and some instruments of music. I hated to be at home–and have no enjoyment abroad. After dinner having left with my fellow traveller one of his mercantile friends, in order to keep off the foul fiend I went to hear music at churches–saw some pictures of Parmegiano in the Servi which put me in mind of my little Charlotte and Crisp who used to call her the little parmegiana.*

This morning WEDNESDAY, I was honoured with a visit from il *Conte Bujovich*, the particular friend of Mr Barretti and had great reason to regret my not having seen him sooner: he is so good humoured, friendly and obliging. He had undertaken to get for me some particulars relative to the 1st establishment of music in the 4 conservatorj, which hitherto I could not get: and was so polite as to attend me to the Doge's palace–showed me several pictures I had not seen before, took me into the Doge's appartments, thro' which I saw him (for the 1st time he having been ill ever since my arrival) pass in procession to St Mark's Church. I followed him thither (his robe was gold tissue) and it was *scarlet* or rather crimson day, with the senators. Count Bujovich conducted me thro' the palace into one of the great organ lofts of St. Mark's Church. I there met with *Latilla* who was beating time to the mass, opposite to Galuppi who was in a *toga* and surplice doing the same on the other side but with a role of paper: Latilla only beat with his hand. From hence I had a fine view of the Doge and senators, of the choir, orchestras etc–but I could not get up my spirits, for the poor Moiana (who was a R. Catholic) had been confessed and had had the Host brought to him in procession thro' the streets to give him the Sacriment. I saw the procession stop in the street under my window, and the people all on their knees but knew

* Charlotte was Burney's fourth daughter (to Garrick his 'Little Dumpling Queen'); and Crisp was Samuel Crisp, disappointed playwright, lover of music, one of Burney's longest-standing friends and an intimate of the whole Burney family.

not that the Host had been carried to him till after it was gone. This
was a terrible apparatue to the poor man–who is young, worldly, and
neither a philosopher nor a hero. I dreaded facing him after this, so
went out to dissipate. I heard music again at the church of the *Celestia*,
but was not easily to be pleased. After dinner I went into the poor
man and found him sorting his papers. He sent the maid away and
begged me to burn a great parcel, I believe from his poor wife–whom
I pity from my soul, for I now see not the least chance of his recovery.
By what he now spits I should think a mortification was coming on–
'tis not red as before, but a black kind of corrupted blood. I believe no
one ever did recover who discharged such stuff.–To night he lies
quiet and fancies himself better, took me by the hand and said he
loved me dearly and hoped to thank me here or elsewhere for my
kindness. Indeed what I have done was more humanity and as a duty
than partiality to his character, proceeding from similar sentiments –
but I see him now in a more favourable sight than ever I did, he's
almost arrived at that period when one forgives every thing–and it
seems to be in human nature to see the living on the bad side, and
the dead on the good.

THURSDAY 16. Moiana had had a bad night and to day will be
critical. He says he's a little better, but I perceived him much more
feeble than yesterday. What he expectorates is not so black.

In going out this morning I stept into 2 or 3 churches. That of S.
Sebastian is a very large and ancient one. There are many good pictures in it, almost all by P. Veronese, who lies buried there. The
organ-loft in particular is admirably painted and well preserved. At
the alter of the Chapel *di Casa Crasso* is a S. Nicholas and a most
beautiful little angel by Titian. This church requires a week to examine. In the Chiesa de' Frari there are 2 pictures of Titian much
admired, but the largest at the great alter, an Assumption on wood, is
to my thinking spoilt–'tis so dark that none of that painter's beautiful
colouring appears. The other at the alter *di Casa Pesaco* is in great
beauty, and one of the few whence one can now judge favourably of
Titian's colouring. A beautiful head of a youth on the right hand and
2 boys in the clouds. At the alter of the sacristy is a good picture of old
Bellini the Virgin and Child and 2 little angels playing an instrument
below–one on a kind of guitar the other on the flute. This painter one
would think was very fond of music, as I hardly ever saw a picture of
his without persons playing on instruments. Of Pordenone too, who
was a notable performer on the lute, and rival of Titian, there are
several pictures (but grown dark) in a private appartment belonging
to this church. In the church of Santa Maria Maggiore is the famous
St John the Baptist by Titian and Noah's Ark a very extraordinary

picture by Giacomo Bassano. An immense number of creatures are here exquisitely painted–the great alter piece is by P. Veronese and there are many other good pictures by old Palma, Roschi, Varottari, Tintoretto etc, but there was such cursed music playing all the time I was there that it was impossible to stay longer. I went twice to the Jesuit's church to see the celebrated Martyrdom of S. Lawrence by Titian, but both the church and picture were so dark I could make nothing out. At the nun's church of St Catherine is an alter-piece by P. Veronese in great beauty: 'tis the Marriage of the Saint. In the church of S. Giobbe is a famous picture of Gio. Bellino with the Madonna in alto, and below SS John the Baptist, Job, Sebastian, Dominic, Frances and Lewis with 3 very beautiful angels playing on instruments. This painter lived in the beginning of the 15 century. In the Church of St Anthony after this*

My visit with Signor Galuppi to day in company with Signor Latilla was long and comfortable, and I was very glad to find that time has spared the person as well as the genius of this excellent composer. He is a lively, sensible, and agreeable natural character–in figure little and thin–but has the look of a gentleman very much. He's between 60 and 70 which he bears very well and seems likely to live 20 years longer. I shewed him my plan–and we talked it over and talked over music and musicians very cordially–i.e. with similar sentiments. His definition of good music I think admirable–'tis tho' short very comprehensive. It should consist of vaghessa, chiarezza and buona madulazione.† He and Latilla recollected the names of all the great masters of the conservatorios and had patience to let me write them down. Buranello‡ was so obliging at my request, as to promise me a piece of his composition which has not yet been made public, as a relick and testimony of friendship. I have already had several of his best things copied. He showed me his house, his wife, a good looking gentlewoman, rather fat, and an admirable picture of P. Veronese which has been long in his wife's family: 'tis a sleeping child quite naked and lying at its ease, with its heels higher than its head–well preserved–the head very highly finished–a fat little *colluppy* thing– the nails of the hands and toes not finished–a sweet brat! not unlike thee Dick.§ The linnen on which he lies is charmingly tumbled. He

* There seems to be a discontinuity here in the manuscript.

† 'Beauty, clearness, and good modulation' (B).

‡ Balthazar Galuppi, sometimes called Buranello, because he was born on the island of Burano, near Venice.

§ Most likely Richard Thomas Burney, born in King's Lynn on 20 November, 1768. He was the son of Charles Burney by his second wife and in his childhood was generally known in the family as 'the beautiful Dick'.

If 'collop' is 'a thick fold of fat on the body', then 'collupy' might well be rendered as 'chubby'?

shewed me his working-room, with a little clavichord in it–but the whole house clean and tidy. The floors here of the better sort of houses are very beautiful, of a composition of marble pebbles etc ground to a fine powder-co-cement and made into a paste and seem as solid and high polished as the finest real marble. The poor Galluppi seems hurt at the encouragement and protection some blockhead priests–among whom is Farlanetto, get – employed as composers here–indeed except Sacchini, his 2nd, he stands so high above the present race of musicians here that he seems a Goliah among dwarfs. His family has been very large, but all his children, except 3 or 4 are now well married. I fancy him a good and regular family man. He said he would come and see me, but I begged him not as I was so much out, he would lose his time and I should be no gainer. Mr Richie and Edwards had been to see me in my absence this morning.

After dinner I went to see La Scola di S. Rocco which is open only on festivals. It consists of 2 immense rooms one over the other, entirely painted in pannels as large as cartoons by Tintoretto. The stair-case too is finely painted by the same master as well as the treasury, which contains such a quantity of gold and silver objects and other things as I never before saw. There was a great crowd and many beggars–who here might be truely said to starve in the midst of plenty.

The better sort of women here who walk in the streets or rather quays and passages, for streets there are none, wear black silk hoods big enough for veils and capucins, and black silk peticoats over all, like the skirt of a child's frock, so that from the binding of this petticoat to the bottom of the veil is all that can be seen of a woman's gown and shape. The cuffs appear generally trimmed, and the gown is laced behind like a child's frock or dust gown. I was again to night alla casa Grimani where there was a prodigious large company of the 1st nobility among whom was the son of the present Doge. I was rather late and it seemed as if they had stayed for me, at which I was terribly shocked: it was with difficulty I could suppose such an attention to one of so small figure and consequence. My reception from the padrone della casa, by whom I was cordially embraced, as in the general custom here; from La Signora Bassa and all those I had seen there before was extreamly flattering. I am ashamed to say that this concert, I was told was designed as a regale for me in particular. The band was numerous–Signor Sacchini at the harpsichord and to sing, there was an abate who sung in the most exquisite taste: and with great difficulty Signora Regina Zocchi had been prevailed on to come–she had been brought up as an orphan, but of a good family at the Hospital of Gl'Incurabili and had the advantage of being there under Hasse, but she is now well married and well received everywhere she chuses to go. She is now under 30 with an agreeable figure and a pleasing countenance. She has a powerful voice and sings charmingly with great execution in allegros and expression in slow movements. But now comes the most curious part of the tale. I was obliged by general solicitation to sit down to the harpsichord (I had not seen one since Madame Brillon's). I would just as readily have submitted to the discipline of the salt canals of Venice, as this ceremony–but there was no retreat. I played a voluntary, for I could neither see nor remember anything I was so frightened. However the politeness of the company extended to general applause and compliments without end from the professors. I then presented her excellence Signora Bassa with a movement of my own which I had transcribed with design to play it first–but durst not. Her excellence received it very graciously and seemed even much obliged by it. She looked at it a great while and entreated me to give her the style of it–which I could not refuse–then she sate down to the harpsichord (while the company was going) and practiced it, submitting to and even begging my instructions and correction. Then she made me play it again and again and I was sorry it was not longer and better for her sake–she admired the fingering of it and if there is any belief in man Signor Grimani was sorry I was so soon to leave Venice. This lady is a widow but lives very retired–sees no company at home, and never plays but at the houses of very particular friends. She is of the Justiniani family here, one of the first of the patricians. She desired me to see her niece la Contessa Tamara Giustina at Bologna–and Signor Grimani insisted in my writing to him from any part of the world where he could be of the least use to me. Poor Moiana worse and worse–was almost choked to night with the blood he had not strength to expectorate–and becomes weaker and weaker every moment.——

FRIDAY 17. This morning Conte Bujovich and Dr Reghillini honoured me with a long visit, after which I went to make visits, but found nobody at home except Conte Torre Tassis. He shewed me all his musical treasures, as elsewhere related and was very polite. There is now at Venice the second son of Sir Armine Wodehouse and a son of Sir John Hind Cotton–our servants are already acquainted–they go to Bologna to night, have a paotte or boat to themselves and would let me have a place–but I cannot leave this poor man till some of his friends arrive. In consequence of my old acquaintance with Sir Armine I waited on Mr. Wodehouse this morning, but he was out. However his servant has been here to say he would return my visit in the afternoon and should be glad if it would suit me to go with them to Bologna. Moiana's father is arrived, but now it is too late to pack and pay time enough for setting off to night. I have a great deal to do of visits and business. Such thunder, lightning and rain! but it will cool the air which had been so intensely hot for several days past, even to the Venetians–and I hope tame the insects and vermin, which are so furious. There is no bearing them. I am no saint, God knows, but I am certainly a *martyr* to the bugs, fleas and gnats ⟨which are here well entitled . . .⟩*

SATURDAY, 18. Taking leave etc is always a melancholy business. Last night I was prodigiously well entertained by being admitted by means of Mr. Edwards, *into* the conservatorio of the Mendicanti, where I *saw* as well as *heard* a charming concert performed in all its parts by females. After this I went with the same gentleman and D. Flaminio Tomj, who sings with more taste than any man I ever heard in my life, except Palma, to Signor Grimani's–accompanied him in 3 or 4 songs and then played 2 or 3 hours to a great deal of company who made a great fuss about very little matter, God knows. I am too old and knowing to become vain now, or I should have had my head turned with the applause I received last night, both here and at the Mendicanti, where I likewise played a great deal. I made Signora Bassi a present of a movement of one of my printed lessons and that has given rise to innumerable petitions for songs, solos, etc. I was invited *into* the music school at the Mendicanti for to night and had an offer of the same interiour entertainment at the other 3 conservatorios, but Satan avaunt, I will positively set of for Bologna to night.

TUESDAY. 21 AUGUST. After taking a melancholy leave of several people at Venice on Saturday and consigning a large box of books I had purchased in all the towns of Italy from Turin to the last mentioned, to the care of Mr Richie, I set off in the corriera, a kind of barge with a covered place in the middle for passengers, at 1 o'clock Sunday morning. Poor Moiana had but a very few hours to live–was wholly insensible when I came away. I left his father with him, who promised me a letter at Bologna. The company I met with in this passage boat was like that in Noah's ark–composed of all kinds of cattle–but not an animal to speak to but a Frenchman, who soon entered into conversation with me. However beds were spread on the floor and we all pigged together–the courier, one female and all–slept and grumbled the greatest part of a terrible thundring, lightening and rainy night, and in as much noise, tho' less danger, as on board a ship

---

* The last six words of a very tightly compressed addition to the text as originally written are illegible: they are close to the bottom of the page and appear to have been cut into.

in the most furious storm. All I could see of the country was flat and marshy.

At 10 on Sunday morning we got out for mass and dinner at a small village in an unpleasant flat country, where I saw no trees but willows. Here we got into a larger vessel. Thus far we were on a canal, but now we mount the Po. The country grew a little better by degrees and we supped on board pleasantly enough. We pigged it as the night before and a little after day light arrived at *Francolino*. Here every thing was depacked and put on carriages, We went in a kind of post-coach with 4 horses to

FERRARA

where we dined. It is a very large old town, now very thinly peopled. I visited the principal churches. In that of S. Benedetto is the tomb of Ariosto. It is clean and elegant. His bust is in white marble and a Latin epitaph which I was at the pains to copy in my tablets but which I find is in M. de la Lande, so I shall not insert it here. The streets are long and wide, but no trade seems carried on but that of r—n.* From hence we set out in the same coach to Bottissedi 10 miles from Ferrara. The country is ill cultivated. I saw few trees but willows–there seems to be some trade carried on here in the basket way. At Bottissedi we met all our baggage etc, which was put in a boat after waiting 3 hours in the hottest weather I ever felt. The canal on which this boat went was for 4 or 5 miles so narrow and full of weeds that it could hardly pass–it is entirely among high reeds–nothing else to be seen on either side–it resembles the Po Dyke and several others in marshland Norfolk. At *Malalbergo* we got into another vessel upon a different canal, several feet higher than that we left, and in this we were all night, only going 20 miles to Bologna. The banks of this canal were pleasant, and if it had not been for the voracious gnats it would have been an agreeable voyage as the weather was fine.

BOLOGNA

In the morning AUGUST 21 we entered Bologna soon after it was light. The environs are rich and charming. At the gates we left our baggage, which was carried to the custom house, where it was slightly visited and the fees but small. I had always great fear of this dogana on account of books which I had been told were always sent to the Inquisition to be examined, but no such thing happened to mine. The Frenchman I mentioned above sticks close to me. He is in great

* Religion.

distress: his story is this—he shewed me his papers. He is of a noble French family, had been an officer in that service all the last war but having run out a great deal of money and run into debt very considerable sums—which his friends have refused to pay, he was forced to quit France about 9 months before. His money is now all gone except 3 zechins. He intends staying at Bologna till October and then to try to get a commission in the Russian troops at Leghorn on their return from the archipelago. His family is so angry with him for his extravagances that he has no hopes of further assistance from them. His name is Louis de St. Croix. I saw a letter from one of his relatives, which gives him not the least hope of an accommodation, and he is so deeply in debt, having 3 lettres de cachet out against him in France and his commission forfeited etc I know not what he will do. I cannot afford to do anything for him except giving him a dinner now and then. He would be glad to go with me to Naples—he had been 3 years in Italy before he was thus involved or had lost the favour of his family and knows very well the *Carte da pais*, but I am afraid of expence and of aventuriers.

Bologna looks melancholy, tho' parts of it are very magnificent and beautiful. The porticos before the houses are very handsome and convenient—the best I have seen in Italy, the pavement is as smooth and pleasant to walk on as a chamber. Every street in the town has these porticos. The rest of the street is paved with small pebbles and bad enough to walk on. Fruit abounds here, particularly melons which are so sweet, so good and so cheap I have learned to eat 'em—a *bajoch* each in the streets which is only equal to an English ½ penny. Figs, grapes, apples, pairs etc in proportion. Here the trade is chiefly that of the belly. The people are very poor, but fat and contented: 'tis reckoned one of the cheapest places to live in throughout Italy. Clergy in very great abondance, and the churches immensly rich. The Duomo or S. Pietro is of a prodigious heighth. It is modern—1600—the façade is very striking and the inside spacious and noble. S. Petronio the oldest and largest building in Bologna is Gothic. Here Charles 5 was crowned by Pope Clement 7 and in this church is the famous meridian of Cassini.* I popped upon it by accident just at midday. It was finished 1655. The light of the sun enters at a hole in the top of the church, and falls upon the line below, upon which are marked the signs of the zodiac. There was music by Signor Mazzoni at the church of the Dominicans—S. Michele in Bosco—to night ⌊the night after my arrival⌋

---

* This meridian line, laid down by Giovanni Domenico Cassini 'consists of pieces of red and white marble inlaid, of a hand's breadth; but those pieces in which the signs of the zodiac are cut, are a foot square' (Keysler, *Travels*, vol. 3, p. 283). An inscription gives the length of the line as one six hundred thousandth part of the circumference of the terraqueous globe ('about 200 feet').

but I was too late. However I was rewarded by finding the walk delicious. The church is on the top of a hill out of the gates, which commands the most beautiful prospect of the city and environs imaginable. This church is richly ornamented but the arrchitecture is not very beautiful. The organ was playing when I entered for the procession in which was a bishop mitred but it was out of tune and coarse–not played well.–I was tired and went not to the theatre. M. de St Croix was with me, it grieved me not to ask him to supper or to lend him a shirt which he wanted while he sent his only 2 shirts to be washed–but as I said before, I'm afraid.

This morning, WEDNESDAY, 22nd all lost in visiting people who were out. Mr. Baretti's friends, the abate *Zanotti* and Montefari Caprara–both from home–one at about a mile or 2 from Bologna and the other at Leghorn; Guarducci at Florence, Dr Gentile out–and a Dominican fryar to whom I had a letter too far to visit this morning. Farinelli too lives out of town, and I must have a coach to make that visit. However I have sent a messenger with my letter to the abate Zanotti and desired him to write a word or 2 of recommendation to Padre Martini whom I must absolutely see ere I depart from Bologna: he's necessary to my plan in all its parts. His library of musical authors only has cost above 1000 zechins. His 2nd volume (I got the 1st at Venice) is in the press, and wanted to talk with him about it– S. Croix has taken a lodging at 15 pauls (20th part of nine shillings) a month–that, cheap as it is will eat up half his 3 zechins and what he will have to eat himself, I know not.

WEDNESDAY night. I went to P. Martini, with an introductory letter from the abate Zanotti, and a present from the Abbé Roussier at Paris of his Memoire Sur La Musique des Anciens Grecs. He read Zanotti's letter and then Baretti's to Signor Zanotti which was inclosed. I found he had been apprised of my journey from Turin and Milan, and said he was very glad to know a person of such merit and of such an uncommon curiosity. We presently became very well acquainted and went to business. I shewed him my plan, at which in several places he nodded and smiled, bravo! polito! etc. I then enquired after his work. The 2nd volume, he told me was in great forwardness and would be published in a couple of months, but this will not finish his plan, as there are to be five volumes but I hardly think he can live to publish them for he is very old and infirm, has a terrible cough and looks dreadully, but 'tis a good natured and worthy being, I do believe–'We are both on the same sea' says he–'Yes, but we steer different courses,' I said, 'and shall carry our goods to different markets'. I then shewed him the catalogue of my books and he was surprised at some of them, which he said were extreamly rare,

[88]

of others he took the titles. He then shewed me *his* catalogue which is indeed immence. *I* surprised several great booksellers with mine, but in my turn I have been surprised. His books on music and relative to that subject amount to 18000 volumes some of which have cost him dear. For one in particular, written in Spanish 1613 he paid 100 ducats–about 20 guineas–at Naples, the place where it was printed–'tis a thick folio. He shewed me this and a great many of his most curious books–of which he has 2 rooms full–with one of MSS and one for practical music or compositions. He has invited me to come to him as often as ever I can during my stay at Bologna–and we are immediately after to open a correspondence and eventually assist each other with every information in our power.

From hence I went to the *play*–there is no opera–and to my great surprise found it was an *Italian* tragedy–Cyrus. I had never seen one before and was much pleased with the opening, but soon grew tired of the long speeches and declamations. They were past all bearing tedious. Thomyris, queen of the Amazons, came on dressed in a very equivocal manner, for in order to give her a marshal look, she had her petticoats trussed up before above her knees which were very discernable, as well as her black breeches. She seemed in the attitude and circumstances of one going to p—s–but the audience clapped violently as they constantly did at the worst things in the play. There was a great deal of religion in it and such anacronisms that J. Ch—t, the Trinity, free will and predestination were not forgotten, and when Cyrus is dying he is examined by the Jewish Priest (a principal character in the play) as to his religious opinions and makes to him his *profession de foi*. This kind of spectacle has been so long neglected in Italy that it seems wholly to have been lost and that, after a second birth, it is now in its infancy. However the language is plainly capable of great things, as it can support dignity without the trammels of rhyme. The actors too are good, as to propriety and variety of gesture, but in voice, a monotony reigned here as in the Italian pulpit. The passion for dramas in music has ruined true tragedy as well as comedy in Italy–but the language and genius of this people are so rich and fertile that when they become heartily tired of music, which they seem in a fair way of being ere long, by abundance–the same love of novelty which has made them fly from one style of composition to another, with such rapidity, often changing from a better to a worse, will drive them to seek amusement from the stage without music, merely for the love of novelty, and in that case, where the sock and buskin are cultivated with all their force, and the writer and actor have an opportunity of displaying all their powers and are even obliged to make use of every resource with which the national language and genius abounds, they will undoubtedly surpass the rest of Europe in the dramatic as well as in other arts. But ere this can happen much must be done towards refining the national taste, which is at present too much depraved by farce, buffoonery, and song. The inattention, noise and indecorum of the audience too are quite barbarous and intolerable. The silence which reigns at London and Paris is an encouragement to the actor as well as a comfort to the hearer of judgment and feeling. In Italy the theatres are immence and in order to be heard thro' space and noise they seem in a perpetual bawl. It is more like an harangue of a general at the head of an army of 100,000 men than the speech of a hero or heroine in a palace, to one or a few of his subjects. This allows of but few modulations of voice. All the passions are alike noisy–the tender and the termagant.

THURSDAY. 23. Again this morning with the *good* Father Martini –'tis a title I have great reason to give him–he has loaded me with kindness and obligations, for besides shewing me his most curious MSS and printed books, he has made me a present of some and has taken measures to procure me others and to serve me in Florence and Rome. In short I never esteemed and loved a man more upon so short an acquaintance: my heart is as open to him already as if I had known him these 20 years and the frankness seems reciprocal, as he answers all my questions without hesitation in the most candid and open manner imaginable. He has told me the whole extent of his plan, has given me his opinion upon several disputable points, and has communicated to me his catalogue of books and MSS with entire confidence. He has likewise begged a copy of my plan and of the catalogue of my books, and we have mutually promised to assist each other with books and intelligence in a correspondence which I hope will last many years.

Signor Farinelli lives out of the town of Bologna about a mile, and as I was not certain of finding him at home I sent a messenger this morning to acquaint him that I had a letter and prints for him from Mr Strange in England, and would wait upon him with them whenever it would be most convenient for him to receive me. The messenger had not been gone an hour when behold Signor Farinelli himself comes to P. Martini's in order to speak to me. I cannot describe the pleasure it gave me to see this extraordinary personage, who had so enchanted all Europe by his uncommon powers. He is tall and thin, but looks very well for his time of life, is lively and well bred. He took hold of both my hands upon entering the library of P. Martini at the Franciscan Convent and said he was impatient to see who it was from England that had favoured him with a message. He staid and chatted a considerable time during which I told him my chief business in

Bologna was to see two such illustrious men as himself and P.
Martini—Ah, he said, what he is doing will last, but mine is past and
already forgotten.—I told him his wonderful talents would never be
forgotten in England, as the grand children of those who were so
happy to hear him there still talk of him, and those who remember
him, can bear no other. They say, upon hearing any new and great
singer from Italy—Ah, this is not Farinelli.—Our conversation ended
by an invitation for me to dine with him, and begged I would name
the day and invited P.M. to meet me: upon which I begged my good
padre to name the day and Signor Farinelli the hour that would be
most convenient to both, and Saturday is fixt on for him to send his
coach to fetch us. As yet he knows not my errand into Italy. Upon
parting he took hold of both hands and in English said *kiss me?*—The
men here, who are intimate always kiss the cheek at meeting and parting. I staid a good while longer with the good padre—and talked writ
and rummaged very comfortably the whole time.

FRIDAY ST. BARTHOLOMEW. This morning I went to the Palazzo
Zampieri and saw such a delicious collection [of] pictures by 1st rate
masters as I never had met with before in one place. The principal
are a holy Family of Raphael so fresh and so beautiful, it seems but
just finished—such grace in all the heads! such beauty in the features!
such harmony of composition! the children, Jesus and St John so
charming: such drawing in the right hand of the latter, who points at
the former! such sweetness in the countenance of St Anne! and such
lively tints in the flesh, particularly the knees of the young St John as
enchanted me. A St. Peter weeping—by Guido—reckoned the best of
all his works—M. Cochin thinks it nearer perfection in all its parts
than any other picture in the world. The colouring is fresh and it is in
Guidos strong manner. A curtain is always kept before it and it is
shewn last, pour faire bonne bouche. An angel, a single figure pointing upwards with the right hand, by the same—of this Mr Robertson
has a copy—the colouring a good deal gone. A capital picture by Albano of cupids dancing in a ring, fresh and charming. Abraham
repudiating Hagar, by Guercino, in great beauty. This I instantly
knew by Mr. Strange's print, which is very like, but I was sorry to
hear from the person who shewd the pictures that it had not pleased
him so much as that of Bartolozzi who had been here with Mr.
Dalton—2 or 3 more pictures with small figures by Albano, very fresh
—several capital things by Hanibal Carach, particularly in the ceilings—
The Samaritan, one of his best designs but the colouring a little gone.
Several fine things by Lodovico Carach, particularly a Jupiter and
Hercules, truely terrifick—and a copy of Corregio's famous Holy
Family at Parma—this is grown dark. There is a very fine copy by

[91]

Guido of the St. Cecilia I saw yesterday of Raphael. I could get nearer this picture than the original, and could not with my eyes or glasses discover any strings upon the viola da braccia, but 6 pins are very visible; and the bridge and frets: how the former stands up without strings I know not. A large picture by Spagnolett, one of Rubens and one of Vandyke with 2 sweet naked children in it. A small picture by Guido highly finished – 'tis the ascension of the Virgin amidst a concert of angels, who sing and play upon all sorts of instruments except the *viol da braccia*. A picture of Julio Romano – dark – another of Guido in his *maniere forte*, extreamly well preserved. In short there are pictures of all the great masters except Corregio, Dominichini and Paul Veronese. One of Perugini, Raphael's master, well kept, but it is stiff and the out-line hard. There is a fine head of an old man by Titian etc etc. I am the more particular about these pictures as neither M. de La Lande nor the book called Pitture di Bologna is so – as the former only mentions 3 or 4 and the latter no one particularly. From hence to S. Bartolomeo, just by to hear music, which was very poor and poorly performed. After dinner an itinerant band stopt under my window who executed several sinfonies and single movements extreamly well – 'twas the best I had heard here. However the music of the churches here, which the common people hear every day, is a good school for them and enables them all to sing with taste and expression of the right sort. Again at night to S. Franciso – read – transcribed and borrowed.

SATURDAY. Spent the morning with P. Martini in his library till we went together in Signor Farinelli's chariot to dine with him. It is a pretty ride. The house is new, not quite finished: 'tis flat all round him, and the Italians have nothing like taste in laying out gardens. However his house commands a fine prospect of the city of Bologna and of the collines near it, is elegantly furnished with a great number of pictures which are either by great painters or of great personages. He shewed me his house before dinner. He has some charming pictures by Zimenes and Morillo 2 first rate Spanish painters and Spagnaletto. His large room where is a billiard table, is furnished with the pictures of great persons, chiefly crowned heads who have been his patrons, among which are 2 Emperours, 1 Empress, 3 Kings of Spain, 2 princes of Asturias, a King of Sardinia, a prince of Savoy, a King of Naples, a princess of Asturias, 2 Queens of Spain and Pope Benedict the 14th. In other appartments are several charming pictures. Sir Benjamin Keen was a great favourite with him, and he speaks of his death not only as a great loss to the 2 courts of England and Spain, but as an irreparable loss to himself and all his friends. He shewed me several pictures painted in England in the manner of

Teniers, by a man in a jail – I forget his name – which Lord Chesterfield had given him in the politest manner imaginable. Upon my expressing some desire to write his life or at least to insert particulars of it in my history – ah, says he, by a modesty rather pushed too far, if you have a mind to compose a good work never fill it with accounts of such despicable beings as me. However he furnished me with all the particulars concerning Domenico Scarlatti I desired – and dictated to me very obligingly while I entered them in my pocket book.

SUNDAY 26. All the morning writing and reading at the Franciscans – this is a day of jubilee here, and equal to that of our Lord Mayor in London. After dinner upon the great piazza or square in the theatre constructed for the fair by the majistrates which began at the assumption, the 15th inst. and which lasts the whole month, the usual popular festival called the porchetta (or little pig) is kept in memory of the extinction of the civil war about 1278, in which by the accident of a pig running across the street, the stout Antonio Lambertazzi head of the Ghibelline faction was killed. In this amphitheatre, after a popular spectacle diversified every year, peacocks, cocks and hens and money are thrown to the people and lastly a pig ready dressed. The Cardinal Legate attended in a balcony and threw money to the mob. The crowd was prodigious – stages built all round – and the windows and even tops of houses were crouded with people. It began by a pageant, a kind of mock triumphal carr, with ordinary girls dressed very fine in it, preceded by others in procession. There was next represented the palace of Armida into which she conducted Rinaldo. Then appear two of his followers in quest of him armed cap-a pied, upon which a huge dragon comes out of the cave under the palace to attack them together with 2 griffins all spitting fire and made hideously frightful. These are vanquished and then the 2 champions go into the palace and carry off Rinaldo in spite of the threats and entreaties of Armida. He is put on board a vessel and sails out of sight upon which more monsters appear all in flames and set fire to the palace while Armida flies a way on a fiery dragon. The whole of this was comical enough – as it was all burlesque – sometimes the machinery of the monsters took fire and burnt the men underneath, upon which they throw off the whole apparatus and appear half naked to the spectators. The scrambling for the money, the poultry etc too afforded great diversion.

My French man was of the party to night and after it was over he explained himself pretty plainly – he wants me to lend him a *few* zechins to live upon till he gets something from his friends. I thought I should have got quit for 2 or 3 dinners which I have already given him and treated him at the coffee house, the play etc. but he's very pressing and I don't like it. Somebody, I forget who, cautioned me against French acquaintance in Italy, and they were right. I have now to manage with him, not yet having learned to pronounce clearly and with energy the monosillable *NO*. Different bands of singers about the streets in abundance. Poor Moiana died about 10 o'clock the morning after I left Venice. I have had a letter from his father whom I left with him. – He was but 33 and seemed perfectly well during the whole journey – cut off in one week! it is truely melancholy and makes one doubt one's own longevity. I believe he over-heated himself at Venice by walking at a season when the heat is such that scarce a creature stirs without a gondola,* and the day he was seized he was upon a party of pleasure to visit the islands round Venice and there eat and drank improper things. He was naturally *gourmand* and 2 days before his illness he made the Flemish gentleman and me stare by the quantity he eat, but in these hot countries stilness and temperance are absolutely requisite, or the blood already boiling becomes corrupt and unfit for the purposes assigned it.

MONDAY 27. Ere I quit Bologna it is necessary to remark that the publick fountains of this city are extreamly noble, particularly the Neptune by the famous John of Bologna, the finest figure in brass I ever saw – true dignity and muscular strength –. The supporters of these fountains, which are always playing are beautiful sirens seated upon dolphins who press their breasts from whence the water is thrown to a great heighth and distance. This fountain was erected in 1563. There is in the piazza publica in a niche of the town house a figure of Pope Gregory 13th in brass. It seems of a common size, but yesterday five or 6 of the mob scrambled up to it – one sate on the leg – one on the arm etc and they all appeared pigmies.

This morning was wholly spent at the *Institute* and it was not sufficient for half what there is to see. The fine copies of the best antique *statues* of Rome and Florence give a good *avant gout* for what one has to enjoy in those cities. The chief pictures are the Story of Ulysses from the Odessy, by the famous Pellegrino Tibaldi master to the Caracci. The drawings and designs are admirable – bold, masterly expressive of the great subjects he paints. I saw a fine book of prints from these designs finely engraved and had no other objection to buying it but that the price was 6 zechins. The Stanze Ostetricie is a wonderful collection of models of all parts of the *uterus* and matrix in every state, and of the fœtus in all situations for the use of young

---

* This sentence was later revised to read: 'He certainly over-heated himself at Venice by walking at a season when it is said that only Dogs and Englishmen are seen out of doors at noon, all else lie down in the middle of the day, and when he was seized he had been upon a party of pleasure to visit the Islands round Venice and here he eat and drank intemperately.'

students in midwifery and anatomy. These were made by the famous Dr Galli for the use of his scholars and purchased afterwards by the senate. Other preparations have been made by Signora Anna Manzolini from 1750 to 1758 to shew in what manner it receives nourishment in the womb. There is in wax and coloured after nature all its appearance from the 1st month to the time of its birth, and the whole seems admirably calculated for the use of midwives and young students.

There are six rooms of natural history full of curiosities. There are Egyptian mummies, Grecian, Roman and Etruscan antiquities a large room full–an ancient systrum* I observed such as is drawn in Blanchine, Kircher and others. It seems now only fit for a child in a nursery. What use the ancients made of it I know not.† Among the old paintings by Immola is a guitar and a concert of different instruments with a lady playing on the harpsichord much admired, by Niccolo dell'Abbate (see lives of painters for the time when they lived). In short, the description of all I saw would be tiresome–as it may be found better arranged and written in a 100 books–all I do is by way of memoranda for myself.–After dinner I went to make extracts from the books and head of P. Martini. From thence I went to the Dottoressa ⌊Laura Bassi⌋–had a very polite and easy reception–upon naming P. Beccaria and shewing his recommendation in my tablets we were instantly good friends. This lady is between 50 and 60 but, tho' learned and a genius, not at all masculine or assuming. We talked over the most celebrated men of science now alive in Europe. She was very civil to the English in eugolies of Newton, Halley, Bradley, Franklin etc. She shewed me her electrical machine and apparatus –'tis a plain plate of glass placed vertically–two cushions covered with red leather, portable and convenient. The receiver a tin *forked* tube: the two forks with pins at the ends are placed next the glass plates. She is very dextrous and ingenious in her experiments of which she shewed my [me] several. Signor Bassi, her husband, she told me after Dr Franklin's first account of the similarity of electrical fire and lightning, and of the method of preserving buildings from the effects of the latter by iron rods, had conductors erected at the Institute, but the people of Bologna are such cowards and were so afraid of these rods bringing the lightning upon 'em–instead of the contrary that he was forced to take them down. Benedict the 14 one of the most enlightened and enlarged of the Popes and patron and a native of

---

* See page 230.

† This sentence was deleted and the following substituted later: 'But it seems to have been an instrument of sacrifice among the Egyptians as a bell is rung in R. Cath. churches at the elevation of the Host.'

Bologna, wrote a letter to recommend the use of these conductors, but it was so much against the inclination of the Bolognese that Signor Verati desisted entirely and they have never since that time been used here. There is an apparatus and a room apart for electricity at the Institute but the machines are old and very inferiour to those in use at this time in England. It is remarkable that this university has no correspondence with England nor is it able to purchase our Phil[osophical] Transactions. The salaries are small and the money allowed for the support of the Institute all appropriated. This I was told by the keeper or *custode* who shewed me the appartments. My visit with this learned lady was very agreeable and she was so obliging to offer me a letter to Signor Fontana at Florence, one of the 1st mathematicians in Europe. From hence I went to take a melancholy leave of Signor Farinelli. He pressed me very much to stay longer at Bologna and even scolded me for going so soon. I found him with Raphael* upon which I prevailed on him to play a good deal. He *sings* upon it with infinite taste and expression. I was truely sorry to quit this extraordinary and amiable person. He pressed me to write to him if ever there was any thing in Italy which he could procure or do for me. I stayed with him till it was so late I was in danger of being shut out of the city of Bologna—the gates being shut every night as soon as it is dark.

APPENINES

FRIDAY 31 AUGUST. I am now for the first time quite alone at a little village called Feligare 24 miles from Bologna upon the top of the Appenines ⌊and have leisure to enter in my journal from my tablets what I could not accomplish ere I left Bologna⌋. I intended setting out for Florence on Wednesday 29th but was told by several people there would be the most famous musical performance at Bologna on Thursday which happens in the whole year, and this was confirmed by P. Martini, who told me that considering my errand there it would be very wrong not to stay, as on that day would be the annual perform-

---

* The account which Burney gives of his day with Farinelli is much fuller in *Tour* 1773 than in the Journal and this reference can only be understood if the printed version is consulted. In *Tour* 1773 Burney writes (p. 211): 'Signor Farinelli has long left off singing, but amuses himself still on the harpsichord and viol d'amour: he has a great number of harpsichords made in different countries, which he has named according to the place they hold in his favour, after the greatest of the Italian painters. His favourite is a *piano forte*, made at Florence in the year 1730, on which is written in gold letters, *Rafael d'Urbino*; then Coreggio, Titian, Guido, etc.'

The 'Raffaello d'Urbino' was made in 1730 by Giovanni, Ferrini the assistant to Bartolomeo Christofori who invented the pianoforte action. The instrument was bought by Elisabetta Farnese, Queen of Spain, who bequeathed it to Farinelli.

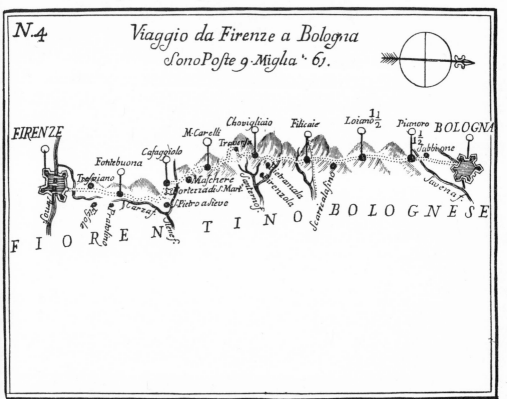

4. Bologna to Florence. Between Bologna and Pianoro the traveller passed over the River Savena by means of a bridge and had to pay a Paul for every vehicle with two wheels. The roads between Bologna and Filicaie were sandy and hilly and travellers in two-wheeled vehicles were obliged to take a third horse for this stretch, and those in four-wheeled vehicles two extra horses with a man up.

ance of the members of the famous Filharmonic Society* which has subsisted above 100 years. This determined me to stay as much as if the same words had been pronounced by the Oracle of Delphus. I never till this day was able to meet with Dr Gentile for whom I had a letter from Mr. Martinelli, but at last after several fruitless attempts we met at my lodging to which place he came to fech me – I found him to be a sensible lively and agreeable young man, with a pretty engaging person and figure. A gentleman from Parma of his acquaintance

* The Accademia Filarmonica was founded in 1666 by Marchese Vincenzo Maria Carrati. Membership was granted only to those musicians who were of outstanding ability, judged on the result of a rigorous test, as composer or performer.

who lodged in the same house with me and who had brought me a letter from Dr. Righi at Parma met him and we prevailed on him to dine with us. He had been about 6 weeks in England but could speak no English. He entered heartily into my *business* and gave me several musical anecdotes. He likewise lent me a curious composition to copy of the famous Perti of Bologna which is constantly sung there on good Friday. After dinner I went to my Daddy good P. Martini who was so kind to lend me his MSS canons of which I copied what I wanted – he had before lent me for that purpose old Doni,* which is an exceeding scarce book. I made extracts from that too.

WEDNESDAY morning I staid at home to write ⌊letters for England⌋. In the evening to S. Francisco again and afterward meet Dr. Gentili at the coffe house. Several musical people happened to be there and he contrived to make us converse together. One was a celebrated counter tenor singer. I went from thence to try a fine Amati fiddle for which 50 zechins were asked. If I had been flush I believe I should have offered 30 as it was a very fine instrument.

THURSDAY morning. After seeing a church or two in my way I went to S. Giovanni in Monti to hear the Philharmonic performances. There was a great deal of company there. Dr. Gentile met me there and among the rest who should I spy there but the celebrated little German Mozart who 3 or 4 years ago surprised everybody in London so much by his premature musical talents.† I had a great deal of talk with his father. I find that they are at Prince Palavicinis. The little man is grown a good deal but still a little man. He is engaged to compose an opera for Milan. His father has been ill here these 5 or 6 weeks. The Pope has knighted the little great wonder. In the evening there was more company than in the morning at the church of S. John. I was charmingly placed between the two finest pictures in Bologna, the St. Cecilia of Raphael in a chapel on my left and a very large and capital picture of Dominichini, in which are the 2 dicky birds, on my right. I had a dismal and unaccountable head ache this whole day. After dinner, which did not, as sometimes it does cure it, I laid myself down on the bed in hopes a little sleep might be more

---

* The principal works of Giovanni Battista Doni were a treatise on ancient Greek music *Compendio del Trattato de' generi e de' modi della musica* (Rome, 1635), a supplement to it *Annotazioni sopra il compendio . . .* (Rome, 1640) and *De praestantia musicae veteris* (Florence. 1647).

† While he was in Bologna Wolfgang A. Mozart, aged 14 years, was admitted a member of the Accademia Filarmonica, on 9 October, 1770. He was given an antiphon to set in four parts, which he completed in less than an hour (K86).

The Mozarts had arrived in London via Paris on 23 April, 1764 and Wolfgang made a tremendous impression both at Court and with the public, in tests of skill and in concert performances. Father, son, and daughter left London on 24 July, 1765, and England on 1 August 1765.

METASTASIO,
FAUSTINA,
FARINELLI,
COPO AMIGONI

AL MERITO INCOMPARABILE
DEL SIGNORE
LUIGI MARCHESI
CHE NELL' AUTUNNO DELL' ANNO MDCCLXXIX. IN FIRENZE
NEL REGIO TEATRO DI VIA DELLA PERGOLA
RAPPRESENTA CON APPLAUSO UNIVERSALE LE PARTI
DI CASTORE E DI ACHILLE
NEI RESPETTIVI DRAMMI.

Nche in mezzo all'orror di notte oscura
O d'ogni bel piacer motor primiero
Gran Genio d'armonìa, cui diè natura
Forte sovra ogni cor soave impero,

In qual estasi bello ogni alma fura,
Per Te MARCHESI, allor che Achille altero
Dolce cantando d'occultar procura
In gonna femminil spirto guerriero!

Oh se il destino a Troja invido tanto,
Mostrato avea pria di mill'anni, e mille
Di Guerrier così caro i pregi, e il vanto,

Ilio forse non fora arsa in faville;
Ma l'irritate Dee vinte al suo canto
Rapito avrian, non palesato Achille.

IN FIRENZE L'ANNO MDCCLXXIX

PER GAETANO CAMBIAGI STAMPATORE GRANDUCALE X CON LICENZA DE' SUPERIORI.

A POSTER IN PRAISE OF LUIGI MARCHESI

efficacious – when soon after I was disturbed by a violent knocking at my chamber door and upon opening it 3 strange gentlemen came in. I neither knew who they were nor their business – however told 'em in Italian, they did me a great deal of honour: they muttered something in return. We sate down and stared at each other some time in an awkward way, when I heard one say to another in English 'I fancy we are wrong' – upon which I accosted them in the same language and found they were all English or at least subjects of England who hearing of me in Bologna came to make me this visit. I soon recollected one of the faces, which I had not seen since the year 1750, to belong to a Mr Keeble a painter and great acquaintance then of my brother. The other is his friend and fellow traveller whose name I forget ₍(Fuseli)₎, the third a Mr. Barry a young (I believe Irish) painter just come from Rome where he has been some years studying. The 2 former have been in Italy and Spain 15 or 16 years. We went to the church and heard the music together. I found Keeble was known to every body as he had been a considerable time in Bologna. Dr Gentili came to see me there and several others – and there was one of the compositions that pleased me so much that I really thought it operated on my head medicinally, for I found it much easier. This charming music was composed by the Abate Zanotti to whom I had a letter from Baretti. He was not in town the whole time I was in Bologna, but it was his letter that introduced me to P. Martini – old Caroli beat time to his composition. After these performances were done I went to take leave of the very good Father Martini who waited for me in his study, it being late, beyond the monastic hour of seeing people. He was quite prepared for me with 3 recommendatory letters one for Florence, one for Rome, and one for Naples, found still more curious books to shew me of which I took the titles, in hopes of meeting with them one time or other. He had told me the day before that as he should not be at the Filharmonic meeting himself, he should rely on my judgment and account how matters went off and were conducted – and now, after it was over I told him my feelings at every single piece: after this I was going to take leave when he says, 'won't you stay for the words to be written to those canons?'. I had the day before sung with a young franciscan his scholar out of a prodigious large book of his canons, several very pleasing ones for 2 voices only, of which I seemed to express a desire to have one or two, and this excellent father remembered it and had set a person to work for me – who was writing when I came into the study – but as he has usually 2 or three amenuenses there I did not mind him. Well we parted, on my side with sorrow and on his with a recommendation to be careful of my health and to write to him often.

Now to pack and pay–but no chaise to be had–all the returned chaises which are one half cheaper, gone–and I was unable to get off till near 12 next day FRIDAY 31 AUGUST. But ere I quit Bologna, with which I had great reason to be satisfied, let me by way of memorandum for myself set down the names of the pictures which pleased me most in two or 3 of the principal palaces there. I had not time to see more. At *Piazza Tanari*, where I visited the lady of the house niece to Signora Bassa of Venice, a handsome fat, and good-humoured young woman–a most veautiful Virgin *en extase* by Guido–St. Augustin by Guercino fine and well preserved–assumption ditto– Death of Abel by Franceschini, Adam and Eve admirable, Cain running away at a distance, and the pale Abel dead on the ground–Head of Magdalen by Guido charming–goats and other creatures by Salvator Rossa, good–Judas's Kiss by L. Carracci fine–Venus by Annib. Carrach charming. Diana naked and sleeping ditto by ditto–The Baths of Aug. Carrach luxurious–Madonna and Child by Guido in his finest manner, she is extremely beautiful and giving suck to the Bambino, a young St John on the left hand warm and finely coloured– copy of la Madona della Rosa of Parmegiano by L. Carrach, the original is at Dresden. She is asleep and the Child 3 or 4 years old lies playing on her lap.–A Sybil fine of L. Carrach.–St Cecilia of Franceschini most beautiful and charming. She is playing on the modern violin with 4 strings, and an angel holds the book. Nothing can be more exquisitely imagined or finished. He was scholar to Guido–Portraits of 4 favourite Bolognese women by the Carracci–Birth of Alexander by L. Carrach, a fine picture. A bagpiper and guitar player, beggars, by An. Carrach–a beautiful little Albano, the angel driving the devil out of paradise–a S. Carol, by Carlo Dolce, great–a beautiful Magdalen by Crespi ditto Spagnoletto–Sybil by Immola, highly finished. A little galary with drawings and designs by Guercino, Guido etc–with a head in red chaulk of the latter by himself.

Piazza Bonfiglioli. A picture of Caravaggio pleased me very much as it was different from all other paintings I had ever seen, bold, yet high finished and pleasing. Annib. and Lud. Carrach have many fine things here, ceilings as fresh as if not yet dry. A Sybil by Guido–a sweet little sleeping Cupid like that of Strange by Guido.–Charming Cleopatra by Guercino. Painting, sculpture, and music, three very pleasing portraits by Brizzi, scholar of Raphael: a 6 string base is the symbal of music–a country concert on the 1st of May by Lonardini, very old, the Queen of the May on a throne, a bagpipes and fidler playing on a violin with 4 strings very plainly to be seen. At the bottom of the frame are the following lines

Pictures to remember · Fine prospects along the road

'Di Colascion scordato al rauco Suono
'Guidan di Maggio il di pazzi Festori
'La Lor Contessa à l'Eminenta Trono'

A Holy Family, small, by Raphael–the lid of a virginal painted by
Guido, framed. 3 figures, one a girl playing on a violin–Fame–and a
young lutanist. N.B. The violin has 4 strings only. Magdalen by
Guercino, fine. A lady of the house of Bonfiglioli admirably painted in
an old fashioned old lady's dress with a nightrail.–Susannah and
Elders by Cavandini, charming–another ditto by ditto, not quite so
good but a fine picture.–The flight into Egypt by water, an angel at
the helm of Lud. Carrach, wonderfully beautiful.–Tiarini's life of
Santa Catarina di Bologna and others–sweet!–ceilings of Carrach
exquisite and quite fresh–Tasso's whole poem by ditto on the walls
of an out building. Admirable designs, but a good deal spoilt etc

The city of Bologna has in every street fine lofty piazzas, which are
charming to walk in–one may sometimes walk a mile without going
from under them, and so well paved with broad bricks that few of the
rooms in common houses are so smooth.–

In going out at the Porta Fiorentina the country is very beautiful–on
the right hills covered with vines and villas–in front the Appenine
Mountains and on the left a rich plain, chiefly laid out in gardens for
the use of the city. A little further on the hills are on the left hand, and
soon after on both sides. These hills at 8 or 9 miles from Bologna have
nothing on them but what nature has planted, but even that discovers
a great disposition to fertility. The bed of the river is without dis-
charge at this time of the year, and quite dry. Before I reached Fili-
gare, the hills were almost covered with chestnut trees and laurel for
underwood. The air after a great heat became fresh at night and made
me so hungry I was ready to eat the horses–but alas! nothing to
eat–it was Friday. However I got some maccaroni, eggs and cheese,
and submitted to my fate, intending to take my revenge at dinner next
day, but behold it was Saturday–giorno magro ancora! However
eggs, mushrooms, boiled rice and bad fish was all my fare. The morning was so cold on these mountains that I was forced to walk several
miles to warm myself–but in the evening in descending the hills it
became again intolerably hot. At Pianoro 12 miles from Bologna a
very pretty valley on the right at the foot of the collines covered with
shrubs. At about 2 miles further it was that we mounted the highest
of the Bologna hills–an extensive prospect on the right, of barren
mountains, but the shrubs and trees made it beautiful. A little further
a wild but magnificent prospect from the summit in front opened
itself. There seems neither trade nor husbandry going on thus far, the

road quite empty, but good almost all the way from Bologna. A little village between 2 rocks on the edge of a mountain with a little church on the summit. The rocks seldom appear in this country, so that there seems soil enough for anything, if encouragement to industry were not wanting. Here and there one sees a bit cultivated, with a vineyard, a corn field etc which plainly shows what *may* be done elsewhere. On these hills I was very dry and asked for fruit, but none was to be had but pears, which though ripe were so sour that they put me in a violent sweat–and in such a climate! only 44 deg. Lat! The last day, in the evening after passing the highest of the Alpi Appenini, the weather grew warmer, the country pleasanter, better cultivated, with here and there a villa and vineyard, and always a row of cypress trees before the former. Within 6 miles of Florence the road and country are charming and tho' still among high mountains they are all covered and fertile –not an inch of land hereabouts is left waste–all is cultivated with great art and this has the appearance of the richest part of Italy I have yet seen. Within a mile or 2 of Florence, *Arno's Vale* appears to great advantage from the hills which one then begins to descend. There is now a fine prospect of the city of Florence but which from hence does not look so large as I expected nor indeed as I found it.

FIRENZE · FLORENCE

At the fine gate on the Bologna side built as a triumphal arch for the entrance of the late Emperor I was stopt a little while for gentle visit of the custom house officers, but nothing was demanded–the persons employed to uncord my trunk followed me however to the inn, and I expected either a more severe examination of my baggage or a demand of fees–but no–it was only for the jobb of carrying it up stairs to my appartment, and upon my giving them a paul they departed well satisfied. I mention this for the honour of Florence. I found things however much dearer here than at Bologna–1 paul a day more for a servant, 3 more for board and lodging etc. It is truely a fine town, tho' some parts are grown dark and old, and some of the streets are narrow, but all delightfully paved with very broad stones, so that one both rides and walks as much at one's ease, as if in Westminster Hall. I put up at the Black Eagle *l'aquila nera*. The rooms are very lofty, so that the bed rooms which are up 2 pair of stairs seem *nel mondo della luna*. But the great evil and plague of *all* Italy for strangers is la buona mancia, or buona mano, fees which all servants, and what is ridiculous, masters and shopkeepers demand after you have paid perhaps an exhorbitant bill. It was, in coming from Bologna to Florence, the 1st time I had travelled quite alone–I gave the *vitturino*, whom I was obliged at short notice to take to myself, without a partner or being on *return*, almost the double fare, which is usually only 30 pauls the passage–and I gave him 5 pauls la buona mana and yet he teared my heart out for more. I knew it to be more than an Italian would have given him by at least 2 pauls and therefore was determined to give no more and we had a battle: but these people like English hackney coach-men are never to be satisfied.

I would not take a servant the 1st night, but lounged about the town by myself always keeping the street whence I came in view–for I have the English pride and shyness about me so strong that I abominate the thoughts of asking the way. I found nothing very curious in the streets except The Centaur by John of Bologna, which is bold and admirable.–

SUNDAY 2nd SEPTEMBER. I got up early to write, and between 6 and 7 I heard the tread of many people in the streets and upon looking out at the window, I saw a great procession of people dressed in whitish uniform that I took to be Dominicans, some with tapers in their hands. Upon enquiry I found these were nothing more than a company of psalm-singers La Compagna. They say all the companies of artisans here go to church in this manner singing psalms and hymns in parts. The institution is very ancient as it is mentioned by the historians to have been practiced by Lorenzo il Magnifico, who with his courtiers used to go thro' the streets singing in 3, 4, 5, 6, and even 8 parts. This company stopt before a church, just after they had passed the inn where I was lodged and sung a chearful hymn in 3 parts very well. They are called *laudi* and the singers laudisti–see the word laudi in the Crusca Dictionary–most of these singers in early times were blind–ciochi–orbi. At 9 I went to see the bridges over the *Arno*. I had great impatience to see this famous river, which divides the city of Florence into two, but found it almost dry. At this season it has very little water in it, as it is usually fed from the melted snow of the Appenines. However the water was very muddy, there having been a heavy shower a day or two before–but at best it is not a considerable river compared with the Thames or even Seine. One of the 3 bridges of 3 eliptical arches is very beautiful–and on them all are fine statues and prospects. Houses on the quays are neatly built like those of Paris: but always with more taste as to architecture. I stept into 2 or 3 churches, but finding the people at their devotions I retired without examining pictures etc, as it would appear very odd to us in England if a foreigner in the time of Divine Service were to enter a church merely for such business; but in Italy it is more common, as there is more to be seen in their churches, and I believe in general that the people are more intent upon their own business of prayer than we, and less likely to observe strangers. At the Duomo, however, I entered and examined the architecture and statues, which are innumerable, tho' mass was singing in the quire–but one may do this in St. Paul's or Westminster Abbey without giving cause of scandal as the quire is remote from the isles and many parts of the church. In looking for Dante's monument which I could not find I blundered on that of Squarcialupi the first on the left hand on entering the great western door. He was a celebrated organist and composer in the time of Lorenzo il Magnifico, and so much beloved by that prince that upon being told of his death by one of his courtiers with some degree of levity he was so angry as to tell him he should have been much more pleased if Squarcialuppi had been able to bring him the news of *his* death. I copied the following inscription upon this monument.

Multum profecto debet musica antonio Squarcialupo organiste is enimita arti gratiam conjunxit ut quartam sibi viderentur charites musicam asciuisse sororem florentia civitas grati animi officium rata ejus memoriam propagare cujus manus sepe mortales in dulcem admirationem adduxerat civi suo monumentum posuit.*

On the right side opposite to this is the monument of the old and famous painter Giotto, cotemporary and friend to Dante, with an inscription copied by M. de la Lande who says there are 2, but I could only find one. While I was examining these monuments etc the organ began to accompany the choir. I never heard a sweeter toned instrument–whether, like St Pauls, it is meliorated by the building or no, I cannot tell; but it pleased me exceedingly. The building is of a prodigious heigth–for the measures see de la Lande–the organ too had the advantage of being extreamly well played by Signor Matucci the present organist. From hence I went to the church of the convent al Santa Trinità where I heard a mass in music set by Signor Valente, which I thought but indifferent any more than the performance both vocal and instrumental. Signor Sabbatini one of the principal violins here played a concerto which was not very striking in any one particular. In coming home to dinner I saw a fountain by Mich. Angello Buonaroti which was admirable–the 2 principal figures are Alexander and Clytus, the former full of grief for the wound he has given the latter who is just expiring in his arms. I never saw anything more striking or better expressed.

After dinner with Count Vander Hagen and the young stupid

* 'Great are the obligations which music owes to Antonio Squarcialupo the organist, who added such beauty and grace to this art, that the three graces seemed to have admitted him among them as a fourth sister. The inhabitants of Florence, in gratitude to the divine raptures with which they were often inspired by the harmoniousness of his music, erected this monument in memory of their admirable fellowcitizen.' Keysler, *Travels*, vol. 2, p. 43 (1760), where the Latin version differs slightly.

Swiss I have often met and mentioned, to the Palazza Pitti. It was too late and much against my will that I went then as we were obliged to hurry away from the finest things in the world for fear of not seeing the rest. On the ground floor of this palace are fine paintings in fresco by Gio da San Giovanni, Cecco Bravo, Ottavio Vannini, and Francesco Furino. They represent the arts and science coming to Lorenzo il Magnifico and to his father John de Medicis born in 1360 then only merchants and great men among the Florence aldermen, who had been gonfonalieri, or mayors of that city. But the time when these great macaenatis lived is a proof that the Italians had the sciences among them ere the sacking of Constantinople in 1452 or 82*–I forget which. Lorenzo died much advanced in years 1492. This settles a point of musical history much disputed. The arts and sciences are personified and presenting to these great patrons their symbols. See de la Lande. Up stairs the fine pictures are innumerable by the very first rate painters and most of them admirably well preserved. In the hurry with which I was forced to run thro' the apartments those which caught my eye the most were the famous *Madonna della* Sedia with a glass over it of Raphael as fresh and beautiful as if just painted. How superior to all others is this divine artist! In the next room another of his, a Holy Family, all beauty and grace with Leo X between 2 cardinals, and in the appartment following a large and capital picture of this Prometheus by himself.–A head by Coreggio in crayons small but beautiful–a little Albano, sweet! 2 large landscapes of Rubens in great beauty, different from all other landscapes I had seen. *La Venere Matta*–Mars going to leave her–all the monsters of war calling upon him–a woman behind with arms uplift in seeming despair and children admirably expressed and Venus herself naked and far more beautiful as less flemish than his women are usually–with such flesh and such colouring as made all the other pictures in the room look dead. A charming Perugino subject a mother and children all very beautiful, in his way. 4 Titians well preserved. 2 large pictures by Andrea del Sarto and many others of this painter–good. Leonardo da Vinci. Paul Veronese, Salvator Rosa and all the great masters have here some of their best works. Pietro da Cortona has painted the ceilings in the most pleasing and luxurious manner imaginable. It grew so dark I was unable to see half this charming collection–but I hope to be able to return.

From hence into the Boboli Garden and to the comic opera, and after that I travelled all night with Count Hagen to Figline about 20 miles from Florence where I was told all the 1st rate musicians of Italy were assembled to celebrate a sort of jubilee held every 25 years

* 29 May, 1453.

in honour of the protectress of that town, Santa Massimina. We arrived about 7 in the morning, found the roads and town very full of country people as at a wakes but very few *gens comme il faut*. Great preparations were making in the great square for the diversions of the evening. At 11 was a great musical performance but not what I expected as to performers—the heat, that of the black hole at Calcutta—such a crowd and such a *hive*! The music of the mass was really pretty, full of new and elegant passages—there was however but one good singer, Abate Fibietto, a tenor whose voice and taste were charming. He sung a motet with such execution, precision and taste as I never remember to have heard. At 4 began the games, which had been 3 months preparing. That of this evening (they last 3 days) was to represent the story of David and Goliah, and it was really well told by the peasants of the nighbourhood. There were 20,000 people assembled without guards and yet no accident or confusion. The 2 armies met of the Children of Israel and the Philistines—a fine giant for Goliah and a sweet little David—horse men and foot without number dressed a l'antique and in uniforms—the stage dresses of the opera houses all round were borrowed for the kings and generals. Above 1500 men were employed on both sides. The sacred story was well told and David, mounted on a fine chariot received the applause of the whole company. In the evening I went to vespers and heard there the whole story *sung* in an oratorio set by Signor Feroce. The principal violin, Signor Modele and his son played a duet concerto very well in the morning. The Maestro di Capella whose music pleased me so much in the morning was likewise Signor Feroce from Florence—at night fine fire works and a general illumination.

We set out about 11 and arrived at Florence about 4 Tuesday morning. I was unable to get out till after dinner—and the evening was lost in search of persons I was unable to find. However I met with Signor Molini, brother to Signor Molini of London and to the bookseller at Paris, who will be useful in finding books for me and in telling me the state of music here etc.

WEDNESDAY 5. This morning visited in vain Sir H. Mann and after a long hunt for the dwellings of Guarducci and Ricciarelle to whom I had letters, I was informed that the former had left this city about 10 or 12 days to go to his own house at Montefiascone, in the road to Rome: and that last Saturday Ricciarelli set out for England. This is being rather out of luck: but pazienza! From hence I went an hour or two into the Maruscellana Library, but found the books chiefly modern—no MSS or printed works not to be found elsewhere. Thence to the church of the Servi di Maria and the Anonciata, where is the monument of Andrea del Sarto and a great number of paintings by the same, but chiefly spoilt by being too much exposed to the air and weather. After dinner and additions to my journal I went to the opera of Le Donne Vendicate by Piccini.

THURSDAY 6. Went this morning to the famous gallery where there are such immense quantities of fine things that one is quite lost amongst them. 3 or 4 different galleries of antique busts and statues – a large room full of the heads of the great painters, painted by themselves. In one of the galleries are pictures of the Medicean family. In another of the famous generals of every country – of ancient philosophers. The ancient statues Greek, Roman and Etruscan of marble and metal amount to 300: one gallery is filled with Roman Emperors, their wives and children etc. There are several Apollos, one *sedens* with a lyre without strings, but there have been plainly 5. A young Apollo and a young Venus in a room apart – charming. Another Apollo standing, an elegant figure, but the lyre is modern and good for nothing – without strings, likewise. Morpheus under the figure of a boy *sleeping*, in black marble, fine and well preserved, poppies in his hand. The Gladiator and a Roman soldier admirable, Cupid and Psyche charming. Leda receiving Jupiter's embraces – Diana, beautiful. Several Venus's which have their merit, but the famous Venus of Medicis I have not yet seen, 'tis reserved pour faire bonne bouche. The cabinets of curiosities require years to examine – one of antiques consisting of idols, talismans, sepulcral lamps, hyeroglyphics, medals, minerals and fossils. Among the antiques I discovered a *sistrum* which I considered a good deal. This had but 3 iron rods tho' intended for 4 as one for which the place was plainly to be seen, was lost. They were all lose in their sockets and produced the same sound – that is the sound of the whole instrument. How this was plaid on or tuned is not certain – whether the iron rods were struck one at a time by a plectrum or swept one after the other I know not, but I suspect this to have had strings attached to these iron rods as there are plainly 4 holes beneath to fasten them to or to pass them thro', and the iron rods in that case could only serve as pegs or skrews to give them the proper tension. | All this must be reconsidered |.

There is a chamber for mathematical instruments with a sphere and globe each 7 feet in diameter. The mosaic tables, the cabinets of precious stones, ivory, amber, lapiz lazuli etc are numerous and wonderfully beautiful, but I hated losing the time they required to look at them, which I could have spent much more to my satisfaction over the pictures and statues. Marsyas tied up to be flead is admirable. An antient Greek philosopher, perfect. A marine Venus, Greek. Fine copy of the Laocoon by Bandinelli, and of an antique boar. Bacchus sedens, Greek statue. A faun ditto – Venus genetrix Greek statue –

Ganymede ditto–a Bacchanal, all fine. Mars in Ethiopian marble Greek statue, very rare–a beautiful little Mercury, all motion–a large Ceres, drapery wonderfully transparent thin and fine. Promethius larger than the life, but fine. An antique boar, all perfection.–The different states of putrifaction in wax by Gaetono Zummo are so wonderfully minute and exact as to make one shudder–what patience! and what a passion!–I have not yet seen the Tribuna. Afternoon, went to the old ducal palace, saw the wardrobe which is full of dead pomp and vanity–immense quantities of gold and silver plate–of jewels, crowns etc which gave me no more pleasure than they now do the 1st owners of them. In the great hall below are admirable statues by Mic. Angelo, John di Bologna, Donatelli, Bandinelli etc. The pictures in the ceiling are all by Vasari–many are now taken down to be cleaned. On the sides are painted in fresco by Salviati–the victories of the Florentines over the Pisans, the Sienese etc. From hence to the Physic-Garden which is small and inconsiderable.

I yesterday saw the famous chapel of St. Laurence, the mausoleum of the Medici family, but as its chief merit lies in the materials it struck me so little that I forgot to mention it. However as a building 'tis fine. It is of an octagonal figure, vaulted on the top like a cupola, but what it is chiefly admired for is its being incrusted over with porphyry, agate, touch-stone, jasper, lapis lazuli, oriental alabaster and other very rich materials. The arms of all the cities belonging to the Tuscan State are on these walls in mosaic. The inner ceiling of the dome is of pure lapis lazuli. At the alter are pillars of crystal, a full ell long. There is a statue of the Virgin weeping for the death of Christ by Mich. Angello, very expressive. This seems the place to see the works of Mich. Angello, John di Bologna and Bandinelli. The former was brought up at the expense of one of the gran dukes–they shew in the gallery his 1st attempt at sculpture at 14. It is a grinning head, which so struck the duke that he sent him to Rome to study.

It is astonishing how gutterally the Florentines speak particularly words with a hard C or Q. Instead of cor–horr–very strong–contra– hontra etc. for qui-*huigh*

Fruit is not so good or so plentiful as at Venice or Bologna. I suppose the cold from the neighbouring hills prevents it from ripening or at least as early as at those 2 places. The grapes are not yet ripe and the melons have little taste. One seldom hears music in the streets here, and never good, as at Venice and Bologna. The best I have yet heard is that of the *laudisti*. The weather is still hot here and no rain has fallen for some time. There have been showers on the mountains which have disturbed but not filled the Arno. I shall not go on to Rome till it is cooler. I find my blood inflamed–my legs swell

and I have a general pruriency in my skin and yet I have such a bad
opinion of Italian surgeons I want courage to let 'em bleed me, tho'
I believe it would do me a great deal of good. I know not the names
or qualities of medicines here or I would take a rumbling purge–a
strong dose of jallop [jalap] if in England. Indifferent food and wine,
heat of climate and fatigue have all contributed, I believe to boil my
blood.

FRIDAY 8. I have spent the whole morning in the Grand Duke's
gallery, where I have received more pleasure than the works of art
ever gave me before. I was there from 8 till past 12: went again over
what I had seen yesterday with new wonder and delight. I shall
mention only things that struck me most; among which the famous
Etruscan antique *Chimæra* is a most curious and fine piece of sculpture, 2 heads and a serpent's tail–this last broken.–Bernini's mistress,
a fine bust with the wound in her cheek he gave her when she disturbed him at his work. 2 fine Roman pillars with bassi relievi well
preserved. All their instruments of war by land and sea are sculptured
on them; among which antient trumpets, which are more in the shape
of horns than like the modern trumpet. A Flora full of grace greek–a
little plump–Antinous a beautiful bust. Agripina, drapery fine–bust
of Cicero, ditto of Sapho, head only antique–fine. Leda a Gr. statue
beautiful. Wrestler or rather gladiator, fine. Seneca a most admirable
bust. Roman matron and consul, fine figures, well draped–Mercury,
very fine–Otho and Vitellius, two of the finest busts in the world.
Bachus by Mich. An. fine–Vespasian good bust–female bachanal
with charming drapery–Endymion beautiful and in a fine attitude on
his left knee and holding up his right hand to prevent his being dazled
by the brightness of the moon which he adores–Ael* Cæsar, extreamly
rare–Faustina young and old, fine–2 busts of Marcus Aurelius
most beautiful–Mars and Venus, 2 large Gr. statues standing by each
other, he seems going away and she entreating him to stay–a most
famous and beautiful bust (head only antique) of Alexander, regret-
ting there being no more worlds to conquer–Venus Nutrix, charming,
a child on her knee to whom she has been giving suck–Æsculupius
and a philosopher 2 fine Gr. statues–a Victory ditto–German soldier
admirable for muscular force and animation–a Ptolomey, extremely
rare–Euripides very fine bust–with all these and more I was much
pleased, but upon entering the Tribunal I was in raptures.–There are
6 of the most capital Greek statues and the best preserved in the
whole collection–and the Apollo Belvedere, the Farnese Hercules
and the Laocoon at Rome excepted, in the whole world. There are
3 Venus's–the famous faun–the wrestlers and the spy whetting his

* 'Augustus Caesar' in the Osborn MS.

knife while he listens to persons framing a conspiracy, commonly called *l'arrotino*, or the whetter.

The most beautiful and perfect of the 3 Venus's and of all that are to be found under that denomination in the whole universe, is usually known by the apellation of the *Venus of Medicis*. It was found at Tivoli in the Villa Adriani but broken in 5 places. However it has been extremely well repaired by Bandinelli. It is supposed from a passage in Lucian to have been the work of Praxitiles then in the temple of Gnidus, tho' a greek inscription on the base gives it Cleomenes son of Apollodorus the Athenian.

ΚΛΕΟΜΕΝΗΣ ΑΠΟΛΛΟΔΟΡΟΥ ΑΘΗΝΑΙΩΣ ΕΠΩΕΣΕΝ

but this inscription is supposed to have been put there by a sculptor who either cleaned or repaired it, and it is written on a different piece of marble joined to the base. There are 2 little Cupids in front, and a dolphin on the side, on which account sometimes it is called the Maritime Venus–it is quite naked and the marble clean and white, its head turned towards the left shoulder, one hand before her breasts without touching them, and the other at a distance from the body, below the waist. Nothing can be more perfectly feminine and beautiful, the feet, the toes, the legs, the thighs, the body–breasts and face of the most exquisite simmetry and beauty. Upon entering the Tribuna this Venus between the other two, was so clean and fair, that I supposed it a copy, but soon saw its superiority not only in colour to all the rest but in every other particular. However the 2nd Venus the *Venus pudica*, (*Venus Virgine*), the Urania or Celestial Venus, seems coming out of a bath, one hand is adjusting her hair, the other holds the drapery with which her legs and thighs are entirely covered is admirable–inferior to nothing one has seen but the former. The 3rd called *Venus Victrix* (the apple or golden prize in her hand which is adjudged to her by Paris) the *Venus Maritata*, is larger than the other two, but in any other place would be charming. The 2nd is said to be the work of Phidias. Then the wrestlers which are young and less than men grown up: but all the limbs and muscles as well as the attitudes which are extreamly difficult are admirably designed and expressed. 5. the Spy or Whetter *l'Arrotino, Rotatore* is admirable–the attention in his countenance, while he whets his knife and listens to what seems going forward at some distance is wonderfully well expressed.

The 6th and last of these famous statues is the *Faun*, which I shall dwell on the longer as the subject leads to my *business* here. He is a musician, playing on two instruments at once; namely the *cymbal*, or *mandrice* with his 2 hands and with his right foot the *scabila, crupezia* or soffiatura. The cymbal is the same kind of instrument as that I had seen and heard at Figline, namely 2 brazen basons beat one against the other to mark the steps or time of the soldiers march. It is used among the Turks, has from thence been introduced into the German troops under the name of the *teller*–is in the Prussian army and was brought to Florence by the late Emp. when Gr. Duke–but the cymbalists have all deserted, and at present this instrument is not used by the troops here. The soffiatura (see Blanchinus) is a pair of bellows under his right foot, which I suppose communicated wind to a kind of flute or whistle like the toys we have for children, which imitate the cuckoo and other birds.

There are round the room (which is a rotund with an arched dome lined with mother of pearl, the floor inlaid with marble of various colours) a great number of small statues, some antique, but chiefly of John de Bologne which are very good: and against the wall innumerable and inestimable pictures, 3 by Raphael in his 3 different manners. The 1st a Holy Trinity, very *Peruginish*–that is to say very like the style of his master, hard and dry–the 2nd the same subject, a little Jesus and St. John more free and pleasing–the third and best is the famous St. John in the Wilderness, of which I saw a copy at Bologna. It seems so fresh and perfect in every particular as if art could go no further ('tis *this* of which Mr. Robertson has copied a copy.) Among the statues 2 little Morpheus's sleeping antiques in the prettiest attitudes imaginable, obliged me to look at them. St John by Carlo Marat a single beautiful but effeminate portrait. A sweet Baccantino in marble. Rubens' and Parmigiano's wifes by their husbands–la Madonna addolerata, a repetition of the sweet picture I saw at Bologna by Guido–a concert by Bassano, admirable–the heads all known–there are 3 of the Bassanos in it, namely his father, son and nephew, with their wives and family–Titian and his wife are on the right, behind, as invited to be of the audience. An exquisitely high finished little picture by Vanderwerl, not at all Flemish in the design.–Head of Raphael by Vinci, well preserved, but rather cold. Another small picture by ditto.

On the left hand of the Tribuna from the door is a little antique Apollo of grecian sculpture, of which I took particular notice as he holds in his left hand an instrument which rests on his shoulder in the manner of a violin and in his right hand something that has been taken for a bow; but I take the instrument to have been a lyre and the flat piece of wood or stick in the right hand to have been a bacchetto or rod such as is used for the dulcimer and instruments of percussion. However the manner of holding this instrument which has something of the shape of the viol da braccia, the finger board and the manner in which the left hand is placed which seems capable of shortening the strings by pressure of the fingers and lastly the stick, or if you will, the bow held in the right hand and placed across the instrument naturally suggest to a hasty observer that this was really a violin played upon with a bow by friction, but the shape of this stick resembles no bow I ever yet saw—indeed this is the only antique instrument I ever yet saw either in sculpture or in books, that was held in this manner, resting upon the shoulder, but I shall look at it again and if possible get a drawing made of it.

I forgot to mention the 2 famous Titians in the Tribuna the one is his wife and other his mistress lying down naked in the character of Venus and both in the utmost perfection. They are hung over each other. The wife is uppermost and has a child or Cupid playing by her. She rests on a cushion into which her arm sinks in the most natural and beautiful manner. This is handsome, but the other below is exquisitely beautiful and an admirable drawing and graving are made from it by Mr. Strange, but the colouring of this is far superior to any picture I ever saw of Titian. All the mezzo tints are still preserved in their greatest perfection and it is beautifully voluptuous in the highest degree.

In the evening I heard vespers performed by a great number of priests and laymen with only a little organ, a violoncello and 2 violoni for accompaniment in the Church of the Annunciation—'tis the vigil of that feast and a fair—the streets are very full and noisy, all the gay and young people seem to be in them. The music I heard sung to night was all in the old coral style of the 16th century. After this full performance in the great choir, there were others in different chapels, where boys sung in the organ loft, with tenors and bases below. Night—the people are surely all mad here—there is such a noise of whistles, little bells, trumpets etc in the streets as I never heard at Barthol'mew Fair.* The fair of the annunciation began this evening and the humour is for the better sort to drive up and down the streets in coaches and the rest to walk on foot. A great number of people are come out of the country, from the mountains and all are alive and merry. The country women's dress here is quite theatrical and coquettish. It consists of a small Leghorn hat bound with ribands placed in a roguish manner on the side of the head or turned *down*, a little, over the forehead, in front, with a great number of coloured ribands tied in

---

* A fair held annually in West Smithfield, London, from 1133 to 1840 on St. Bartholomew's Day (24 August, old style). It was an important market for cloth, cattle, pewter and leather, and in addition attracted large gatherings of people with its exhibitions, side shows, performers of all kinds, quack doctors, and the like. After 1840 the fair was held at Islington, was last proclaimed by the Lord Mayor in 1850, and was abolished as a nuisance in 1855.

little knots and fluttering about at the top of the body of the gown, which is always of a gay party coloured stuff, and a shepherdess wand in the hand.

SAT. 8. This morning every body is in gala and I went with Signor Giosep. Molini, brother to him in London, to the church of the annunciation to hear the mass. It is a good creature this Molini and very civil and useful to me. As to letters here, I am quite unfortunate–out of 6 that I had, not one has yet taken place: Guarducci gone to his house a great way off–Ricciarelli set out for England–Mr. Perkins, to whom I had a letter from P. Martini out of town as well as Dr Fosse: a Dominican to whom I had a letter, I have not yet found. And Mr. Richie wrote to Sir H. Man in my favour, but I have been twice and have not seen him. At 1st out–I asked the servant the best time to come again–he named 11 next day. I went, and a message was brought me that Sir H. was very sorry he could not see me as he was very much engaged–and as no other time was mentioned for my return I'll see him ⟨   ⟩ before I'll go after him again. He can be of no use to my business as it lies chiefly in the *public* libraries and places where I must *pay* for admission if I was his brother; and I detest dancing attendance after little poeple who fancy themselves *great*. After the mention I know Mr Richie made of me, if he had chosen to see me, he would have sent to the inn to name an hour–and as an Englishman, I am certainly entitled to an audience–but–thank Heaven, I want him as little as he does me.

At night went again to the opera of Le Donne Vendicate–it was to be the last this season–and I never heard such applause. The house was very full and the best natured audience I ever saw. In one of dances there was a great ⟨shower⟩ of a printed sonet or copy of verses in praise of the two principal dancers thrown from the slips which flew all over the house and were scrambled for by the audience. Before this I was in the fair–and at the Annunciata–la via de'Servi leading to this church at 2 continued rows of coaches going different ways from one end to the other. It was very troublesome to those on foot, like me, who don't chuse the expense in dry weather, finding that of books and other purchases take off my spare pence very fast. At the church I heard again old music in 8 parts as in the morning. This evening I met with Mr. Perkins for the first time, and Dr. Fosse in the street, and at the opera Mr Fothergale found me out and came to speak to me. I had dined with him at Count Firman's in Milan.

SUNDAY 9. This morning between 6 and 7 the laudisti passed my window again in procession, and stopt at the church ⟨   ⟩ to sing a psalm very well in 3 parts: the music was lively and agreeable, and now the Gr. Duke's guards pass, they are all young noblemen. At 9 went to the Convent del Portico about a mile from Florence, via Romana, to hear a very solemn mass for the last consecration of 8 nuns. It cost more than 300 zechins. The music of the mass was composed by Signor Soffi, Luchese. There was a trio in the 1st part of it for Manzoli, Verole, and the 2nd maestro del annunciata–Verole beat time, the composer not being present, to the choruses. The band, vocal and instrumental, was very numerous. Manzoli sung a motet charmingly, very well composed by Monzi of Milan; but with less voice, I think, even in a small church, than he had in the opera house, when in England. Luckily I had a coach to day for the 1st time since I came to Florence. I say luckily, for such a rain fell all at once as I had never seen, even in Italy, before. When I returned to Florence there was a river, or rather a torent running through all the streets we (I had Molini with me) got however to Mr. Perkins's but could not get out till the shower was over. He is a deep musician, I find, and has made several curious discoveries on the violoncello; we had a long dish of music and chocolate, and set our horses very well together. After dinner I visited il proposto Dr Fosse, who is to carry us to morrow to the famous Laurenzian Library.* He is very intimate with the librarian Signor Bandini. After this little Linley came to see me after dinner. He has been 2 years with Nardini. We went to the Cascina, a ⟨farm⟩ a little way out of Florence belonging to the Gr. Duke, where it is the fashion to walk and ride. Then went to the *Bottegone* or great coffee house, and afterwards to the comedy of il *Saggio Amico*, by Goldoni, which I had seen before since I came to Italy, but forget where. It was in another theatre from that of the opera buffa near the Duomo–a very pretty one, and larger than that of the comic opera. The play was dull, but there was a superb Turkish dance and as to scenes and dresses, I never saw one so rich–it lasted full ½ an hour, after which I was tired and *re*tired, for I could not possibly get a seat. But before the play just as it was growing dark, I met in the streets a company of laudisti. They are called Fratelli della Venerabil Compagnia D.S. Maddalena de' pazzi e S. Giuseppe in S. Maria in Campidoglio. They had been at Fiesole and were proceeding in procession to their own little church. I had the curiosity to follow them, and got a book of the words they were singing–Laudi da Cantarsi da'Fratelli etc. in Italian. They stopt at every church in their way to sing a stanza in 3 parts, and when they arrived at their own chapel, in to which I went there was a band of instruments to receive

* The Mediceo-Laurentian Library was founded by Cosmo de' Medici (1389–1464) who enriched it with collections of classical and oriental manuscripts of the highest importance. It survived many vicissitudes before it was opened to the public by the Grand Duke Cosmo I in 1571. Bandini, mentioned by Burney here, described the collection in a catalogue of 13 folio volumes (1764–78).

REDICOFINI

THE PONTE
MOLLE, ROME

them who between each stanza which they sang played a symphony. They performed vespers in canto fermo assisted by their chaplain. It was very decorous and certainly very innocent. These companies are numerous, and some of them have subsisted near 500 years. The 1st mention I find of 'em is in the Magliabecchi Library in a folio MS of Laudi Spirituali for the Compagnia of Friars of the Church of all Saints 1336, in Florence of the order degli *umilitati*.

MONDAY 10. This morning went with Dr Fosse to the Laurenzinian Library. He introduced me to the Librarian Signor Bandini, who has written the life and published some of the posthumous works of the famous G. Bat. Doni. He shewed me the only book of MSS upon music in the library: here the books are all chained to desks and can only be read in that place–however there is a seat and convenience for writing. This vol. of MSS contains the following works.

Guido aretinus* musica–de musica intervallora quo ad voces prima ordīs

Joanni Tinctoris de proportionibus–this is the Gram. Ant. who gives the invention of contrapunto to the English.

Micrologus Guidonis Lib.2

Ejusdem–Rithmus–Explicit Micrologus in Musica

Ejusdem. Dialogus de Musica.

Ejusdem Formula Sonorum

Ejusdem Epistola ad Michaelem Monacti

De manibus vocū, anñ Boetiū

Incerti auth.

Enchiridion Musice incerti aut.

Laus Musice–incerti aut.

Aurelianus de Musica

Regule de Contra puncto. incerti auth.

Johan de Muris

Exordium Musice–incert aut

Regule Contrapuncti Joan Ocrobi. Carmelite

Dialogus de musica. Incert. Aut.

The micrologus begins: Explicit proportionale Musices Nnomīe dm Incipit Musica secondus Dictā Guidonis Carmina ejusdem –etc.

I was hurried and could write no more–but Padre Martini has had the whole book copied and I saw it at Bologna.

* The names of a number of the most important early writers on music are to be recognised in this list, among them: Guido d'Arezzo (Guido Aretinus *c*.900–*c*.1050, Johannes de Tinctoris (*c*.1446–1511), Anicius Manlius Torquatus Severinus Boethius (*c*.475–524), Reomensis Aurelianus (*c*. middle of 9th century), Johannes de Muris (early 14th century).

From hence I went with Dr. Fosse who has the keys to the library del Palazzo Rinuncini where is a neat and well chosen collection of books in a very elegant room. I found there a printed copy of the 1st opera that was ever performed entirely in music* and made extracts. After dinner went to a great *accademia* at Mr. Hempson's an old English gent. where I heard Nardini, little Linley, the master of the house, who plays on the common flute in a particular manner, blowing it thro' a spunge–a person from Perugia who played on the viol d'amore–etc, etc, and saw a great deal of company–among whom was the famous improvisatrice† Signora *Corilla*, with whom I had a good deal of chat.

TUESDAY 11. All the morning spent in the Magliabecchi‡ Library which pleases me more than any one I have been in–there is more to my purpose in it. I made extracts from an old missal of the XIth century–from an old book of Laudi Spirituale in the Gregorian Note Canto Firmo in 1336–with a preface giving an account of that institution which still subsists. I have employed a person in the library to copy the preface of the 2nd opera that was composed, at Florence 1608 which is historical–took an account of the MSS of and upon music etc —— but I must return–

After dinner (being sent to) I visited Sir H. Mann–found him in bed with the gout and Lord Tilney with him. They were both abundantly civil–the former lamented his not having seen me sooner –blamed his porter for not telling him I had been there before or mistaking the name etc etc–a fib costs an old courtier but little. He invited me to dinner next day–I was engaged–Lord Tilney invited me to a concert at his house that night–engaged–the English spirit of

---

* Burney refers here to *Euridice*, based upon a poem by Ottavio Rinuccini and set to music by Jacopo Peri (1561–1633). It was first performed in Florence in 1600 to grace the festivities which followed the marriage of King Henry IV of France with Maria de' Medici.

† Corilla, or Corilla Olimpica (Fernandez or Maddalena Morelli) was perhaps the most celebrated of the Italian improvisers, who sang verses extempore to the guitar and other stringed instruments 'upon any subject moderately susceptible of poetical amplification' (Baretti). An account of a performance by Corilla as reported to him is given in *A View of Society and Manners in Italy* by John Moore, M.D. (1781): 'After much entreaty, a subject being given, she began, accompanied by two violins, and sung her unpremeditated strains with great variety of thought and elegance of language. The whole of her performance lasted above an hour, with three or four pauses, of about five minutes each, which seemed necessary, more that she might recover her strength and voice, than for recollection; for that gentleman [Mr. Ramsay] said, that nothing could have more the air of inspiration, or what we are told of the Pythian prophetess. At her first setting out, her manner was sedate, or rather cold; but gradually becoming animated, her voice rose, her eyes sparkled, and the rapidity and beauty of her expressions and ideas seemed supernatural.'

‡ Particularly rich in the early productions of the Italian press, the library was based upon the collections made by Antonio da Mario Magliabecchi (1633–1714).

independency was strong upon me or I might have got rid of my engagements.–However we set our horses together very well at last, after a little kicking–professions were very strong on the side of the knight–and I seemed to have got the length of the noble lord's foot. After this to a private accademia, where the best thing I heard was little Linley.

WEDNESDAY. In the morning visited Dr Bicchiere and had a power of antiquarian talk about music–but I heard nothing new. He quoted and referred to books which I had already seen and started no game, except by asserting that he had either seen or heard of a machine at Berlin for taking down extemporaneous pieces of music as fast as played on a harpsichord–which I much doubt.* From thence to Mr. Hempson's where Nardini and Linley met me to breakfast. The former played an old solo of Tartini delightfully–gave me a MS harpsichord lesson of his own, and a solo of Tartini. The little man played a great many of Nardini's things and old Mr Hempson shewed me his books and curiosities. Dined at Molini's in a family way. After dinner visited Dr Guadagni, who was extreamly obliging. He is prof. of Experimental Philosophy at Pisa. He shewed me all his books and instruments which are innumerable: of these last the chief part are English–he reads and corresponds with English writers. He made me a present of a very old music book by Orlando di Lasso. From hence went with Molini to see Campioni, who is married and settled here, as Maestro di Capella to the Gr. Duke. He was very civil–shewed me his books and compositions in MS–I am to go there again to hear him and his wife who plays the harpsichord. I had not my plan to shew him, which he much desired to see: Nardini had borrowed it to copy. At night to a great accademia, where were all the best company of Florence. It was at the house of Signor Domenico Baldigiani. Nardini led, and played a solo admirably, little Linley played a concerto very well–Mr Hempson one on the flute–la Mellini, a young lady sang very prettily and some *misses* played and sang vilely. The master of the house is a good gent. harpsichord player, they say, but did not perform. There were 2 harpsichords one played by Signor Frei and the other by an abate–but only in accompanying. When most of the company was gone I was *dragged* to the harpsichord tho' not to

---

* Burney returns to consideration of this claim in the account of his German Tour. He enquired at Berlin and was told that such a machine had been successfully produced, but that it had since been accidentally destroyed by fire. He recalls that a proposal outlining a mechanism of this kind had been put to the President of the Royal Society by the Rev. Mr. Creed in 1747: in this device specially ruled paper moving at a steady rate over two cylinders–one dispensing, the other receiving– was to be marked by pins or pencils fixed at the ends of the several keys of the instrument and so record in the correct position on the stave the notes as they were struck.

execution. They pretended to be pleased, but I was by no means pleased with myself and came home very sulky–O, but I forgot–the Corilla sung–and not ill——

THURSDAY 13. Attempted a great deal of business to day but with little success. Went 1st to the Magliabecchi Library, where I continued writing till the custodii and all the people wished me a 1000 miles off, then went with Molini to hear a famous female player on the harp, but the house was full of folk and tomorrow is appointed. Then went after the widow of Piscetti to see the famous harpsichord of Zarlini, but that business cannot be done till tomorrow. Then, after a permission or faculty for having a drawing made of the little *fidling* Apollo in the Gr. Duke's gallery, but referred till tomorrow. After dinner several other things were in vain attempted, till it was time to go to the Corilla's. There was Nardini, the little Linley, Signor Frei and 2 or 3 more of her particular friends and we begun to be very comfortable and *she* in a very good disposition to satisfy my great curiosity concerning the manner of pronouncing and accompanying poems *al l'improvistà*, when, behold! a heap of disagreeable people came in and spoilt all–there was nothing but politicks going forward, and every other subject but music and poetry. The nearest thing was started to the former was the question I put concerning the first use of euneuchs as singers,* which was discussed a long time, but to no useful purpose for me, tho' several of these people were doctors or abati–all was conjecture of or quotation from old books–in short I was obliged to come away from hence without my errand–and vile procrastination! Hopes only are given of better success tomorrow or next day.

Sat. [FRIDAY] 14th. I this morning heard Signora Anna Fond play on the harp, Mr Perkins on the base and saw the church of Sn Croce which contains the tombs and monuments of Mich. Angello–Galilei–Michele–Aretino and many other celebrated Florentines. 'Tis a very large and lofty old church. and has some good pictures by Vasari and others. I likewise this morning saw in the house of Pis-

---

* Eunuchs were employed in church choirs from very early days (perhaps as early as the 10th century in Constantinople) but it was with opera, and with Italian opera particularly, that their fortunes, from the 17th century onward, were most closely linked. There were strict laws – civil and ecclesiastical – against the practice of castration undertaken merely to preserve a soprano voice in a male singer; but the demand for such a voice was so great and the financial rewards to a successful castrato were so rich that there were always those to be found who were prepared to undergo the operation and specialists who were prepared to perform it.

The castrato dominated the vocal music of Italy for the best part of two centuries, and the peculiar qualities of the male soprano voice continued to fascinate composers long after the 18th century: Meyerbeer was the last operatic composer of repute to write for a male soprano; his *Il Crociato in Egitto* (1824) was designed specially for Velluti.

cetti's widow the famous enharmonic harpsichord* made for Zarlino, 1544. al Pesaro–and have copied his description of it from his own hand writing on the fore-board. I there got acquainted with a very clever man, il Canonico Domenico Cavalea, who made me a present of a book and invited me to his appartments at the Duomo to talk and see books on the Hebrew music. After dinner I went–and found he had been thinking about my plan, which I had shewed to him in the morning. He gave me some notes he had made on D. Calmet. He is a great Hebraist and now writing a great work upon the Hebrew language. He has promised to send me his remarks upon the accents of the Hebrew, which he thinks were the ancient notation for sound–or musical notes. After this to Signor Menze [Mengs] a very eminent painter here, who is engaged by Mr Harris at Madrid to paint a large picture for an altar-piece at Oxford†. He shewed me the design which is charming: it is only of 2 figures–our Saviour when he appears to M. Magdalen in the garden: it is the moment of the Noli Me Tangere. She is kneeling before him and has infinite expression in her countennance. I found M. Mengs a very sensible and agreeable man, and forgot my hurry so much as to stay chatting with him a couple of hours. From his appartments to the play a little while. I find the Italians excellent comic actors and had they better pieces to represent, I believe they would beat all the world. Dr Fosse to night shewed me several books of ancient laudi which he had been so kind as to ferret out for me.

SAT. 15. I am now winding up my bottom here‡ and have so much to do that I can get no time to tell it–3 hours in the morning spent in the Magliabecchi Library–then visited Signor Campioni, with whom I stayed 2 hours. He has a very great collection of music ancient and modern, particularly of motets of the 16 and 17 centuries–of prints–of gessi§ and of pictures, for his wife is a very good paintress– was at work upon Titian's Venus–and likewise plays the harpsichord prettily. Campioni has a very elegant house, well furnished and seems very well off here–is very desirous of corresponding with me in

---

* Burney does not mention this instrument in the *History*, but it is referred to in the article 'Spinet' in *Rees* XXXIII, where it is stated that Zarlino had the instrument made at Venice. It was later sent to England 'but the mechanism and tone were so bad, that no tuning could render its sounds agreeable'.

† The painting had been commissioned by All Souls College, Oxford, to be put up over the altar in the Chapel. Mengs was at Madrid at the time (1769) and Mr. Harris (the future Lord Malmesbury, then *chargé d'affaires* in Madrid) helped forward the negotiations between the College and the painter. The fee was 300 guineas and the painting was finished in Rome in 1771.

‡ Winding up my bottom, ending my time, here.

§ Gessi = casts. The word 'casts' is written above gessi, neither seems to have been preferred.

England, and was very obliging. After dinner visited the famous Dr.
Perelli the professor of Pisa. He is well read in ancient music and
ancient authors, has a great number of anecdotes concerning both,
reads English and has promised to *think* for me. After this made other
visits of *partenza* and finished the evening at Maddalena Morelli's,
detta Corilla–where was music and a great deal of company.–Found
an invite to dine with Sir H. Mann, but ——

SUNDAY morn. 16. To draw to one point what I have seen and
heard at Florence I shall begin with what concerns antient music–the
little Apollo seemingly playing on a fiddle–Antient modern–the
missals in the public library–the 1st establishment of laudisti in 1336.
The tomb and epitaph of Squarcialuppi, the harpsichord of Zarlino–
the 1st drama in music at Florence 1600–extracts from old authors
etc.–As to modern music, Signor Nardini, Signor Campioni and
Signor Dotel Figlio, who are settled here in the Gr. Duke's band–and
Manzoli and Varole who are singing birds of passage excepted Florence is worse off than any great town in Italy–there is worse music at
the theatres, the accademias, in the churches and in streets than elsewhere, and less frequent. Not one great harpsichord player or good
lesson* could I find, or one celebrated and standard Florentine composition.

In taking leave of Sir H. Man at my visit of partenza I begun to
think I had judged too hardly of him before, for he then expressed so
much concern at his not having been able to wait on me, on account
of his gout, at not having been able to cultivate my acquaintance or to
be of any use to me, that I could not help believing a little of it: and to
see how much good nature and civility embellishes the person of him
who bestows it, to day I found out the Sir H. was a very handsome old
man: that his countenance was full of grace, intelligence and dignity,
which circumstances had before escaped me–but indeed he was ill in
bed with the gout. I thought it right to wait on Lord Tilney, who
seemed a plain good natured man, and had invited me to his house. I
found him surrounded with English news papers which he had just
received. I was not sorry I called for he was very civil; and expressed
concern he had not seen more of me, but hoped we should meet at
Naples, where he spends all his winters, etc etc. He shewed me his
house which is a very good one. Mr. Cox an old English gentleman
and Mr. Peachy a painter were with him. He has a room hung with
pictures which he has had painted to imitate tapestry–which are

---

* From the beginning of the 17th century to the end of the 18th the term lesson
was used to denote pieces for the harpsichord and other keyed instruments; usually
separate pieces, which in their collected form made up a suite. Lesson was also used
interchangeably with sonata.

very like–but surely 'tis having long hair dressed to resemble a peruque. Upon taking leave of Mr. Perkins I received many civilities, and he made me not only a present of a book written by himself upon the violoncello, but of a celebrated mass by Perti, and a bookfull of MS. motets by the greatest masters of Italy. Mr Joseph Molini, from whom I have received such assistance at Florence has been so kind to undertake to send my books, collected here and at Bologna to England directed to his brother. They began a second time to be too much for my trunk and would have been a possible embarrasment at the entrance into the Pope's territories, or at least upon going into Rome, where they say all books are examined by the Inquisition.

It is astonishing to what shifts the poverty of the Italian common people drives them. But it must be confessed that they are very ingenious in finding ways and means to raise money, for it is utterly impossible to make a bargain with them so clear and strong, as to escape new demands and disputes. If the agreement be for 5 zechini they'll swear it was for 5 and ½–this is not ingenuity indeed, but impudence–but here comes the mark of genius. After disputing the matter with them for an hour, which is perhaps more precious to you than the matter in debate, if they find you resolute, at length, to show moderation and a good disposition, they'll say–'lustrissimo, a few pauls shall not occasion a difference with so accomplished a cavaliere we'll e'en split the difference–Sometimes they'l bring your zechins again and tell you they want 2 or 3 grains of weight; and at other times, by way of change, if it be a postillion or vitturino, he'll tell you that it will cost him a zechin or 10 pauls to go out of the gates which will eat up all his profits, that he's a poor man with a large family, which perhaps, if he's a good actor will excite compassion and incline you to pay the pretended amande for him. All these arts have been successfully practiced on me, but yet, it is not just from such rascals as these and the camerieri of the hotels, who have always an understanding with them and a share in the plunder, to judge of all the inhabitants of a country.

After a 100 plagues of this kind which make one ready to tear one's flesh, I got into the chaise–but all was not over–at the gates going *out* of Florence, my baggage was all unpacked, and my trunk abominably tumbled, which had not happened to me before. But ere I quit this subject, I must write down by way of memorandum that the camereira at the Aquila Nera, is a true barone–a d—d confounded rascal–who with the figure and gravity of an ancient Roman, occasioned me all these plagues. He told me 2 or 3 days before my departure that he advised me to go to Rome with a vitturino di ritorno, who was a very worthy man, well known to the house, had a good chaise and horses

and would use me very well. This proposal I did not immediately fall
into, as I thought it would be more expeditious to go with the *procaccio*
or post, but upon talking with this last I found I should save no time
as he would be 5 days on the road as well as the other – so I een decided
to strike a bargain with the vitturino and I asked *my friend* the cameriere what he would have. He said 7 zechins and I should have a very
good bargain as he would bear all expences and let me sleep more than
the proccacio: but the proccacio only asked 5 zechins, and ¼ of a paul
per pound for baggage, allowing 60 pounds free. I desired to speak to
the vitturino and he at dinner was ready. I liked his countenance – and
offered him 5 zechins. He made many difficulties but at last consented
upon condition I would let him take in another at *Siena* – agreed provided he was a gallant huomo – but just at his going away the waiter
said it was Saturday night and no vitturini could stir out of the gates
on the Rome road next morning without paying a zechin – I proposed
a 1000 expedients, but all in vain the waiter would not yet part with
me. At length it was agreed that if I set out immediately after dinner
on Sunday I should reach Rome before dark on Thursday – which was
what I wished and determined to do, as every body says the entrance
into Rome from Florence is the finest and most striking thing imaginable to a stranger. – All this I thought well settled – so did my friends –
I drew up an agreement in writing ready for the vitturino to sign. A
little after 2 comes my man – but with a face of sorrow, said it was
impossible for him to go with me, as he had a horse lame etc – but his
brother would do every thing he had promised and use me very well.
This I did not like, and grumbled at being turned over to a stranger
and to one who had not been present at the bargain – O it was his
brother – that *he* was the principal and would be answerable for the
performance of every article – yes, yes say the cameriera 'tis his
brother and exactly the same thing. Well it was late and I submitted
tho' not with a good grace. *He* signed the article – the brother could
not write – but just before this comes the waiter and says the vitturino
must still pay 10 pauls to go out of the gates – well I was sorry for it –
but I had nothing to do with it and would pay none of it, well they
borrowed of me the 10 pauls – when I was going a way in order to be
clear,* I said you must tell the driver of the 10 pauls you owe me –
that I have received 2 zechins earnest, which I shall return at Rome and
then I shall have 5 zechins to pay – 5 zechins et *mezza* Signor says the
vitturino – only 5 I protested – the waiter was appealed to – oh 5 and ½

* This rather confused passage appears thus in the Osborn MS.: '. . . to be
clear, I said you must tell the driver of the ten pauls you owe me, and that he has
received two sequins earnest – so that I shall have only 3 sequins and ½ with the
extra baggage, to pay at Rome as 5 sequins was the original agreement . . .'

Signor–well, as I said before, they kindly propose to split the difference, and I, in a hurry and tired to death with disputing consent–And
it was my good friend the cameriera who brought word that, tho' it
was so late, by a *new* regulation of which they were not apprised
yesterday, the poor vitturino must pay 10 pauls for going out of the
gates–all which I found after was a d—d lye. This I said I had nothing to do with when a fresh dispute arose–but the good of all this evil
is, that I should never have been able to speak Italian with tolerable
readiness in the short time I had to stay in Italy had I not been frequently provoked by these fellows to scold and sputter out every word
I could muster in my own defence. Passion is an excellent stimulus to
the tongue–and there can be no better practice than a dispute in
which one is interested, as it provokes one to exercice every power of
expression in hopes of victory, or, at least self defence. But after all
it is not just I must repeat from such fellows as these to judge a whole
nation, ⌊and at Venice and Naples among higher classes I have met
not only with politeness and civility, but probity and simplicity of
character, but friendship⌋.

The country going out of Florence towards Rome, is very mountainous, but rich and well cultivated. The hills are all covered with
vines and olives, but these last are so like willow-trees that they give a
marshy look to places that are really scorched up for want of moistior.
We lay at Barberini a small village about 20 miles from Florence,
between Tavernelle and Poggibonsi. The vitturino who talked of
setting out at 4 next morning lay in bed till past 6, and I was forced
then to call him and we had a sad battle for he now absolutely says it
will be impossible to reach Rome on Thursday–sets me at defiance–
says I may do what I please–the article drawn up and signed between
me and the other is nothing–for he can neither write nor read and he
plainly says that the other vitturino and the cameriere *m'anno man-
giato**–that it was all a lye when they talked of his being brother to
him–they are no relations. What scoutatles!†–but at length, I'm on
the road to *Siena*, still in a mountainous country; but all these inequalities of ground in a rich soil, well cultivated, must produce fine
prospects at every instant; and from Florence to Siena there is an
eternal variety.

---

* 'had been feeding upon me' (the Osborn MS.).

† Burney deleted this word and substituted 'scoundrels', which appears in the
Osborn MS. The word 'scoutatle' has not been traced, but it would seem to contain
something of 'scourer' = sharper, vagabond; and of 'scoubanker' = an untidy,
idle, lounging person, sneak-thief, rascal.

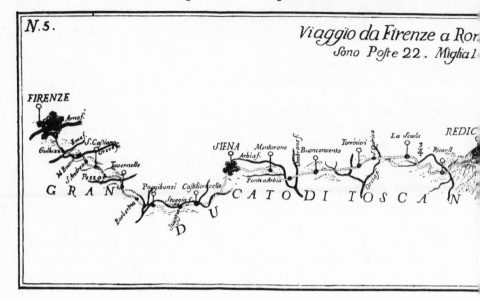

SIENA

This city is much fallen off from its ancient splendor, however there are still de beaux restes–some churches and palaces well worth visiting. And as to the cathedral it pleased me more than any one I had seen in Italy: 'tis quite compleat. The front is the most elegant thing I ever saw; very rich both in work and materials. The symmetry is a little hurt by the campanille or steeple appearing on the right–the inside too is charming. The mosaic story of the Bible on the pavement, admirable. A few good pictures too in fresco, and in a little chapel on the right 2 by Carlo Maratt and 2 fine statues by Bernini, a St. Jerom and a Magdalena the former full of dignity and the latter of expression. In the library are 29 very large missals, curiously written upon vellum in the Gregorian black note upon 4 red lines–dated anno milesimo quadragesimo quinto–very elegantly illuminated, and for this they are most curious as their antiquity is not very high. The drawing of the figures is hard and dry but coloured very beautifully. The large pictures in fresco on the walls of this library are by Pinturicchio from designs of Raphael and not by Perugino as M. de la Land advances. They are stiff and in Raphael's first manner, but fresh and finely preserved–but the 3 Graces in Greek sculpture are charming, tho' the middle one has lost a head–the other two by a spirit of barbarism are turned from the light. They were once in the church, and perhaps not so saintly as they should be for that place, but why they should be in the dark here is not easy to say. The grand place Piazza del Campo is

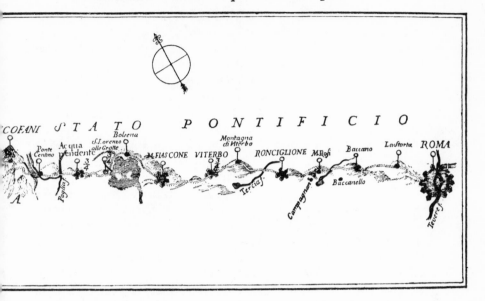

a kind of amphitheatre on a slope seemingly scooped out, where once a year they have still games called gli pugni – and horse races. There is a large fountain and in the Palazzo della Signoria, or town house, are many good pictures of the Siena school those of Sodomo and Salimbeni please me most. These were all done during the time of the republic which ended in 1555. The Spaniards were master of Siena for 2 years, after which the Florentines under Cosmo Primo took possession of it 1557.

On the Roman side of Siena the country begins to be very naked, consisting of arable land, just now ploughed up. At the third milestone it begins to be barren and uncultivated, at the 8th mile stone more cultivated and fine land with vineyards. We travelled all night, for at 12 o'clock, when we arrived at Terreniezi [Torrenieri] 3 posts from Siena – all were in bed, and so sound asleep, it was impossible to wake them. At Saraoliccico they would not take us in, nor give the poor ho[r]ses either hay, corn or water. We travelled on in this manner (I was almost petrified with cold though the day had been very hot) till 6 in the morning, and then stopt and a hedge-wine-house – where, though I was dying with hunger, thirst and fatigue, everything we found disgusted me it was so dirty – all was filth and misery. However I laid me down on a thing called a bed till 10 o'clock and then got up to the vilest supper, breakfast and dinner all in one, that I had ever yet seen – with wine more sour than vinegar, and bad water – bread black etc etc.

At 12 TUESDAY set off through a terrible country, burnt up and
barren, pass by Radicofani an old fortified town on a hill like old
Sarum. Here I began first to see the smoke of the turf and stubble
which they burn here as in Wiltshire for manure, to which is attributed in a great degree the mall'aria. This continues to the very gates
of Rome and extends more than 40 miles round it–a light coloured
earth, quite bare, with rocks and sharp, loose stones. Here again it
grows intolerably hot. On both sides Siena, for 40 or 50 miles are
little pyramidal mile stones. A house and vineyard in this desolate
country was quite refreshing to the sight: it seemed a very paradise.
At the 50th stone from Siena a little cultivation and fertility appear on
the right hand, but a few green trees only on these mountains, have at a
distance that appearance though left still arrid–the road up and down
hill eternally. At the 52d mile stone, we enter the Pope's territories
and pay the gabello–a mezzo paulo–3d–this happens 4 times–1st at
Centino–2d Aquapendente–3 Lorenzo and 4 Montefiascone. The
Pope's territory is divided from Tuscany by a river terrible in winter
says the vittorino but now dry–over which there is a good bridge of
stone built by Clement 11th. The country very bad till Aquapendente–which is in an agreeable wild but charming situation–among
rocks and cascades–but the hills are covered with green of some sort
or other. There seem to be some good houses and churches, but I
could not stop to examine. Beyond it the country is somewhat more
pleasant and cultivated. We slept at S. Lorenzo, a village surrounded
by pleasant hills. I supped with 2 fryers, one of which was mad and
2 vitturini–sad fare and beds–was very near having the mad priest
for bedfellow, but compounded with having the other in the same
room with me, tho' in a different bed.

Pass in the morning WEDNESDAY 19 along the Lago di Bolsena
which is 30 miles round and often 9 or 10 broad. It appears at a distance like a vast river–large fishing boats on it–great fogs–the hills
round it covered with smoke from the fires where they burn stubble
etc. This air is at least very unpleasant, but I had such a notion of its
want of salubrity that I feared to draw my breath lest I should inhale
the poison. But for the smoke and fog, the road by the side of this lake
would be delightful. All the people here have agues and putrid
fevers; but they have been worse this summer, so as to be thought
contagious. I was a little alarmed at these accounts but too far advanced to retreat–but little rain had fallen here, tho' much at Florence. They live most miserably–sour wine, black bread and little or
no meat–and all their food dressed with rancid oil, which I so detest
and loath that I could vomit with thinking of it. In this road there are
olives and vines on each side and the lake at a little distance. We

passed by the town of Bolsena which is upon the lake and is said to have been the ancient capital of the Volscians. It has an old castle and fortifications. Keep near the lake till near *Montefiascone* a hanging wood on the left an open and pleasant vountry, but now much burnt up. It is pretty well cultivated and seems a good corn country.

I visited Signor Guarducci at his new house, called here a palazzo. He had received news of me already from Mr. Hudson in England and received me in the most hospitable and obliging manner—made me drink chocolate etc and loaded me with provisions and excellent wine, a basket of cakes of all sorts that he had received from a nunnery in the neighbourhood and 2 bottles of delightful wine made at Montefiascone on his own estate. This is one of the most famous places in Italy for wine—shewed me his house which is truely elegant and at the same time comfortable—says he has quitted the stage and intends to live here with his family, having a mother living and brothers and sisters. Tho' so heavy and solemn on the stage in a room he is lively, obliging and agreeable—he had only a priest with him. There is a charming prospect on both sides his house—the Lake Bolsena on one side and Viterbo on the other. He read my plan with great attention and seemed to interest himself very much about me—said many very civil things of my design and his expectations that I should make not only a useful work but one still more general and pleasing than that of P. Martini, which he and most people think rather dry and too learned for the generality of readers. He wrote me a letter to the famous Merula at Naples and promised to write to me if any thing occurred during my travels. I hope to see him at Florence in my return where he has a sort of winter house. He was so obliging as to sing me a delightful song of Sacchini's composition which begins thus—

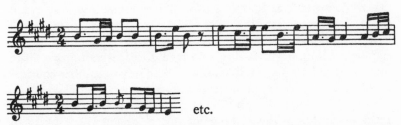

etc.

which I accompanied on a little octave spinet or rather virginal, miserably out of tune—but he sung it divinely—such smoothness taste and expression! and the few notes he put in, so select that I was truely charmed. He treated me with 2 long and learned cadences. He says the English love only a few notes in gracing, but they must be good—that they have been of great use to him—but this is rather civil than true, I believe, for he was a very chaste singer when he arrived in England. The Italians all say now he is the 1st in Italy and I can venture to say so with truth, as far as I have yet heard. Mansoli's voice is much dropped and his is better than ever it was in England. I have not yet heard Nicolini–who they say is nasal. He was at Siena this summer and pleased there, but is now at Lucca where they dont like him.–Nor have I heard Aprile the crack of Naples, who, however, has, they say, a thin voice and embroyders too much. Caffaride is 63, Mansoli 57, Nicolini 43–and Guarducci 41. By way of memorandum let me say here that as to eunuchs the Italians are so much ashamed of the practice of making them that every single city says it is not there, but names some other place. 'Tis like the north in Pope.*–To the article Venice, add that at Florence I heard the Corilla in a *Scena* of an opera by *Latilla* with recitativo and air both accompanied by Nardini and Linley in which the music was charming–full of expression and new passages.

I left Guarducci with regret, and got to Viterbo by dinner. There are always 2 high mountains covered with trees in sight a little to the left of Viterbo, which is a pretty town–the entrance into it is gay thro' an elegant gate. There are 3 or 4 fine fountains always playing in it the 1st at coming in–one of them is 800 years old. The Duomo is an elegant compleat building but no extraordinary pictures in it–tho' the sacristan told me those by Bonefiani were very much esteemed a forestiere [stranger]–Inglese–had bid 1500 crowns a piece for 'em. There are two or 3 of Romanelli that seem good. It was the beginning of a fair at Viterbo and there was a song at the inn door sung dialoguewise by a man and woman accompanied by the man on a tamborine–pleasing enough. It cost me half a paul.

Set out at 3 from Viterbo where I dined upon *magra* with rancid oil that made me sick 24 hours–with an officer in the Pope's service of about 29 years of age. He was of Siena and spoke good Italian–had good natural parts and school learning but talked ignorantly of other countrys. All uphill work thro' and by a great chesnut grove till the summit of the Montagna di Viterbo. There is here another considerable lake. We were forced to alight and walk down the hill which was so steep it was with difficulty I kept my feet. Here it grew dark so that I can say nothing of the next 6 miles to Ronciglione where we lay and

---

* 'But where th'Extreme of Vice, was ne'er agreed
Ask where's the North? at York, 'tis on the Tweed;
In Scotland, at the Orcades; and there,
At Greenland, Zembla, or the Lord knows where
No creature owns it in the first degree.
But thinks his neighbour further gone than he.'
                                        Pope, *An Essay on Man*, Epistle II.v.

set out next morning at 5 for Rome thro' Monterosi, Baccano and Storta, a wretched village 9 miles from the Porto del Populo where there was the same *magra* entertainment–truely Lenten to me–for I could not eat it–however I got 2 or 3 eggs tolerably sweet and away to Rome. There is nothing on this side which announces the capital of the world–a desolate, brown, barren country–no houses or villas appear till within 3 or 4 miles of the city–which from hence tho' situated on 7 hills seems in a bottom. From Storta to Rome we were on the ancient Via Flamina* which is so broken in many places and was so dusty now and hot that I never travelled in more misery–2 or 3 bits of old tours are still remaining but nothing considerable till the sepulture of Nero on the right hand, now much defaced by time. Here the villas begin to appear all white, like those throughout Italy–and by small degrees the city begins to appear on the right, but one does not see the vast cupola of S. Peter till within 3 miles ½. We descended by degrees and lost sight of the city again at Acqua Traversa and soon after pass Ponte Molle over the Tibur at 2 miles from the gates of Rome. These 2 miles are all suburbs–this bridge was formerly called Pons Emilius. It was here was fought the famous battle between Constantine and Maxentius which determined the fate of the pagan religion and gave the Xtians possession of the capital of the world. The Tibur here is very muddy tho' there had not been rain lately at Rome–but there are often showers in the night upon the mountains here and in Tuscany which disturb the Tibur and Arno in the dryest times at Rome and Florence. At approaching this celebrated city one has sensations and a curiosity not easily described tho' not hard to imagine–one looks on every stone and stick with veneration [and] eagerness.

ROME

It was about 5 o'clock of a very hot but fine evening, SEPTEMBER 20 when I arrived at the Porto del Popolo at which I was stopped sometime for a pass to the dogana which cost a paul and a penny. I was much pleased with this delay as it gave me an opportunity of feasting my eyes with this grand and noble spectacle–'tis a large open piece of ground within the fine gate del popolo with an obelisk in the middle with 2 beautiful churches and 3 handsome streets in front. This gate was built by Mich Angelo and ornamentated on the inside by Bernini –the 2 statues of St Peter and St Paul on the outside are by Mochi–

---

* The Flaminian Way was the great trunk road which in Roman times stretched 222 miles northward from Rome to Arimium on the Adriatic.

the 2 churches in front one on each side the long and fine street called il Corso, are of white stone and so exactly alike as to be called the Gemini. The column is called la Guglia d'Augusto Piazza del Popolo, vice Flaminia. It was brought from Elyopolis [Heliopolis] in Egypt by Augustus–is ornamented with hyroglyphics–and was dedicated to the sun. This pillar, which had lain long on the ground after the declension of the Roman Empire was erected again by Sixtus Quintus. The twin churches are called Santa Maria de'Miracoli and Santa Maria de Monte Santo. There is likewise another church in sight called Santa Maria del Popolo. The middle street, il Corso, is above a mile long and 'tis here they have their horse races. Down this I went to the dogana and the ceremony of examination was soon over and fee a trifle. From hence go the Piazza de Spagna, at Damon's, where I took up my abode at 8 pauls lodging dinner and supper a day.

FRIDAY 21. All the morning was spent in unpacking, getting together my letters and preparing for business. After dinner I went after the Abbé Grant who was out, but seeing a fine church and fountain in the place where he lives, Piazza Navona–I went to examine them. The church S. Agnese is a very beautiful building like our S. Paul's in little. There is much good sculpture within and rich materials–the fountain is from designs of Bernini and admirable 4 great colossian figures representing the 4 capital rivers in the world. From hence I went to Mr. Byers, who received me very kindly. He had already been apprised of my journey and errand by Mr. Lumisden. He had 2 great professors with him, who came to see his designs for Sir W. Wynn's house, which is a noble one indeed. I had the pleasure to see and to hear it explained. I likewise saw some good landschips by Delany and Deane 2 young Englishmen of great merit–and some good pictures. I shewed him and Mr. Norton for whom I had brought a letter from England my plan and talked over. They started a good deal of game for me and promised to ferret out more. From hence to Mr. Beckford with Dr Bever's letter–whom I found together with Mr Vyse an agreeable young gent. to whom Dr Bever had written about my plan ere I had determined to go to Italy. This was rather lucky, as he goes to England in a few days on account of the death of his father. In the same house lives the Duke of Dorset to whom I had the honour of being introduced–he had an accademia and much company, chiefly English–I was very well received by all, and his Grace invited me to dine with him next day. There was a very pretty concertino by 3 hands only, but all good. Mr Vyse has been collecting materials for me already: has got a large cargo of solfeggios by Lio, the score of an opera by Jomelli etc–

SAT. 22. Such a busy day! This morning I breakfasted with Messrs

Beckford and Vyse–who were kind enough to accompany me to St. Peters over the bridge by the castle of S. Angelo–Messrs Nevy and Fuselier, the young artist who came over with Dr. Armstrong were of the party. To describe what I saw or what I felt is equally impossible –all my *great* expectations were surpassed–the approach, the vestibula the grand scala–the mosaic–at the whole I was in a delirium. From hence to see the Apollo Belvedere–the Laocoon, the Antinous etc–all most exquisite–the very first statues in the universe! Dined very agreeably at the D. of Dorset's–went out again with Mr Beckford after dinner again to see the Coliseo or Amphitheater–the Rotundo or Pantheon and innumerable other fine remains of antiquity.–Church of St. Gieronimo pictures of Carach–Dominichini and Guido–concert by this last–after which to Mr. Beckford's concert, consisting of 12 of the best hands in Rome, led by Celestini–and 3 voices, viz Signor Cristofero of the Pope's chapel who sings very much in Guarducci's way and is little inferior to him in delicacy, Grassetto–a boy made a eunuch by his own choice against the advice of his friends in order to preserve his voice, which is a very pleasing one, and he is moreover in other respects a very promising singer; and a buffo tenor, a very comical fellow.–Here was a great deal of company– among which the D. of Dorset, Mr. Layton, Abbe Grant, Mr Jenkins, Mr Vyse, etc. etc.

SUNDAY 23. This morning to see the Transfiguration of Raphael in the *original* in the church of St. Pietro Montorio. It is in mosaic at St Peter's as well as the St. Michael of Guido, St. Jerome of Dominichini and St Petronella of Guercino–the 4 1st pictures in the world. Then to see the sweet aurora of Guido perhaps the most pleasing and poetical picture ('tis a ceiling) in the universe. After this to the Colonna Palace: could only see the 1st floor. The collection is immense–the hall or saloon the largest and most beautiful I had seen and filled with pictures by the very first rate painters. In this gallery among the statues of which there are many, is a faun in the action of playing on the crotolus or cymbalum, which he holds in such a manner with his thumbs as would bruise them at every stroke. In one of these rooms is an old man playing on a harpsichord with the broad keys white and the sharps black by Tintoret: black and damaged. From hence to dine with Mr. Beckford, Vyse and Byers. After dinner I visited Mr. Morison, Mr. Jenkins and saw in the street the Abbe Hertford. Then I drove round a great part of Rome with Mr. Beckford, going out at the Porto del Popolo–over Ponte Molle, turning on the left and coming in at St. Peters–then with ditto visit the Forbes family–went to the English coffee house, saw many of my countrymen and artists of Scotland and Ireland–and afterwards to Signor Crispi a celebrated

[131]

Maestro di Capella here, where was a great deal of music. Signor Crispi played many of his own compositions and his wife sung etc.

MONDAY 24. Made 2 or 3 visits and then went to gli Santi Apostoli to hear Te Deum and to see the Pope and cardinals. There were 2 large bands and an immense croud. The music was composed by Signor Mori: Cristofero sung charmingly. The airs were pretty but the chorusses poor stuff – called on Cav. Pirenese found several ancient instruments.

After this went with Mr. Beckford to St. Paul's out of Rome – fuori delle mure. This church is remarkable both for its antiquity; for the richness of its marble columns, and for its size. It was 1st built by Constantin the Great in 324. It is supported by 80 pillars some fluted and some round; 40 of the middle or broad isle (there are 5 isles) are 34 ft. high. These Corinthian pillars were taken from the tomb of Adrian. They have been lately cleaned and are truely magnificent and beautiful. There are few things in Rome which give one a higher idea of ancient grandeur: 24 of parian marble fluted with Corinthian capitals; 16 Cipiline ditto., 28 porphyry, 6 granite – 41 white. As to size this church is 244 ft. long – without reckoning the tribune of the alter – and 140 broad says de la Lande. – Others give it 780 long and 260 broad. Dined with Messrs Beckford, Vyse, Byers, Nevy, Fuseler, Delany etc. After dinner went to see the Pope pass in procession to the Portugese church – afterwards to see the Forbes family – where was music – saw there the church of St Peter illuminated – then to the D. of Dorsets, where was more good music.

TUESDAY 25. Had this morning the honour of being presented by Mr Jenkins to his Eminence Card. Aless. Albani, principal librarian of the Vatican and prefect of the pontifical chapel: was wonderfully well received. He took me by the hand and said *Figlio mio* you shall have what you want but write it down in the form of a memorial etc. – asked if I was English – said he would recommend me to the prelate Apamea Prefetto della Vaticana who knew more about those matters than any body – went from hence to Mr. Jenkins's and drew up the memorial – then went to Mr. Byers's to meet the Abate Elie, *custode* at the Vatican, who has promised to ferrit out all that can be found for my purpose in that library. I am to have a list of books – MSS. music etc and then to chuse what I wish to have copied. After this visited abate Hertford, an Irish fryer and antiquary – who is likewise very musical and a good maker of violins – he has likewise promised to hunt for me. I hope by the time I return from Naples something will be found for my purpose by so many able enquirers. After dinner the abbé Grant made me a long visit, he's going out of town for a month but has promised to think of my business in his absence from Rome. Mr Jenkins called on me at 7 to carry me again to Card. Albani's. We were immediately let in thro' an army of more than 20 servants and found the good cardinal in his night cap with only a canonico with him. Upon presenting to him the memorial he immediately called for his secretary and gave him orders how and to whom it should be directed, during which time he talked freely with us about English views and politicks etc. The secretary soon returned with the memorial sealed up and directed to the prefect of the Vatican. Upon going away I found Mr Jenkins kissed his hand, he held it out to me who offered to do the same, but he would not let me. He seems a wonderfully good natured old man.

From the Cardinals to see the illuminations and hear the music at the Portuguese Church. All Rome is again illuminated, as last night, and in a gallery over the church door in the street was a band of 100 instruments playing as loud as in England formerly at the fire-work music for the last peace but one.* From hence went to St Peter's which was again light up – it was on the outside of the cupola and church that the lights were placed, together with the Vatican palace and colonade.

WEDNESDAY 26. Went early to the post house and in my way back stept into S. Andrea delle Fratri a pretty church, which before the reformation belonged to the Scots. It has nothing in it very remarkable except 2 angels in marble by Bernini. From hence, in my way to Villa Rafaele, stept in to Santa Maria del Popolo. The most remarkable things in it are 2 very elegant organs designed by Bernini and the Assumption in the 1st chapel on the left, by An. Carrach. To the Villa Rafaele I had a monstrous long, hot and dusty walk. It is now occupied by a Mr. Wiseman, a music-master and copyist, who is an Englishman that has been here 19 years. He now speaks broken English like an Italian. The house is large and pleasantly situated in the midst of a garden. There are still some ceilings and other frescoes of Raphael left upon a smooth solid ground made of marble pouder and whites of eggs. There is his mistress on the wall and a fine study of naked men shooting at a target with arrows, in which representation are fine attitudes. There are many charming grotesque paintings too by John de Udine from his designs. Mr. Wiseman often makes concerts here for our noblemen and gentlemen – the late Duke of York made a concert there during his residence at Rome. I went home thro' the Medici Gardens, a shorter way than I came which was out of the gates at the back of them and the old walls of Rome. From hence, with Mr. Leighton to the Marchese Gabriele, but he not being up,

* Handel's Firework Music was performed at the fireworks given in the Green Park, London, on 27th April, 1749, to celebrate the Peace of Aix-la-Chapelle.

en attendant we went to the Palazzo *Farnese*, where we saw the famous *Hercules*–one of the 1st statues in the world. The *Flora* another, which is very much celebrated–but the head, the arms and feet have been but ill restored by Guglielmo della Porta–who succeeded so well in restoring the legs of the above mentioned Hercules, that when the original legs were found Mich. Angello would not have them changed. The antique legs are now in the Borghese magazine– for the fine proportions of this Hercules, the Apollo Belvedere, the Antinous, the Laocoon the Gladiator and Venus de Medicis see the article Design in the Encyclopedie.* The statues and busts here, of a lower class, are innumerable, but that of Caracalla should be distinguished from the croud. In the *Galery*, which contains the finest of all the works of An. Carrach, there were 20 or 30 artists drawing and copying different things which shows the great esteem it is in. The whole ceiling of this gallery was painted in fresco, by An. Carrach– 'tis full of taste, poetry, learning, fine design and fine colouring–I never was more pleased: 'tis as poetical as the Aurora of Guido. 'tis admirably preserved and the whole is in the best taste of antiquity. In the middle is Bacchus and Ariadne–in two triumphal cars, his is gold and drawn by tigers–hers' silver and white deer. Old Silenus on his ass, almost dead drunk, precedes them–the 2 pictures on the sides are Pan offring the wool of his goats to Diana, and Mercury bringing the apple to Paris–this is charming, Mercury flies well and the attitude of Paris is good. There seems a difference between the two natures, and the landscape in the back ground is fine. The two great pictures on the sides are Galatea and the Triton, Cephalis and Aurora and Morpheus sleeping, which is truely charming. At the ends are Polypheme playing on the syrinx† to Galatea and the same monster throwing a huge stone at Acis. There are 4 less pictures–such as Jupiter receiving Juno in the nuptial bed with the cincture of Venus: Diana caressing Endymion: Hercules playing on the tambour de basque [tambourine] or castinets to Iole: and Anchises removing the cestus of Venus. At one end is Andromeda chained to the rock, at a distance Perseus fighting the monster and her family weeping her situation on the shore. And at the other end Perseus petrifying with the head of Medusa, Phineas and his companions. There are little

* *Encyclopédie, ou dictionnaire raisonné des sciences, des arts at des métiers, par une societé de gens de lettres*, edited by Diderot and d'Alembert, was the largest and most important encyclopedia so far undertaken in Europe. The first volume was published in 1751 (Burney was a subscriber) and by 1780 the work had been completed in 35 folio volumes, text, plates and index. Not only does the *Encyclopédie* enshrine the thoughts of the 'revolutionary enlightenment' on scientific, social, philosophical political and economic questions; it preserves exact descriptions of the industrial and craft processes which formed the technology of the age.

† See page 230.

pictures likewise of Apollo and Hyacinth – and Jupiter and Ganimede etc. There are many things painted by Dominichino and An. Carrach together – as well as many other very poetical and charming by Carrach alone. Below, in a small room by itself is the Toro, one of the most famous remains of antiquity. This group of 6 figures bigger than the life, with several others that are less, together with the rock on which they are all supposed to stand, are cut out of one block of marble. The story is Dirce fastened to the horns of a wild bull by her hair, with the figures of the 2 persons that bound her namely Zetus and Amphyon sons of Lycon King of Thebes endeavouring to throw her and the bull into the sea, to revenge Antiope their mother for the injury done to her by the husband of Dirce at her instigation. From hence I had drawings of many curious antique instruments. From hence we returned to the Palace of the Marchese Gabriele who is a notable composer. I there met and heard the famous Mazzanti – put 5 or 6 questions to them about musical history no one of which was answered. This Marchese has £2,000 worth of prints and a number of good pictures together with a fine library. In the afternoon went with Mr. Leighton to the prelate Monsigno Reggio – who is likewise a pretty good composer and performer on the harpsichord and violoncello. He has got 2 or 3 delicate toned harpsichords and a good library. He had with him an old abate belonging to the Vatican with whom I had much talk about ancient music and MSS – it was a concerted thing, our meeting here – then, 1st taking an airing, we went to the D. of Dorset's where was more music.

TIVOLI

THURSDAY 27. Came here in a party of 4. Mr. Grey an Eng. Gent. Le Conte Hegen – and a German Gent. We set out so early I could see nothing till we came within smell of the solfatara or sulphurious lake. With great difficulty we got to it. The water which is white and muddy stinks abominably – it is incrusted over in floating little islands upon which nothing grows but reeds – 'tis called solfatare – Lago di Bagno – Acqua Solfa etc – 'tis warm, but not hot enough to occasion that saming [curdling] ebullition in many parts of the lake. This must be owing to the force with which it rises from the springs below. From hence we saw nothing remarkable till we came to an antique round tower which was erected to the memory of a youth of 9 years old of the family of Plautius. From hence it is not far to the Villa Adriani – which was a celebrated country house of the Emperor Adrian. We walked about here till we were heartily tired and found nothing left entire, but there are ruins of innumerable fine things. A great number of the cento camere are still standing – an amphitheatre is in part left, pillars, capitals, and bases are scattered about and in the rubbish are innumerable pieces of verd' antique [green marble], granite, porphyry, Parian marble etc with which one might load 100 waggons. After mounting the hill at Tivoli the 1st place we stopt at was the Villa d'Estense, built by Card. Hypolitus D'Este, son of Alfonso Ducca di Ferrara, 1542. There are in the house many antique statues and busts and in the gardens, which are famous fountains and water works innumerable, with some ancient Roman buildings. The rooms are painted in fresco by Zuccheri in imitation of Raphael and John de Udine. There is a very fine prospect from the house as far as St Peters, at Rome, which can be seen very plainly here almost 20 miles off. It belongs now to the Venetian State and is sometimes inhabited by the Modenese Ambassadour en villegiature [on holiday]. Tivoli is in a very wild and bold situation, upon the side and summit of a high hill, or hills, for the streets are broken and uneven – but the most beautiful things in it are the temple of Vesta or of Sybele and the Cascade both of which are famous and merit well being seen – as the one is a beautiful work of art in the best time of the Romans quite in the Greek taste, and the other of nature. The temple is round with fluted pillars of the Corinthian order. It is pretty entire except the top, and being placed on the summit of a hill within sight of the cascade and a great part of the town and country has a fine effect. The people here seem all starving and look remarkably wretched and desparate. They have more the appearance of banditti in the streets than the inhabitants of a civilized nation in a large town. The weather was intolerably hot – I never felt so faint and unfit for labour of any kind in my life – and perhaps this will in some measure account for the idleness of the people between Tivoli and Rome – where nature does all their work – they might have 3 crops a year off the ground, but hardly get one. The country is now quite naked, barren and depopulated in all appearance – quite as bad on this as on the other side Rome – everything is burnt up – and neither man or house to be seen for miles, on the road.

ROME

FRIDAY 28. All this morning was spent in the Vatican Library till past 12 – and afterwards till 2 with Signor Santarelli, chief of the Pope's chapel. I had great pleasure and satisfaction in his conversation. He seems to me to think the deepest and with the most taste of any one I have yet conversed with in Italy. He has long been employed in writing an account of the music of the church and particularly of the Popes chapel. He was, unluckily at dinner when I called in my way from the Vatican, but so civil he, met me on the stairs–made many apologies for not having been able to find me, as he had heard my servant had been at his house etc. I stayed with him upwards of 2 hours and shall return in a day or 2, as I find him more enlightened than any one I have yet conversed with.

After dinner Capt. Forbes played the cicerone and accompanied me to the Capitol or Campidoglio, where I saw so many fine remains of antiquity, it is impossible to remember half–tho' I confined myself to the statues only, without seeing the pictures; but first we went to see the famous Tarpeian Rock, just by, which is not so inconsiderable as Bishop Burnet makes it, though now several feet lower than in his time–'tis now, according to Mr Byers's measure 9 ft. and the pavement is raised above the level by the rubbish of ruined buildings 22 ft. The most striking things on mounting the Capitol are the trophies of Marius or Trajan–2 Roman mile stones–No. 1 on the Appia–and another with a brazen globe on it, in which 'tis said are the ashes of Trajan–the 2 sons of Constantine are on the 2nd pedestal: 2 colossal figures of Caster and Pollux, holding each a horse by the bridle–tho' antique the sculpture is not admired. In the front of the senators' palace is a fine figure of Rome, the head is wanting–but the rest is admirable scupture. The architecture, which does not strike me much is from designs of Mich. Angello. In the middle of the square is the finest equestrian statue in bronze of Marcus Aurelius, which has been preserved of ancient sculpture. The horse moves and the emperor speaks. One day when Carlo Maratt was studying these figures–'March, says he, to the horse, do you forget that you're alive?'. I only went into the musæum, or Palazzo de' Conservatore–at the entrance are 2 fine military statues of Julius Cæsar, and Augustus after the Battle of Actium. The feet and hand of the colossian Apollo brought by Lucullus from Pontus–it was 41 ft high so that the great toe is as thick as the body of the Abbe Grant, who is rather corpulent. Urania and Thalia, both with single flutes. The bassirilievi of Marcus Aurelius or Arco di Portogallo which was in the Corso is charming sculpture. The dying gladiator, one of the first statues in the world, finely preserved–Cupid and Psyche standing and kissing each other with innocent fondness his hand delicately supports her chin 'tis charming. Agripina, sedens to the last degree exquisite: such drapery and expression as I never saw in sculpture. Antonius, by some preferred to that at the Belvedere. Upon the walls of the stair-case are incrusted the plans of ancient Rome, found in the church of S. Como and S. Damien in Campo Vaccino.

There are 7 great rooms all filled with antiquities–the gallery–the

miscellanea-then the great hall-the philosophers-the emperors-
that of Hercules-and that of vases. Galery, two children playing with
a lyon, in mosaic, very ancient-a colossal bust of Trajan and a
Ceres-etc. Miscellanea-a faun holding grapes in one hand and a kind
of cross in the other, with fruit in a goats' skin upon the left shoulder.
At his side is a trunk of a tree, to which is hung his siringa*-of 7
pipes-4 of the same length, and 3 ditto shorter-which could only
produce 2 different sounds. There are here several fine busts, as that
of Jupiter Ammon-a youth, unknown-a very beautiful head of
Bacchus etc. Sala grande-Hygia, goddess of health-the falling
gladiator-2 fine centaurs in black marble of which the hips of the
men and shoulders of the horses run into one another by such
insensible degrees that it is impossible to say where they begin or
end-2 pictures in antique mosaic-one with pigeons is very famous.
These were found in the *Villa Adriani,* and prove the art to be very
ancient. Stanza de'Filosofi contains a further collection of illustrious
personages in the sciences and in letters. Zeno a whole figure-the
best busts here, seem to be those of Pythagoras, Virgil, Hiero, Pito-
doris, Aristomachus, and Diogenes. In the Emperours Chamber a
fine Flora-a large Venus, not very beautiful-busts of Caligula with
a look that terrifies one, Messalina, Adrian, Julia daughter of Titus,
Nero, with his rascally look-Sabina, Adrian's wife, dressed like
Ceres-and Faustina, which is charming. Lucius Verus, Commodus
etc. Chamber of Hercules, one Apollo bigger than the life standing,
holding on one side a very large lyre, almost as big as a Welsh harp-
the belly of it placed at the bottom, is equal in length to the strings.
There are two small projections upon it not easy to account for-as the
places to which the strings were supposed to be fastened are plainly
above. With such an instrument as this something might have been
done; it is placed on a griffin. *Stanza del Vaso.* In this room is a
wonderfully fine antique vase, round it an Etruscan basso relievo representing Jupiter, Neptune, Apollo, Vulcain, Mercury, Mars,
Hercules, Diana, Minerva, Juno and 2 women I could not make out.
There are in this room an infinite number of inscriptions which I had
not time to try to read. These are the chief of what I could remember
next day. One ought to go again and again to see so noble a collection
of the finest remains of antiquity collected in a place so celebrated.

At dusk I went to an accademia at Crispi's, who had been to see me
and left a card, as I was out. There was a pretty good band and much
company, among which the Marchese Gabrielle at whose house I had
been a day or two before-several of his things were performed as well
as of Signor Crispi-but neither of them has any originality of style or

* See page 230.

thought. No one sung while I was there but Madame Crispi, who has facility of execution and some taste by dint of practice–but her voice is false and coarse. After the company was gone she and her husband sung some of the Marchese's *Duettini*, and Crispi with a young professor played on 2 harpsichord some sonatas written by the former for one harpsichord accompanied by 2 violins and base–it was caw me, caw thee,* between the two authors. From hence to the D. of Dorset's who made a concert *for me* on purpose that I might hear a girl sing who is much admired at Rome as a promising subject, but by some accident she could not come. However there was a good deal of English company and a very agreeable concert–the Grassetto and Corri sung very well.

29th. SATURDAY. This being a holyday, there was nothing to be done at the Vatican, so I returned visits. Almost all the English here have been to see me, as Messrs Leighton, Gordon, Scot, Forbes, Byers, Jenkins, Trent, Vyse, Beckford, Abate Grant, Abate Hertford, Mr. Rutherford, Mr Morison etc. But 1st I went with a Mr. Wiseman to seek old music–picked up an oratorio by Stradella in the beginning of the last century, and the person of whom I bought it is to carry me to S. Filippo Neri's church on Monday afternoon to try to find there the music of the 1st oratorio that ever was composed. Then, to the church of La Maddalena Frazole to hear one of the best organs and organists of Rome, but was rather disappointed in both. After this I mounted the Antonius pillar from whence is a clear prospect of the greatest part of the city of Rome–'tis 190 steps high, and 8 or 10 in the ground.

In the evening went with Mr. Leighton, by appointment, to Mazzanti's where I had a fine dish of music and saw all his curiosities –he sings in a very rich taste, but has now but a thread of a voice. He has a great collection of Prenestine's† music and has given me leave to have what I will copied. He is famous for singing the poem of Tasso to the same melody as the Baccarolli do at Venice, with infinite taste, accompanying himself with the violin. I got him to write down the melody. He has composed a great deal himself–such as operas, motets, quintets, quartets and trios for violins. He plays the violin himself pretty well, and has the best Steiner I ever saw. Has studied the theory of music very much, has an abridgement of the Modulation of Prenestina very well done.

SUNDAY 30. Went this morning to S. Peters to hear Mass where I staid 2 hours and had a delightful contemplative lounge–from hence to Signor Santarelli, with whom I spent 2 hours more very profitably.

* 'Scratch me, says one, and I'll scratch thee', perhaps.
† The Latin form of the name of Jean Pierluigi de Palestrina was Praenestinus.

He had looked out several very curious things to shew me, among which 2 MS volumes of extracts from curious authors and anecdotes concerning the lives of musicians by himself when young–his own book printed, but not published; El Cerone–for which P. Martini gave 100 Crowns–Osservazioni per regolare il coro pontificao etc del Andrea Adami, which is very curious and useful towards the history of church music–it seems compleat to the year 1711 and Signor Santarelli's book comes up to the present time. This latter is divided into the different centuries since the time of our Saviour–as Secolo 1° 2° 3° etc–and gives all his authorities from ecclesiastical history–'tis in 4to. The former has heads well engraved of the popes and cardinals who have most encouraged and patronised music, and of all the most celebrated maestri di capella and cantatori of the Pope's chapel, beginning with Palestrina. With regard to the famous *Miserere* of Allegri, he says its beauty and effect arise more from the manner in which it is performed than from the composition–there are many stanzas to the same music–and the singers have by tradition certain customs and expressions and graces of convention, which produce great effects–such as swelling and diminishing the notes altogether; accelerating or retarding the measure, singing some stanzas quicker than others con certe expressioni e gruppi etc. There is no organ or other instrument ever used in the chapel. The singers are 32–8 trebles–8 contr'altos–8 tenors and 8 bases. These are all in ordinary–there is likewise a number of *extras* ready to supply the places of those who are sick, absent, and infirm, or dead–so that the number of singers is on common days never less than 32 and on festivals nearly doubled. They are all in a kind of purple uniform.

vide in other journal p 7

Their pay not great–and at present little notice or encouragement is given to subjects of superior merit belonging to this establishment so that music here begins to degenerate and decline very much–not only for the little estimation it is in among the great, but on account of high salaries given to fine voices and singers of great merit in the number of operas throughout Italy and indeed all over Europe. By little and little all those embellishments and refinements of convention as well as the simplicity and purity for which the music of this chapel was so celebrated, will be lost–formerly even the canto fermo of this service was infinitely superior to all others by its purity and refinement.

He says that at the sacking and burning of Rome by the Duke of Bourbon 1527 all the music and memorials of the chapel previous to the time of Godimel, Palestrina's master, were destroyed–which occasions a chasm in the history of church music, not easy to supply.

A frustrated author · Sta. Maria Maggiore

It seems as if Signor Santarelli was prevented from publishing his work which has been printed off ever since 1764 for want of a patron. He is Knight or rather Capellano di Malta, and wears a cross and a small ivory star, but is so sensible of the indignity with which music is treated at present by the first dignitaries of the church, that he has but small hopes of the success of his book, which has been a work of many years and seems well worthy the patronage and protection of his Holiness, for the use of whose servants as well as for the service of music in general it is in a particular manner calculated.

After dinner with Capt. Forbes to see the original of the famous St. Michael of Guido in the church della SS. Concezione de' Frati Cappuccini. This picture is copied in mosaic at St Peters. The angel's face is truely divine and the attitude (tho' some think it rather affected) animated to an amazing degree, tho' the face is feminine. From the print of this my friend Mr Davis of Watlington, Norfolk made a charming picture for his Watlington sign. The angel's dress is blue–the scarf rose-colour and the sandals white. From this church to Dioclesian's baths, out of the remains of which is the large and famous church of the Sta Maria degli Angiole built. This was the great hall of the Thermes* and is a wonderful fine building, full of granite and other rich and beautiful marble pillars: 'tis in other respects the plainest and the least encumbered with ornaments, alters and chapels, of any I have seen. There are many good pictures in it by Dominichini, Vanni, Muziano, Romanelli, Carlo Maratti etc. This church is likewise famous for its meridian by Blanchini in 1701 the most ornamented of any I have seen. The entrance into it is thro' a beautiful rotund in which are 4 niches for tombs and those of Salvator Rosa and of Carlo Maratt are among them, but not worthy of such eminent artists.

From hence to Sta Maria Maggiore one of the largest and most beautiful churches of Rome, and it has its name from being the largest that is dedicated to the Virgin. The inside of the church affords the most noble and majestic prospect that I have ever seen: on each side of the broad isle is a row of Ionic white marble pillars, with Corinthian pillasters over them. The length and height are immense, and it seems calculated for an Egyptian hall of the utmost grandeur and magnificence. The outside front of white stone is fresh and noble. The 2 great arcades of the nave are supported by columns of oriental granite. The chapels are immensely rich, and ornamented with

---

* The thermæ were public buildings founded in, and after, the time of Agrippa (63 B.C.–12 B.C.) which combined warm baths (and cold) with facilities for exercise, especially for the game of ball. In some, there were covered colonnades which offered space for conversation and instruction: theatres and libraries were also incorporated.

[141]

porphyry and oriental marble pillars and paintings by Guido and several great masters. On one side of the church is an Egyptian obelisque 43 ft high, on a pedistal of 22. The Empr. Claudius brought it from Egypt. On the other side is a beautiful pillar of white marble, fluted, and of the Corinthian order, brought from the Temple of Peace.

S. John Lateran – the 1st. church in the Christian world. It is amazingly rich, has 335 columns of the most beautiful marble. Those which support the organ are of Giall' antique [yellow marble], near 30 ft. high. The 2 columns of granite which support the great arch are near 40 ft. high. There is a vast number of statues in niches, ornamented with verd' antique pillars. The pavement too, is curious. The statues are all of white marble, by eminent sculptors, bigger than the life – among 'em are the 12 apostles. There are beautiful bronze and oriental marble pillars to support the great altar, which are said to be brought from Jerusalem. There are in this church many precious relicks the shirts of St Peter and S. Paul, a piece of the True Cross – and of the robe of Christ, tinged with his Blood – the linen with which he wiped the apostles feet at the last Supper – that which covered his face at the last Supper – the robe of the Virgin, with a drop of her milk, etc. The Egyptian obelisk in the front of this church is the largest in Rome – its height is 140 ft. All these obelisks were dug up and erected by Sixtus Quintus – this was found 14 feet under ground in the ruins of the circus. The front of this church is noble, but that of St. Peters – that of Sta Maria Maggiore and this, seem to eyes accustomed to Gothic buildings more like palaces of an enormous size in front, than churches. The Batistiere, just by this church, is a round building richly ornamented, and is said to have been that in which Constantine the first Xtian Emperor was baptised. From hence to S. Filippo Neri or the Chiesa Nuova, where I expected to hear an oratorio, but those of the winter are not yet begun. It was in this church that the oratorio took its rise. – After this, to the English coffee house, where I met near 20 Englishmen, chiefly artists. – Then to the D. of Dorset's concert – he had the girl to sing this evening who was expected on Friday. She has a fine firm voice, and a pretty way of singing; but her shake is very weak and imperfect; and she is moreover a very young musician.

MONDAY 1st OCTOBER. The weather is now as hot as ever I felt it at midsummer, in England; especially in the afternoon – the mornings are cool and pleasant, but there is no stirring without a coach or great fatigue the rest of the day. I have a very stupid disagreeable servant here, who prates me to death – he's my utter aversion – he seems to have no understanding for any one thing except his own interest, and in that he has an instinctive cleverness. He is every moment bringing

rascally people to ⌊sell me bargains and⌋ for the *buona mancia,* who
have never done the least thing for me and have consequently not the
least claim; but he would not take that trouble for *them* even, he's so
lazy, did he not go halves in the plunder. In order to get rid of him, I
was determined to give him 6d a day less than usual and he stood out
yesterday and seemed determined not to stay longer, which I was very
glad of for he knows nothing, and does nothing, except shew me the
way to people's houses. We parted last night and this morning I was
my *own man,* and ventured out by myself, I had to go to the Vatican,
as far as from our house in London [Poland Street] to St. Paul's and I
had never tried to find a street alone, before. However, I set out and
was got about half way thither, when I met a great number of people,
which increased every moment, till at last the street became impass-
ible either in latitude or longitude, and I was quite hemmed in, and
what should come close by me 10 minutes after, but a cart with 2
priests, masqued, and a poor devil in it going to the most disgusting
execution in the world. He had murdered a woman, by throwing her
out of the window, or some such thing, and was to be amazzato,
knocked on the head; to have his throat cut and to have his hands and
feet amputated while he was panting and bleeding. It seemed by the
account I had of it more like another murder, than the execution of
justice. He seemed more dead than alive when I saw him, and will
run in my head a long time–the procession was very solemn. There
were priests on foot of all orders–singing the Service of the Dead in
canto fermo–and the 2 in the cart were Venetian noblemen devoted
by the rules of their order to this dreadful task of attending criminals.
They are called *Confortori.* One held close to his eyes a crucifix while
the other talked to him.

I found my way tolerably well to St. Peters–went in and heard the
service in the Roman chant, and a service in the style of Palestrina,
without the organ. I adored the Transfiguration–the St. Jerome–St
Petronella, and the angel Michael and then, with difficulty made out
the Vatican Library, found there the Abate Elie waiting for me and he
and I were alone there near 4 hours, for it is vacation time–and, but
for the letter which I delivered to day to the Arch Bishop–I could not
be admitted. Most of the morning was lost in hunting after the large
vol. of Provençale Songs No. 59 among the Queen of Sweden's
books* mentioned by Crescembeni; but, unluckily, the books have all
been moved, and the numbers changed since he writ; so that it was

---

* Christina, Queen of Sweden, abdicated in 1654 and a year later settled in Rome
where she died in 1689. Her books passed by succession to the Ottoboni family,
whose head was Pope Alexander VIII and through him 1900 of the Queen's manuscripts were placed in the Vatican Library.

impossible to find it. However, in the search, I found other things – among which a vol. of provençale romances, older than that I wanted, in which the musical notes are only points and accents – it was written in 1188. If Guido was the inventer of the scale, it is plain that it had not reached Provence, or at least had not been adopted there. 2 Greek MS. missals with little marks in red ink form the vocal characters without lines or spaces and are different from the accents which were in black. I found one of the 5th century without any singing characters at all. I read and made extracts from some other MSS. and then found my way back to the castle and over the bridge of S. Angello very well. After dinner I was to have gone to ransack the library or archives at S. Filippo Neri for the 1st oratorios in music, but it was not open to day. So I went to Capt Forbes in hopes of having him for my ciceroni this even, but found he had been ill and blooded. So I staid and drank tea and fiddled with him – heard a person in the same house sing very prettily. Afterwards had a comfortable dish of tea – and then with Mr Nevy, looked over all Santi Bartoli's designs from antique basi relievis for antient instruments. From hence to the D. of Dorset's concert, met a good deal of company there, among which Mr. Leighton, an Abate, Mr. Trent, a French gentleman, Mr. Scot etc. The former brought me a long list of rare books on music which an abate of his acquaintance had found for me in the Barbarini Palace. – My fool is come again – I hate a new face, so that I am not sorry to keep even *his* near me. It is not worth changing for the few days I shall remain here – I now stay for rain only – in going to Naples it will not be quite safe without.

TUESDAY 2. This morning book hunting – after which I had a very long and curious conversation with Signor Santarelli of which I wish to remember every word. It is inconceivable how civil and friendly he is, and how communicative. He shewed all his most curious books and papers – promised me extracts – has found a great many useful and scarce ⌊books, tracts and compositions⌋ for my purpose: such as ⌊Storia Musica di⌋ Bontempis which I have been unable to get all over Italy; all the works of Luca Marcuzio in score; a mass of Morales; motetti of Palestrina etc etc. He has promised to have copied for me the most celebrated compositions of the Popes chapel with some of the canto fermo, as handed down pure from the time of S. Gregory, of which he was so obliging as to sing several parts to let me know the manner of performing it in the service of the chapel and to crown all his civilities, made me a present of a book out of print, absolutely necessary for my purpose, concerning the choir of the pontifical chapel by Andrea Adami. He saw I was eager after the book and gratified my longing in the most polite manner imaginable: *his* copy of this work was the dedication book to Cardinal Ottoboni, and finely bound in morocco and gilt. This author begins at the time of Palestrina and comes down to 1711 – but Signor Santarelli has promised to supply the deficiencies of those two periods from his own notes. He accounted very naturally for the little effect the famous Misereri has, when performed in other places – and told me a story relative to this subject. – The Emperor Leopold a great patron of music and even a good composer himself entreated the Pope to grant him a copy of it – which was granted – but when it came to be performed at Vienna, neither the Emperor nor any one who heard it could believe it to be genuine – upon which his Imperial Majesty sent a complaint to the Pope against the maestro di capella who had sent the copy – His Holiness, quite in a rage would not hear the poor man's defense, but ordered him from his presence and took from him his employment. – However, after some time he got an opportunity of explaining the thing to one of the cardinals – who with great difficulty got the Pope to hear him. His Holiness did not understand music and could hardly comprehend how the same notes could sound so different in two different places. However he desired the maestro di capella to write down his defense, which was admitted and the Emperor desired the Pope to let some of his musicians go to Vienna to instruct the Germans in his chapel how to perform the Miserere – which was likewise granted but a war breaking out at that time with the Turks which called the Emperor from Vienna nothing was done towards perfecting his choir.

In the afternoon a violent thunder storm and showers made it so soon dark I could not see either the Barbarini, or Chigi Palace as I intended. Mr Nevy and I tried to see the Lodovisian, but it was shut up. We walked in the gardens which are laid out in walks and ornamented with antique statues; but all weatherbeaten and spoilt. We saw a little oval church of Bernini's belonging to the Noviciate Jesuits, which is pretty, and went out at the Porta Pia, where the Pope usually walks, and saw the Villa Albani at a distance. This gate was built by Mich. Angello, and has some fine things in it, but was never finished. – From hence to Mrs. Forbes's where I saw a great collection of old music, written by and belonging to Salvator Rosa – she lives in his house and some of his descendants are still alive in it. I saw his satirs in MS by himself and many songs and cantatas written, set and copied by himself.

WEDNESDAY. All this morning at the Vatican hunting the book of Provençale poetry with the notes, which at last was found. It turns out to be more old French than provençal – it is, however, very old and curious. The notes are gregorian – upon 4 and sometimes 5 lines.

No mark for time nor different length of notes. But I have chosen 3 to have copied, with one still more antique in another MSS book. I saw and examined the following numbers: 966, which is a Cronique Francoise in ryme–3062–one of the Q. of Sweden's books with Bourdelot's name in it–*Icy commence le livre du chevalier des dames*–in octave stanzas, in a very old French hand-writing–it seems as if Spencer had seen this book ⌊in his Knight of Dames⌋–No. 1490 and not 59 among the Qu. of Sweden's MSS. was the book I wanted–it is called Cantilene Lingua Gallica antiquæ vulgo' Canciones, desunt initio, paginæ nonnullæ–The MS. by Marchetto di Padua dedicated to il Re Carlo and Roberto of Jerusalem must be old–for I find il Rè Carlo began to reign 1282 and il Re Roberto 1303.–In the Qu. of Sweden's MS. the old songs are more obsolete French poems than provençal–there are some Flemish among them–by Guillaume de Bethune–d'adans li Bocu ou Bossu, d'Arras–Martin le Beque de Cambrai etc–this last is well illumined with a little man in a blue dress playing on a bag-pipe, another in a blue robe with the front of an organ in his hands, like the St. Cecelia of Raphael–2 long pipes and 7 others gradually diminishing in size.–There is a great MS. Folio score of an old oratorio among the books left by Cardinal Ottoboni, but without name or date. No. 3204 is a fine MS. of prose romances– 3205 contains above 50 different provençal poets, among whom one *Richart*, Re d'Inghilterra. No. 3206 small ditto–3209 ditto Fol. etc.–

After dinner went with the Forbes's, Mr. Solley and Nevy to see the Vatican Pallace–the most striking pictures only, I can find time to mention, as I was obliged to see things so quick one upon the other, it is not possible to be minute–and if I did not set down the chief objects I should even forget them, my journey is so like a dream, that the last object effaces all the rest and leaves not a trace behind.– Stanze di Rafaello. A great suite of appartments of which the 4 principal are celebrated by the works of Rafael. These pictures, all in fresco have suffered very much by time–but more by the brutality of the German soldiers belonging to the army of the Constable of Bourbon, who took Rome by assault in 1528, and made guard rooms of these appartments in which as there were no fire-places, they made fires in the middle of the rooms so that the smoke and damp exhaled from the walls have sacriligeously injured these incomparable performances.–The School of Athens has suffered the most–at first one wonders how these works became so celebrated–and asks *Raphael ubi est?* But upon examination he is soon found, in the grandeur and clearness of the design–in the learning–in the elegance–in the beauty–the grace and above all the truth and propriety which reign throughout. Deduct for time–accidents–and ill usage–and he is still in these works the god of painting, and design.–In the Sala di Costantino his chief scholar and assistant, Julio Romano, painted from his designs Constantine haranguing his troops before the battle against Maxentius.–The Cross appears in Heaven carried by two angels–'tis the moment of their saying–*in hoc signo vinces.* The composition is admirable, the figures drawn and arranged with grace, but there is no fascination of colouring left to impose on the spectator.–The second great picture–perhaps the greatest of all, is the famous Battle of Constantine, which it is impossible to admire sufficiently–each figure in this as well as in the next divine work, the School of Athens, should be studied first separately, and then in composition. The figure of Constantine in the former, the old soldier over the body of his dead son–the fright of the half-drowned horses in the Tyber, and the diabolical grin of Maxentius–together with the two single figures of modesty and liberality, painted by Rafael himself, and engraved by Strange, are beyond all praise. In the School of Athens, notwithstanding it is so hurt, there are so many things to admire that one knows not where to begin.–In this picture entirely painted by Raphael himself, there is so much learning, clearness and propriety and the subject moreover so agreeable that in giving way to my own feelings I dont hesitate in pronouncing it the greatest or at least the most agreeable work of this divine master.* The architecture, the disposition and expression of the figures, by which we may know each philosopher and his sect, is astonishing! The pictures of Perugino and of Raphael himself are on the right hand. The Incendio del Borgo is full of expression and natural incidents. In the Miracle of Bolsena Raphael is a fine colourist, or at least 'tis better preserved than the rest –'tis a priest who doubts of the real Presence in the Sacrament, upon which blood appears upon the white wafter.–In St. Peter drawn from prison by an angel–the angel is charming–The Dispute of the Fathers concerning the Sacrament is great–and Mount Parnassus agreeable, except Apollo playing on a modern fiddle, which is little and childish, but in the 1st drawing and print it was a lyre and changed after to a violin in compliment to a famous performer on that instrument in the Pope's service, whose name I am unable to learn. In the picture which is very high over a window, Raphael has introduced the most celebrated Italian poets, and himself, near Homer and Virgil. The 3 muses together, and Sapho all are grace and beauty–

THURSDAY 4. Every morning I have a levée of copyists, booksellers

---

* Burney seems to have felt that the judgement expressed in this sentence was drafted in terms that were too emphatic, for he edited it to: '. . . and the subject so agreeably interesting that in giving way to my own feelings without seeking for professional authority, I should not hesitate in pronouncing (for myself only) that it is the greatest or at least the most pleasing work of this divine master.'

etc, who bring me such stuff! but I am on my guard and pick up curious things now and then. – This morning in a party of 3 I went to St. Sebastian's Church a mile or 2 out of Rome to see the famous catacombs, which but ill rewarded the trouble – then to Capo de Bove or Metellus's Tomb,* which is a little castle S. Angello, walls 3 ft thick – passed by fine ruins of the Roman Emperor's palace – went to the Capitol to see the pictures which are in great numbers and very fine ones – particularly the Ariadne of Guido – St. Cecilia of Romanelli (fiddle 4 strings) Orpheus by Brille, Triumph of Flora in procession Sybil of Guernico, sweet single figure writing – ditto Dominichini, Cleopatra kneeling to Augustus, Guercino – Andrea del Sarto, 3 heads, charming etc –

Afternoon went to the Villa Albani which is new and fitted up with infinite taste – it is full of the most precious remains of antiquity – the house is cleaner than any one I have seen in Italy – the gardens extensive – the semicircle or coffee house elegant and full of fine statues and bassi rilievi, among which some Etruscan where are musical instruments of which Mr Jenkins has promised me drawings – Abbé Wynkleman too has written about 'em. The statues etc which struck me most in the villa are the Antinous in alabaster – Lucota and Child and Minerva in the gallery – Jupiter Sarapis – Etruscan bassi rilievi, vases, etc, etc.

FRIDAY 5. Went to see the Palazzo Doria Pamfili – fitted up and furnished in a modern and elegant manner: the windows all of large looking glass plates, and the mirrours the largest I ever saw. It was here that the great entertainment was made for the Emperor in 1759. In the 3 first rooms are an infinite number of charming landscapes by Claude Lorrain, Poussin – Brille, Annibal Carrach and Dominichini – Gasparo del Sole's angel playing on a 4 stringed fiddle, an old man holding the Book, pretty – Cain and Abel by Salvater Rosa, fine – Madonna and young Jesus 2 single figures by Albano, all beauty. In the gallery another Claude Lorraine, said to be the best he ever painted – Bassan – Gesse – P. Veronese – Geurcino – Magdalen by Vandyke, all good – a charming Guercino – the sweet sleeping Child and Madonna praying over it, in my parlour – Diana and nymphs with Calista's pregnancy discovered, by Albano – fine landscape of Dominichini, with a glowing sky all in a blaze – Romanelli, sweet – a beautiful and affectionate Magdalen by Titian well preserved, and in all the beauty of his best colouring. Nocturnal Concert by Lanfranc – singular – the lights come in white patches from above – a modern fiddle and harpsichord in it –

---

* The words 'Cecilia Metalla's' have been written in over 'Metellus's'. The hand that made the alteration is not necessarily Burney's own.

At 4 this evening Signor Santarelli made me a long visit in which we had an uninterrupted musical conversation which, on his part, was curious, historical, and full of anecdotes. I could wish to remember and write down every word of it, but neither time then nor reminiscence will allow it. We went together to the celebrated painter il Cavalier Battoni, who is always visited by the great: the Emperor Prince of Brunswick, Gr. Duke of Tuscany, arch D. of Austria. Duke of York etc have all been with him and painted by him over and over. He has a very large house and lives in a great way. He received me very politely and conversed a great deal together on the arts. We were then introduced to Madame and the Misses. He has two daughters.* The eldest is a scholar of Signor Santarelli and sings divinely with more grace, taste and expression than any female in public or private I ever heard. She was so obliging as to sing 6 or 8 capital airs in different styles, and all charmingly but her *fort* is the pathetic. She has a good shake and well toned voice an admirable portamento with great compass and high finishing in all she attempts. Indeed she does infinite credit to her master for he has contrived to unite the falset so with the real voice, that 'tis very difficult to say where it begins.

From hence to Signor Crispi's academia and then to the Duke of Dorset's. I had at dinner to day a very agreeable and useful conversation, *al mio proposito* ⌊on my business⌋, with M. Reiffenstein, a man of the 1st taste in the fine arts now at Rome: he enters heartily into my plan, and has promised to think for and of me when he meets with anything to my purpose–and is well informed of the present state of music in Germany–

SAT. 6 Went this morning with Mr. Wiseman and a copyist to the Convent of S. Girolamo della Carità, where S. Filippo Neri lived 33 years, and began his institution *dell' oratorio* with others among whom was Pietro Spadari d'Arezzo (I believe the composer and author of a musical treatise in the Mazzarine Library at Paris). Here, from all Saints Day, till Palm Sunday, upon every feast day are oratorios composed by the 1st rate masters and performed by the best hands and voices in Rome. Over the door of a small chapel up stairs is the following inscription. Primū Beati Philipi Nerii Florentini Oratorium. anno Dñi M.D.LVIII.

In the church I saw Dominichini's famous and charming picture of St. Jerom in his last agonies receiving il santo Viatico, 'tis one of the 1st rate pictures in Rome and perhaps in the world–at St Peters 'tis

---

* This sentence caused Burney a great deal of trouble. It was altered to: 'He received me very politely and was so obliging as to converse with me on the fine arts for a considerable time. We were introduced to [la Signora and the signori . . . deleted] his Lady and two daughters. The eldest is a scholar . . .'

well done in mosaic–but what I came to this church for, was to seek old music and copies of the 1st oratorios. Those of the last century are in great disorder and ⌊the papers⌋ imperfect for the most part. However I brought away 6 or 8 vols. to examine at home with the permission of the prefetto, a sensible and obliging friar–*chemin faisant* I saw a second time the fine Farnese Hercules and Flora.–In an old oratorio of il Cavaliere Alesandro Scarlatti à quattro voci con violini, violetta, ouboe, flauto e tromba, called after the name of all the characters–Maria Vergine, S. Giovanni, Nicodemo ed' Oria, Scarlatti is called Maestro di Capella della Real Capella di Napoli–and in this composition the overture is very much in the catching style of Handel's and Lulli's–there are several accompanied recitatives both with and without ritornellos–which proves that Rinaldo di Capua is not the inventor of them, as is now said and believed by many in Rome.–In the afternoon I went with Celestini to visit il Signor Abate Orsini, a great collector of books on the subject of music as well as of musical compositions. Here I saw some very useful things for my history, particularly a kind of drammaturgia or list of all the operas that have been performed in Rome for above 100 years past; several of these operas he has, printed in score; by which I saw the progress of the drama musicale. In examining these compositions, and those of Scarlatti, Buononcini etc which I saw this morning at S. Girolamo's Convent I see that it would not be difficult to trace all the *melody* of Handel's works. His choruses are longer and more full; but of these the church abounds in 4, 6, 8, 10 & 12 parts for voices. He had the merit of adding to the noise and confusion of so many different parts as many different instruments.* I had great pleasure and satisfaction in this dillettante's library and conversation. *He* is likewise a brother author, having written a history of dancing among the ancients. Hence to Mrs Forbes's, a very sensible and agreeable Scots family, that lives in the same house as Salvator Rosa did, and as his descendants still live–it consists of a mother and 2 daughters one of which paints admirably–and a son in the army with whom I go to Naples.

SUNDAY MORNING. Church hunting for organs and pictures. Of the former no good one: of the latter a fine picture of a taking down from the Cross by Dan. Volterra in the church of Sa Trinità de' Monti–it is a fine composition and full of expression, particularly the group of women on the left hand; but the coloring is a good deal gone. However 'tis reckoned one of the 4 best pictures in Rome which are

---

* This sentence and the preceding one were altered as follows: 'His choruses are longer and more full and spirited; but of ecclesiastic choruses the church abounds in 4, 6, 8, 10 and 12 parts for voices. Handel had the merit of adding to the harmony of so many different vocal parts as many instrumental.'

1. Transfiguration Rafaele, 2. St. Jerome Dominichini, 3. The taking down from the Cross D. Volterra, and 4. St. Romualdo, of Andrea Sacchi. In the little church of St Romualdo the subject is the Saint in the Hermitage, 'tis a fine and pleasing picture. From hence to S. Gregorio Maggiore, in which at the great altar is another picture of Andrea Sacchi–a very pleasing one of Mattoni–in one of the chapels –in the cimeterio a fine picture by Annibal Carrach–and in St. Andrea nel Monte Celio, a little church just by, are the 2 famous concurrent pictures in fresco of Guido and Dominichini–the former seems too red and does not please me so much as the latter, which is charming–especially the little Boy who hides in his mothers' lap part of his face from the sight of the scourging St.

After this I dined with the D. of D. [Duke of Dorset] and then went with his grace to ALBANO. In the way thither saw the Circus of Caracalla, which is very entire. The most striking objects on the road are the remains of aqueducts, ancient sepulchers, etc. On the Via Appia a little before Castel Gondolfo, they shew the place where Milo killed Clodius. The D. took a band of music with him to Mr. Leighton's at Albano whose guests we were, and we had music all the evening, with delightful singing by Bacchelli, commonly called the Mignatrice. She has a very sweet voice with infinite taste–has a good shake, great flexibility, and is more free from affectation of any sort than ever I saw in an Italian singer; but though she sings so admirably, 'tis not her profession, which is that of painting. However, she is much stronger in the former than the latter. She seems a perfect mistress (has learnt 5 years) and embellishes and changes passages better and more at her ease than any female I ever met with. Upon the whole, her singing is not so much in the great style of an Opera Queen as in that which I should wish a lady of fashion or private gentlewoman to be possessed of.

MONDAY 8. This morning with the Duke's valet de chambre to see all the curiosities and beautiful prospects in and about Albano, such as Pompey's tomb and that said to be of the Horatii and Curiatii, some part of an acqueduct very entire in a vineyard just by Albano down a precipiece where a horse could not go–the garden and Lake Nemi at the Capuchins which is charming. Then the famous Lake of Gondolfo close to the Pope's castle or summer residence, with the emissario, or outlet said to be made by the Romans in the time of the Republick at the Seige of Veia, 398 years before J.C. in consequence of an oracle which said that the city could not be taken till the lake was drained. This work extends through the rock under the mountain to the opposite side. It was performed in a year and is still entire–I returned to Albano thro' the beautiful avenue called la Galleria, which is quite arched over with trees, and is a mile long. The air and prospects here are charming. In the evening we all walked out, saw the Pope ride out –and the young noble students at their games. Met here Franchi, the famous composer. At night had music again; and the Mignatrice to sing.

ROME

TUESDAY 9. Arrived here about 12 with the party I went with to Albano. After dinner visited Santarelli, who had been after me 2 or 3 times, and had left a letter to tell me that he had found the 1st oratorio, dell' anima et del corpo of 1600. I had been long in search of this, and found it worth my seeing on account of the preface and instructions to the performers as well as the music. After this went with Corri to the Mignatrice, who sung 2 or 3 songs admirably. Then to the Duke's to hear another cantatrice–but she was a poor business– her singing would be bad among English misses. –Finished the evening at Mrs Forbes's, who has got me for a trifle, the original music book of Salvator Rosa in which the words, and music and writing are his own.

WEDNESDAY 10. I begun this day with the purchase of MSS music to the amount of 8 zechins; then I had a long *Conversatione Tartinesca* with Nicolai about his master Tartini. He likewise has procured me copies of curious things to the amount of 30 pauls. From him to Mr Jenkins's to consult ancient sculptures for drawing of instruments, which he has kindly undertaken to make for me. For the same business I went to Mr. Byers's, where several things were fixt on to my purpose. After this paid Mazzanti's copyist 23 pauls for 2 of the most celebrated masses of Palestrina. After dinner, a long conversation with M. Zink, the famous miniature painter from Vienna about German music and musicians. All the afternoon with Messrs Gordon, Finch, and Scot; at night music at Mrs. Forbes's.

THURSDAY 11. Went out a virtù hunting with Messrs Finch and Scot, saw the Pantheon, Corelli's and Raphael's monuments and several churches; then went to the Chigi palace, but could only see part of it. From hence to the Barbarini Palace, where there is an immense collection of pictures and statues, but all miserably dirty and disorderly–the Palace is now fitting up for the prince's marriage. The great hall ceiling is very beautifully painted by Pietro da Cortona; and on the right hand is a fine copy of the Transfiguration of Raphael, by Julio Romano, for which great sums have been offered by most of the princes in Europe. Prima stanza, or room, carto[o]ns of Pietro da Cortona and Andrea Sacchi, with the Esther and Ahasuerus of Guercino, which Strange has engraved. Colouring a good deal gone. The lyre and plectrum of the Apollo, about which Doni has written

2 folio volumes; the latter modern. A good picture of Mich. Ang., Carravaggio; a statue with a sistrum perfect. Narcissus very fine. 3 old heads and a child by Titian very good. A fine bronze statue of Marcus Aurelius. Meleager and Atalanta charming. Sleeping Pan 7 pipes, perfect; this is the 5th or 6 statue in Rome. Good picture of Leonardo da Vinci, Meleager and deer, good sculpture–2 little Albanos. Death of Germanicus by Poussin, very fine. S. Girolamo by Guido, 2 Bassani, large, Romanelli–concert with large harp and harpsichord –large Bassan, good landscape–Magdal. of Guido inestimable, 1200 guineas have been offered. Rafael's mistress by himself, left hand clumsy, but all the rest divine–this is on cloth–but there is in another room a fine copy by Jul. Romano on board.–Fine Bassan. St Cecilia playing on a large double harp, by Lanfranc. Titians' naked mistress lying down–2 little boys, one p—g in the hands of the other. Pan, with siringa, pipes 3 and 3 etc etc.

Monte Cavallo. Saw this in a great hurry–carto[o]ns for S. Peter's by Carlo Maratti and Pietro da Cortona. Fine S. Mich. Tonans and dragon by the latter. Little chapel alter piece, Salutation of Guido sweet; the ceiling and sides painted by ditto in fresco, fine Rafaellish picture of the holy Family in the Conclave. S. John by Rafael–N.B. this is the 3rd I have seen–1 in the Palais Royal at Paris, 1 at Florence in the Tribuna and this. That at Florence is thought to be the 1st and best. Madonna and Child, very large and fine by Carl Maratt. St Peter by Guido, Madonna and Child beautifully fresh, by Rubens. Charming Guercinos and beautiful Andrea Sacchis. Ascension of Dominichini, charming as usual. Santa Proseda by Poussin with the famous original Santa Petronilla by Guercin, which is in mosaic at St Peter's etc. etc. . . .

After dinner went with Counseller Rieffenstein and Conte ⟨   ⟩ who has been in England with the Prince of Anhault Dessau, and the miniature painter, to the Villa Pamphili about 2 or 3 miles from Rome. We crossed the Tiber in a boat and passed by S. Peter's; here I saw and heard the hydraulic organ.* Many fine prospects. Aqueducts. Fine furniture, and ⌊all kinds of⌋ fine things. In the evening at a charming concert, to which I was invited by the D. of Dorset, there was an excellent German flute player from Saxony, a good tenor singer from Naples, Torelli Veronese, and the Mignatrice. They sung songs and duets most exquisitely, accompanied by Celestini, Corri etc.

FRIDAY MORNING 12. It has rained in the night and the weather is still unsettled. I staid at home writing all the morning: dined with

* It is not clear where Burney heard this organ: nor is it clear what sort of organ it was.

Messrs Gordon and Scot–an English party but had first a long and agreeable conversation with Mr. Morrison, whom I find admirably well informed about antiquities; and tho' no musician, to be depended on for references to classical remains and sculpture that is genuine.–After dinner I went to Crispi's academia which was the best of all those I had heard at his house. I subscribed to his quartettos 2 or 3 of which were played after the company was gone and pleased me much more than his sinfonies which are too furious and noisy for a room or indeed for any other place. He made me a present of his duo, which I heard and liked much the first night I saw him. There was a young man Signor *Ruma*, who played the violin in a very delicate and pleasing manner. From hence to visit Signor Rinaldo di Capua, an old and excellent Neapolitan composer, whose music has often given me great pleasure. He is not in great fashion now, tho' he composed an intermezzo here for the Capranica* last winter which had great success–I found him in person not unlike Mr. Smith the English composer. He is very intelligent and reasonable in conversation. He thinks composers have nothing to do now but to write themselves and others over again, and the only chance they have for obtaining the reputation of novelty and invention must arise either from the ignorance or want of memory in the public–as every thing both in melody and modulation that is worth doing has already been done over and over again.† He confesses that tho' he has written full as much as his neighbours yet out of all his works perhaps not above *one* new melody can be found, and as to modulation it must be always the same to be pleasing. What has not been done is only the refuse of thousands, who have tried and rejected it, either as impracticable or displeasing. The only chance a man has for introducing new modulation in songs is in a short 2nd part in order to fright the hearer back to the first, to which it serves as a foil by making it comparatively beautiful.–I had not my plan to shew him but he's to meet me on Sunday at Mr. Morisons. We not only agreed in the above sentiments, but likewise about the noise and tumult of instruments in modern songs. This conversation was in a coffee house and shortened by the intolerable clamour of 2 disputants who out-Heroded Herod to a stunning degree.–Went with Mr. Solly, ⌊an English traveller with whom I became acquainted at Rome and formed with him a lasting friendship which still subsists⌋ for the rest of the evening to the Forbes's where we had an agreeable *chatation*.–I had a monstrous deal of writing to do, but was unable to

---

* A theatre near the 'Panthéon'. It had six rows of 28 boxes and was not distinguished architecturally. It was used for comedies, opera buffa and similar works.

† Burney inserted a reference sign here which is picked up on the opposite page of the Journal with a statement '⌊Let Haydn, Mozart and Beethoven answer this assertion⌋.'

set about it, for a cold in my left eye, which was so bad I could hardly open it. SAT. 13. With Mr. Byers–Piranesi–Nicolai–Rinaldo di Capua etc–after dinner lounged with Mr. Scot and Capt. Forbes–took my leave of the Pantheon and began to pack and pay.

SUNDAY. All hurry and confusion–just on the point of setting off for Naples. Made several visits and after a d—d squabble about the post chaise of which we were disappointed 20 times, we at length procured a good looking one, and set out at ½ past 4 for Villetri in our way to Naples. It soon grew dark and we could see nothing of the country, but at setting off from the *porta di S. Giovanni*, there seemed but little to regret. The wind was violently high and at the end of the 1st post it began to rain. This was only a single house, called *il tor di mezza via* [Alla Torre]. The next post was Marino, a town which I had seen when I visited the environs of Albano. The 3rd Faiola and the 4th Vellatri. In the morning (MONDAY) which was a very bad one, the first thing we were able to see, was the famous or rather infamous Palus Pontina or marsh of Pontini now called by the Italians Paludi Pontine, which extends more than 30 miles on the left hand of the road, and which has never yet been drained, not withstanding the repeated attempts made both by the ancients and moderns.* It is to this stagnant water and uncultivated land that the mall'aria on this side the Campagna of Rome is attributed and one shudders with horrour at the sight of this bog and the sickly and putrid hue of the inhabitants. I am rather of the opinion of Padri Ximenes and Contatori, in their history of Terracina, that the obstacles must be insurmountable, as the ancients, who were so industrious and who performed such great works in aqueducts, roads and fortifications have failed in this project, and am inclined to think with this last author that the springs and quicksands are so innumerable that the draining of this country is not practicable. The road to Naples lies between this fen, and the Appenine Mountains which are on the left. Here buffalos and black pigs abound–both of the colour and ugliness of the d—l. The towns and posts we stopt at to change horses on this marsh were Cisterna, Sermonetta, Casenuove, Piperno, and Terracina. The woods on the hills by Sermonetta are very pretty–on the right is seen the promontory of Monte Circello [Circeo] where Circe is said to have changed Scylla into a sea monster, and Ulysses' companions into sea-hogs. This country was inhabited by the ancient Volsci and Sezze, then *Setia*, was their capital. Terracina was the Anxur of the ancients and belonged to the Volsci. Here we came to the Mediterranean

* The Pontine Marshes stretched from Velletri (on the right of the road and not as Burney wrote, on the left) south to Terracina and west to the coast. The region was reclaimed during Mussolini's regime.

N.6. *Viaggio da Roma a Napoli*
Sono Poſte 19. Miglia 155.

ROMA

AllaTorre
1¼

Marino

La Faiola

Nemo

VELLETRI

Caſefondate
1¼

Cari
¾

Ciſterna

Sermoneta Bagliano

Sezze

Caſenuove

Piperno

Maruti

S T A T O   D E L L A   C H I E S A

Sea, and travelled near it all the way to Naples, generally on the shore.
It was very windy and the sea foamed and beat against the rocks which
are here very high in a very grand and terrible manner—I never had
seen it so enraged. Here we paid the gabella of 3 pauls to the Pope
and soon after entered the Kingdom of Naples, where the finest road
begins I ever had travelled; it was made 2 years ago for the new Queen
when she came from Vienna. It is smoother than our best turn-pike
roads and in general, covered with excellent gravel. At the town dell'
Epitasio, we were not asked to shew our pasports, but our money: from
hence to Fondi we travelled thro' a grove of myrtles of all sorts, very
beautiful though not now in blossom. The weather cleared up and we
found the air pure and delightful. At Itri a populous town, we were
obliged to stop to have a buckle mended in the harness, and had a mob of
more than 100 miserable looking wretches round us, who eyed us as
curiously as if we had been wild beasts. There were several ruins of
antient buildings, sepucres etc. It grew darkish ere we reached
Mola[-di-Gaeta], a Neapolitan sea port on the Mediterranean, where
we lay. 'Tis a remarkable dear place to strangers; but we escaped for
⅔ of what the landlord asked. We were obliged to go to the custom
house on getting out of the chaise, and underwent a severe visiting of

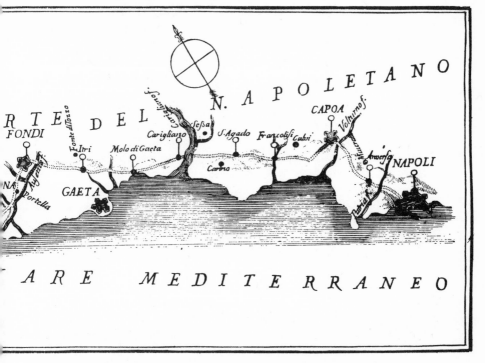

6. Rome to Naples. At Itri the traveller paid a toll on entering the territory of the King of Naples. The River Garigliano was crossed in a ferry boat: the fee was 3 Carlins for every chaise. At Anversa a second toll was paid to the King of Naples. A passport was required for this journey.

our baggage which was all a farce to draw money from us. We paid here in different fees to officers, porters etc of the custom house 12 carlins. In the night there was a dreadful storm of thunder, wind and rain.

TUESDAY 16. We were very glad to get out of this truely cut throat place. The morning was bad, but soon cleared up, and by the time we reached Garigliana, where we crossed the river of the same name in a ferry boat, we began to rally our spirits, and to enjoy the road, which was delightful, and the air which was refreshing and pure. This river which had 3 fine names among the ancients, Clanius, Glamius, and Liris, is now as much a puddle as the Tyber, and tho' much swelled by the late rains, very inconsiderable. Horace speaks of it very poetically –

Rura quæ Liris qüieta
Mordât aquâ Taciturnus amnis. L 1. Od.31*

* 'Nor lands, where Liris' waters stray
And – silent – eat their banks away'
John Sherwin, 1843.

From hence to Sant' Agata [Agado], which is only a single house at the corner of the road that goes to Sezza which seems a pretty large town and looks very pretty from the road. The country from Sant' Agata to Francolisi and to Capua, at this time of the year, looks very brown and unpleasing to the eye, except when there are trees and vinyards: but rich as the soil, and mild as the climate is, much ground lies waste and uncultivated tho' so near the capital of a kingdom which has one of the finest seaports in the universe. Capua is now but an ordinary town but has a good bridge over the Volturno, and is well paved with lava cut in large squares, but I suppose both the bridge and pavement were repaired when the new road was made for the Queen, as M. de la Lande complains of both. This is not the ancient Capua which detained Hanibal with its attractions when he should have pursued his victory at Cannæ by marching on to Rome–the ruins of the ancient Capua are still to be seen 2 miles off the modern. The country round the old city was always mentioned by the ancients as the finest and most delightful in all Italy. In the cathedral of the new Capua is a very fine figure of our Saviour in the tomb, which is very much admired. Our pass was again examined at Capua, which detained us just long enough to see the church. To the person who brought us our pass, a fee of 2 or 3 carlins was necessary; but we did not think it quite so, to give money to the soldiers who came with him, merely to fleece us if they could.–From Capua to *Aversa*, the next post, is a rich country full of vinyards, with more houses in sight than is usual in Italy. Here the road was new covering with cingle [shingle] and gravel, which after the rain, rendered the sides very disagreeable, otherwise, from Fondi to Naples there may be said to be the finest road in Europe. All the way from Capua are high trees, up which the vines run, which are now loaded with grapes. The people are just beginning the vintage. From Aversa till within about a mile of Naples, the country is flat, but the richest that can be imagined, truely abounding with corn, wine and oil; all which are produced by the same land, at the same time. The trees up which the vines run are usually mulberry, which are so stript early in the summer by the silkworms, as to be ready to receive the vines without shading them from the sun or otherwise embarrassing them.–Within about a mile of Naples hills appear on each side, covered with olives, vines and houses, which afford a rich and most beautiful appearance. Ere we got to the gates we were stopt twice by custom officers merely to extort money from us, for they refused to examine our baggage. There is more of this scandalous open robbery alowit in the Kingdom of Naples, than anywhere else in Italy; it is tormenting strangers and disgusting them, without either use to the public or government–

NAPLES

The entrance into Naples is through a fine fauxbourg of which the streets are very wide, well built and well paved with lava. It is amazingly populous and has the air of bustle and business beyond even London or Paris. We went to the house of Luigi d'Arc, a Frenchman, to whom we had been directed by several who spoke well of it. I was met by a valet de place or servo di piazza, who had been thoroughly recommended to me by a gentleman at Rome his name Battista. We arrived about 5 o'clock and at night went to the Teatro de Fiorentini, to hear the comic opera of Gelosia per Gelosia set to music by Piccini. This theatre is as small as Mr. Foote's in the Haymarket,* but higher, as there are 5 rows of boxes in it.† Notwithstanding the court was at Portici and a great number of families at their *villeggiaturas* or country houses, so great is the reputation of Signor Piccini that every part of the house was crowded, and indeed this opera had nothing else to support it, as both the drama and singing were bad. There was however a comic character performed by Signor *Casaccia* a man of infinite humour. The whole house was in a roar the moment he appeared and the airs were full of pretty passages and in general most ingeniously accompanied. There was no dancing, so that the acts of which there were 3 seemed long.

WEDNESDAY 17. This morning Capt Forbes and I had a coach between us at 16 carlins a day and 2 la mancia. Thus far we have been perfectly of one mind: if anything he is too *facile* on the road, and rather than dispute with the rascally inn-keepers he would pay pauls instead of pence. But they always expect to be bated down and ask accordingly.

We went first to our minister's Mr. Hamilton, who, unluckily, is out of town, where he continues till the 3rd of next month. Our next visit was to Mr Jamineau the British Consul. There we were let in and extreamly well received. I had a letter from Mr. Beckford to him, and moreover soon put him in mind of an old acquaintance with him in England at Mr. Greville's. He is very well bred and rational. He entered much into my undertaking and has promised all the assistance in his power. We are invited to dine with him on Saturday. His

* The first small Haymarket Theatre was built in 1720; it was rebuilt in 1747 when it was taken over by Samuel Foote, actor, dramatist and superb mimic. He made the theatre prosperous and in 1776 sold it to George Colman: it remained in use until 1820, when it was demolished and the present Haymarket Theatre, designed by Nash, was built a little to the south of the site of the old theatre. It was opened in 1821.

† De La Lande, *Voyage* (3rd edition, vol. 5, p. 447), says the theatre had four rows of boxes, with 15 in each.

house is finely situated on the bay, full in view of Mount Vesuvius, which is every day expected to make an eruption of lava. It has thrown up fire for several days past. I wish very much for the eruption to begin before my departure from Naples.* To Dr Cirillo and to Padre *della Torre*, but both were out, then to booksellers. After dinner to music at the Franciscan's church–where the 3 conservatorios were to furnish music and musicians for a great festival of 8 successive days, morning and evening: 'tis a large handsome church, but too much ornamented. The architecture seems good, but it is so begilt that it almost blinds one to look at it, and in the few interstitial parts where there is no gold laid on there are tawdry flowers painted in abundance.

The band was very numerous, consisting of above 100 voices and instruments, in a long occasional gallery totally covered with gold and silver gilding. Tho' the band seemed a very good one, and the leader very careful and attentive, yet by its great length it was impossible the performers could be always together. The composition which in many movements was admirable, was by Signor Gennaro Manni, who beat the time. The opening was in a rough Handelian style, after which, this species of overture was made an accompaniment to a chorus which was well written. Then several airs and a duet succeeded which pleased me infinitely. There was fancy, contrivance and light and shade, and tho' the singing was not of the first sort yet there were a counter-tenor and a base voice which pleased me much–the former was one of the most powerful I ever heard–it made its way through the whole band in the loudest and most tumultuous parts of the chorusses. When he had an air to sing alone, his shake was good and his style plain, but his *portamento* a little deficient: rather savouring of what we call, in England, the cathedral manner of singing thro' the throat.–The air which was given to the base was as ingeniously written as any one I ever heard. The accompaniments full without destroying the melody of the the voice part. Instead of shortening or mutilating its passages, the instruments seemed to continue and finish them in giving the singer time for respiration. In a duet between two sopranos the accompaniments were likewise admirable, as they were in a chorus in which were many solo parts.–After this the author did not seem so happy–there were some trifling and some heavy movements in which there was no other novelty than in throwing the accent upon the wrong note, for instance, upon the 2nd instead of the first or, in common time, upon the 3rd instead of the 4th. This even may have its merit in comic operas where some humour is seconded by it, but surely such a poor expedient is beneath the dignity of church music where a gravity and decency of style should be pre-

* ⌊The natives, like Esop's frogs, might say "tis sport to you, but death to us.'⌋

served even in rapid movements, but the same rage for novelty which has occasioned such sudden revolutions in the music of Italy, gives birth, some times to strange monsters.

From hence we went to the Mole, which is wonderfully beautiful, being enriched with a fine prospect of the city a view of the whole Nepolitan navy, consisting of galleys, men of war, 4 in number and merchantmen. There was likewise riding at anchor a 36 gun French frigate and a 70 gun Spanish man of war. One sees here, likewise, Portici and Mount Vesuvius, which seem near the sea but are a mile or 2 distant: and there is likewise an unbounded prospect of the Mediterranean. On the landside appears the palace on Capo di Monte, which is the highest hill in sight towards the north. From hence we went a catalogue hunting to booksellers, but without success. The streets are, in general, strait and wide, and there are many open places not made out into direct squares like those in London but well paved, well built and full of people, which to me have a better look than ponds, trees, or gardens –

THURSDAY 18th. This morning we were visited by Dr Cirillo in consequence of the having yesterday left our names and direction at his house. He speaks better English than any foreigner I have ever conversed with, and is an agreeable man. He undertook to make several enquiries for me and to procure some of the Neapolitan national music, which is quite singular being totally different both in melody and modulation from all I have heard. Last night in the street there were 2 people singing alternately one of these conzoni, accompanied by a violin and *calascione*. The singing is noisy and vulgar, but the accompaniments were admirable, and well performed. The fiddle and calascione part was incessantly going during the song part as well as the ritornells. The modulation surprised me very much: from the key of A♮ to that of C and F was not difficult or new – but from that of A♯ to E♭ was astonishing, and this was done without offending the ear, and the return to the original key so insensibly managed as neither to shock the ear or for it to be easily discovered by what road or relations it was done.

My first visit this morning was to Signor Piccini, and it was long. I found him dressed ready to go out. He seems to live in a good way; he has a good house and many servants and attendants about him. He has a son studying at the university of Padua. He is about 4 or 5 and 40 – looks well, and is a lively agreeable little man, rather grave for an Italian so full of fire and genius. I first of all presented him with Signor Giardini's letter, which he read and told me he should be extreamly glad if he could be of any use to me or my work – I then communicated to him Mr Hobart's proposal for coming into England, with Mr Wyseman his agent's letter, and an article to sign, in case he approved of the terms proposed; but he by no means comes into them. The offer was £400 for 8 months – during which he was to compose 3 new operas and to arrange and patch up pasticcios. In the 1st place he said he would by no means be plagued with these pasticcios which would take up all his leisure time and produce him neither honour nor profit; that the 1st proposal was for *two* new operas – that he asked to have the printing of his own opera songs by which Guarducci had told him much was to be gotten. I explained this matter to him and told him that Signor Guarducci had not been long enough in England to know how short lived opera songs were; that the last new opera made the preceeding soon forgotten; that only the *favourite* songs were printed and that for a small price, which nothing but the number sent to the shops and abroad by a dealer in music could make it worth while to publish; that when once in England, his name was so well known and his compositions in such high favour he might do what he would and enact new laws of publication; that he would find protection every where, and might employ his leisure hours either in teaching at a very high price ladies of great quality, or in compositions for instruments, which would turn to good account. In answer to this he said he could get £400 by only 2 operas in Italy – without the expence or risk of going so far as England; that he would not undertake so long a journey for less than £800 sterling, that the proposal was made only for one year; that the expence of going to and coming from England would make a considerable hole in the 400 proposed, if he travelled at his ease, which he had been accustomed to; that he had often travelled and found it necessary to have the hand always in the purse (*sempre la mano in borsa*) etc; that though the printing his songs should produce but small profit, yet whatever it *was*, he thought it belonged to him more than to any one else. I told him no one could be so good a judge of his affairs as himself; that I would not attempt to persuade him to do what he thought contrary to his interest and inclination. I could only say that he was certain of a very good reception from the public as well as individuals of my country who were all prejudiced in his favour by the great pleasure they had already received from his compositions. He said the offer might be a good one to a young man not known or established here; but to him who always knew how to employ his time to advantage it was no kind of temptation.

He then of himself *ex mero motu*, returned to *my affair*, and repeated his desire to be of some use to it. I then asked him the following particulars concerning the conservatorios –

1. The antiquity of the establishments. 2. Their number and names. 3. The number of masters and scholars. 4. The time of admission and quitting etc.

IN THE GARDENS OF THE VILLA PAMPHILI, ROME

THE GROTTO
OF POSILIPIO

As to the 1st article they are of ancient standing he says, as may be seen by one of the buildings which is ready to tumble down. 2. They are in number 3 viz. La Pietà, Santa Maria di Loretto and S. Onofrio. 3. The number of scholars in the first is 120; in the 2nd 200; and in the last about 90. There are to each 2 principal maestri di capella: the 1st superintends and corrects the compositions of the students, the 2nd the singing, and gives lessons. There are assistant masters which are called maestri secolari – 1 for the violin, 1 for the violoncello, 1 for the harpsichord, 1 for the oboe and 1 for the French horn etc. 4. Boys are admitted from 8 or 10 to 20 years of age – when taken in young they are bound for 8 years; but when more advanced it is difficult to get in unless they are already far advanced in the study and practice of music. After having been in for some years if no genius is discovered, they are dismissed to make way for others. Some are taken in as pensioners who pay for their teaching, and others, after having serv'd their time out, are retained to teach the rest, but in both these cases they are allowed to go out of the conservatorio at their pleasure. He says there is a register of both masters and scholars in each conservatorio.

Mr Jamineau and Dr Cirillo both say that it is absolutely forbidden to castrate boys in these music schools – that they chiefly come from Leccia in Puglia, but are first tried here or elsewhere as to the likelihood of voice and then taken out by their parents to be cut*: but this is even forbidden under severe penalties unless with the consent of the boy, and there are instances of its being done even at the request of the boys themselves, as was the case of the detto il Grassetto at Rome.* But as to these previous trials of the voice, it is my opinion that this cruel operation is but too frequently performed without trial or at least without sufficient proofs of a dawning and improvable

** This passage was revised to read '. . . by their parents for this barbarous purpose, but it is death by the laws to those who perform the operation and excommunication to all concerned in it, unless it be done, as is often pretended, on account of some disorders which may be supposed to require it and with the consent of the boy. . . .'

Three methods of performing the operation were traditionally available. In the first the child was bathed in warm water and decoctions of plants and the testicles were pressed and bruised with the fingers so as to break them down and so prevent their further growth. No cutting of the skin was necessary. A second made the testicles 'so frigid as at last quite to disappear and vanish, this is done by cutting the Vein that conveyed their proper Aliment and Support, which makes them grow lank and flabby, till at last they actually dry up and come to nothing. Another Method was, to take the Testicles quite away at once, and this operation was commonly effected, by putting the Patient into a Bath of warm Water . . . some small time after they pressed the Jugular Veins, which made the Party so stupid and insensible, that he fell into a kind of Apoplexy, and then the Action could be performed with scarce any Pain at all to the Patient.' *Eunuchism Display'd*, a translation by Robert Samber (1718) from *Traité des Eunuchs* by Charles Ancillon (1707).

voice–otherwise there could never be found such numbers of them in every great town throughout Italy without any voice at all–or at least without one sufficient to compensate for the loss.* Indeed all the *musici* in the churches at present are made up of the refuse of the opera houses, and it is a very rare thing to meet with a tolerable voice upon the establishment of any church in Italy.† The virtuosi who sing in the churches occasionally on festivals only, are usually strangers paid by the time.——

From Piccini I went to Jomelli's, but he was out of town–from thence to Signor Merula, who was sick in bed–then to Lord Fortrose's, who was at Pompeja——

After dinner to the Franciscan's church again where there was a larger band than the day before, the whole conservatorio of the Pietà consisting of 120 all dressed in a blue uniform attended. The *sinfonia* was just begun when I arrived, it was very brilliant and well executed–then followed a pretty good chorus–after which an air by a tenor voice, 1 by a soprano, 1 by a base, 1 by a contr'alto and another by a different tenor, but worse singing I never heard before in Italy: all was unfinished and scholar-like the closes stiff, studied and ill-executed; and nothing like a shake could be mustered out of the whole band of singers. The soprano forced the high notes in a false direction till they went to ones brain and the base singer was as rough as a mastif, whose barking he seemed to imitate. A solo concerto on the bassoon too in the same incorrect and unmasterly manner, drove me out of the church ere the whole vespers were finished.

From hence I went directly to the opera, which to night was at the *Teatro Nuovo*. This house is less than the *Fiorentini*, is older, and more dirty. The entrance to it for carriages is thro' very narrow streets and very inconvenient. This burletta was called *Le Trame per amore*– and set by *Signor Giovanni Paesiello, Maetro di Capella Napoletano.* The singing was but indifferent. There were 9 characters in the piece and yet not one good voice among them. However, the music pleased me very much. It was full of fire and fancy. The ritornels abounding in new passages, and the voice parts with elegant and simple melodies such as might be remembered and carried away after the first hearing or be performed in private with a small band or even without any other instrument than a harpsichord. The overture, of

---

* According to Samber 'when they used to cut children in their most tender Infancy, there were 200 Eunuchs made, which proved to be good for nothing': the children were thus made doubly miserable, they were maimed in body and their voice was good for nothing 'and it is certain, nothing in *Italy* is so contemptible as a Eunuch that cannot sing'.

† '. . . any church ⌊throughout Italy which confirms what Santarelli had told me at Rome⌋'.

one movement only was quite comic, and contained a perpetual succession of pleasant passages. There was no dancing which made it necessary to spin the acts out to a rather tiresome length. The airs were very much applauded tho' it was the 14th representation of the opera. The author is engaged to compose for Turin at next carnaval, to which place he is soon to set out. The performance began about a quarter before 8 and continued till past 11 –

FRIDAY 19. It rained all the morning, so furiously and incessantly that I could not find in my heart to take out servant or horses. In the evening I went again to St Francesco's Church and heard the performance of the scholars of another conservatorio, namely *Santa Maria di Loreto*. They appeared all in a white uniform with a black kind of sash. The singing was a little better, but the instruments hardly so good. The 1st air, after a smart *sinfonia* and chorus, was sung by an inoffensive tenor–then another by a soprano not quite so, after which a 3rd air by a base voice, the direct contrary of inoffensive, such a bawling stentor with a throat so inflexible sure never was heard before. The divisions* were so rough and so strongly marked they became quite grotesk. If it had not been for the serious effect his performance had on the the melancholy audience no one could possibly have supposed it to be serious–a solo on the coarsest double base that ever was played on would have been soft music to it. After him a midling counter tenor which so strong a foil could not make one relish–and then another soprano by not at all a hopeless subject, his voice was well toned and he had a little improvable shake–in short this was the only promising singer I had heard for two days. But to the poor voices, there is such a slovenly, ignorant and unfinished manner to be added that they sung the people out of church as fast as they came in. There was a young man who played solo parts in the ritenellos with a kind of clarinet which they call here a vox humana, another on the trumpet, and a 3rd on the hautbois, but in an incorrect and uninteresting manner. The boys who sung had very poor cadences to their songs, which after the 2nd parts returned to the first and these were always repeated after the da capo.† At night when the rain had quite ceased Mount Vesuvius burst out violently.

SATURDAY 20. This morning I heard at the same church the boys of the 3rd conservatorio, namely of S. *Onofrio*–these have a white uniform. The performance was much about the same speed as that of the other two.–These celebrated seminaries which have heretofore

---

* Passages in which there is a rapid succession of consecutive notes in runs.

† This sentence was clarified in *Tour* 1773: 'The boys who sung had very poor cadences to their songs, which, as they normally had second parts, were always repeated in the *da capo*.' Presumably repeated from the beginning without change or embellishment.

produced so many great professors, seem at present but low in genius, but perhaps these institutions like others are subject to fluctuations, and after some time like their neighbour Mount Vesuvius they will blaze again with new vigour. Dined to day with our consul Mr. Jamineau who is very intelligent polite and friendly. At night such a deluge of rain we were glad to get home as fast as possible, where all the amusement we had besides writing, was to go upon the leads to see the fireworks of Mount Vesuvius.*

SUNDAY 21. The conservatorio of S. Onofrio consists of about 100 scholars who are taken in from 8 years old to 20–the costs to the children's friends for the first years is considerable but for the last nothing, as they are able to teach others. I find in the Notizie di Napoli published in 1690 mention made of the seminario di S. Onofrio, as an old establishment then see p 148–'Questo principio da una Miseria grande accaduta nella Nostra Città, per la quale molti poveri ragazzi, andavano dispersi Sens' ajuto alcuno. Quivi s'allevano col santo Timor di Dio, e si fanno attendere alle Lettere, ed alle Musica, nella quale riescono molti buoni soggetti'.† The principal director or governor of this foundation is the 1st magistrate of the city of Naples, and it seems originally to have been well endowed as all the houses in that quarter have the image of S. Onofrio painted on them, which proves them to have belonged to it, but these estates have been all dissipated and at present the boys maintain themselves and the house by their own labour, by being let out for academias or concerts.

This morning set out with a large party on foot to see La Grotta di Posolipo [Posillipo]–or Pausilepase [Pausilippo] subterranean grotto; 'tis full ½ a mile long, 50 feet high and about 20 wide. Upon the top of the mountain on the left hand at the entrance of this grotto, is Virgil's tomb. We passed thro' this grotto, which is cut out of the solid rock, to Lago d'Agnano. The country after coming out of the grotto is amazingly rich and beautiful; 'tis in the form of an extensive amphitheatre and covered with vines, figs and olives, among which there had been corn. 'Tis about a mile from the grotto to the Lake Agnano. In the way thither is an ancient tomb, which was repaired and beautified by Philip the 2nd. The malaria in summer rages more about this lake than elsewhere in the Neapolitan state: 'tis about a

---

* The passage from 'Sunday 21' . . . to 'academias or concerts' appears between square brackets in the Journal. Burney explains why in an editorial note: '[The following period within the Hooks for Introduction to the account of Conservatorios. p. 92]', (a reference to some other material).

† 'This had its beginning in the great poverty which occurred in our city as a result of which many poor children would have been wasted without help from any one. There they grew up in holy fear of God, studied literature and music in which many good people did well.'

mile round–and now belongs to the king. It did belong to the Jesuits. There is an infinite number of ducks and teal upon it; the sea formerly used to come in here, but at present 'tis fresh. On the side of this lake. next Naples, are the Sudatorj di S. Germano; a chamber built upon a place whence arise out of the earth extream hot sulphurous vapours, and the Grotto de' Cani in which a dog being held to the ground in about a minute becomes totally senseless, and in appearance dead, but being taken into the air recovers in about 2 minutes, but if held any longer time than is sufficient to occasion this temporary suffocation he will never recover.* From hence on the left hand of the lake we mounted or rather clambered up the Monte Secco thro' a narrow way to the Solfatara, which is a plain about a mile round, and seems plainly the ruin and remains of an ancient volcano: 'tis still burning in several places, and in one is so furiously hot as to hiss and made a violent noise like that of a great fire when water is poured on it. At its mouth there is genuine salammoniac, cinaber and sulphur–a piece of iron sweats in it immediately in large drops of water. Here are alum pits–and much genuine flower of brimstone is found about the mountain–some places are so hot as to burn one's feet. There is likewise here a boiling spring. It seems hollow underneath, by the noise it makes when a heavy stone is thrown on it with violence.– Between this and Puzzuoli we saw the ruins of an amphitheatre, with some of the most beautiful and perfect ancient Roman brick-work I ever saw–and several temples, but so ruined 'tis not possible to guess at their original forms. Puzzuoli is an ancient sea port and now very populous. Here we got some bread, cheese and wine with which we were refreshed a little after the greatest fatigue I ever felt. After this delicious repast we saw in very good humour the ruins of the temple of *Jupiter Serapis* which are exceedingly beautiful. There are still standing 3 noble fluted Corinthian pillars, and many broken ones lying about–bases, capitals etc. The form of the temple was a square, and the great alter in the middle round. The statues and best sculpture are carried to Portici; but there still remain sufficient to make it the most noble reste of antiquity I have seen out of Rome. Enough subsists to show the form of the temple and of the great alter. The floor is of very large oblong squares of marble, and every thing points out a building of the highest taste and magnificence.–Near this temple is the *Monte Nuovo*, which was thrown up in a sudden eruption during one night only in 1538. Puzzuoli was famous for *intaglios*. Here are

* 'This experiment is repeated for the amusement of every unfeeling person, who has half a crown in his pocket, and affects a turn for natural philosophy. . . . The fellows who attend at this cave have always some miserable dogs, with ropes about their necks, ready for this cruel purpose.' Dr. John Moore, *A View of Society and Manners in Italy* (1781).

the ruins of Caligula's bridge to Baia. The sailors and children offer to strangers little seals and bits of porphyry, agate, lapis lazula etc which they have picked up in diving under water. – Contrary to all my expectation we got caleshes here to carry us to Naples for 6 carlins each – 3 apiece, not 18d English – 'tis 7 or 8 miles. It was a very rainy evening, and all were dog tired.

MONDAY 22. This morning the same party set off at 8 o'clock in caleshes to Pompej – we had to go from Santa Lucea and we carried thro' the whole semi-circle of the city which is by far the most busy and populous of all Italy. We met an incredible number of these calashes, which run with amazing rapidity. They have but one small horse, but are so light that they seem to fly with them. They are not wider at bottom, tho' they carry 2 persons than a fine lady's waist in old fashioned times. One of the riders or rather passengers holds the reins, but is wholly under the direction of the master of the carriage who is in fact the driver tho' he rides behind – for he will on no account part with the whip. They cost about 10 or 12 carlins a day. We passed thro' Portici and bespoke our dinners – stopt at the Carmelites to see the place in their church thro' which the lava passed in the irruption of Mount Vesuvius in 1737, and thro' their gardens, and at Torre del Greco just by is still seen an immense quantity of lava left there in this eruption tho' much has been carried away to pave Naples and the publick roads and towns in its environs. In 1760 another eruption crossed the great road to Pompej and Salerno, and ran almost to the sea. The remains of this eruption seem like black cinders and are spread over a great deal of fine land on the left hand of the road. One never loses sight of Vesuvius all the way to Pompej. We called at Mr. Hamilton's country house just opposite to it, but he was rode out: however we met him a mile or 2 further and I delivered him my letters and a copy of my plan. – The country is covered with vines and other fruit trees all the way to Pompej – which is itself in a vineyard covered with vines that were then loaded with ripe fruit of which we all eat our fill. The entrance into the city has been dug out entire.* A burying ground has been discovered – and at the entrance an osteria or inn – a whole street with its ancient pavement is made out very entire. There is a place a part for foot passengers on each side like those in the streets of London, but narrower: a portico too runs along the houses. Several shops are distinguishable particularly a colour shop, well painted in fresco, with the god Mercury as the protector of trade. The rooms of the houses are small but the floors very beautiful in mosaic – and the walls painted in general with great taste in fresco on a cement which has the smoothness and hardness of marble, which has been

* Systematic excavation of Pompeii was started in 1763.

the means of these paintings being so well preserved; the best are carried to Portici as are the statues, busts etc. However all is kept open here, and they go on digging without filling up as at Herculanum and else where—the king allows but 2000 ducats a year to this great work. It is more than a mile and ½ in length.

We walked to the further end thro' the vinyard—here we found a temple with the alter-pillars and rooms round it for the priests still standing, then a gentleman's house with the several appartments entire, in one of which were found the bones of 14 or 16 persons all entire—it is supposed, and naturally, that the family driven from one place to another by the eruption and fire, at length assembled in the room of the master or mistress of the house and there all perished together. All the offices of this house can be made out. The entire skeleton of a woman still remains in the attitude she died in, sitting by the side of a large boiler or copper below stairs—several utensils are entire. From hence to a theatre which is not quite dug out but seems pretty entire—the streets leading to it are beautifully so—with rows of columns well preserved. The guard room for the soldiers, with an immense number of human bones was distinguishable—as was a prison with the bones of people in irons. In short this city, stript as it is of all its best remains, which are carried to Portici, afforded me more pleasure than any antiquities I ever saw. It was destroyed in the year 79, on the same day as Herculanum, which we went to next. It is about 14 or 15 miles from Naples to Pompej.

Herculanum is a subterranean city in Portici on the side next the sea. Nothing is now left open of all that has been discovered but the theatre.* It is from 70 to 100 ft. below the level of the road, and all this depth is lava—Pompej was covered with ashes, cinders and pumice stone and is not many feet lower than the level of the fields and road. But Herculanum was deluged with liquid fire, which had come from Vesuvius and had raised all the ground from thence to the sea side near 100 feet—it is much more difficult to dig in the latter than the former. After the fine things I had seen at Pompej in open day light I was much disappointed in descending with flambeaux into Herculaneum—nothing but bear walls and the meer out line of the theatre are left. It is stript of every thing which one has heard and read so much about—so that except the the satisfaction of knowing there is *nothing* either to see or to languish after, and for which one might accuse one's self of neglect for not seeking, and the vain glory of saying

* In 1719 Prince Elbeuf discovered the site of Herculaneum by accident when looking for marble to go into a villa he was building at Portici. Excavations led to the discovery of superb statues in marble and bronze. The site is built over by the modern town of Resina, and systematic excavation has not been possible.

one has been in Herculanum, it is I believe a much less entertaining descent than into a coal pit in one's own country.

We dined very well at Portici for 4 carlins each and drove home most furiously thro' a high wind and violent rain and finished the evening by going to the Teatro Nuovo for the 2nd time to hear Paisiello's opera, where it pleased me full as much now as before and in the same places. The overture is full of comic and original passages, the airs are very pleasing and far from common.* If he has any fault 'tis in repeating passages too often even to 5 and 6 times, which is like driving a nail into a plaistered wall–the 1st 2 or 3 strokes fix it better than more–for after that number it either grows loose or recoils–thus an energy is often given by reiterated strokes on the tympanum, but too often repeated they cease to make an impression and seem to obliterate those already given. I still think this opera too long for want of the intermezzi of dancing. –

TUESDAY 23. Did not stir out the whole day–had the rheumatism in my right shoulder and a cold or stye in my left eye. I tried to cure both with writing. In the afternoon I had a very obliging letter from Mr. Hamilton not only with an invite to dine at his house at Villa Angelica, but likewise to remain there some days. And at night hearing in the street some genuine Neapolitan† singing, accompanied by a calascioncina, a mandaline and a violin, I sent for the whole band up stairs–but like other street music, it was best at a distance–in the room it was coarse, out of time, and out of harmony, whereas in a street it seemed the contrary of all this. However, hear it where one will the modulation and accompaniment are very extraordinary. In the canzone of to night they began in A♮, and without well knowing how, they got into the most extraneous keys one can imagine without however offending the ear. After the instruments have played a longish sinfonie in A, the voice begins in F and stops in C.–that's not uncommon or difficult–but after another ritornell from F he gets into E♭–then closes in A♮ and at other times gets even into B♭ and D♭ without giving offence, returning or rather sliding always into the original key of A, the instruments going all the time in quick notes without intermission.–The voice part is very slow, a kind of psalmody, the words of which there are many stanzas, are Neapolitan. It is a very singular species of music, as wild in modulation and different from that of all the rest of Europe as the Scots and 'tis perhaps as ancient, being among the common people merely traditional: however

* This sentence was edited to: 'The overture still seemed comic and original, the airs far from common though in general plain and simple.'

† This was altered later to 'some genuine Neapolitan or rather Calabrese singing ...'

the violin player promised to write it down for me. They played several other Neapolitan airs, all different from other music. A little before Xmas ⌊the musicians of this sort come from Calabria⌋ to Naples and *their* music is wholly different from this–they usually sing with a guitar and violin not on the shoulder but hanging down.–Paesiello has introduced this music into his comic opera now in run. Piccini promised to procure me some of these wild national tunes. Another sort is peculiar to Apulia, with which they set the people a dancing and sweating who either are bit or fancy themselves to be bitten by the tarantula. Of this last Dr Cirillo has promised to procure me a specimen. Signor Serrao in a dissertation on the subject and Dr Cirillo who has made several experiments in order to verify the fact are both of opinion that the whole is an imposition of the people of Apulia to gain money–that not only the case but the malady itself is a fraud, Dr Cirillo having never been able to provoke the terantala to bite either himself or others upon whom he has tried the experiment. However the whole is so thoroughly believed by some innocent people in the country that when *really* bitten by other insects or animals that are poisonous they try this method of dancing to a particular tune, till they sweat, which together with their faith sometimes makes them whole. They will continue the dance in a kind of frenzy for many hours even till they drop down with fatigue and lassitude.

MEMORANDUM FOR ANCIENT INSTRUMENTS

Nel Tempietto della Villa Albani Sotto la, Dea Cibele c'e' Stromento antichissimo di Musica–Do. Cestius's tomb–Do. Vespasian's arch, via Sacra–palazzo Verospi Todini Gallery for Musical Instruments. Musea Kircheana for fibia, with Mr Morison.–Sanbrook Freeman Esq has an antique faun with a siringa in perfect conservation of most beautiful greek sculpture of which Mr. Jenkins from who he had it has a copy–See Winckleman's History of Art 2 vols. 8vo in French and inedited antiquities Ital. Fol.–Roma antica e Moderna del Venuti 40.–Studio delle pitture di Roma del Abate Titi–de Obilisco Caesaris augusto e Campi Martii ruderibus nuper exate Commentarius auctore aug. Maria Bandinio–Roma 1750–Admiranda Romanorū antiquitatum. Santo Bartoli 1693.

MEMORANDUM FOR HISTORY

St. Cecilia in sculpture playing on the violin in the church of S. Agnesia, Piazza Navona at Rome–for the Tarantula see Dr Serrao's dissertatio on that subject in Latin–Palazzo Chigi Mercury playing on a hautbois by Salvater Rosa–the Scots Magazine for 1761 Rhythmus of the Ancients–genuine ancient Scots tune Gill Morice.–M. de Reitter Maestro di Capella Imperiale à Vienna–chiesa Nuova S. Filipo Neri where the oratorio was 1st instituted and where I found the notes of it and of several other oratorios.–At Pisa S. Stefano dei Cavalieri, the organ fatto del Cavalier dell'acciaia, inventor of the folding or portable harpsichord.–1614. Antiphonaica and graduale de Tempora in Roma, della Stamperia Medicea. Tomo Primo, p. 21–impertinence of Zarlino, Mazzante–Sirce del Franco 1770 favourite opera at Rome–Dr Blaire's Dissertation upon the Poems of Ossian, which likewise see–Aurisicchio's Church Music at Rome–Feroce, organist at Florence–Lidarti (Clari) at Pisa–Piccini composing this year for Naples–Palermo and Venice–Tarrantino–Alessandro Scarlatti–Feo–Leo–Durante–Jomelli–and Piccini all brought up at the conservatorio of S. Onofrio. Brav'orbi at Bologna see memorandum book——

WEDNESDAY 24. Set off in a large party, at 8 o'clock in fine weather this morning for Pozzuoli–passed thro' the Pausilipan Grotto–and saw a great number of galley slaves working at the road by the sea side chained 2 and 2 and guarded by soldiers. At Pozzuoli (Latinè Puteoli) are many antiquities which I had not time to examine. In the market place is the base of a statue of Tiberius in marble with fine figures on it. Here we were to put to sea in a shaloop or skiff to cross the bay, but ere we set sail what an imbroglio! what a noise, and what quarrels! We got in–then fresh difficulties, demands and squabbling– we got out and tried to get caleshes–here a new imbroglio–but ere it was finished we were called on by our cicerone an old waterman of the place, to enter the boat, as all was adjusted. At my first entrance, I was made giddy and felt sickness come on very fast, tho' a fine day and but little wind. We past by the ruins of Caligula's Bridge, as 'tis called, tho' some think it only a defense against the force of the sea. There are 14 piles still standing some of which have parts of arches still remaining which manifestly, I should think, proves it to have been a bridge–Suetonius mentions a bridge of boats which Caligula built over the bay and passed in triumph and 'tis thought by some that he first intended it of brick and stone but finding the sea too deep afterwards finished it with boats. From Pozzuolo to Baia is a league; the prospect of the castle of Baia, of the promontary of Misenum, the island of Nisita on one side, and the town of Pozzuoli on the other, afford the finest prospect imaginable when in the middle of the gulf or bay, but I was so sick as not to be able to enjoy much of it, or indeed to see as I kept my eyes shut as much as possible to prevent giddiness. We were carried on shore on the watermens shoulders at a place called the Campi Elisj, or Marchetto di Sabato, between the castle of Baia and Misenum. From hence we walked by tomoli antichi, ancient tombs, to the Piscine Mirabile, or ancient reservoir of fresh water, from which the Roman fleet used to be supplied. One descends by many steps to the arches which are very entire, then to the Cento Camerelli, or 100 cells built by Nero either as a labyrinth or prison—one goes out of one little room into another by little doors of a gothic form pointed at the top—it is not very certain for what purpose they were built. Then to the Mare Morto and port of Misenum. All along the shore on this side are still to be seen the ruins of villas belonging to the first people of Rome such as Sylla, Marius, Pompey, Cæsar, Lucullus, Hortensius, Agripina, Nero etc. At Baia were the most famous and fashionable baths of antiquity. There all the gay, galant and polite world used to resort in autumn, but now all lies in ruin—several earthquakes at different times have swallowed up the greatest part of these villas and towns or tumbled them into the sea—however enough remains to render it certain that it was a place well inhabited and full of temples and palaces.

From the Mare Mortuum we came back to the boat into which we were carried and sailed along the coast by the castle of Baia to the Lucrine Lake, where we were again carried on shore, where we saw the tomb of Agripina and the ruins of the temple of Diana—of Venus—of Mercury etc. Into this last we were carried on men's shoulders as it was several feet under water. The dark rooms called le camere di Venere, we entered on all fours almost, as the passage is extreamly low and difficult. In these rooms and in Agrippina's tomb are still on the walls and ceilings paintings in fresco and pretty elegant bits of sculpture but blacked spoilt by the torches. Here most strangers write their names with char-coal. These temples give one even in ruin, great ideas of magnificence and splendour. Here are on the coast still famous hot baths, so hot as to boil eggs—one of the water men stript, and went in with 4 eggs and soon returned with 'em boiled, and himself in the most violent sweat I ever saw in my life. If I had had a proper shirt I'd have gone in myself for my rheumatism, which was at this time very bad in my right shoulder. From hence we went to the Lake Avernus—and Sybil's Grotto—into which we entered and marched near a mile under an ancient arch which used to be 3 miles long, but has been broken and filled up by earthquakes: at the end of a mile we were carried on men's shoulders thro' water in to the Sybil's bath. At coming into the air we walked along the Lake Avernus to the temple of Apollo at the end, and mounting a hill behind it, had a most beautiful prospect of the lake and its banks—near this is Monte Nuovo. After the prospect from the hill at the back of the Temple of

Apollo on the Lake *Avernus*, we went on in caleshes to see the ruins of the ancient city of *Cumae*, passing thro' the *Arco Felice* a very beautiful piece of ancient brick work: 'tis 55 ft thick and 70 high–20 wide in the arch. The ruins of Cumae are upon an eminence in a vinyard that commands a wonderful land and sea prospect–the grapes here the best I ever tasted. Not far from this vinyard, in another, is the Giant's Temple in which was found the colossal term* of Jupiter which is in Naples near the Palace. In our way back to Pozzuoli we saw a great number of ancient tomoli on both sides the road. We dined at Pozzuoli and returned to Naples in the most alarming weather imaginable after which we went again, Wednesday 24, to Piccini's opera but were too late for the overture. The house was very full and the music pleased me more than the first time. The airs are not so familiar as those of Paesiello, but there is much better writing in them–some accompanied recitatives especially, in which tho' several different parts are going on at the same time there is a clearness, and, if one may so call it, a *transparency* which is wonderful. The singing as I before observed, is wretched, but there is so much *vis comica* in *Casaccia* that one never thinks of his singing–but for want of dancing the acts are necessarily so long that 'tis wholly impossible to keep up the attention, so that those who are not talking or playing at cards, inevitably fall asleep.† I have been since informed that dancing is only allowed at the king's theatre(n)‡

THURSDAY 25. Made visits–to the consul–Messrs Brydone and Fullerton and Mr. Terney. This last I found at home and had a long and agreeable chat with him–he's a very sensible man, with a gravity in his manner not at all disagreeable. I had young Oliver to dine with us to day to pick his brains about conservatorios and musical people– he has been in that of S. Onofrio 4 years. Hunted for curiosities in the book way on stalls, but unsuccessfully–Messrs Barnard and Crofts have been here before me. This morning in my walks called on Mr. Lee an English banker to enquire after Mr. Morrice, now in Sicily. Mr. Lee had heard of my journey and business and was very civil and conversible.

THURSDAY 25. After dinner I went again to hear the boys of S. Onofrio at the Franciscans' church and had my pocket picked of a fine

---

* A statue or bust, sometimes without the arms and terminating below in a pillar or pedestal out of which it appears to spring.

† '. . . it is so much the fashion at *Naples*, and indeed, through all *Italy*, to consider the Opera as a place of rendezvous and visiting, that they do not seem in the least to attend to the musick, but laugh and talk through the whole performance, without any restraint . . .' Samuel Sharpe, *Letters* (1767), p. 78.

‡ This sentence was later squeezed into a small space left at the end of a line. The n may be taken to indicate note.

new cambrick handerchief for the 3rd time tho' I buttoned it up at my entrance and had not taken my hand off it two minutes. But the pickpockets of Italy as the politicians, I suppose are superior in, subtilty to those of other countries. I heard a Litany here by Durante: the rest of the music, which was but young, was by the young man who beat time. The instrument I took before for a clarinet is here called *voce humana*;* 'tis an agreeable tone, has a great compass, but was not well played on. A concerto on the violin was introduced where hand and fire were discovered but no taste or finishing.

No opera to night, so came home to write and to admire Mount Vesuvius, at which Capt. Forbes and self constantly gaze after dark from the leads of our house. It begins to be very furious. The honourable Mr Hamilton the British Minister at this court whose taste and zeal for the arts and whose patronage of artists is well known throughout Europe being out of town when I first arrived at Naples, did me the honour to invite me to his house at the foot of Mount Vesuvius, called Villa Angelica as soon as he was apprised. See Mem:Book.

FRIDAY 26. This morning before we set out for Mr. Hamilton's I made a visit to Signor Jomelli who arrived at Naples from the country but last night. He is extreamly corpulent, and in the face not at all unlike what I remember Handel but far more soft and polite in his manner. I found him at an instrument, writing. He got up very politely to meet me and made many apologies for not having been to wait on me, which were indeed unnecessary, as he was but just come to town, and at the point of bringing out a new opera, which must have occupied his time and thoughts sufficiently. He had heard of me from Mr. Hamilton. I gave him Padre Martini's letter, and after reading it we went to business immediately. I told him my business in Italy, and shewed him my plan, for I knew his time was precious, and moreover was fearful of being too late for Mr. Hamilton's dinner. He read with great attention and conversed very openly and rationally, said the part I had undertaken was much neglected at present in Italy–that the conservatorios of which I told him I wished for information, were now all at a low ebb, tho' formerly so fruitful in great men. He told me of a man of great learning who had been translating David's Psalms into very fine Italian verse, in the course of which work he found it necessary to write a dissertation on the music of the ancients, which he had communicated to him–that he was a fine and subtil critic had differed in several points from Padre Martini–had been in correspondence with Metastasio, had a long letter from him on the subject–all which he thought necessary for me to see–had promised to procure one of his books and to make us acquainted.–Spoke

* Edited to 'There was again a solo on the instrument called here *la voce humana*'.

very highly in praise of Alessandro Scarlatti as to his church music, such as motets, masses etc.–promised to procure me information concerning the conservatorios and whatever else was in his power, as soon as ever his opera was on the stage, of which he promised to let me know the time of its first public rehearsal. He took down my direction and assured me that the instant he had got rid of his opera, he should be *tout à mois*. Upon my telling him that my time was very short, that I should have been on the road home but for his opera which I so much wished to hear, that besides urgent business in England there was great likelihood of a war,* which would keep me here a prisoner–he said in answer to that, and with great appearance of sincerity, that after I was in England if anything occured he would not fail of sending it to me; in short I went away in high good humour with this truely great composer who I look upon as clearly the first of his profession in Italy and if I except Hasse, who is at Vienna, in the whole universe. Were I to name the living composers of Italy for the stage according to my idea of their merit they would be in the following order. Hasse–Jomelli–Galuppi–Piccini–Sacchini etc–

Capt Forbes and I went to the Minister's in a chariot the same road as before when we visited Pompej–that is through Portici–Resina by Herculaneum–and Torre del Greco etc. His Villa Angilica is but a small house which he fitted up himself–situated opposite and within 2 miles of the foot of Mount Vesuvius in a very rich and fertile spot as every one here abouts is, that is not covered with fresh lava. He has a large garden, or rather vinyard, with most excellent grapes. The Captain and I were received with great politeness by the Minister and his lady. After dinner we had music and chat till supper. Mr. H. has 2 pages who play very well one on the fiddle and the other on the violoncello. Tho' my companion was not invited to lye there nor did intend it, yet he was easily prevailed on to pig in the same room with me who was, and a field bed was put up on the occasion. As soon as it was dark our musical entertainment was mixed with the sight and observations of Mount Vesuvius, then very busy. Mr. H. has glasses of all sorts and every convenience of situation etc for these observations with which he is much occupied. He favoured me with a sight of his MS. of which he has just sent a copy to our Royal Society, in which a very ingenious hypothesis is well supported to prove that most of

---

* France had suffered severe losses at the hands of the British in India, Europe and Canada during the Seven Years' War which started in 1756. The Peace of Paris (1763) brought an end to hostilities, but France still counted Britain its worst enemy and started to rebuild its forces, particularly its naval forces, to challenge British power. British policy was not accommodating, and political conflict continued between the two countries and was reflected throughout Europe. It was this tension which Burney was reacting to.

the mountains in this part of the world have been formed by volcanos. Tho' at 3 miles distant from the mouth of the mountain, were heard the reports of the explosion before we saw the stones and red hot matter thrown up by them, which proves as light travels faster than sound, that they must ascend from a great depth, and we were certain that they mounted near 1000 feet above the summit of the mountain. The sight was very awful and beautiful, resembling in great the most ingenious and fine fireworks I ever saw. M. H. who has studied very closely this mountain and all its symptoms for upward of 6 years read us very entertaining lectures upon it, and is now of opinion that it is on the eve of some great event or considerable eruption. The sound was more deep than that of thunder which proves the cavern to be of an immense size and depth.

After supper we had a long dish of musical talk relative to my history. All his Etruscan and other antiquities not sent to England are at Naples. He says nothing is allowed to be copied at Portici, and not a pencil suffered to appear there, and of him the Neapolitans are more suspicious and jealous than of any one else. I wished very much to have a bit of the Greek MSS. recovered on music–tho' a satire against it–but till the court publishes it nothing can be obtained, no more than of the entire ancient instruments found in Herculaneum and Pompej. However, I shall get a sight of them and be enabled to judge of their construction and the correctness with which they are copied in the books given a way by the King to most of the crowned heads and universities in Europe. M. H. will give me letters to the governor of each conservatorio at Naples and comes thither himself on Monday, when I am invited to a concert made on purpose for me at his house in order to give me an opportunity of hearing Barbella and the best performers of Naples and conversing with the cleverest people.

Mrs H. has a very neat finger and plays the harpsichord with great delicacy, expression and taste. Mr. H. is likewise a pretty good performer on the violin; but are both so tired of the music of the Neapolitans as to be glad to return to that of Corelli, ⌊Geminiani⌋, Handel, Vivaldi etc for the sake of harmony and variety–indeed the general run of Neapolitan music is noisy and monotonous, but while such composers as Jomelli, Piccini, Merula, Mann⟨a⟩, Paesiello etc are in it one would think no complaint need be made of a scarcity of good music.–The mountain was very turbulent all night.–

In the morning SATURDAY 27. Mr. H. very much to my wish proposed a journey into the neighbourhood of M. Visuvius, *on* it was not adviseable. The most daring, even Mr. H. himself during the efforts it makes to throw out lava, and at a time when the crater is full, and while such perpetual showers of immense red hot stones and such quantities of sulphureous smoke are thrown out, dare not ascend the mountain itself; as it is uncertain where the stones will drop, or which way upon a sudden change of wind the smoak may be driven. I was very glad to be under the guidance and direction of so excellent a cicerone and lost all desire for ascending the mountain to gratifie a vain curiosity against his opinion and counsel. We therefore set off only with an intention to visit the lava of former eruptions and to coast round the foot of Vesuvius as far we could with safety by keeping always to the windward. Capt. Forbes and I for this purpose set off in Mr. Hamilton's chaise, while he preceded us on horseback–we had two servants behind. It began to rain ere we had got two miles from the Villa Angelica. We stopt at a gentleman's house in a rich vinyard within a mile of the foot and left there our chaise and the horses, and ventured on foot towards the mountain. It held up a little while and we got among the remaining bits of vineyards that had been overwhelmed in the late eruptions, when it began again to rain. I was prepared for the worst by having a flannel waistcoat, leather stockings and old good-for-nothing shoes, with a great coat. Capt. Forbes had on a silk suit. We escaped a little while in a hovel belonging to a poor old man who saw his vinyard destroyed but 3 years ago and a mountain of a mile round raised upon it in less than a day's time. He has now only a few small slips of it left upon which there are most exquisite grapes of that sort with which Lacrimæ Christi wine is made. He brought us more than we could eat. I had before taken shelter under the leaves of a remaining bit of another vinyard, during which time it was impossible to resist the tempting ripe clusters. We heard the mountain roar, felt its throes under our feet–saw huge red hot stones thrown up within a mile of us.

At last after being dripping wet, it held up and we began our march over ragged lava which cut our shoes and feet to pieces and upon which it was with the utmost fatigue and difficulty we kept our balance–this was the scoria a scum of the lava of 1760. At length we gained the foot of one of 3 new mountains of cinders, ashes, and lava formed by that eruption. We mounted by a way which only Mr. H. and a few of his friends have used. When we had gained the top we saw all the 3 mountains and their mouths, whence all the lava etc had proceeded, and this shewed us in miniature what we showed [should] have seen on a greater scale on the summit of Vesuvius during quiet times. After this we descended and scrambled along as well as we could sometimes on all fours, to the fresh lava of 1767, the last which has appeard. This is very dark, nearly black, and has taken such shapes as great quantities of hasty pudding* or cow-dung would have done on

* A pudding made of thick batter.

A CONCERT

AN ITALIAN KITCHEN

TWO ITALIAN CHARACTERS

uneven ground. Sometimes it is formed into great Brobdignagian curles. Sometimes one can fancy the figures of mishapen monsters – sometimes the bases of large columns etc. Upon this which is solid lava, the difficulty of walking is not so great. This had proceeded from a new aperture at the foot of the mountain, as indeed all the different lavas seem to have done, the mountain not having force sufficient to throw out liquids at the top – all that comes from thence being chiefly stones, ashes and cinders.

After it held up tho' I only walked in my waistcoat the fatigue threw me into the most violent sweat I ever was in. After visiting the different kinds and streams of lava and going to the foot of Vesuvius we returned to the gentleman's house where he had left our chaise and horses: 2 gentlemen came out to salute Mr. H. and his companions and pressed us very much to drink chocolate with them. They seemed under great apprehension of a new eruption by the symptoms of the preceding night. They had heard the mountain roar and seen it throw out huge stones and cinders all night – and one of 'em said to Mr. H. mi pare Signore, Minacciari nuova Rovina. From hence we had a pleasant ride to Villa Angelica whence Capt. F. and I parted off about 5 in the evening and arrived at our lodgings in Naples before 7. We found ourselves too stiff and tired to go out any more or indeed to do any thing more than sup and go to bed. The Capt. found a letter from his mother at Rome, and told me there was something that concern'd me in it; and at the same time gave me joy. I could not conceive for what, when he read as follows 'The English papers say that Dr B—'s daughter is married to one of his own name – I hope felicemente and with his concent.'* If it had been otherwise the Captain's manner of breaking it to me would not have been the most gentle in the world.

SUNDAY 28. It *has* rained all this morning with such fury that not a creature was to be seen or heard in the streets of this populous town. After dinner I had a head-ache which took away all desire of going out tho' it held up – but I can get no shoes here that will keep out the water and a coach is 18 carlins a day, which I grudge confoundedly when not absolutely necessary, and to day there was no particular formality or ceremony to perform. – In order first to bully, and then to sooth my head ache I determined to go out, and to try the medicinal power of music at Piccini's opera, and this last tho' it did not cure, alleviated and diverted the pain. The house was very full and the actors in great spirits. I was to night for the first time soon enough to

* Charles Burney's eldest daughter Esther married her cousin, Charles Rousseau Burney, at St. Paul's, Covent Garden, on 20 September, 1770. They were both brilliant harpsichord players.

hear the overture: it is very pretty and fanciful, consisting only of 2 movements, which trimmed* the fiddles; but Piccini never suffers them to sleep. With what pleased me before, I was more pleased now, and am now more and more charmed with the originality, and resources of this author. As I went home it rained furiously, my head ache returned and I went supperless to bed with no inconsiderable fever upon me, which burnt me up the whole night. In the morning however a little sweat came on, which I encouraged, and about 10 got up and went out. This was

MONDAY 29th. I keep the exact number of days in the week and month lest I should overstay my time—just as one counts the clock in the night previously to a journey for fear of over sleeping ones self, and tho', in general, things have gone on more awkwardly here than any where else that I have been in Italy, yet time gallops at a great rate and besides my own family and business which require my attendance in London there is constantly another weight on my spirits which is the apprehensions of a war, that would either oblige me to stay all the winter in Italy, or ruin my health and indeed greatly affect my affairs by the fatigue, difficulty and expence of travelling home thro' Germany and in danger too of being taken prisoner in a long sea passage at which on the meer account of sickness, I very much shudder. Every body here talks of war, and this morning for the first time since I came from Florence and the 2nd since I left England, at the Consuls I took up an English paper, which I found full of hostile intentions such as impressing men, fitting out a vast fleet, the answer from Spain if not satisfactory being regarded as a declaration of war, etc.—all this helped to vex and allarm me exceedingly, but Pazienza!, I must trust to fortune, who is always playing me some de—d trick or other.—All this bad morning was lost in visits which had very remote relations with business, but in the afternoon we went to the Minister's, Mr. Hamilton, at whose house there was much company and the chief musical performers of Naples. The former composed of the French ambassador, consul, and several officers, together with our consul Mr. Jemineau, Lord Fortrose, Messrs Methuen, Brydone, Fullerton, Tierney etc. Among the performers was Barbella and Orgitano, Lord Fortrose's master and one of the best harpsichord players and writers for that instrument here.—But Mrs. H. herself is a much better performer on that instrument

---

* Burney was determined to find the exact words to indicate the nature of the music and the demands it made upon the performers. He first wrote 'trimmed' in the sense of 'to beat, thrash, trounce': this was deleted and 'sweated' was substituted. This did not suit either, and '2 movements, which operated as a s[u]dorific to the fiddles' was preferred. None of these alternatives appeared in *Tour* 1773 where we are told 'the violins were confined to hard labour'.

than either him or any Italian I have heard since I crossed the water. She has great neatness and more expression and meaning in her playing than any lady I ever heard, for ladies, it must be owned, tho' often neat in execution, seldom aim at expression. Barbella rather disappointed me; his performance has nothing very superiour in it now. He is not young indeed, and solo playing is never wanted or minded here; so that teaching and orchestra playing were his chief employments. The best thing he did was to play me the famous Neapolitan air which the people here constantly play at Xmas to the Virgin: this he performed admirably with a drone kind of bag-pipe base.–As a solo player he is far inferior to Nardini and indeed to several others in Italy, but seems to know music and to have a good deal of fancy in his compositions with a spice of not disagreeable madness. Mr H. introduced me to the French consul, who is a real connoisseur in music, perfectly well acquainted with the different styles of all the great composers of Europe, past and present, and discriminates very well the *fort* and *foible* of each.–To him I communicated my plan and with him I had a very satisfactory conversation. In order I believe that I might have more time for conversation with Barbella and this gentleman there was a supper party selected, of about 10 or 12 and we staid till near 2 o'clock.–Barbella is the best natured creature imaginable, his temper as one of the company said is as soft as the tone of his violin. I sate next him and picked his brains about old Neapolitan musicians.–Mr. H. had offered to write me a letter to all the governors of the conservatorios, but Barbella very obligingly offered to get me all the information I can desire of these celebrated seminaries, and Lord Fortrose, with whom he is every morning has invited me to meet him there when ever I pleased. So that from Barbella and a young Englishman, Mr. Oliver, who has been 4 years in the conservatorio of S. Onofrio, I shall have a clear and perfect account of all that is necessary for me to know concerning this part of my enquiries. I gave Mr. H. a list of my wants which he has promised to consider and supply to the utmost of his power. Unluckily he goes back to Villa Angelica to morrow.

TUESDAY 30. This has been a very busy day. In the morning we set off from our lodgings with the artists Messrs Forester, Design, Robertson and Myers to the church of the Carthusians called by the Italians la Chiesa, e Certosa di S. Martino, situated on one of the highest hills about Naples, upon which stands close by it the Citadel or le Fortezze ò Rocche, detti Castelle della Città di Napoli–commonly called Castello di S. Elmo or Eramo–this castle is chiefly hewn out of the solid rock and seems most amazingly strong. There are arches cut in the rock for flanking all the avenues and entrances. The

Carthusians are very rich, and give a great deal away in alms, besides entertaining all strangers who come recommended by any person of consequence in Naples. We might have had an excellent Irish dinner provided for us, if we had chosen to ask Mr. Hamilton for a recommendation – as it was we were very well entertained with the fine things and pictures we saw of which there are a great number. The most striking pictures are those of Spagnolet, one of which is wonderfully fine – 'tis a dead Christ supported by S. John, with the Virgin in tears and Mary Magdalen kissing his feet. Every part of painting seems perfect in this picture except that the back ground is become too black. There are a great number of pictures by this painter, particularly the 12 prophets admirably coloured, which are painted in the corners at the top of the arches in the quire. There are above a 100 of this painters pictures in this monastry tho' so scarce elsewhere. Lanfranc and Luca Giordano have painted many of the ceilings, and there is besides a very fine Nativity (left unfinished) by Guido – some of the heads are charming particularly that of a woman in white on the right hand, but some of the men seem too red – 'tis however a very large and valuable picture – but the boast of the place and collection is the little Crucifix of Mich. Angello, which is not above a foot and ½ high – this is the picture in which the expression is so strong that the painter was said to have crucified a man in order to represent from departing life the agonies of that situation. – Besides these and many more fine paintings, the treasures of this monastry are almost inestimable, in gold, silver, precious stones etc –

The prospect from hence of the city, sea and country is amazingly grand and beautiful. In descending from this mountain, I waited on Lord Fortrose, who received me in a most polite and hearty manner. He is really a lively, sensible and accomplished young nobleman, in person very manly and pleasing he has great talents and taste – he both draws and paints very well, understands perspective, rides, fences, dances, swims and plays on the harpsichord. – Messrs Brydone and Fullerton were with him, and the conversation was lively and agreeable – Barbella was just gone – I shewed his lordship my plan into which he entered very comfortably, and promised his assistance in getting information and curious things from the musical people here. From hence I went to Mr. Hamilton's – *he* was out, upon which I enquired for his lady, who tho' at her toilet came out to me. She is very sensible, shewed me pictures and music and told me of Paesiello's burletta called l'Idolo Chinese,* and played some of the airs – which I liked so well, and the plot of the drama that I expressed a desire to have the whole copied. It seems a very witty satyr on the Pope, which

* First performed in 1767.

is more likely to take in England than elsewhere. She immediately called for one of the pages to enquire after a copyist for me then invited me to her toilet in order to finish our chat. She had a pretty Sicilian girl waiting upon her whom she made sing and accompany herself on the tambour de basque. The air was simple and national. It begun, after a long sinfony on that monotonous instrument something like this

Then Mrs H. gave me an account of her journey into Sicily and Malta—Mr H. had yesterday lent me his M.S. [manuscript] account of Etna, written on the spot while in Sicily. Upon my saying Mr. H. was out she said, no he is not out to you, he's writing in his study and you may go to him—and sent the Sicilian songstress to shew me the way. Mr. H. was so obliging as to leave off writing to shew me his Etruscan vases and other antiquities and to lend me a MS. account of a voyage into the Levant by a French gentleman of his acquaintance, in which he speaks of the music of the Turks and Greeks—signed an order for me and my friends to see the Museo at Portici which is to be sent to the Marchese Tannacci to have his signature likewise.—Another invite for Saturday to hear a remarkable fat Dominicain sing buffo songs, and on Sunday to go into Mrs. Hamilton's box at the new opera of Jomelli.

In the afternoon I went with the same company as in the morning to Capo di Monte—it was so far and so high we went in 3 caleshes. It is a palace of the King of the 2 Sicilys not finished, but contains the greatest number of fine pictures I ever saw in one collection. The cameos too, medals, intaglios and other antiques are innumerable. All these belonged to the house of Farnese and came by succession to Don Carlos by the Treaty of Vienna, who brought them from the Dutchy of Parma to Naples. They have not been long here as no account of them is to be found in the old books which describe Naples. The palace was begun in 1738. The library here is one of the best in the Kingdom, under the care of Padre della Torre, to whom I had a letter, but unluckily he is still out of town. There is on the 1st floor a suite of 24 rooms all full of excellent paintings by the 1st rate masters such as Rafael, Coreggio, Titian, Mich.Angello, Julio Romano, P. Veronese, Albano, Parmegiano, Carach, Guido etc. There are more Coreggios and Parmegianos in this collection than in any other in the world–for which it is not difficult to account, as they were brought here from Parma.–The charming holy Family by Rafael which is repeated in the Palais Royal at Paris and in the Palais Pitti at Florence is all beauty and the best, I think of the 3. There are 2 other Virgins of Rafael in this collection. There are 8 pictures by Annib. Carach here–that of Rinaldo and Armida pleases me the most. The hero holds a mirrour for her to dress her head by. The colouring of the female Bacchanal is much admired, but I think 'tis too red and looks as if the nymph had been flogged. There are 5 large pictures of Schidone a scholar of Carach, but an imitator of Coreggio–he was of Parma–his works are very scarce. There are 2 concerts by Coreggio, and a holy Family, a Danae of Titian most exquisitely coloured and preserved; this subject Titian has often repeated. A Magdalen, and a Knight of Malta by the same–2 pictures by P. Veronese, one of which is upon a canvas of 6 pieces sown together, which prove how distressed this great painter must have been for money: 2 very good pictures by old Palma, 1 of which is Moses striking the rock, and the other the waters changed to Blood. The 4 seasons by Bassan–and several pictures by Ricci which have their merit–and 2 battles by Bresciano, delightful. A flight into Egypt, Love stript, Astronomie and Geometry, by Parmigiano, charming. A S. George by Rubens, an Ecce Homo and S. John by Guido–Rachael by Albano, delightful. The last Judgment by Mich. Angello very fine–'tis small and is supposed to have been done before that in the Pope's chapel. Ancient paintings found in the palace of the Cæsars at Rome, a celebrated cartoon by Guilio Romano, and 10,000 other things that I forget.–

The prospect of town and country at descending the stairs most rich and beautiful–the fields now begin again to be green as in spring. This fine day after so much rain makes every thing appear charming.– But I wish I were at home, for all that, most heartily–for, besides the war, they were talking this morning of the plague being feared in London, as 'tis supposed not only to be in the Baltic but in Holland, and ships from both these places are now obliged to perform quarentine.

WEDNESDAY 31 October. This morning I went with young Oliver to his conservatorio of S. Onofrio, and visited all the rooms, where the boys practice, sleep and eat. On the 1st flight of stairs was a trumpeter screaming upon his instrument till he was ready to burst–on the 2nd a French horn bellowing in the same manner–in the common practicing room was a dutch concert,* consisting of 7 or 8 harpsichords, more than as many fiddles, and several voices all performing different

* A concert in which every performer plays a different tune.

things in different keys–other boys were writing in the same room, but it being holiday time not near all were there who study and practice in the same room. This method of jumbling them all together may be convenient for the house and may teach the boys to stand fire, by obliging them to attend their own parts with firmness whatever else may be going forward at the same time. It may likewise give them force, in obliging them to play loud in order to hear themselves, for nothing but noise can pervade noise, but in the midst of such jargon and continued dissonance it is wholly impossible to acquire taste, expression or delicacy–there can be no polish or finishing given to their performance and that seems to account for the slovenliness and coarseness remarkable in their public exhibitions, and for the total want of taste, neatness and expression in these young performers till they have acquired it elsewhere. The beds which are in the same room serve for seats to the harpsichords etc. Out of 30 or 40 boys who were practicing I could discover but 2 that were playing the same piece. Some of those who were practicing on the violin seemed to have a great deal of hand. The violoncellos are in another room and the wind instruments, such as the flutes, hautbois etc in a 3rd.–The trumpets and horns either fag on the stairs or top of the house.– There are in this college 16 castrati, and these lye by themselves in a warmer appartment upstairs than the other boys for fear of colds, which might endanger or injure the voice. This is the only vacation time in the whole year, but on Monday term begins, and I shall then return and hear them take lessons of the masters. They then begin the winter practice of rising 2 hours before daylight, from which time they continue their exercise, an hour and ½ at dinner excepted till 8 o'clock at night, and this constant perseverance for a number of years, must, with genuis and good teaching produce great musicians.

From hence a book hunting at stalls, old shops etc–and in my way home, visited the cathedral or Duomo, which is a large and noble building, with 2 large organs in it, 2 good statues of S. Peter and S. Paul by Finelli. The cupola is painted by Perugino* and the angles by Dominichino: 6 alters by ditto. The church of S. Gennaro, which is very rich in marble and silver pilasters etc–and that of S. Paul Maggiore, which is likewise very much decorated–all the pillars are of granite–

After dinner to the theatre of S. Carlo to hear Jomelli's new opera rehearsed. There were only 2 acts finished, but these pleased me infinitely. The overture was short, and rather disappointed me, as I expected the 1st movement would have been made more of, but as to the songs and accompanied recitatives in general they are all good–as

---

* Perugino did not in fact paint the cupola: it was done by Giovanni Lanfranco.

I don't recollect one that is so indifferent as not to seize the attention except a short bravura before the duet. The subject I believe is Demofonte—the names of the singers as yet I know not, except Aprile the 1st man and Bianca the 1st woman who have both great merit. The former has rather a weak and uneven voice, not constantly steady as to intonation—but has a good person, a good shake, and much taste and expression. The latter has a sweet and elegant toned voice constantly in tune with an admirable portamento—I never heard any one sing with more ease or in a manner so totally free from affectation. The rest of the singers are all above mediocrity: a tenor with both voice and judgment—sufficient to make one attend—a very fine contr'alto—a young man with a soprano voice, and way of singing full of feeling and expression, and a 2nd woman far from despicable.— Such performers as these were necessary for the music, which is in a difficult style more full of instrumental effects than vocal—sometimes it is rather recherchée, but admirable in its tout-ensemble—learned often in modulation, and in melody full of new passages. This was the first rehearsal and the instruments were rough and unsteady, not being as yet certain as to the exact time or expression, but as far as I am yet able to judge the composition is perfectly suited to the talents of the performers, who tho' all good, yet not being of the very first and most exquisite class are more in want of the assistance of instruments to mark the images and enforce the passion which the poetry points out.—

The theatre is a noble and elegant structure: 'tis an oval, or the section of an egg, the point next the stage being cut. There are 7 rows of boxes sufficient to hold 10 or 12 persons in each. In every row there are 30 boxes except the 3 lowest which by the Kings box and the door under it reduces them to 29. In the pit are 14 or 15 rows of seats, which are very roomy and comfortable, with leather cushions and stuffed backs each seperated from the other by a broad rest for the elbow. In the middle of the pit there are 30 of these seats in a row.

Nov. 1st. I never knew what thunder, lightning a rain were till I came into this country—all last night torrents of water came down without ceasing, with such bursts and flashes of thunder and lightning as were far from pleasant. In the morning, being all Saints Day I went at least a couple of miles to the church of the Incurabili where I was told there would be good music but found it miserable. From hence to several others where I found only bad music ill performed. In the chapel or sacristy of which up in a gallery* lye in sarcophagi in the form of large trunks the remains embalmed of many of the

---

* This sentence is more lucid in the Osborn MS.: '. . . bad music, ill performed. In the Chapel or Sacristy of one of these, up in a gallery. . . .'

Neapolitan kings and their children and ministers.—Then a chaise hunting, but in vain—one to which we were entitled by a contract with Damon at Rome is not to be found all over Naples: the English of which will be hiring and paying for one that will be worse than that to which we have a claim for nothing.

Dined with a large English party at Mr. Tierney's and as it rained most violently the whole evening, there was no stirring from thence till 10 o'clock at night.

MUSEO AT PORTICI

FRIDAY. November 2nd. I went this morning with the former party of artists to the museo at Portici, having had an order procured by Mr. Hamilton from the Marchese Tanucci addressed to Signor Camillo Paderni for that purpose. The infinite number of fine things in this amazing collection made from the choicest things found in Herculaneum, Pompej and Stabia are not to be described. Not a pencil must appear, so that memory alone is all one has to trust to and each fine thing defaces the other in these transient views.—In the cortile are a great number of charming statues particularly those on each side the door of the museum, of the 2 Balbus's father and son— the father's is by far the most agreeable countenance, but both are statues of a high class. There is on the right hand, among many other good statues a Vestal of most exquisite beauty as to sculpture: the drapery is in a noble style and the whole figure graceful and charming. There are on the walls a great number of inscriptions. Ciria the wife and mother of the 2 balbi, 6 ft. high, veiled—the drapery admirable. All the way up the stairs there are bronze statues *saved out of the fire*, literally, for they are still black by having been overwhelmed in red-hot lava. We did not see our cicerone, Signor Paderni, till we were at the top of the stairs.—He is not so old as I expected him—is very civil and very intelligent.

There are 14 different apartments, all filled with antiquities of different kinds. I despair of remembring them all in exact order or number, but the 1st was filled with antique instruments of sacrifice, 2nd. lamps and lacrimatories—3rd musical and chirurgical instruments, among the former are a great no. of broken bone and ivory tibiæ—but none entire—3 systrums, 2 with 4 cross bars and one with 3. Crotoli—tambours de basque—siringa with 7 pipes etc—but the most extraordinary of all is a species of trumpet found at Pompej, about 11 months ago. It is a good deal broken, but not so much as to make it difficult to conceive the entire form, it having the remains of 7 small bone or ivory pipes inserted in as many of brass all of the same length and diameter which surround the great tube, and seem all to terminate in one mouth-piece. Several of the small brazen pipes are broken, by which the ivory ones are laid bare, but it is natural to suppose that they were all blown at once and that the small ones were unisons to each other and octaves to the great one. It used to be slung over the shoulder by a chain, which chain is preserved and the place where it used to be fastened to the instrument is still visible. No such instrument as this has been found before either in ancient painting or sculpture, which makes me the more minute in speaking of it. When we got to the inn where we dined Mr Robertson an ingenious young artist of our company was so obliging as to make a drawing of it by memory, in my tablets, which all the company, consisting of 7 agreed was very exact. Among the chirugical instruments are several different kinds of probes, a cathiter etc with a compleat case of instruments of different kinds, well-preserved. In the same room are tripods and a glass case filled with priapi of different sizes and fancies, one larger than the rest with bells to it and others with wings. It is supposed (and even mentioned by Juvernal) that the women used to wear these about them as amulets and charms against barrenness. A watering pot with a priapus for spout. One of the tripods is of most beautiful sculpture in bronze, supported by 3 satyrs or priapes – each holds out his right hand quite open and has a droll, laughing countenance. Each has only one ear, one leg and one foot, but these are amazingly well carved or molded. The part from whence the figure has its name is furiously erect. These were chiefly found in Herculaneum, which as well as Capua, and Baia were frequented by the most licentious and voluptuous among the Romans, and Venus was in a particular manner honoured and worshipped at Herculaneum.

4th room had ancient weights and measures for the most part very ingeniously contrived. – Glass utensils of different sorts and f ms, which prove the ancients to have been in possession of that material in great perfection. 5. Vases, urns, and lacrimaria of most beautiful forms and preservation. 6. a compleat kitchen, with all kinds of culinary utensils – in earthenware and metals – pots, basons, pans, dishes etc of various forms – even the stamps and molds for pastry figures, and letters to mark the bread and pyes with are preserved – this was approaching very near the art of printing. 7. In the room adjoining are several eatables found entire, such as bread, baked and unbaked, flour – dates – corn or burned wheat, black indeed but entire in its form. – Eggs – almonds – figs – dried oil, wine etc. 8. Instruments of husbandry. Horses, bulls etc. 9. A delightful room surrounded with busts in bronze and marble placed alternately, of the most beautiful sculpture and preservation, among which a young Alexander and an old Seneca admirable. In the middle of this room is a bronze statue of

Mercury Sedens of the utmost beauty and perfection, nothing just out of the mold could be more beautiful or perfect – 10. In the middle of this room is a drunken young faun lying down and snapping his fingers, with such an expression of fun and jollity as is not to be conceived but by seeing the figure: he lies on a skin of wine at which he seems to have been sucking, and upon 2 tables, I think in the same room are two wrestlers companions of bronze and of exquisite sculpture. These figures seem to me equally perfect with any of the finest statues in the world, such as those at Florence and the Belvedere. – At the further end of one of these rooms are all the volumes as yet found in papyrus etc. of which only 4 have been made out – these are Greek, one upon the Epicurean philosophy – one upon Rhetoric – one upon morality and one against the musical system of Aristoxenus by Philodemus.* They appear to be only a black cinder. I saw 2 pages opened and framed of the Greek MS. against music. Every lover of learning laments the slow way in which they proceed in opening these volumes. All that have been found hitherto were in Herculaneum – those of Pompej were supposed to have been wholly destroyed by fire.

11. Remnants of wearing apparel – such as part of a purple robe wrapped up in linnen – gold lace without silk threads – bracelets – rings – jewels – ear-pickers – combs – ornaments of youth, called *Bullæ* in form of a heart of gold and worn by the young nobility till they arrive at puberty: *rouge* boxes with rose coloured powder still entire. In a glass, dry colours for painting. Medals, gemms, cameos, and intaglios of the most beautiful workmanship. 12. Bucklers, helmets etc some very beautiful and well shaped – some like a flapped hat etc. On one is represented in rilievo the whole history of Troy: large figures in terra cotta – urns etc – 13. In another room fragments of mosaic – one is very beautiful, with 3 women playing on different instruments, and dancing, one on the tibiæ pares† – one on the cymbalum and a 3rd on the tambour de basque. Sundials. One on a little piece of copper in the shape of a hare with the tail for gnomon – this seems to have served as a watch and to have been made for the pocket. A Roman folding foot-rule. Compasses etc. – 14. Portable furnices – some from whence our modern kitchen tea kettles seem to have been imitations. There is a place for fire in the middle and for water on the out side round it: the forms of these are very elegant. The lanthorns

---

* A pupil of Aristotle, Aristoxenus of Tarentum was born about 354 B.C. He was the first to lay down a scientific foundation for music. The only substantial work of Philodemus (born *c.*100 B.C.) to survive is the one mentioned by Burney, which was unrolled and published at Naples in 1793. It is neither historical nor technical, but purely philosophical, asking if music is worthy of praise or blame.

† See page 230.

and candelabriæ are wonderfully injenious: the stands for lamps of all heights very convenient and beautiful—and for a side board lamps of different sizes and heights hanging to a tree—very ingenious and elegant, struck me much.—Ink stands, wooden pens—styles—tablets upon which the wax was to be spread—an instrument to scratch out or erase—and a case for styles like our modern pen cases.—There is still dried ink in one of the stands. All the above are in appartments separate from the paintings, but the floors of each room are very ingeniously covered with most beautiful antique mosaic, *tale quale*, such as they were found in Herculaneam, Stabia and Pompej. The designs and colours of them are exceedingly beautiful, and each appartment of the 1st. 9 or 10 rooms has each a floor still more beautiful than the other. Some are like our modern painted floor cloths, and others like the patterns on beautiful carpets.

ANCIENT PAINTINGS AT PORTICI

After dinner we went to appartments in the old palace on the other side the street to see the paintings recovered in Herculaneum etc. They shew that painting and design were well known among the ancients—and that they were not ignorant even of perspective. Some architecture I saw painted in which the columns are thrown back according to the modern rules are a convincing proof of this—these pictures in fresco or detrempe* and chiefly taken off the walls must not all be supposed of equal goodness—some one may imagine to be done by *house painters* of no great reputation when alive—but amidst a great deal of bad and midling are many elegant designs well executed.

My hunt throughout Portici was for ancient instruments—among those I found in the collection of ancient paintings I found representations of a great number of lyres of different forms, one with a pipe across the top which is not to be met with elsewhere—one in the shape of a quadrant—but that in the picture where Chiron is teaching the young Achilles to play on it is the most perfect—it has 11 strings, which several others in this collection have—tho' there are likewise some with only 4.—A crotolo well represented—a siringa with the 5 longest pipes of different lengths and the 4 shortest of the same one with 11 pipes.—Two long great flutes of metal, they must have been very loud and shrill, are of the same length and blown at the same time.—9 Muses with symbols, a nymph or priestess with a systrum in one hand and a patura in the other. NB. The Systrum seems to have

---

* Détrempe (distemper: Italian, tempera) is a mixture of powdered colour with water and some glutinous substance. Unlike egg tempera it is mixed with size or gum and given opacity by whitening. It is less permanent than egg tempera and less suited to fine work.

been chiefly used in sacrifices, for the same purpose as the little bell rung in Rom. Catholic churches in the time of mass and at the Elevation of the Host. Among the statues here are two of bronze remarkably fine – namely, one of Drusus and one of a Vestal.

The most remarkable pictures and the largest are the Chiron and Achilles I mentioned before – Theseus vanquisher of the Minotor – the expression of gratitude in the young Athenians is charming. Some kiss his hands, – some prostrate themselves, and others embrace his knees. – The Minotaur is weltering in his blood below under the figure of a man with a bull's head, which is not met with elsewhere. – It is observed by artists that the ancient painters failed more in the clair'-obscure [chiaroscuro] than in any other part of painting. One of the largest and best pictures in the collection puzzles the curious to find out the subject. There is a Hercules, a child suckled by a goat, a winged divinity crowned with laurel, with an ear of corn in one hand, and with the other pointing to the child. The Goddess Flora, sedens, and behind her Pan with the siringa of 11 pipes – Pilades and Orestes, – with Iphigenia – Another picture with Pilades and Orestes in chains, led to King Toantes before the statue of Diana. Iphigenia and 2 of her women appear in the piece. A small picture of a faun kissing a naked nymph with his right hand pressing one of her breasts and the other lifting up her head – she has one arm over his neck with which she seems to press him – 'tis a voluptuous representation – his crotolo or cymbalum are lying on the ground. There is a centaur with a young man on his back in full galop – the centaur touches with one hand a lyre with 3 strings which rests on his crupper, and with the other he strikes the half of a crotolo against the other half in the hand of the young man. In the appartment of statues under a 3rd custode are the following in marble: 3 Muses, a Roman senator – young Bacchus – Pythagoras – young Homer fine manly figure – Autumn and a priestess two admirable statues – Euripides – a Roman matron, a young brother and sister found at Pozzoli – Cicero, head modern, Jupiter Sedens, Venus – Apollo – alabaster columns modern – verd antique, a large dog, an admirable modern cast etc – At night went to a little neat new play house just opened – there was a comedy in prose – a Turkish story ill told and not well acted.

SATURDAY 3. Dreadful wet day – could do nothing in the morning but stay at home and fret at that and the great likelihood of a war, which one hears of from all quarters – how I shall get home, or when, it is not easy to tell – but this is only another piece of my usual ill luck, that demon which never quits me. – In the evening went to Mr. Hamilton's where I staid till 2 in the morning – it was very chearful and the conversation much of it to my purpose – Lord Fortrose was there, and very lively–Andrea del Sarte's anatomical figures, where all the muscles and bones of the human body are laid bare–all the heads of Raphael taken off by means of oiled paper–cameos and intaglios in abundance were introduced.–In talking over the trumpet found at Pompej, Mr. H. says it was found in the corps de garde room–which proves it to have been a military instrument and the true clangor tubarum of the ancients.

SUNDAY 4. Went this morning to St. Gennaro to hear the organ and to see the chapel and pictures in it by Dominichini–after which to the house of D. Carlo Cotumacci, whom I heard play and talk a great deal about old times. He was scholar to the Cav. Scarlatti in the year 1719 and shewed me his lessons, in Scarlatti's own hand writing. He had 4 sons–Pietro–good for nothing–Domenico, famosissimo.–Nicolo–abate–Carlo, pittori–2 daughters–one that died young, and one who died just before her father–her name was Flamina. He was born in Sicily–his son Domenico in Naples.–

Vinci was scolari e maestro in the old conservatorio of the Povere Giesu Christi as was Pergolesi–This latter spit blood and died of a consumption and of fatigue–Durante, scolare e maestro di S. Onofrio–Jomelli and Piccini were both of this conservatorio under him–Il Cotumacci was Durante's successor. The old man plays in the old organ style very full and learnedly as to modulation, and has composed a great deal of church music, of which he promised me a copy of 2 or 3 curious things. He has had great experience in teaching. He shewed me two books of his writing in MS. one on accompaniment and one on contra punto. I take him to be upwards of 70 years old.

At night, after visiting Padre della Torre, taking a giro sul corso, seeing all the fine folks in gala there, and hearing and seeing the salute of a 74 gun Spanish man of war, I went to the opera and was there honoured with a place in our Minister, Mr. Hamilton's box. It is not easy to imagine or describe the splendour and grandeur of this theatre when doubly illuminated as was the case to night. In the front of each box there is a mirrour 3 or 4 ft long by 2 or 3 wide, before which are two large wax tapers. These by reflexion being multiplied and added to the lights of the stage and to those within the boxes make it too much for the aching sight.–The King and Queen were there in a large box in the front of the house, which contains in height and breadth 4 others. The pit and all the other boxes were wholly filled with well-dressed people it being gala day. The stage, the scenes, dresses and decorations were extreamly magnificent, and this theatre is superiour, I think in these particulars [as] well as in the music to that of the great French opera at Paris. It surpasses all that poetry and romance have painted. But with all this, I must own, that in the magnitude of the building and the noise of the audience, one neither can hear voices or instruments distinctly, and I was told that on account of the K. and Q. being present, people were much less noisy than on common nights. There was not a hand moved by way of applause during the whole representation, tho' people seemed much pleased with the music–but to say the truth it did not afford me the same delight as at the rehearsal, nor did the singers, tho' they exerted themselves more, appear to such advantage. Not one of the present voices is sufficiently powerful for such a theatre, when so full and so noisy. The 1st woman Signora Bianchi whose sweet voice and simple manner of singing gave me and others much pleasure at the rehearsal did not satisfie the Neapolitans, who have been accustomed to the force and brilliancy of a Gabrieli, a Taiber and a De Amici–there is too much simplicity in her manner for these enfans gatés, who are never pleased but when they are astonished. As to the music, much of the claire-obscure was lost, and one only heard distinctly those course and furious parts which were meant merely to give *relief* to the rest.–The mezzotints and back ground were generally lost and little else was left but the bold and coarse strokes of the composer's pencil.

During the performance Caffarelli came in to the pit and Signor Giraldi, who was in Mr. Hamilton's box proposed to make us acquainted and at the end of the performance carried me down to him. He looks very well and has a still very lively and animated look–perhaps more manly than ever: he does not seem above 50 tho' he is said to be 63 years old. He was very polite and entered into conversation with great ease and chearfulness. He enquired after the Duchess of Manchester and Lady Fanny Shirley who had been his patroness when in England, which he said was in the end of Mr. Heydeggar's reign. He introduced me to Signor Gennaro Manno, a celebrated Neapolitan composer who sate just behind him. Signor Giraldi had been with him before to fix a time for bringing me to his house at 2 o'clock on Tuesday, and we are to meet at Lord Fortrose's for that purpose–indeed it is to his lordship that I am indebted for this and many other opportunities of information given me while at Naples. The house was emptying very fast, so that I took my leave of this sire of song, who is the oldest singer in Europe who still continues the public exercise of his profession–for he frequently sings at convents and in Churches yet tho' he has for some time quitted the stage. Mrs. H. was not at the opera–but her box was very full, chiefly of English–Mr. H. Lord Fortrose–Messrs Fullerton, Methuen, Brydone, Forbes, Solly etc–

There are 2 or 3 good dances in the lively way–the Italians are not pleased with any other–indeed as I have before observed, all their dances are more pantomime entertainments than anything else, in which the scenes are usually pretty and the story well told. The subject of the first dance was l'isola disabitata*–of the 2nd the humours of Vaux Hall garden, in which were introduced Quakers–sailors–women of the town–Savoyard show boxes etc–and in the 3rd dance at the end of the piece it was the people of Thrace who figured at the nuptials of Creusa and Cherinto characters of the opera.–The 6 principal dancers are gli Signori Onocuto Vigano, Giuseppe Trafieri–Francesco Rafetti–and le Signore Colomba Beccari–Anna Torselli, and Caterina Ricci–the 1st man has great force and neatness and his *à plomb* is as exact as Slingby's–and the Beccari's *many twinkling feet* not inferior to those of Radicati.

MONDAY 5. This morning to the conservatorio of S. Onofrio to see the boys take their lessons and to hear some of the best of them play. They were all hard at work and a noble clangor they made, not to be equalled by

> a 100 mouths, a 100 tongues
> a 100 pair of iron lungs
> ten speaking trumpets etc

However the ears of both master and scholar are respected when lessons in singing are given–as that is done in a quiet room, but in the practicing rooms the noise and dissonance are not to be described or imagined.–However I heard in a quiet room 2 of the boys accompany each other in a solo on the violin by Giradini and one on the base by the performer. The first was but indifferently played, but the 2nd was both a pretty composition and very well executed. I find all over Italy that Giardini's solos and the overtures of Bach and Abel are in great request, and very justly so as I have heard nothing equal to them of the kind since I arrived on the continent.

From hence, as I was going to P. della Torre I met him in the street and he went with me to my lodgings where he staid and conversed very chearfully and with great abilities on several curious subjects. I first started music and shewed him my plan–after which he told me of several books of which I am in possession–but frankly confessed his want of depth in the subject. However he promised to make his assistant ransack the King's library for me, in search of materials–told me some particulars relative to the Greek treatise on music by Philodemus, which is not a poem on music as M. de la Lande says nor a satjre against it as others say, but a confutation of the system of Aristaxenus, who being a practical musician preferred the judgment of the ear to the Pythagorean numbers or the arithmetical proportions of meer theorists. Ptolomy did the same afterwards. I shall try to have a little talk with P. Antonio Piaggi about it

* The Uninhabited Island.

yet ere I depart, he it was who opened and preserved the MS. and it is he who is now superintending at a foundery, the casting a new set of Greek characters exactly resembling those in which it was written and in which it is to be published. – After this we had a dissertation on Mount Vesuvius, upon which P. della Torre has written very learnedly a book which is much esteemed. – And then the subject was changed to optics and the improvement of telescopes and microscopes upon which he has likewise made many experiments and published several treatises. – When this good father, with whom I was much pleased [left] we went to Mr. Hamilton's to dine, but as he dined later than we had imagined, Mrs. H. proposed our going out to take a ride with her in the coach. – Among other things we went to see one was a great festival at the convent of La Donna Regina, una bellissima fonzione – at which were several bishops and a great deal of good company, with music, on account of two Turkish slaves who being converted by loss of chains and gain of money were this morning to be baptised. One was more than 40 and the other upwards of 30 years old. They looked very silly (the only thing that could incline me not to suppose them knaves) and the gens comme il faut seemed to laugh in their sleeves. The nuns of the monastery were all at the grate except one whom Mrs. H enquired after, but she was not allowed to come down, lest she should be the more confirmed in her repugnance to taking the veil into which her friends seem determined to teize [her]. –

The dinner at Mrs. H—ltons was very comfortable as the company was select. After dinner came a fat friar to sing buffo songs – and Nasci to accompany him and to play some of his own music. Both were excellent, the former in humour and the latter in a graceful and easy manner of playing the violin. –

After this Mr. H. took me in to his study to shew me his charming Coreggio – the subject is a naked Venus who has taken Cupid's bow from him which he is strugling for, during which time a satyr is running away with his quiver: 'tis a wonderful fine picture and reckoned equal for the number of figures to the S. Gerom at Parma. After this Etruscan vases and other antiquities of the highest antiquity and value, other curiosities, both natural and artificial, curious books etc – then went up stairs to tea, where we found, a Neapolitan prince and princess – 2 or 3 ambassadors, Lord Fortrose, the French consul, with a number of English etc. After tea more music – then supper with a select party, and a delightful chat till near 2 in the morning when I took leave Mr. H and lady, with infinite regret as their civilities and kindnesses to me all the time I have been here have been so great that I can never forget them.

TUESDAY 6. Time is so short now that I can only give an index to memory for the future. This morning after chaise hunting I visited Jomelli, Piccini and Signor Baragine to whom I had a letter from Mr. Vyse, which, till now, I have not been able to deliver. I found him a very pretty kind of man, very musical and one of the governors to the conservatorio of S. Onofrio–which makes my late acquaintance with him a loss–After this we went to Lord Fortrose, with whom we were to dine–but first I was to see his medals, cameos, intaglios, Etruscan vases, pictures etc–which I did with great delight.–The engagement to Caffarelli was put off, by his recollecting that 2 o'clock would be his hour for sleeping and saying that he would come and see me at Lord Fortrose's after dinner.–There was a very large company– among which Barbella and Ortigano were invited on my account.– There was likewise the French consul M. D'astier who flatters me exceedingly.–After dinner a complete band was assembled in the gallery and we had music there till past 11 o'clock–Barbella pleased me to night much more than before–he is very certain of his tone and has a great deal of taste and expression; if he equalled Giordini in brilliancy and in fulness of tone his playing would be unexceptionable and perhaps superior to most of the players in Europe. Orgitano played the harpsichord pretty well too, and Signor Consorte, a musico, was there to sing.–There was likewise a pretty good solo hautbois.– We had all given Caffarielli over–when behold he came in high good humour and contrary to all expectation was prevailed on to sing. Many notes in his voice are now thin, but there are still traits in his perform- ance sufficient to convince one of his having been an amazing fine singer. He accompanied himself and sung without other instrument than the harpsichord. Expression and grace with great neatness in all he attempts are his characteristics–both Barbella and he are Bolisari- us[e]s, rather in ruin than otherwise, but what remains of them is but the more precious for it.–Cafarelli said we should have a whole day together, which would still be too little for all we had to say, but upon being acquainted with my resolution of setting out for Rome to morrow night after the opera, he proposed meeting me again with Lord F to morrow morning. It is impossible for any one to do the honours of his house better than Lord F. We were all at our ease and very chearful and happy–and after supper Barbella played several Calabrese, Lecese, and Neapolitan airs, and a lullaby of his own *per la Natale* which is excellent and was very well expressed.

WEDNESDAY 7. Went, after other jobbs, with Mr. Fullerton and Capt. Forbes to P. della Torre at the foot of Capo di Monte–it is the most chearfully obliging creature I ever saw. He can't be less than 70 yrs. old and yet is as badin [playful] as a young man of five and 20–he and his assistant had been hunting in vain thro' the King's library, which belonged to the Farnese family and was brought from Parma, for materials al mio proposto–he shewed me several books and MSS I already knew but nothing else–no inedited MSS or scarce book but his own dissertation on sound published in his works in 9 vols. 8vo.– Elementa Physicæ, auctore P. D. Johanne Maria de Turre–vide–To. 8 De Sono. p.113–Napoli 1769 Donati Campo–vide likewise Memories de l'Academie Royal 1741. D. Ferrein Dissert sur la Formation de la Voix.–After this he shewed us his telescope and microscopes, in both which he has made great improvements–especially in the latter–by means of a spherical globe of pure crystal glass, the smaller the better. He blows it himself, thro' a clear flame–1st melted and then made spherical in Tripoli earth*–It magnifies the diameter of an object, if the glass be of the smallest class 2560 times–the common microscopes magnifie about 350 times.–After shewing the whole process he was so obliging as to give me 2 globules–one of which magnifies about 150 times and the other 500 times.

From hence I went to Lord Fortrose's to meet Caffarelli–and now I have mentioned his name let me write by way of memorandum that he has bought a dukedom for his nephew after his own death, Duca di Santi dorato. He is very rich, yet often sings for hire in the convents and churches. He has built a magnificent house for himself and over the door is this motto, Amphion Thebas ego Domum–N.B. one *with* stones and one without.–Visits di partenza, banker etc–then home where I found Signor Fabio the 1st fiddle of the opera of S. Carlo who dined with us and brought his violin 'tis but a coarse player, tho' a fat good natured man. He sung several buffo songs and accompanied himself very well on his fiddle and after dinner he had a 2nd who came to accompany him in one of Giardini's solos etc.–I got from him the number of hands employed in the great opera orchestra: 18 1st and 18 2nd violins, 5 double bases and but 2 violoncellos which I think has a bad effect, as the double base is played so coarsely throughout Italy as to produce no musical sound nothing but meer noise.

I stole away to Barbella with whom I had an appointment but could not find him for a long time. I was in a great fright, as I depended on him for particulars of the conservatorios, old composers and performers of the Neapolitan school etc.–However with the assistance of Orgetani I at last found him–heard one of his scholars play a solo of Giardini very well, and got all the intelligence I wanted of him–

Then went home to pack and to pay which lasted till 2 o'clock in the morning, when we left Naples in order to go to Rome.

THURSDAY was a fine day and I found great part of the road through Capua, and over the Gariglione very pleasant–chiefly a garden full of

* A fine earth used as a polishing powder.

vines and olives. The rain had made the country look better than when I travelled thro' it before–the leaves still on the trees–tho' about Naples off.–M. de la Lande says they remain on 6 weeks longer than in France and spring is 6 weeks forwarder here than there. We got to *Mola* by a little after 6–and escaped the custom house rumage for 6 carlini.–

FRIDAY 9. We were called at one o'clock this morning. I would not go to bed–as it was a cursed one and every thing upon it wringing wet. 'Tis meet I should set down that this house is infamously bad in all respects, but in a particular ⌊manner⌋ for theft and imposition.–When we stopt at it before they asked 25 carlini for what was worth 12 at most, and for which after a remonstrance, they took 16, but now tho' I looked upon it as a precedent for the demand at our return they insisted upon its having been 16 pauls, and not carlins. They are all thieves and assassins. I recollected before I was 100 yards from the house that in the fresh demand on us for more money I had laid down my netted cap–but it was gone past recovery.–I lost patience more here than throughout Italy–and every road in it is not strewed with flowers–nor does one meet with the manners of the golden age or patriarchal hospitality. It rained most part of the night, in the morning a few hours of fine weather shewed here and there a beautiful and fertile spot. But I was too stupid and drowsy to enjoy it. The end of the Kingdom of Naples was the end of the good road. It used to be the worst in Italy, till made the best for the approach of the new Queen. From Fondi to Terracina is along the Mediterranean shore– the sea there is always very furious. On the right hand the rocks and mountains are very bold and sublime–they have very much the appearance of ancient volcanoes–montagnolis–lava–scoria etc according to Mr. Hamilton's hypothesis. At Terracina we stopt to dine at the most miserable and unfurnished inn I ever entered. It rained the whole afternoon except just before sun-set when we got out and walked thro' a wood chiefly of the cork oak and olive trees, which were as green as in July.

We lay at *Piperno* a little town belonging to the Pope and set off SATURDAY 10, at 1 o'clock, too early to see much of the horrid Pontine fens.–The weather cleared up at sun-rise and was very fine till we got to Villetry where we dined, got post horses and set off for Rome furiously at 2 o'clock, but had so many accidents and stops on the road that I thought we should never get there.–All about Velletri the country is charming, full of inequalities of ground, vinyards, olives, etc and has a very rich and cultivated appearance–the ridiculous ceremony of a dogana here is too bad–it is like those about Naples merely to levy money on strangers for scoundrels without doing either the King or the State any service–In this stage a broken breast-piece, and a broken wheel stopt us 3 several times, and such a furious rain came on as I never yet had seen even in Italy–Between Marino and Torre di Mezza Via, the roads grew so bad from the torrents of rain that poured in on each side that it became a very rapid river, so deep and violent that I really begun to think we were in imminent danger of being drowned. I tried to get this book out of my sac de nuit and was preparing to try to escape shipwreck with it as my most valuable chattel*–But after travelling more than a mile in *hot water*, or rather cold we found the torrent lessened by outlets at the sides, and, at length got on the cause-way above the water which roared on each side. This furious rain continued till we got to the gates of Rome and afterwards–for I had a packet for Lord Weymouth, which Mr. Hamilton had consigned to my care for the post, and tho' I stopt to write one myself to England–all this time there was not the least remission.–I thought the man and horses who carried me to the post would have been overwhelmed.

ROME

SUNDAY 11 NOVEMBER.–Having a little recovered the fatigues of my Neapolitan journey, this morning I renewed my operations again at Rome. I find a great number of English come here since I went away. I went this morning to the convent of Saint Ursula to see the ceremony of a nun take the veil. I accompanied Mrs and the 2 Miss Forbes–who were in high dress as was all the company which was very numerous of the first people in Rome. I was close to the alter and saw and heard every word that was uttered. The 1st ceremony was saying mass–then came Cardinal de Rossi in great state, while the organ was playing and mass was singing with instruments, all performed by nuns and ladies of the convent in the organ loft–the music was very pretty, but ill performed–the organ was bad and too powerful for the band. Most of their best hands were occupied in the convent with the internal ceremony–the external was all in the chapel. When the cardinal was robed, the young lady was led in by a lady of the 1st rank in Rome and brought to the alter in exceeding high dress, her hair beautiful and curled en tete de mouton all over her head. Her gown was the richest possible; embroydered, and I believe embossed blue and silver silk–a large stage hoop, and great quantity of diamonds. The train of her robe dragged I believe near two yards on

---

* An additional passage was later written in here: 'If I had not been kindly and wisely prevented leaping on a little bank of dust by my fellow traveller Capt. Forbes seizing the skirt of my coat and stopping me'. The text then continues 'But after travelling more than a mile thus in bodily fear we found the torrent lessened. . . .'

the ground, she was more a pretty sort of young person than a beauty –looked very pale when she came in and more dead than alive–she made a very profound curtsy to the cardinal who was on the alter seated in his mitre and all his rich vestments to receive her–she threw herself on her knees and remained there some time while some other parts of the ceremony were adjusting–then walked up to the cardinal who said Figlia mia–che domandate?–when she said she begged to be admitted into that convent as a sister of the order of St Ursula–Have you well considered what you ask?–She said chearfully she had, and was well informed of all she was about to do–then she kneeled down again and kissed the cardinal's hands and received from him a little crucifix which was likewise kissed–then she retreated while the cardinal said mass, which was sung at the same time in the organ loft– she on her knees the while. After this was over, there was a sermon, and that being over she was led by the cardinal into the convent, where she was stript of all her finery and ornaments–had her hair cut off and came to the grate in her religious dress to receive the white veil–with which she was invested by the Lady abbess at the grate, the cardinal etc standing by. After this more pretty music badly performed, the organ playing all the sinfonies and accompaniments overpowered the violins and had a bad effect, tho' neatly performed. By this time the veil was on and she came to the convent door to receive the congratulations of her friends and the company–but first with a taper lighted in her hand went round the convent to salute all the nuns who had likewise tapers in their hands–when she was at the door with her veil and crown on, but face uncovered I, among the rest went close to her, and found her much prettier than I had thought–a sweet mouth with the finest teeth in the world–lively, speaking eyes and a genteel shaped visage–she would anywhere else have been called a pretty woman–but here, so circumstanced, a beauty. At the alter she changed countenance several times–1st pale, then red–and seemed to pant and be in danger either of crying or of fainting, but she had recovered before it was all over, and at the convent door was very chearful, talked to several of her friends and acquaintance and seemed to give up the world very heroically and thus ended this human sacrifice!

There I met with my old acquaintance and scholar Lady Stanley (Miss Owen) who was in tears and I believe more surprised to find me here than I her ladyship*–She invited me to dinner–where, after 2

* Other old acquaintences were remembered later: 'Here I met with my old acquaintance and scholars the honourable Mrs. Hampden (ci-devant Miss Graeme) and Lady Stanley (Miss Owen) who were in tears and, I believe, more surprised to find me here than I at meeting them. Sir John Stanley and Lady invited me to dinner. . . .'

or 3 visits I went–but 1st found 2 right welcome letters from England–one from Venice and a drawing of the little fidling Apollo from
Florence–that from Venice was written by Count Boujovich, and
inclosed many very valuable particulars of the Venetian conservatorios
and school of music.–Dined in a family way with Sir John and Lady
Stanley, had a great deal of agreeable chat about old times and an
invite to their conservazione in the evening and a general one while at
Rome. From thence I went in Sir John's coach, there was no other to
be had, so full is the town now, to the Chiesa Nuova to hear an oratorio
in that church where that kind of drama first took its rise. There are
two galleries–in one an organ and in the other a harpsichord–in the
former the service was begun by the vespers in 4 parts a la Palestrina
–then the Salve Regina à voce sola, after that, prayers, and then a little
boy not above 6 years old mounted the pulpit and delivered a discourse
by way of sermon which he had got by heart, and which was made truely
ridiculous by the vehicle thro' which it passed. Then the oratorio of
Abigaille set by Signor Casali consisting of 4 characters, and divided
into 2 parts was performed. The 2 first movements of the overture
pleased me a good deal the last not at all–the minuet, as usual
degenerated into a jig of the most common cast. The rest of the music
was pretty common place–no new melody or modulation, tho'
nothing vulgar. Signor Cristofero sung the principal part very well, in
Guarducci's smooth and polished manner–he made 2 or 3 excellent
closes, tho' rather too long. This fault is general all over Rome and
Naples; a long winded licentiousness in all their cadences, which very
much wants curtailing and correction. A few select notes with a great
deal of meaning and expression given to them is the only expedient
which can render a cadence desirable as it should consist of something superiour to what one has heard before in the air, or it becomes
impertinent. This abuse is not of very ancient standing, for in a serious
opera of old Scarlatti composed in 1717 there is not one ad libitum
to be found.* Between the 2 parts of this oratorio (there are no more)
there was a sermon by a Jesuit delivered from the same pulpit from
which the child had desended. I waited to hear the last and only
chorus, but tho' it was sung by book it was as light and unmeaning
as an opera chorus which must be got by heart. With respect to a
true oratorio chorus† accompanied with instruments in the manner of
Handel's I have not heard one since I came into Italy. When this
performance was over I went to the D. of Dorset's concert where I

---

* Later edited to '. . . composed in 1717 there is a place for no cadenza ad libitum
to be found'.
† Later altered to read '. . . as an opera chorus which must be performed by heart.
With respect to a masterly and dignified oratorio chorus. . . .'

met many English, and finished the evening at Sir John Stanley's where I met many more. There was the D. of Dorset–General Patterson and lady–Sir Thomas Heskett and lady–Lord Lincoln–Messrs Leighton–Coffin–Fothergale–Gordon–Scott–Glover–Lord Carmarthen and several more I cant remember. Sir T. Hesket introduced me to General Shovelhoffe, who has great concerts here, and he invited me to one for to morrow night.–I renewed my acquaintance with the pretty Mrs Hampden, who had been my eleve when she was Miss Græme–and would have gladly been so now, she said if I had been to winter at Naples, whither she is soon going. Mr. Leighton has given me a thick book filled with the choicest compositions of old Scarlatti whom Jomelli rates so high.

MONDAY 12. This morning after a long musical chat with Wyseman, Parsons, etc at home, I went to Mr. Byers and found there a letter from Mr. Beckford written at Geneva–and in it a drawing by the famous Mengs of an ancient lyre at Florence and his judgment on the fidling Apollo there. From hence to the Vatican library where I found the Abate Elie, who had not copied all the things I wished, tho' he had some–he had even forgot several of the extracts I had required--so that I was forced to hunt them out again in among the MSS.–⌊The books are all inclosed in archives, and nothing is seen in entering the Vatican Library but painting and sculpture⌋. In short this proves that nothing is well done here especially but what one has done or does one's self.* He has promised the whole for this day sen'ight–and not sooner could he undertake them, so that there would be no getting away before Wednesday in next week, if the corriera had a place for me. After a long re-examination of the MSS. in the Vat. Library I went into the Popes or Sistine chapel–which I was curious to see on many accounts, first as it is the place in which the famous Miserere of Allegri is performed on Good Friday–2ndly as it was here that church music took its rise, and where it was brought to its highest perfection by Palestrina–and 3rdly where, at the altar piece is Mich. Angello's greatest work in painting, or perhaps of man –the *last Judgment*. It is astonishing what dreadful ideas and figures his dark imagination has produced. Not anything in the Inferno of Dante or Paradise Lost of Milton is more terrible, but it is greatly discoloured and the ceiling by the same painter is in many places broken down; in 2 or 3 places of several feet in breadth–the sides are of Pietro Perugino and the best things I have seen of this famous master of the divine Rafaele–I went up into the orchestra with respectful curiosity to see the place sacred to the works of Palestrina.

* Later altered to: '... proves that nothing ⌊is⌋ well done here especially ⌊by commission. It is necessary to watch others, or to act for⌋ one's self'.

This chapel is only used on Corpus Cristi day, in Passion Week, Wednesday twice, Thursday twice, Good Friday and Saturday.

The orchestra seems hardly big enough to contain 32 performers, the every-day number of singers in the Pope's service–and on great festivals the super-numeraries are taken in.–There was only a large lectern or wooden desk for the score book of the maestro di capella and a marble bench at the back and sides. This orchestra is placed at the right hand corner from the alter facing the Pope's throne which is near the alter on the opposite side. There are places for the cardinals at the sides and a small place for foreign ambassadors to stand in just within the rails opposite to the alter, but no other strangers are ever admitted within the rails–nor is any one but the performers ever suffered to enter the orchestra during the service. The rails or grate, which is diamond squares gilt, seem to take off one 3rd of the whole room which is very lofty and magnificent, but now very dusty and out of repair–the floor is marble mosaic.–After this I went to the Pauline chapel used only once in the year, when it is finely illuminated with wax lights.* I wanted very much something of a smart waistcoat to wear with my blue English cloth frock, which I thought would be easily found abroad wherever and whenever I pleased–but at Naples they asked me 12 zechins for what I wanted and refused 10 which I offered. This made me postpone the purchase till I came hither and now 'tis far too cold for silk cloathes and time is too short to get any-thing made so that I determined to try the Roman Monmouth Street, alias the Jews Quarter–which is at an immense distance from every habitable part of the city like Rag Fair†–However I was in a walking humour and set off from St. Peter's–but when I came thence the stinks, beggary, and wretchedness of the place and people made me shudder–however I had the courage to go but not without trembling into 3 or 4 infernal holes called shops, but met with nothing I would pick up off a dunghill and had my walk but not my dinner for my pains, as I was too late for this last.*

In the afternoon I drank coffee at the Cavaliere Battoni's, and met there my good friend Santarelli–his scholar the Signorina Battoni sung sweetly with noble simplicity and a truely pathetic expression, several songs of Hasse, Piccini etc–after this I went and bargained with the corriere to carry me to Lyons. He does not go this week–so that I must stay till Wednesday se'night, which I am sorry for, tho' it will afford me an opportunity of collecting my papers and which I could not have done by next Wednesday–After this at the Muscovite General Schovelhoffe's to a great academy. Sir Tho. Hesket presented

** Over this passage is written in red chalk 'Not printed, nor was it worth writing'.
† The Houndsditch market in the City of London for the sale of old clothes.

me to him last night at Sir John Stanley's, and he then invited me to his concert, where I fancied myself in London–except 3 or 4 the whole company was English.–D. Dorset, Lords Carmarthen, Lincoln and Tilney–Sir John Stanley–Sir Tho Hesket–Messrs Hampden–Leighton–Gordon–Scot–Johnes–Fothergale–Cotton–Ladys Stanley and Hesket, Mrs Hampden and Earl–with a great many more English gentlemen, whose names I cannot recollect. The little Mignatrice Bichelli was there and another girl–the former sung very well and the other *will* sing. There was nothing extraordinary in the instruments. The General set Mrs. Hampden and Lady Stanley, my two old scholars and children upon my bones to get me to the harpsichord–and after more fuss than it was worth I was forced to comply, which I did about as comfortably as I should have done to be dragged thro' a horsepond and it had, so great was my fright, much the same effect. However, all were very indulgent, and *seemed* pleased.–Indeed I have had this kind of sweating to carry off humours, in every town in Italy since I broke the ice at Venice–here at a dozen places and at Mrs. Hamilton's and Lord Fortrose's 2 dozen times; but I have long had other pursuits than the glory of a good player–and he that wishes either to gain or keep professional fame, must be a constant slave to that and to his instrument.

TUESDAY 13. Il Cavalier Piranesi while I was at Naples had sent his draughtsman all over Rome in search of ancient instruments–and he had made drawings from several of the most antique and curious. However as I came here to see with my own eyes I determined to examine the originals and compare the copies myself–for which purpose I set off this morning as soon as it was light in company with Piranesi's young man–and walked about till I was ready to lye down in the street. However I was glad I took this method of having the drawings correct, for several things had been mistaken and omitted, and others were very obscure till I had seen the whole figure who held or played the instrument, and sometimes even seeing the whole group in a basso rilievo was necessary to my forming any conjecture about the occasion and manner of playing it. (Vide drawings and explications among Roman papers)–

I had but just time to step into the pretty church built by Bernini of St. Andrea della Noviciata–to hear music composed by Casali and led by Nicolai–I heard a pretty sinfony and a good chorus à due cori–Stopt a moment in my way to the Campidoglio to see the paintings of Dominichini at the church of S. Andrea della Valle–the Tribunal–many parts of St. Andrews history–the 6 greater virtues between the windows and the angles of the cupola are his.–After dinner sorting papers and chatting with Mr. Byers whom I esteem most sincerely.–Then to Sir John Stanleys–Mrs. Forbes's and to the D. of Dorset's music–There all the Englishmen were, that had been the night before at General Shoveloff's. It is very agreeable now to meet all these people as we are well-acquainted and they are very civil to me. I was again obliged to play to night a lesson (sonata) of Pugnani's at sight to oblige the Duke and Mr. Hampden.

WEDNESDAY 14. Went this morning with the Duke and Mr. Jenkins to the Villa Albani, it was fine weather and the place in great beauty. Mr Jenkins set me right as to several pieces of sculpture that had been restored; particularly the lyre in the hand of a muse, which has 11 strings, and the crotolo in the hand of a young baccante are both modern, lyre with 7 strings in the hand of Apollo ditto–flute in the faun's hand ditto.–N.B. Among the hyroglyphics at the back of the Priestess of Isis, which is Egyptian sculpture there is a systrum and a calascione–in the semi-circular portico in a greek basso rilieve is a lyre under the statue of Esculapius–the left hand playing with the forefinger while the right holds a patera for a libation at a sacrifice–another figure holds the train of this priestess. Under the Jupiter Tonans is another lyre of the same kind with 5 strings played likewise with the fingers and not with a plectrum, which proves these instruments to have been rather harps than lyres: the band across is a sort of sling to hand or hold the instrument by.

From hence we went to the Aldobrandini Palace to see the ancient painting there. The colour is very much gone and much less fresh than that of the Herculaneum and Pompeia pictures–but the design of this and the drawing seem superior. The figure which holds the lyre is charming. Mengs in his Apollo and the Muses at the Villa Albani has imitated the form of this lyre, which has a circular base. I dined at the D. of Dorsets, and afterwards went to Monsignor Reggio's, where I met the custode of the Barbarini Library. Then to Mr Forbes's, where there was music.

THURSDAY 15. Very busy–I had the corriere with me to see my trunk etc–Piranesi's man who had made the drawings from antique instruments to pay 5 zechins. Giacomo Frej's prints to chuse out of–and a visit from Capt. Forbes–Sir Thos. Hesketh and Mr. Glover son of Leonidas, before I could get out. Then things to buy for my journey–such as fur gown, books, and a ⌊folding⌋ white hat–to see theatres–the Alberti is nearly as large as that of S. Carlo at Naples. It has an immense stage and 6 rows of boxes, 36 in each–capable of holding 3 in front–the Argentina and Capranica were shut–but see De la Lande Vol 5–then to Monaldini the bookseller's and old stalls in the corso. After dinner Mr. Morrison and Capt. Forbes went with me to examine antiquities and in our way we saw some fine paintings of Rafael in the church of ⟨   ⟩ and the famous Trinity of Guido in the church della SS Trinità de' Peregrini, e Convalescenti. Near this is the Pelegrini Street full of gold and silver smiths like our Lombard Street.–We saw in our road the Farnese Hercules, the famous statue of Jupiter at the Verospi Palace, 'tis the best extant–and 2 charming pictures on the ceiling of the portico behind it by Albano– 'tis the story of Acis and Galatea, beautifully told.

FRIDAY 16. This morning after a levée of copyists etc I went to Santarelli's and had a delightful confab with him. He delivered to me all the music of the Pope's chapel for Passion Week–several other things belonging to the Capella Pontificia, and extracts from his own book in MS. relative to several points of musical history, all invaluable as it is utterly impossible to get them elsewhere. ⌊This most friendly and honourable man is the only Roman who religiously performed all his promises⌋. He had with him 3 or 4 of his bretheren of the Popes chapel, among the rest Signor Pasquale Pisari who had with him the original score of a mass in 16 real parts full of canons, fugues and imitations; I never saw a more learned or ingenious composition of that sort. Palestrina never wrote in more than 8 real parts, and but few have succeeded in so many as those; but to double the number is infinitely more than doubling the difficulties. After 3 parts every one becomes more and more difficult, all that can be done on these occasions is to adhere to a simple melody and modulation–and to keep the parts in contrary or at least dissimilar motion. In the composition above mentioned every kind of contrivance is used, such as making the parts answer or imitate each other by 2 and 2–inverting the subjects etc etc. A century or two ago the author of such a composition would have had a statue erected to his honour, but now it would be equally difficult to get 16 people to hear it with patience as to find as many good singers in one place to perform it. Besides all these vocal parts, there is one for the organ often on a regular subject different from all the rest. The ground work is canto fermo, upon which all is built. In some of the movements this canto fermo is made a subject of imitation and runs thro' all the parts. Upon the whole it must be allowed that as this work consists of many different movements and is of a very considerable length, tho' it may be thought by some to require more patience than genuis, yet it seems sufficient to have employed a long life in composing, and to entitle the author to great praise and admiration.

Le Chevalier Tayler died here this morning in extream poverty.*

* According to *D.N.B.* John Taylor, itinerant oculist, died in Prague in 1772. A late addition to the Osborn MS., in Burney's hand, at this point reads: 'I dined with him at my table d'hôte a few days before his death.' *D.N.B.* may have erred.

Burney at the harpsichord · The Villa Borghese

After dinner to Crispi's academia – I arrived late – his new quartettos were performing, and he was so obliging as to make the performers begin again and go thro' with the whole 6. I think these compositions have great merit and are superior to any of his other productions. – From hence to the D. of Dorset's concert where all the English were assembled to the amount of more than 30 lords and gentlemen. Mr. Hampden brought with him two rods in soke [pickle] for me in the shape of 2 of Pugnani's trios for the harpsichord in MS. which I had never seen. I scrambled thro' them at sight as well as I could and received the thanks of *both houses*. Sir Thomas Hesket, a good natured pleasant English character who is very civil to me and has been twice to see me, ere I went to him invited me to dine with him to morrow, but I was engaged to Mr. Earl.

SATURDAY 17. Visited this morning Counseller Reiffenstein and the miniature painter. The former told me of a Chinese organ (the Ching)* blown with the mouth like the instrument found lately at Pompeia – after this went with Messrs Scot, Forbes and Nevy to see the Villa Borghesi or Pinciana Palace. It is but a little way out of the Porto del Popolo, on the right hand in the way to the villa Rafaele. The gardens and park are more free and in the English way than anything I had seen in Italy. The park is 3 miles round and has verdure. The outside of the house is incrusted almost entirely with antique bassi rilievi – Curtius leaping the gulf as big as the life in alto rilieva is inserted in one of the great walls both him and the horse are very spirited. There are in this collection 3 or 4 statues of the first order, such as the Fighting Gladiator, the Hermaphrodite, Silenus and the Infant Bacchus, Seneca in the Bath etc – but in the order I saw them the following are my feelings. Seneca in the Bath of black marble or touch-stone wonderfully fine – the eyes white – expression in the countenance divine but seems rather too young for Seneca. Bernini's David taking aim at Goliah, sling in his hand – 'tis said to be Bernini's own portrait, and is very ugly. A Juno, the best porphyry figure in Rome. – Rome Personified, a noble bust. Marcus Aurelius one of the finest in the world. Apollo and Daphne of Bernini, exquisite. It has all the beauty of cleanliness added to infinite grace and expression. Daphne is branching out – the leaves of the tree and the draperies are so light and fine one would swear they were muslin or laun – Æneas carrying Anchises and his household gods on his shoulders, by the father of Bernini: the old man's right arm is admirably ematiated and scraggy. Lucius Verus the finest portrait bust in Rome. The Gypsie, very pretty in profile. N.B. the head is Bernini's. – The fighting

---

* By ching is usually meant cymbals or gong. Burney may refer here to a china, a small sona or conical flute.

Gladiator most amazingly fine, drawing, attitude and muscular force, with manly grace are all united. – It has been formerly hurt and discoloured by the casts that have been made of it, and now, 'tis too late, crowned heads are refused the privilege of having it cast, the Empress of Russia among the rest. – The only 2 fluted porphyry pillars in Rome are here. – In the same appartment is Faustina and the Gladiator or as some say Venus arming Mars – the 3 Graces supporting an urn or vase, charming heads modern. – Silenus with the infant Bacchus in his arms very fine. – A noble vase with Bacchanals playing on all kinds of ancient instruments, such as the lyre, tamborine, tibiæ pares, castinets, clappers etc – Hermaphrodite most admirable! The 2 sexes strongly marked, it seems in a dream, ⟨. . . 4? words deleted and illegible . . .⟩ – the matrass of Bernini on which it lies, is much admired. – A small Venus rising from the sea, charming. Psyche, excellent, beautiful face. Centaur with young Cupid behind on his back, tying his hands behind him. – Young patrician with the bollo d'oro. – A faun playing on a fife. – Head of Venus, fine. 2 little Cupids, companions, one of which is laughing at a bird in his hand in a very pretty and droll manner. – Gallery of beauties, all ugly –

Dined at Mr. Earle's, where I met Franchi the composer, who promised me some of his works. – The company at dinner were Mr. and Mrs. Earl – with Messrs Worseley, Wilbraham and self. Saw here Antonio Carrara, to whom I had a letter from Garrick – he served Mr. Sharp and has honourable mention made of him in Baretti's book – is very well spoken of by Mr. and Mrs. Earl – went home and wrote two letters to Venice etc –

SUNDAY 18. After I got rid of a heap of people, I went with Wyseman to the church of St. John Lateran, heard high Mass performed in the Colonna chapel by 2 choirs and saw it played by Signor Colista on a little movable organ. The music was by Signor Casale, maestro di capella who was there to beat the time. I was introduced both to him and Signor Colista after the service and the latter upon being entreated to let me hear the great organ very obligingly complied, upon condition that Monsignore il Prefetto of the church was applied to, which is a necessary ceremony in consequence of some injury that was formerly done to the instrument by the malice or ignorance of a stranger who had played upon it. This application was very readily undertaken and obtained by Signor Casale, and I was conducted into the great organ loft by Signor Colista who did me the favour to open the case and shew me all the internal construction. 'Tis a 32 ft. organ and the largest in Rome. It was the first built in 1549, and has undergone 2 repairs since, the one in 1600 by Luca Blasi Perugino (see Venuti p.10) and a 2nd a few years ago under the direction

of the present organist. It has 36 stops, 2 sets of keys, has long 8ths*
an octave below double F. and goes up to E in altissimo. It has pedals,
in the use of which Signor Colista is very dextrous. His manner of
playing this instrument seems to be the true organ style, tho' at present
his taste is a little passé–indeed the organ style seems better preserved in general through Italy than with us, as the harpsichord is not
sufficiently cultivated to encroach upon that instrument. Signor
Colista played several fugues in which the subjects were frequently
introduced in the pedals in a very masterly manner. It seems as if
every virtue in music was to border upon some vice, for this style of
full playing seems to preclude all grace taste and melody, while the
light airy harpsichord kind of playing destroys the *sostenuto* and richness of harmony and contrivance of which this divine instrument is so
peculiarly capable. It is very extraordinary that the *swell*, which has
been known in England more than 50 years, and which is so capable
of expression and pleasing effects, that it may well be said to have been
the greatest and most important improvement that ever was made in
any keyed instrument, should be still utterly unknown in Italy. It is
the same with the beat from the octave or 5th of any note on the violin
instead of the old close shake.–The touch too of the organ which our
builders have so much improved, still remains in its heavy and noisy
state, and now I am on this subject I must observe that all the organs
I have met with on the continent seem inferiour to ours built by
Father Smith, Byfield or Snezler in everything but size. As the
churches are often immense, so are the organs, and the tone is meliorated by the distance, but when near it is intolerably coarse and
noisy. Though the number of stops in these large instruments is very
great they afford but little variety, being for most part duplicates in
unisons and octaves to each other, as great and small 12th, flute 15th
etc–In ours the touch, the tone and imitation stops are greatly
superiour.

From hence I went to Messrs Jenkins and Morrison to collect
drawings etc–and dined with Mr. Byers who has procured some good
drawings of ancient instruments from the best and most authentic
sculpture. Immediately after dinner went to St. Peters where there
was a great funzione for the feast of its foundation. The vespers were
said by Cardinal York assisted by several bishops–there were Mazzanti, Giovanini and Christofero to sing, besides the whole choir and
several supernumeraries. The fat Giovanini, famous for playing the

* This suggests that the organ had a full range of accidentals (sharp and flat notes)
in its lowest octave, whereas it was customary in most keyboard instruments at this
time to tune the bottom octave without four of the sharp and flat notes that normal
tuning would require ('short', or 'broken', octave).

violoncello as well as for being one of the maestri di capella of St. Peters, beat time. The solo parts were finely sung by the 3 singers above mentioned and the choruses by 2 quires and 2 organs admirably performed. There were no other instruments than the 2 organs, 4 violoncellos and 2 double basses. There were some fugues and imitations in dialogue, between the 2 choirs which had a very fine effect. The service was in the large Winter chapel on the left in which is the largest organ. Cardinal York said mass in the morning–when there was a very great congregation.–This poor prince, as he is called here seems a greater bigot than his grand father [James II] could ever have possibly been–not contented with assisting at the vespers, after every body else had done, he came out of the chapel and in the broad isle of the middle of the church he kneeled down before a bench and prayed till I and every one else was weary of looking at him. From hence to the Abate Orzini alla Piazza di Monte Citorio. Thence to the oratorio of Jonathan at the Chiesa Nuova, which not being either well set or well sung, after the 1st part was over I went to another at St. Gerolamo della Carità, which had only 3 characters in it–the subject was the Judgment of Solomon–the tenor was admirable–had great taste and facility of execution–and one of the mothers, a castrato, had a sweet toned voice and sung in a very pleasing manner. The subject seems extreamly well adapted for musical expression, the stern note of the judge, the indifference of the false mother and the tenderness of the true, are all susceptible of musical colouring. The music, far from bad, was by a young composer who had begged employment in order to have an opportunity of displaying his talents. His name is Giuseppe Maria Magherini. From hence to the D. of Dorsets academia–and then to sup with Messrs Gordon, Scott and Byers.

MONDAY 19. At the Vatican to collect the extracts that were made for me and to pay for them. Signor Abate Elie was very reasonable and asked less than I gave him so that we parted very good friends–but 1st he shewed me several of the most ancient and curious MSS. in the Vatican Library–among which is the Virgil and Terence of the 3rd and 5th century. Virgil in the 5th on vellum a fine large and legible character, all the words separated by points–the illuminations are engraved by Santi Bartoli, as are those of the Terence. I examined both for ancient instruments and found some–in the Terence, though very rude, but the miniatures in the history of an Italian family (Justiniani) before the time of Rafaele are exquisite–from hence to see the medals, cameos and intaglios etc–after this to the Belvedere–and then to the Vatican Gallery to see paintings of Giotto which were in the old church of St. Peter, and there I found a species of viol played by a bow. Giotto was contemporary with Dante.–After dinner I was visited by Santarelli and Pisaro then after prints, copyists etc–and to Battoni's, where I met the good Santarelli. Miss Battoni sung a great number of songs and very much to her own honour, to the honour of her master and to my satisfaction.–Leave taken here of the dear and worthy Santarelli, who at my request consented, contrary to his custom, to give Parsons some lessons in singing, and proposed himself a correspondence.–I went to make visits of partenza and finished at the Forbes's by buying the etchings of Salvator Rosa of his great grand daughter as much to serve her, as to please myself.

TUESDAY. A dreadful wet day–however at 11 I went out–called on Byers, Morrison, Leighton etc and then went alone thro' a heavy rain to visit the famous Todini Gallery in the Veruspi Palace.* All the accounts of Rome are full of the praises of this music gallery or as it is called gallery of instruments; but nothing shews the necessity of seeing for one's self more than this gallery for these instruments cannot have been playable for many years; but when a thing is once got into a book as curious, it is copied into others without examination. There is a very fine harpsichord to look at, covered with gilding, but not a key that will speak–It formerly had a communication with an organ in the same room, with 2 spinets and a virginal–under the frame is a violin, tenor and base, which by a movement of the foot used to be played on by the harpsichord keys. The organ appears in the front of the room but not on the side, where there seem to be pipes and machines inclosed but there was no one to open or explain it, for the old cicerone of the house is just dead.† The gallery of this palace is charmingly painted by Albano, as is the ceiling of the portico behind the famous statue of Jupiter. At 6 went out in the most violent rain, thunder and lightening that can be imagined–to make partenza visits and to examine Piranesi's things, from which I had had some ancient instruments drawn. Thence to Mr. Hamilton, the painter whose pictures I saw and whose prints I bought, and in going from his house to the Duke of Dorsets where I was to meet Corri, my prints were so wetted by a hole in the top of the coach, that they were nearly spoilt. They were spread to dry in the Duke's appartment– then a little while music, here, after which to Crispi's where I was engaged to hear his quartettos over again, and a tenor being wanting I played that instrument while Crispi played the base.–These being finished and bows made, I returned to the Duke's–where now

---

* Michael Todini (born 1625?) was an astonishingly skilful maker of musical instruments and mechanical devices. The instruments were acquired by the Verospi family.

† The organ had apparently been set up in a form not intended by its maker.

I found much company, all very civil to Pil Garlic* on taking leave.

WEDNESDAY 21. This night being fixt on for my departure with the courrier, the morning was a very busy one – packing, paying – receiving visits, drawings, prints, and music, not delivered in before. But notwithstanding all this hurry I went with Mr. Morrison and Capt. Forbes to the Kirkeana Museum – which the former had obtained leave to see – still a violent rain, thro' which we tramped. – The museo was shewn us by a young Irish Jesuit, Father Plumket, I think – who was likewise a young antiquary, but Mr. Morrison, whom I take to be the 1st and most sagacious in Rome, set him right in many things. – Ancient paintings, ruins, vases, jewels – intaglios etc in such abundance, that I could have fancied myself at Portici – but what I chiefly went to see were Father Kirchers instruments and machines described in his Musurgia – all now out of order – and the little bronze figure I had been told of at Florence – 'tis not bigger than a pocket crucifix, but very ancient and of the best sculpture – it is quite a caricature, a thin and ghastly naked figure playing on a lyre with 6 strings with both hands and consequently without a plectrum, and singing at the same time – the strings half project and half concave, alternately.

⟨5 whole lines and part of two more deleted
and illegible⟩

Tho' I was in waiting many hours before, we did not quit Rome (the corriere and I) till one o'clock THURSDAY morning. – It was bitter cold – a clear sky and north wind full in our teeth in an open chaise à l'Italienne – and such a chaise! It never had been good for anything, but for my sins it was now at its worst and was going to its long home never to return to Rome again. We jogged on in that kind of stupifaction which people have who are neither a sleep nor a wake, dead or alive. – Besides cold and want of room for expansion of arms, legs etc I had the disagreeable task at the end of every post to dismount which roused me out of my lethargy merely to feel more poignantly the cold and my otherwise disagreeable situation. At Viterbo the hill was covered with snow – however in this way we got to the gates of Florence on SATURDAY at 3 in the morning but could not enter till past 6 – at Florence but an hour and ½ allowed – during which time I went to Molini to enquire after the books and commissions I had left with him – found as usual nothing had been done or thought of in my absence – nay Molini tho' a very obliging good natured man, had so much of his country about him that he had forgot even *what* he had

* 'Poor I', 'Poor me'.

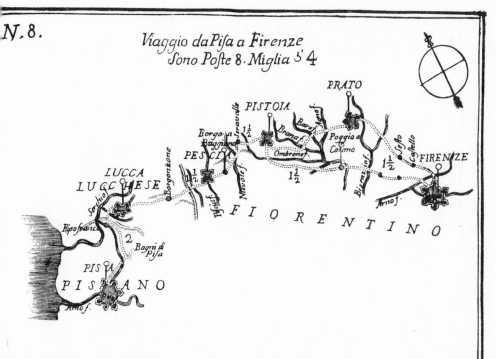

N. 8.

Viaggio da Pisa a Firenze
Sono Poste 8 · Miglia 5̸ 4

8. Florence to Pisa. There were two recognised routes – of equal length – for this journey.

promised to do for me before my return. – 'Tis extraordinary that this inattention to promises runs thro' all Italy. Mr. Molini never quitted me all the time I was at Florence, and really rendered me several singular services – and all the Italians to whom I had letters or was introduced loaded me with favours and civilities when present, and promised mountains while absent; but I have not yet received one proof of the sincerity of these promises, which seem made as things of course to please and keep the people they are made to, in good humour while present, little caring what they may think of them when absent. – In the way from Florence to Pisa the country was all mud and slime, like the banks of the Nile after its retreat – the Arno and other rivers had been so overflowed, that there had been 6 or 8 ft. water in houses, where the water never used to approach. It was a melancholly and comfortless sight – no refreshment to be had on the road. – A miserable piece of black, dry veal which the courrier had brought out with him – was every day produced till we got to Genoa – Friday and Saturday are always giorni magri, and once a month 3 meagre days fall out

[213]

N.20. Viaggio da Genova a Pisa
Sono Poste 16. Miglia 121.

20. Pisa to Genoa. The journey from Lerici to Genoa could be made by boat when the weather was calm in order to avoid the long and little used route over the high mountains.

together, of which I have constantly found the coachmen of diligences, the vitturini and courriers ready to avail themselves—

PISA

It was night 'ere we reached Pisa on SATURDAY—but I ran to see the tour by moonlight and the cathedral by the lamps with which it was luckily for me still illuminated on account of public prayers, devotions and ceremonies for dry weather. The tour is beautiful, not in its deformity of being all awry but in its construction. The cathedral is large and has many fine things in it, brought from different parts of the world at different times—such as pillars of different orders,

materials etc–I likewise here while the courrier waited for me without
the gates visited Signor Lidarti–and had about ½ an hour with him–
he's a decent intelligent man, and was very desirous of obliging me;
had I been able to stay he would have made an academia for me of the
best performers in Pisa. I take him by his Italian to be a German–a
book I had from de la Chevardière at Paris of his writing I could not
get at, but sent it him from Genoa by means of the French consul M.
Reyner–he is a bit of a reader and shewed me about 10 or 12 books
on music, all which I am in possession. He had heard of me at
Bologna from Padre Martini with whom he had been since I was
there. From Lidarti I learned a reason for P. Martini not keeping his
word with me in sending the 2nd Vol. of his history to Florence by
the time I returned there, which greatly disappointed me, as it was
the chief reason for my returning thro' that city–but I find the dedication to the Grand Duke had not been received which prevented other
copies being issued out.–

We had several rivers to pass in the night and about one in the morning it began blowing and raining so furiously, that it took away all hope of embarking at Lerici as we intended for Genoa. In this one night we passed thro' 5 different states from Pisa to Sarzana–namely, the Tuscan, Lucchese, Tuscan again, Modena, and Genoa–at Sarzana we dismounted from the chaise and got on mules, our trunks and baggage with assistance did the same. I had no boots and was otherwise but ill prepared for riding on horseback–however there was no help for it–submission to necessity is the easiest complied with. Here we had a little distance from the town to ford the *Magra* a rapid river from the mountains, now overflowing its banks–at the river a terrible squabble with the muleteers for a trifle with the courier, who let 'em carry off my mule, which I liked very well and I had in its place a wretched one without bridle or saddle with only a halter on his neck–at this I own I was unable to *bridle* my passions–I complained, I grumbled–I alight and walked and at last provoked the courier to send to a cottage and hire a saddle for me to the end of the 1st post— my boots were too big which I had bought at Sarzana, too stiff and unpliant, and hurt me desperately when I walked.–It cleared up a little while, and the 1st 2 posts were not quite unpleasant, tho' thro' a very wild country; but we had still 2 more to go in the night, and these were terrible indeed! such as I shall never forget. During the 1st we had a rapid river to ford 20 times which grew bigger and bigger–such rocks to climb, and descend!–But all this was nothing compared with the last post where the road was always on the edge of a precipiece, with the river above mentioned, now a torrent roaring below, with such noise and fury as turned one's head, and almost stunned one; had it quite done so it would have been for the better; for I neither knew what I did nor what any one of the muleteers or guides said.– At every moment I could only hear them cry out *alla montagna*! which meant to say that the road was broken and dangerous. In short it was so much so that we were obliged frequently to alight and hold by the side of the rock and precepiece. I got 3 or 4 terrible blows on the face and head by boughs of trees I could not see. In mounting my mule, which was vicious I was kicked at once by the 2 hind legs on my left knee, and right thigh which knocked me down and I thought at 1st and the muliteers thought my thigh was broke, and began to pull at it and to add to the pain most violently–It was a long while ere I would consent to mount again, tho' I walked in great misery. Such bridges! such rivers! and such rocks! amidst all the noise above mentioned, to pass, as are beyond all power of description! However, at length, about 11 at night we arrived at a wretched inn, or pigstye–half stable and half cow-house–with a fire, but no chimney, surrounded by boors and muleteers all in appearance cut-throatly personages, with no kind of refreshment but the cold veal and some stinking eggs and water *a bere*; after which repast and dosing in the smoak about an hour we set off again to pursue the same most tremendous road.

It is in vain to attempt to describe what I could not see–but I could feel that we clambered and crawled up and down rocks and mountains on narrow roads at the edge of precipieces and could hear torrents always. At length day broke and discovered to us that we were at the summit of the highest mountain of all the Appenines–and a formidable sight it was.–However it was desirable to see our danger as it put us more on our guard. All this morning, MONDAY 25 [26] on the top of these high mountains in a most furious wind, which I thought would have sometimes carried away both me and my mule– however this was not so bad as darkness and rain, and we trudged and dru[d]ged on tolerably till night, when the wind continued so high the candles in our lanthorns were frequently blown out, and we obliged to stand stock still. It now rained again, and was totally dark, not-withstanding the moon ought to have shone–in short it was so bad the courrier was forced to submit to stop 2 or 3 hours at Leric,* by the sea side, to which we had now descended or rather tumbled and slided, for going down these hills is ten times worse than going up. I lay down on a bed and in a room that made me shudder and had but just got into a feverish and uneasy sleep when I was waked again by bugs and devils.–We had 3 posts to go ere we arrived at Genoa, it was nothing but scrambling up hills merely to get down them again till within 2 or 3 miles of that famous city.–Bad as this country is for travellers I could perceive it to be very much cultivated near the city, and to be extremely fertile in olives, vines and corn which was sowing now under the olives in little slips of land supported by walls one above another.

Whether it was from my fatigue, and the badness of the weather which uglies every thing, Genoa did not answer my expectations. The suburbs are viley paved, full of holes enough to break the legs of men and beasts–but it is well paved within the gates.–The houses are indeed large and noble, but all of stucco plaistered and painted with-out, in a taudry and very bad taste–I expected marble fronts but saw no such thing. Tho' I knew I had letters at the Post office to which we first went, they could not be got on *this day*.–This is a great incon-venience to strangers in many towns of Italy, as particular days are set apart for particular parts of the post office business–as taking in– and delivering out letters for particular places. During the whole time I was here, which was about 3 or 4 hours at most, it rained and blew

* The Osborn MS. has Citri.

with the utmost violence imaginable–3 ships had been lost near the port. Several English were waiting for horses, servants, cloaths etc from Nice–Antibes–Monaco etc without anything to appear in and had been thus confined for near a fortnight to their rooms, unable to comfort or amuse themselves any other way than by swearing as I was told by the barber most d—ly,–G—d D—n—sun Bitch.–

There was at this time no opera at Genoa either serious or comic– an intermezzo only in which Piatti who had been in England was principal–I had a good deal of musical talk with M. Reyner the French consul whose daughter is a famous performer on the harpsichord. To him I delivered La Chevardiere's present of books to Lidarti which I could not get at when I saw him at Pisa. At about 2 o'clock we set off for the 2 1st posts in a dreadful open chaise, raining as I said before most furiously–in this we could only go to *Utri* about 12 or 14 miles from Genoa, always by the sea side. Here we were stopt all night by floods, a river at the end of this town being impassable.–

But here I must not forget to tell my distress at Genoa, the courrier seemed very unwilling to take me any further–dissuaded me all he could from undertaking the mountains of Final etc, said I had best wait for better weather and another courrier–but hearing what had happened to others who had been waiting above a fortnight at Genoa I did not at all like staying behind–but the English of his Italian and French were that he wanted more money–the mule I rode on and that for my baggage with a guide he found eat into his profits and as there were no hopes of the sea, he wanted to get rid of me and my lumber.–As soon as I found this out, I offered to pay for my own mule, which would be about 3 guineas more and this offer removed all his fears on my account as well as his own.–What strange creatures we are!–In passing the former mountains I thought if I once got safe over them nothing should tempt or force me to undertake such another journey–but–now, after the difficulties the courrier made in taking me with him, I began to think the staying behind a worse evil than going even over worse mountains that the former: 2 days and 2 nights we were clambering up and sliding or tumbling down these horrid mountains as far as one post beyond Final.–The night work was indeed most dreadful, the road always on the very ridge of the mountains and the sea always roaring beneath with a strong land wind, which I often thought would have carried me, mule and all into it.–I was frequently obliged to alight and hold by the opposite side of the rock or mountain–and once, the instant I was got off the mule's feet flew from under her and she fell with such violence, that if I had been on her back I must have been dashed to pieces.–Soon after the courrier's horse was missing and 2 of the pedini–and upon halooing after them, we found they were tugging up the precipiece this horse which had fallen down and luckily met with a bush which alone could have prevented his being precipitated into the sea. We were now so high that I thought we should never get down the hills to Final–the road was so bad, the stones so loose etc, that tho' I was walking with the utmost care I got a terrible fall by my feet flying from under me.

Thro' all the Genoese state the language the people speak is a jargon wholly unintelligible. But the people seem a handsomer race than their neighbours–the children have black eyes, good features and fair complexions, but there are no people in Italy said to be more notoriously wanting in probity.–The women wear tawdry linnen capuchins. We passed thro' Final in the night, the mountains on each side the most terrible of all, but one post beyond Final some sailors persuaded the courier to get into their felucca–tho' it blew as I thought a storm–so bad some times that my old guide seemed terrified to death and begged and prayed to be put on shoar.–However all he could obtain was to be rowed terra a terra.–We had a strange variety of weather during the 14 or 16 hours we were at sea–some times the wind poured down the hills in such gusts I thought we must be overset every instant–at others it was so calm that the sails jibed and the men were forced to take to their oars.–However at about 11 at night, FRIDAY 30 NOVEMBER, we got to Antibes in the kingdom of France–here a difficulty was made to let me into the town–and a fuss at the custom house, all to get money, not for the King or the State but blood sucking rascals.–I was so sick at sea the whole day and night I could not swallow a bit or drop of anything and would have given the world for a little broth at Antibes,–but it was a meagre day and nothing to be had but a worse chaise than even I had been in before and this was to carry me to Lyons 370 miles.–

At 1 we set off SATURDAY morning got to Frejus about 10 and stopt there an hour or 2. There are ruins of Roman aqueducts at going into the town, and in it remains of an amphitheatre–this was the only fine day we had all the journey–we were now in Provence and the weather was as warm as in England at the beginning of September–very good roads are cut on the mountains here much different from those in the Genoese state–but in the bottoms they were terribly cut up and full of water. We got to Aix next morning which is a very pretty town–the *Course* is a large fine street–planted on each side–with stone seats for persons who walk to repose on, and a wide road in the middle for the coaches.–The weather changed again now and we got to *Avignon* at night in terrible cold and wind. I could see but little of this famous old town made more famous by Petrarca and

Laura than by the Popes that resided in it–'tis now full of French troops. We were obliged to cross the Rhone here twice which is very rapid and wide.–'Tis the largest river I ever saw.* The bridge is broken. We got to *Pont St. Esprit* SUNDAY morning 2nd DECEMBER when we ought to have been at Lyons–this is a very fine light bridge of 36 arches over the Rhone.–From thence thro' Valence and Vienne to Lyons. Vienne is a large old and very miserable looking town situated on the Rhone. I was on my arrival at Lyons TUESDAY morning– so ill that I did not soon expect to get a way. Here I was much disappointed in not finding the books I had bought at Geneva in going to Italy.†–

I crawled to the theatre and was more disgusted than ever at French music after the dainties my ears had long been feasted with in Italy. Eugenie a pretty comedie preceded Sylvain an opera of Gretry–there were many pretty passages in the music but so ill sung, so false the expression–such screaming, forcing and trilling as quite turned me sick. I tried to observe on the road by what degrees the French arrive at this extreme depravity in their musical expression–and it does not come on all at once. In Provence and Languedoc through which I passed the songs of the country people are rather pretty–I got 'em to sing me some whereever I stopt–and the airs are national and simple– less wild than the Scots as less ancient, but I rather think these melodies the oldest since the invention of Guido's system. From Lyons I travelled night and day to Paris and arrived there quite knocked up and ill on SATURDAY DECEMBER 8th–went however to the concert spirituel at night to hear Mademoiselle Le Chantre more than anything else on the organ.–She did not answer my expectations–is but a *pretty* player, not a great one–her taste is formed from Italian and German compositions but she is often weak and inarticulate and her closes which she is fond of are very poor and both fanciless and fireless–M. Richer brother to Mrs Philidor has a most charming tenor voice–but having only French music to sing it was thrown away. However he was far less bad than the rest–M. Dauvergne is a very dull and heavy composer even in the oldest and worst French style– Bezozzi played a concerto charmingly–all the rest was the screaming of tortured infernals–the sopranos are squaled by cats in the shape of women. M. le Gros with a very fine counter tenor voice becomes by his constant performance in the French serious opera more and more intolerable every day. The motets are detestable. M. the prompter

* This statement is elaborated by a continuation written in pencil: '. . . the largest river I ever saw ⌊and the postillion who had never seen it before cried out *C'est ici qu'il y a de l'eau*⌋'.

† The Osborn MS., in this passage written by an amanuensis, has a late addition in Burney's hand: 'Here I stopped two or three days to refit . . .'

danced not beat the time to them. There was a great deal of men company who seemed much pleased with these intolerable master-pieces, as M. Rousseau calls 'em, to all ears but their own. I went to the Hotel D'Espagne very ill indeed, but by care and nursing all day on SUNDAY I was able to get out on MONDAY–found none of the commissions I had left at Paris in my way to Italy had been thought of in my absence–most of 'em lost–so that I had everything to do myself.

Monday night heard M. Grettry's new opera of les Deux avars – There were several pretty things in it, but he seems to become more and more French in his style daily. They say it is to suit the genius of his language–but this is not true–for the music that Lulli grafted on it was *Italian* tho' at a time when Italian music was bad.

On TUESDAY night I tried to get in but could not to a new serious opera by M. ⟨   ⟩. I lost all my day in hunting after folks I could not find.

WEDNESDAY, found M. Suard and Madame at home, but the Abbé Arnauld is out of town–saw Monnet and the Baron d'Holbach with whom I had a very long and agreeable conversation chiefly about music and found him well read and his taste and opinions what I wished 'em. He gave me several curious anecdotes–among the rest one relative to the quarrels in Spain about music–the partisans for the Italian music and those for the native Spanish having fought at first so many duels about it that 40 or 50 persons were killed when Italian music was first introduced there.–The music to the Dervis's dance at Constantinople several Italians agree is charming–Dr Gatti among the rest. I dined at Monnets and met there the famous journalist M. Frereon–he is by no means the sort of man Voltaire has painted him.*–To day several plots were laid for my being well received by Rousseau–but whether they will succeed I know not yet.–He now, as 'tis said only transcribes music–says he can neither read nor write to any purpose–complains of want of memory, *his* seems the contrary of Cæsars.

Went to a concert to night as I thought but they were puppets, automates–who played the violin, base, flute, harpsichord, organ etc–a better kind of puppet show tho' a worse kind of concert. I did not like it well enough to stay long but went to the Mareshal Ferrant†–neither Caillot nor la Ruette sung–and it went off but flat–and

---

* Fréron was the editor of the *Année littéraire* and had published criticism of Voltaire and his works. Voltaire vented his rancour by putting Fréron on the stage as a character in his comedy *L'Ecossaise* (1760) and had accused him of being not only a partial critic but a thief (*Le Pauvre Diable*).

† *Le Maréchal Ferrant* (The Blacksmith) a one-act opera by François André Danican Philidor.

more over I detest that mixture of old French vaudevilles with Phili-dor's Italian plunder.–

THURSDAY 13. Went early this morning with a letter from Freron, backed by Monnet, to Gui the bookseller one of the two people Rousseau suffers to approach him, in order to contrive an interview between us. He could not go out then but promised to carry me to his lodgings in the afternoon. From hence to the Abbé Morellet, where I found Dr. Gatti–had a long conversation about Turkish music which the Dr. heard at Constantinople at the Dervis's College which affected him, an Italian, more than any music he had ever heard–'tis all instrumental and begins very slow–'tis a kind of dance, a religious ceremony of great antiquity–(see Picard's *Ceremonies religieuses*. T. 7.)–The time and steps are accelerated by small degrees to extreme velocity, the decoises turning round, till at length they fall down with fatigue. The Abbé is a notable musician, has an English piano forte and is a great acquaintance of Echard.–I communicated to him my plan, of which he begged a copy, gave me Diderot's address–to whose hotel I went, but he was out–from hence to M. Flonsel whom I found ill in bed–but he was so obliging as to have his son called to shew me his curious Italian library, consisting of 20,000 vols. all in that language. Out of this number I could find but 2 or 3 on music which I had not already got, and those of no consequence. M. Flonsel has never been in Italy–all these books have been collected in France. He gave me his print and a dedication to him by Goldini, by way of envelope.

After this I came home and wrote a letter to M. Rousseau, which I intended sending to him in case Gui made any difficulty in carrying me–and thence to dinner at the Baron D'Holbach's–the 1st person I saw after I had paid my respects to the Baron was M. Diderot, whom I so much wished to see. We naturally embraced each other as cordially as if acquaintance of long standing–indeed he had been *mine* along time.* We soon grew very intimate–were placed close to each other at table, where there were above 20 persons, and we had a comfortable deal of talk. Madame la Baronne and her 2 sons and 2 daughters were there–the celebrated M. Grimm, to whom I was introduced, and all the rest were men of letters and merit of the 1st order in Paris.–The dinner and conversation were charming and I was sorry to quit them even to go to Rousseau. However I was to return again at 7 in order to meet the Abbé Morellet.–M. Gui was obliged to call at the Lieut. de Police ou Censeur Royal–where I saw all the booksellers, authors and authoresses of Paris. They assemble

* This was amplified editorially: '. . . long standing–indeed ⌊his writing made him⌋ *mine* a long time ⌊ago–1st Vol. Enyclopédie 1751⌋. We soon . . .'

here once a week–it was not unentertaining to see this ceremony–all new books are licenced here.

From hence to M. Rousseau, Rue Grenelle, at a small house, a crayon painters', up 5 pair of stairs. I went up in great sogezzione [uneasiness]–as I knew so much of his character–had heard of the rebuffs many had met with, and as I was prepared by Gui for a cold reception. However we got to the summit at last–and entered a small room with a bed in it–Madame was the 1st person we saw and in a dark corner was the man mountain–in night cap, gown and slippers– for which he apologised–and very civilly placed me near the fire–the reception was far better than I expected.* I began immediately to tell him of my journey and errand in to Italy–and the account seemed to catch his attention and after a little time, I told him that I was very much pleased to find his dictionary in all hands there, and that P. Martini *en faisoit le plus grand cas.*–He said he was very glad of that, as the Italians were the best judges of its merit (Gui printed it). After this I went all over Italy with him–discussed several curious points and pleased him again by accidentally saying I had found music at Venice in the best state of any part of Italy. He was *glad* of that, he said, as it was his opinion when there–then we talked of the conserva-torios, of Galuppi, Sacchini, etc–after which we went to Naples and discussed the opera there and the works of Jomelli and Piccini–then back to Rome–talked over the Pope's chapel–St. Peter's etc–and here I was in luck again.–I said on the 17 of last month I had heard 150 voices at St. Peters sing all together without *noise*–but on Saturday last, at the concert spirituel de Paris–I had been *stunned* by a third part of that number. He laughed out at this–somebody came in after this and I was silent till they had said their say.–Rousseau soon addressed himself to me again–and we talked of the ancient instruments and music of the Greeks–of recitative–of harmony in the last age and melody in this, etc.–He then mentioned his idea of the *unity* of *melody* which he had started without being understood in France at the time he set the Devin du Village†–Upon this I took occasion to tell him it was I who had given a translation of his *pretty*

* This sentence was later altered to: 'Madame ⌊la Gouvernante⌋ was the 1st person we saw, ⌊at her needle almost two double. She took not the least notice of us nor we of her⌋–and in a dark corner was the man mountain–in a ⌊woollen⌋ night cap, great ⌊coat⌋ and slippers . . .'

† *Le devin du village* (The Village Sorcerer) was an intermède (intermezzo) in one act with words and music by Jean Jacques Rousseau, and first performed before the King at Fontainebleu on 18 October, 1752. Burney prepared an English version of the work with additional numbers which was produced at Drury Lane as *The Cunning Man*, 21 November, 1766. In his *Confessions* Rousseau describes the writing and production of *Le devin du village* and reveals the part it (and he) played in the musical polemics of the time.

opera, I now ventured to say, I durst not attempt to flatter him before –and begged leave to present him with a copy of the translation. –He said he should be very glad to see it, and asked if it was that which had been received on the stage a few years ago, and I answered in the affirmative. –All this while we hit it off very well–he is a little figure with a very intelligent and animated countenance, black eyebrows. After this I had the courage to produce to him a copy of my plan, in French which had the appearance of great length, it having been copied wide by the Abbè Morellet's secretary–he said he never read and seemed coy and afraid of it–however he took it in his hand, and began reading to himself–and ere he had got half way down the 1st page he read aloud and seemed caught by it. –When he came* to the harp of David, ma fois, vous aller bien loin–says he–and I felt a little ashamed of the promise to examine it–When he came to the music of the ancients divided into martial, theatrical and ⌊in the contentions at the public games⌋–c'est bon ça–and at the article national music–Ah that's good, tis what I waited for–and at the instruments–he said that would be the most difficult and laborious of all–and then went on with seeming eagerness to the end, and said several very civil things. Ere I went away I got him to consent to let me send him the music of Jomelli's Passions–and the London edition of his *Divin* my *Cunning Man*–and we parted exceeding good friends. He did not bite–nor did I knock him down down†–but said he was very glad to have had the opportunity to conversing with one who loved and cultivated music so much and was very much obliged to me for my visit and communication, so we parted. He came to the head of the stairs whether I would or no.‡ From hence I returned to the Baron D'Holbach's, where I found the Abbe Morellet and M. Marmontel where I supped and stayed till midnight.

We here discussed several curious subjects relative to my history. The abbe, the Baron and all abuse me violently for quitting Paris so soon. M. Morellet did not stay supper. There was a gentleman there M. Kohaut, who played very well on the arch lute. After supper I was entertained and enlightened very much by the Baron's conversation on chimystry–minerals, fossils and other parts of natural history of all which he seems a perfect master–many of the best articles on those subjects and metallurgy in the Encyclopedie are his. –He is a fine character and a very superior man.

* Later altered to: '. . . seemed caught by it. When ⌊I mentioned Don Calmet's dissertation on⌋ the Harp of David, ma foi ⌊c'est⌋ aller bien loin ⌊dit-il⌋ . . .'
† Edited to 'He did not bite nor knock me down'.
‡ Burney later added: ⌊'Shewed me a very large print, a splendid frame, and glazed close by the door; asked me if I knew who it was–oui–c'est notre roy–he nodded assent'⌋–.

FRIDAY 14. To Diderot's at 9 in the morning—by appointment to hear his daughter and discuss my plan. I staid there till 1 and was charmed with his conversation and counsel—I gave him Miss Young's translation of le *Fils Naturel* and promised him mine of Le Divin—he *reads* English as his own language. We discussed my plan article by article—and I was very much flattered by the similarity of our sentiments upon the most essential parts of it. He has pressed me very much to let him see my MS. when finished ere it is printed, which I shall have great satisfaction in doing—as his taste and his learning rank equally high in my opinion—When we came to the articles ancient music—accents—poetry etc he took out of his cabinnet a great heap of MSS. in his own hand writing upon the same subjects which he gave me to make just what use I please of them. After this he wrote me down a list of all his works of which I was not already in possession—gave a little idol from Carribou Island, his address, and a charge to write to him often—then he presented me to his daughter a pretty and amiable young lady of 17, who is a great performer on the harpsichord and has a prodigious collection of the best German authors for that instrument. She played some pieces in every different style—is a great mistress of modulation—has a good finger, but not quite correct in time. The rest of the day in visits etc till night when I went to the Comedie Françoise. The pieces were l'Ecole des Femmes of Moliere and les Playdeurs de Racine.—These seem passées tho' once so famous, and appeared flat and to me far from entertaining tho' well acted.

SATURDAY. All this morning I had my books to collect and send off by a chest of Molini's to his brother in London, which was just ready to depart.—I dined at M. Suard's with the abbé Reynel—another abbe whose name I forget that has distinguished himself in the literary world, M. de la Harpe etc etc. After dinner M. Suard shewed me a Chinese instrument belonging to the abbé Arnauld. It is in form like our sticcado*—thin bars of light dry wood very sonorous which rest on a hollow vessel in the form of a little ship. There are but 17 notes on it—it has no semitones that I could find—and but 5 sounds from a note to its octave. I noted down the scales of 2 or 3.

 etc.

The Abbé thinks this scale to be that of Pythagoras. I stayed late for a copy of Voltaire's Epitre a l'Empereur de la Chine with his own corrections. M. de la Harpe received it by the post house while we

* A form of wooden dulcimer.

were at dinner. He seems the youngest of these literary gentlemen, and the fag. He came in with a huzza! M. Suard made one of his amenuenses transcribe it for the sake of the corrections and then gave the original to me.—From hence to take leave of the good Baron d'Holbach, who besides 2 books he had been so kind to bring me the day before undertook to procure me several scarce and necessary books in German, which he had promised to send to England if they can be found. After this I had to pack etc, which lasted me till ½ past 3 in the morning, when I set off by lamp light for Calais in a little poste chaise with one place.—I got late at night to Amiens 15 posts ½, where I stayed only 2 or 3 hours and then set off for Boloyne [Boulogne], where it was near midnight ere I arrived—the roads, houses and weather all miserably bad—floods every where.

Next morning TUESDAY 18th at 5 o'clock set off again and got to Calais at 10 or 11—I was hurried on board the pacquet in less than 2 hours time, with out having time allowed me to dry or arrange my things or even to get refreshments, as it was expected the ship would sail directly—but ere I had been on board ½ an hour a storm which had lasted several days and had but just subsided returned with redoubled violence—so that several ships which had got out of harbour were glad to return and we all came on shore where we continued without patience or hope of getting away from this dismal place, Calais, till SUNDAY 23rd at 3 in the morning when we set sail with a tolerable fair wind; but it soon grew otherwise, and we had a very disagreeable passage, being 12 hours at sea. However we arrived at Dover without accident on SUNDAY evening and next day, XMAS EVE, to my great joy got home to my family and affairs in London, after an absence of 7 months.

GLOSSARY

In the preliminary pages of *Tour* 1773 Burney gives what he calls an 'Explication of some musical terms and foreign words, which occur in the following Journal'. This is in fact a glossary of some of the terms of art, foreign words and technical terms which occur and recur, throughout the text. Burney's definitions are those current when he wrote, and they are often different from those related to the same terms in our day. It is important that the reader should bear this in mind. As the 'Explication' appeared in the preliminary pages in *Tour* 1773 Burney naturally used the future tense when he was referring to the text as something that was to come. The tense has not been changed in this edition although the 'Explication' follows the text.

In this edition the glossary has been extended slightly: the additions are marked by an asterisk*.

Accademia, a concert.

Adagio, slow, in the first degree: or, when used substantively, it signifies a slow movement.

Allegro, gay, or a quick movement.

Appoggiatura, from *appoggiare*, to lean on; a note of embellishment: it is usually written in a small character, as not essential to the harmony, though most essential to melody, taste, and expression.

Baritono, a voice of low pitch, between a tenor and base.

Bravura, as *aria di bravura*, a quick song of difficult execution.

Cameriere, waiter.*

Canon, a composition in which the parts follow each other in the same melody and intervals.

Canto fermo, plain song, or chanting in the cathedral service.

Canzone, a song.

Collina (*e*, plural), a hill usually not more than 500–600 metres high and still within the zone of cultivation.*

Contralto, a counter-tenor, or a voice of higher pitch than a tenor, but lower than the treble.

Contrapuntista, one skilled in the laws of harmony, a composer.

Contrapunto, counterpoint; composition in parts; this term came from the first music in parts, being expressed in points placed over each other.

Coup d'archet, the attack with the bow on the strings, or the stroke of the bow.*

Dilettante, a gentleman composer or performer; synonimous with the French word *amateur*.

Diminuendo, diminishing a sound, or rendering it softer and softer by degrees.

Double bass, the largest, and lowest in pitch, of the violin family. It is sometimes referred to as the *violone*, but this could also denote a double bass viol.*

Due Cori, two choirs, orchestras, or chorusses.

Expression, the performing a piece of melody, or a single passage, with that energy and feeling which the poetry or passion, to be impressed upon the hearer, requires.

Forte, loud.

Glossary

Fugue, a flight or pursuit; a *fugue* differs from a *canon* only in being less rigid in its laws; a *canon* is a perpetual *fugue*: the first, or leading part gives the law to the rest in both; but, in the course of a fugue, it is allowable to introduce episodes and new subjects.

Funzione, function, ceremony in the church on a festival.

Giorno di magro, fast day.*

Graduale, gradual; an appellation given, in the Romish church, to a verse which is sung after the epistle, and which was anciently sung on the steps of the altar.

Harmony, music in parts, in opposition to melody.

Imitation, a slight species of *fugue*, in which the parts imitate each other, though not in the same intervals, or according to the rigorous laws of a *fugue* or *canon*.

Improvvisatrice, a female who pronounces verses extempore.

Intermezzo, an interlude, or musical farce, usually performed between the acts of a serious piece.

Laudisti, psalm singers.

Maestro di Capella, a composer, or one who directs a musical performance in a church or chapel.

Maestro del Coro, master of the choir.

Melody, an air, or single part, without base or accompaniment.

Messa Bassa, a silent mass, whispered by the priest during a musical performance.

Mezzo Soprano, a second treble, or voice between the treble and counter-tenor.

Miserere, the first word of the 51st Psalm, in Latin.

Modulation, the art of changing the key, or of conducting the harmony or melody into different keys, in a manner agreeable to the ear, and conformable to established rules.

Motetto, *Motet*, a Latin hymn, psalm, or anthem.

Musico, a general term for musician; but now chiefly applied in Italy to a *castrato*.

Offertorio, Offertory, an anthem sung, or a voluntary played, at the time the people are making an offering.

Orchestra, that part of a building assigned to instrumental players or singers.*

Piano, soft.

Plain chant, plain song, or chanting.

Portamento, conduct of the voice: the *portamento* is said to be good, when the voice is neither nasal nor gutteral.

Ritornello, originally the echo or repetition of any portion of a song by the instruments; but, in process of time, it became the general term for symphony, in which sense it will be often used in this Journal, and which will perhaps, be called, *Verbum movere loco*; but though the word *Ritornel* is rather obsolete and has for some time been supplied by symphony, it now wants revival, as symphony, among modern musicians, is usually synonymous with overture.

Saltatori, jumpers, or dancers of uncommon agility.

Sistine, The Pope's chapel is sometimes called the *Sistine* chapel, from Sextus Quintus, who built it.

Soprano, the supreme, or treble part, in vocal composition.

Sostenuto, sustained; or, used substantively, the power of continuing a sound: the harpsichord has no *Sostenuto*, the organ has one.

Spinet, a keyboard instrument in which the strings are plucked as in the harpsichord or virginal: it had but one string to each note.*

Steiner [Stainer], the name of a famous German maker of violins.

Sinfonia, symphony, or overture.

Taste, the adding, diminishing, or changing a melody, or passage, with judgement and propriety, and in such a manner as to *improve* it;

[228]

if this were rendered an invariable rule in what is commonly called *gracing*, the passages, in compositions of the first class, would seldom be changed.

Tenor, a name often given in the 18th century to the viola.*

Vetturino (*i*, plural), driver, coachman.*

Viol, a family of stringed instruments with six strings, fretted finger boards and played with a bow. They were made in many sizes. Originally played sloping across the body, they were later held vertically between the legs, whence its familiar name *viola da gamba.**

Viola (Italian *viola da braccio*), the alto member of the violin family, played on the arm with a bow, tuned a fifth below the violin.*

Violin, (*violino da braccio*), four-stringed instrument, without frets on the finger board, played on the arm by a bow.*

Violoncello, a member of the violin family, played with a bow and held between the knees. Strung an octave below the viola.*

Virtù, talents, abilities; hence

Virtuoso, a singer.

Virtuoso da Violino, a performer on the violin.

Virtuoso da Camera, a chamber musician.

Voce di Camera, a feeble voice, fit only for a chamber.

Voce di Petto, a voice which comes from the breast, in opposition to one that is nasal or guttural.

Vox Humana, human voice.

Vox humana, a tenor oboe: it stood a fifth below the ordinary oboe.*

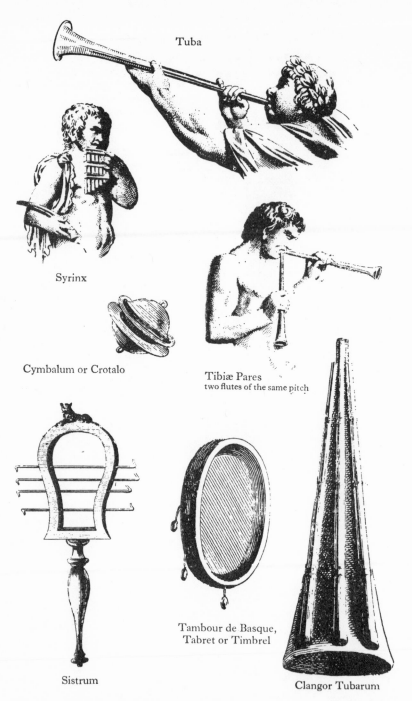

Tuba

Syrinx

Cymbalum or Crotalo

Tibiæ Pares
two flutes of the same pitch

Tambour de Basque,
Tabret or Timbrel

Sistrum

Clangor Tubarum

Some of the musical instruments of antiquity mentioned by Burney. They
are reproduced from plates IV, V and VI of the first volume of Burney's
A General History of Music, second edition (1789).

BIOGRAPHICAL INDEX

has not been possible to identify all the artists, musicians and writers from all ages whose
ames appear in the Journal; or all the men and women whom Burney met – 'Mr. Cox, an
d English gentleman' at Florence, and many other figures more substantial than this, re-
ain obscure. Where the necessary information is available, limitation of space has restricted
dividual entries to the dates of birth and death of the subject and the briefest summary
 his career. Some characters who appear in general reference books have been excluded
together.
 Burney is not always careful about the spelling of names: Mich Ange and Michel Angello
th appear for Michelangelo. Where these irregularities occur Burney's version is printed
st in italic and the more usual version follows. In some cases Burney uses a number of
riants: not all of them have been noted, as it has been assumed that if the reader is put on
e alert by the identification of one he will recognise the others.

bate, Niccolò dell' (*c.*1512–71), Modenese painter: worked in Modena, Bologna and France (1552) where he settled. Influenced by Mantegna and Correggio.95.

el, Karl Friedrich (*b.*Cöthen, 1725;*d.*London, 1787), virtuoso viola da gamba player: composer, concert promoter (with J. C. Bach) in London. 194.

lami, Andrea da Bolsena (*b.*Bolsena, 1663 ; *d.* Rome, 1742), master of the Pope's chapel and acting professor of music. His *Osservazioni* (1711) is a history of the Papal chapel.140, 144.

bano. Albani, Francesco (1578–1660), Bolognese painter: fellow pupil with Guido Reni under Calvaert and the Carracci.40, 91, 100, 105, 148, 153, 184, 206, 211.

egri, Gregorio (1582–1652), Roman musician, best known for his 'Miserere' for nine voices in two choirs.140, 202.

ati, the surname of a family of violin makers who lived in Cremona, Italy, in the 16th and 17th centuries. They made a number of superb instruments.98.

nici, de. Amicis, Anna Lucia de (*b.*Naples, *c.*1740), a celebrated singer, She appeared in London in 1763 in opera buffa, but impressed by her powers J. C. Bach wrote for her in serious opera, and she continued to sing in this form during the remainder of her career. She had fine technique, her singing was 'exquisitely polished and sweet' and young Mozart took special pains to display her powers in his opera *Lucio Silla* at Milan (1773).193.

hault. Dessau. Anhalt, a sovereign duchy of the German Empire (N. Germany), divided among four branches of the ruling house in 1666.153.

Aprile, Giuseppe (1738–1814), of Apulia, an eminent contralto singer: educated at the Conservatorio 'La Peità', Naples, he sang in all the chief Italian and German theatres. Composer and famous teacher.52, 128, 186.

Aretino, *see* Spinello

Ariosto, Ludovico (*b.*Reggio, 1474 ; *d.*Ferrara, 1533), celebrated poet; man of affairs.86.

Aristaxenus. Aristoxenus of Tarentum (4th century B.C.), Greek writer on music, pupil of Aristotle.189, 194.

Armstrong, Dr. John (1709–79), M.D., physician, essayist and poet 'The Art of Preserving Health' (1744). Medical adviser and warm friend of Burney and his family.76, 131.

Arnaud (or Arnauld) (1721–84), Abbé, librarian to the brother of the King of France, prolific writer, historical and polemical on music.18, 21, 22, 221, 225.

Arthur, John(?) *b.*Great Hanwood, Salop, a watchmaker in Paris, where a Jean Arthur is recorded master 1757–89, and as one renowned for his repeater watches.17, 18, 23.

Bach, Johann Christian (1735–82), known as the 'English Bach' son of J. S. Bach. Went to Italy 1756 and to London (1762) where he settled. He wrote successful operas and much orchestral and piano music.19, 50, 194.

Bacchelli. Bicchelli, the family name of a paintress of miniatures, best known because of her art as La Mignatrice. She was an accomplished singer, married D. Corri her teacher and sang in Edinburgh in 1772.151, 152, 153, 204.

[231]

Baglioni, family name of six sisters, all singers. Costanza, excellent actress and pleasing singer, was the best known.52, 54.

Balbastre, Claude (1729–99), organist and composer, in Paris.17.

Bandinelli, Baccio (1493–1560), Florentine sculptor, goldsmith and painter: sought to rival Michelangelo.107, 108.

Barbella, Emanuele (1704–73), outstanding Neapolitan violinist: composer, much influenced by Tartini.177, 180, 181, 182, 196.

Bartoli, Pietro Sante (*b*.Perugia, 1635 ; *d*.Rome, 1700), a painter, but best known for his engravings from antique bas reliefs.144, 210.

Baretti, Signor, brother of G. M. A. Baretti, one of the Johnson–Thrale circle. There were four brothers, this one was probably Amadeo, architect.40, 41, 42, 54, 68, 76, 80, 88.

Barry, James (1741–1806), Irish painter, came to England 1763, visited Paris and Rome: R.A. 1773, Professor of painting R.A. 1782–99. Depicted Burney among water nymphs in a mural at Royal Society of Arts, 1777–83.99.

Bartolozzi, Francesco (*b*.Florence, 1727;*d*.Lisbon, 1815), engraver: studied in Venice and Rome, arrived in England 1764: founder member Royal Academy 1769. Head of school of engraving Lisbon (1802).59, 91.

Bassan, Bassani. Bassano, group name of a family of Venetian painters. The most considerable was Jacopo (*c*.1510/18–92), son of Francesco da Ponte the Elder (*c*.1475–1539).65, 74, 82, 111, 148, 153, 184.

Bassi, Laura (1711–78), eminent in literature and science, doctor 1732, married Dr. J. Verati of Bologna, 1738, experimentalist in physical sciences 1745 to her death.41, 95.

Battoni, il Cavalier, Batoni, Pompeo (1708–87), painter, specialist in portraits of Grand Tourists in Rome posed against antiquities.149, 203, 211.

Beccaria, Padre G. B. (1716–81), native of Piedmont, physicist and mathematician: his writings on electricity were specially important.41, 95.

Beckford, William, (*d*.1799), historian. He wrote about Jamaica, and France (history 1794).130, 131, 132, 139, 159, 202.

Benedict XIV, Pope (*b*.Bologna, 1675), of the family of Lambertini, elected Pope, 1740. He encouraged learning and was a great benefactor of Bologna University.49, 95.

Bellini (Old), Jacopo (*c*.1400–70/1), Venetian painter, father of Gentile (*c*.1429–1507) and Giovanni (*c*.1430–1516).81, 82.

Bernini, Gianlorenzo (*b*.Naple, 1598 ; *d*.Rome, 1680), sculptor, creator of the baroque style which he expressed in single works and in great

architectural schemes in Rome.109, 124, 130, 133, 145, 204, 207.

Bever, Thomas, LL.D. (1725–91), scho learned in the civil law.130.

Bezozzi. Besozzi, an Italian family of virtu wind instrument players established in Par Burney heard the two eldest brothers at Tu and a nephew (oboe) in Paris.220.

Bevis [Bevans] John (1693–1771), physician astronomer: physician in London before 17 F.R.S. 1765; Foreign Secretary R.S. 1766-50.

Blaire. Blair, Dr. Hugh (1718–1800), div Edinburgh. Professor, Edinburgh Univers 1760 (Rhetoric), wrote *Critical Dissertation Poems of Ossian* (1763),172.

Blainville, Charles, Henri de (*c*.1711–*c*.17 violoncellist and teacher, best known for pretended discovery of a new mode betw minor and major (1751), the centre of m polemical writing.68.

Bologna, John of (1529–1608), sculptor, *b*.Do trained in Flanders, arrived in Italy *c*.15 worked in Rome, settled in Florence where achieved repute second only to Michelang 94, 103, 108, 111.

Bonefiani. Bonifazio di Pitati (?) (*b*.Verona, 14 *d*.Venice, 1553), Italian painter of the Vene School.128.

Bontempis. Bontempi, Giovanni A. A. (*b*.Peru *c*.1630 ; *d*.Perugia, 1705), singer compo theorist: published *Istoria musica* . . . in Per (1695).68, 144.

Boscovich, Padre Roger Joseph (1711– eminent mathematician of Ragusa, Dalma Made valuable contributions to geome astronomy, optics; foreshadowed molec theory of matter: wrote elegant Latin ve Died in Milan insane.41, 49, 60.

Bourbon, Duke of. Charles de Bourbon (14 1527), led a troop of mercenaries against R in 1527, when he was killed, by Benven Cellini, it is said.140.

Bourdelot, Pierre (real name Michon, *b*.S 1610;*d*.Abbey of Mace, 1685), Royal Physic compiled material for a history of mu worked up by his nephews and published *Histoire de la musique et de ses effets* (1715). Bradley, James (1693–1762), astronomer divine. F.R.S. 1718; Savilian Professor Astronomy, Oxford 1721, discovered muta of the earth's axis, 1748.95.

Bremner, Robert (1713?–89), Edinburgh m publisher, extended his business to Lond 1762. Published sheet and other music built up a very substantial business.22.

Brille. Bril (Brill), the name of two Flem

painters, the brothers Matheus (1550–83) and Paul (1554–1626);*b*.Antwerp, worked and *d*. Rome. Had an important influence upon the development of landscape painting.148.

rizzi. Brizio (Briccio), Francesco (1574–1623), Italian painter;*b*.Bologna; studied under L. Carracci. Worked as engraver too.100.

rook, Lord. Probably Second Earl, George (Greville) Earl Brooke of Warwick Castle, Earl of Warwick (1746–1816), F.R.S., 1767, F.S.A. 1768.30.

rydone, Patrick (1736–1818), traveller and author. Studied electricity as a young man, travelled through Switzerland making experiments. In 1767 and 1770 travelled as tutor with Mr. Beckford (William, of Somerly) and two others: Italy, Sicily, Malta. Published *A Tour Through Sicily and Malta* (2 vols) 1773 which was a great success. F.R.S. 1772(?).174, 180, 182, 193.

uononcini. Bononcini, Giovanni Battista, one of a family of musicians (*b*.Modena, 1672). A successful opera composer (Rome, Berlin and Vienna), he came to London 1720, composed in rivalry with Handel; left after 1732: later in France, Vienna and Venice.150.

aranello, see Galuppi

urnet, Gilbert, Bishop of Salisbury (1643–1715), during a discretionary absence from England visited Paris, Rome, Geneva, Strasburg, Frankfort, Heidelberg and Utrecht (1685–6) and published a narrative of his tour in 1687. 137.

ite, Lord, 3rd Earl (1713–92), Prime Minister 1762–3, President Society of Antiquaries (1780–92): a great patron of literature and the fine arts and a distinguished botanist.67.

rers, James (1733–1817), Scottish architect and archaeologist. Lived in Rome 1750–90, collected antique objects (including Portland Vase) and Italian romances (for Bishop Percy). 130, 132, 137, 139, 152, 202, 204, 209, 210, 211.

rfield, John: two organ builders of the same name, the younger was organ maker to the royal household (1770–82), *d*.1774.209.

affaride. Caffarelli (born as Gaetano Majorano, near Bari, in 1710), a castrato soprano who enjoyed a fame second only to Farinelli. He made an enormous fortune, bought a dukedom and built a palace. He died in Naples in 1783. 128, 193, 196, 197.

illiot. Caillot, Joseph, Parisian (*b*.1732;*d*.1816), an actor and singer outstanding in comic opera. 221.

almet, Dom Augustin, Benedictine scholar (*b*.Lorraine, 1672; *d*.Sénones, 1757), writer on ancient music and musical instruments.119.

Campioni, Carlo Antonio (*b*.Leghorn 1720;*d*.1793), Maestro di Capella of the Grand Duke of Tuscany, composed chamber music and music for the church.117, 119, 120.

Campognolo. Campagnola, Domenico (*b*.Padua or Venice, *c*.1482;*d.c*.1662), painter and engraver of the Venetian school, follower, (pupil?) of Titian.70.

Caracalla, Marcus Aurelius Antonius Bassianus (186–217), Roman emperor.134

Carcano, Don Francesco, man of letters, member (later secretary) of the Academy of the Transformati, a literary society in Milan: he was a correspondent of the London Baretti.48, 54, 55, 56.

Caroli, Old. Caroli, Angelo Antonio of Bologna (*b*.1701;*d*.1778), eminent musician, organist, composer of operas, oratorios and songs.99.

Carrach, Aug. Carracci. There were three C., all Bolognese: Ludovico (1555–1619), and his cousins Agostino (1557–1602) and Annibale (1560–1609). Of the three Annibale was by far the greatest. Together they founded and conducted a famous teaching academy in Bologna which trained, among others, Domenichino, Reni and Geurcino.91. 94, 100, 101, 131, 133, 134, 135, 148, 183, 184.

Caravaggio, Michelangelo Merisi da (*b*.Caravaggio 1573;*d*.Porto d'Ercole 1610). His 'naturalism' was widely influential, but raised controversy at the time. Of a violent disposition his career was marred and cut off by brawls.100, 153.

Carlin, stage name of Carlo Bertinazzi (1710–83), the last of the great Arlequins of the Comédie Italienne, and one of the last Italians to join the company, 1741.12.

Carmarthen, Lord. Francis Godolphin (Osborne) 1750–99: F.R.S. 1773. F.S.A. 1776. Succeeded his father as Duke of Leeds in 1789.202, 204.

Casali, Giovanni Battista (1715–92) of Rome, maestro di cappella of St. John Lateran, 1759 until his death. Wrote operas and church music.201, 204, 208.

Celestini. Celestino, Eligio (*b.c*.1739–1812), a Roman violin player, amongst the best of his day. Travelled to London (1772) and in German states: composed music for strings. 131, 150, 153.

Chesterfield, Philip Dormer Stanhope, fourth Earl of (1694–1773), courtier and letter writer.93.

Choiseul, Etienne François, Duc du (1719–85), French statesman: foreign minister 1758.17.

Claud. Claude Gellée (Claude Lorraine) (1600–82), *b*.near Nancy, France, he went to Italy *c*.1613 where he settled. He earned a great reputation as a landscape artist which has survived.40, 60, 75, 148.

Clifford, Lady, 'a Roman catholic dowager', sister of the Duchess of Norfolk.13, 15, 16.

Cochin, the name of a family of French engravers. Charles Nicholas Cochin II (1715–90), travelled in Italy (1749), became secretary and historian of the Royal Academy of Paris, and revised Bosse's treatise on engraving.91.

Colista, organist at St. John Lateran Rome in 1770.208, 209.

Colombo, Padre, Professor of mathematiĉs at Padua, and a great friend of the composer Tartini.69.

Cosmo (Cosimo) I (1519–74), Grand Duke of Tuscany, son of Giovanni de'Medici. He captured Siena in 1555. A harsh ruler but a patron of art and literature.125

Coreggio. Correggio, Antonia (1494, or 1489–1534), Italian painter who worked mostly in Parma, particularly in fresco.40, 60, 91, 92, 105, 183, 184, 195.

Corelli, Arcangelo (1653–1713), Italian violinist and composer, particularly for the violin. Settled in Rome under the patronage of Cardinal Pietro Ottoboni. He laid the basis on which the subsequent development of violin technique was built, and established the form of the concerto grosso.152, 177.

Corilla, Signora Olimpica, the name given to the great Improvisatrice, Maria Madalena Morelli Fernandez, of Pistoia.116, 118, 120, 128.

Corri, Domenico (*b.*Rome, 1746 ; *d.*Hampstead, 1825), singer; invited to Edinburgh 1771 to conduct the concerts of the Musical Society: settled there as publisher and singing master. 139, 152, 153, 211.

Cortona. Pietro Berrettini da Cortona (1596–1669), painter and architect, a main exponent of the Roman high baroque style. Apart from Rome he worked in Florence.105, 152, 153.

Cotton, Sir John Hynde (*d.*1752), Jacobite. M.P. 1708–52.84.

Cotumacci, Carlo (1698–1775), a Neapolitan organist and composer of church music, pupil of A. Scarlatti.192.

Couperin, Armand Louis (1725–89), Parisian organist, one of a dynasty of illustrious French musicians. He held a number of appointments and was organist to the king from 1770 to his death.16.

Crescembeni. Crescimbeni, Giovanni Mario (1663–1728), Italian poet and critic. His major work *Istoria della volgar Pesoia* (1698) is still authoritative on the history of Italian poetry. 143.

Crisp, Samuel (*d.*1783 'aged 76'), traveller, disappointed playwright (*Virginia* 1754). The failure of this play drove him to the continent,

but he returned to England in 1764. He li⟨ in retirement, a confidant of Burney and Burneys. He is said to have imported the f pianoforte into England.80.

Crispi, Abbé Pietro Maria (1737–97), Ron musician. At first a devoted amateur, he m⟨ music his profession (1765). He wrote cham music and works for the keyboard.131, 132, 1 149, 154, 207, 211.

Dalton, Richard (1715?–91), draughtsman, ⟨ graver and librarian: travelled in 1749 throu Greece, Constantinople, Egypt; was librari keeper of pictures and antiquarian to Geo III. In 1764 he persuaded Bartolozzi to co to England as 'engraver to the king'.91.

Dauvergne, Antoine (*b.*Moulins, 1713;*d.*Lyo 1797), French violinist and composer. He ⟨ in Paris in 1739 where he wrote instrumer music and later ('50s) operas: in 1753 important *Les Trocqueurs*, an interlude w sung recitative, instead of spoken dialog appeared.220.

Davis, John, of Watlington, Norfolk. He is ⟨ corded from 1728 to 1778, when his will ⟨ proved. Among other property he had interest in the 'Angel' at Watlington.141.

Deane, Hugh Primrose, Irish landscape pain (1740/50–84). He went to Rome under patronage of Henry, 2nd Viscount Palmers⟨ in 1770; he was a member of the Florent⟨ Academy (1776), but was back in London 1777.130.

Delany. Delane, Solomon (*b.*Edinburgh 17 *d.*1784?), self-taught landscape painter. travelled through Italy and settled in Ro⟨ exhibiting in London at the Royal Acader Was in Germany in 1780.130, 132.

Diderot, Denys (1713–84), French savant and ⟨ of the most versatile and important writers the 18th century: best known as animator of *Encyclopédie.*222, 225.

Dolce, Carlo (1616–86), Florentine portraitist ⟨ painter of religious subjects.100.

Dominichini. Domenichino (Domenico Zampi⟨ *b.*Bologna, 1581;*d.*Naples, 1641), one of outstanding pupils of the Carracci. He wor⟨ in Rome and Naples: was a pioneer in landsc⟨ painting.40, 92, 98, 131, 135, 141, 148, 149, 1 185, 192, 204.

Donatelli. Donatello, Donato de Nicolo di B⟨ Bardi (*c.*1386–1466), Florentine sculptor, greatest before Michelangelo and one of most influential artists of the 15th century.⟨

Doni, Giovanni Battista (*b.*Florence, *c.*15 *d.*1647), in the service of Cardinal Barbe⟨ (1622) and travelled through Europe with h⟨ He studied ancient mucic and published

Compendio . . . a treatise on the ancient Greek music (Rome) in 1635, followed by *Annotazioni,* an extension of the first, in 1640 (Florence). *De praestantia* appeared in 1647 (Florence).68, 98, 115, 152.

ᴐrset, John Frederick Sackville, third Duke of Dorset (1745–99). Among other distinctions a member of the Hambledon club, a patron of cricket and one of the committee which framed the laws of the Marylebone club.130, 131, 132, 135, 139, 142, 144, 149, 151, 153, 201, 202, 204, 205, 207, 210, 211.

ᴐtel Figlio. Dothel, Nicolas, flautist *b.*in Germany at the beginning of the 18th century, the son of a skilful flute player. About 1750 he was in the service of the Grand Duke of Tuscany. He composed for the flute.120.

ᴜrante, Francesco (1684–1755), Neopolitan composer and outstanding teacher. A pupil of Gaetano Greco and A. Scarlatti, he was in turn head of the Conservatorio San Onofrio and of Santa Maria di Loreto (1742). His pupils included many of the outstanding Italian composers of the age.172, 175, 192.

ᴚhard. Eckardt, Johann Gottfried (*b.*Augsburg, *c.*1735;*d.*Paris, 1809), an outstanding keyboard player, a composer, and the leading miniature painter of his time.222.

ᴛori, Guglielmo, a celebrated tenor singer born in Italy about 1740, he was for a time in the service of the Elector Palatine. Had a tremendous success at Padua (1770). In 1771 he went to Stuttgart where he died in the same year.68.

ᴚrinelli, Carlo Broschi, detto (*b.*Apulia, 1705; *d.*Bologna, 1782), a phenomenal castrato singer renowned throughout Europe: his singing the only solace to the melancholy Philip V of Spain (1737), at whose court he enjoyed considerable political influence. He returned to Italy in 1760.88, 90, 91, 92, 96.

ᴚo, Francesco (*b.*Naples *c.*1685; still living in 1740), composer, particularly of opera. In 1730 he was director of the Conservatorio de' Poveri at Naples.172.

ᴇrrara, Duke Alfonso di. Alphonse (II) d'Este, Duke of Ferrara, succeeded Hercule II d'Este 1559) and died 1597.136.

ᴚbietto. Fibietti, Abate 'an excellent tenor' (B).106

ᴌorini, Giovanni Andrea (*b.*Pavia, 1704 ; *d.* Milan, 1778), an important composer of church music, pupil of Leo at Naples.47, 60.

ᴚrmian, Carlo Guiseppe Conte di (1716–1782), Governor General of the Province of Lombardy for Maria Theresa of Austria (1759). He was a great patron of learning and the arts.49,51, 54, 55, 58, 59, 60, 61, 113.

ᴚscher, Johann Christian (*b.*Freiburg, Breisgau,

1733;*d.*London, 1800), a celebrated oboist. He had great success on the continent before coming to London in 1768.12.

Fontana, Gregorio (*b.*Tyrol, 1735;*d.*Milan, 1803), physician and one of the foremost mathematicians of Europe: in 1735 he succeeded Boscovich in the Chair of transcendental mathematics at Pavia.96.

Foote, Samuel (1720–77), actor and playwright, celebrated as a mimic and writer of satire. Built the new Haymarket Theatre (1767) and held it until 1777.159.

Forester. Forrester, James (*b.*Dublin, 1729 ; *d.* Rome, 1775). He went to Rome soon after 1752. He exhibited at the Royal Academy (London) in 1761 and Dublin in 1765. He was known for his carefully etched plates of Italian scenes.181.

Fortrose. The style of Lord Fortrose was used by the heirs apparent of the Earls of Seaforth, Mackenzie. Kenneth Mackenzie (*b.*1744, Edinburgh) would have been 7th Earl but for his grandfather's attainder. M.P. 1768–74, F.R.S. 1772, F.S.A. 1776. Died on passage to East Indies with Seaforth Highlanders 1781.164, 180, 181, 182, 191, 193, 195, 196, 197, 204.

Fracastorius. Fracastoro, Girolamo (1483–1553), Italian physician and poet, learned in medicine and belles-lettres.66.

Franceschini, Cavaliere Marc Antonio (1648–1729), painter, founder of the Upper Italian School, worked in fresco, oil and tempera in many towns.100.

Franchi, Giovanni Pietro, Italian composer, *b.*mid 17th century, still writing in 1697.152, 208.

Franklyn. Franklin, Benjamin (1706–90). American statesman and scientist.41, 95.

Frej. Frey, Johann Jacob (*b.*Lucerne, 1681 ; *d.* 1752), line engraver settled in Rome.205.

Frereon. Fréron, Elie Catherine (1718–76), French critic, controversialist, poet.221, 222.

Fritz, Gaspard (*b.*Geneva, 1716;*d.*Geneva, 1782), distinguished violinist and composer for that instrument and the harpsichord: he also wrote chamber music for various combinations of instruments.29, 30.

Furino. Furini, Francesco (1600–46), Florentine painter celebrated alike for his easel pictures and his mural decoration.105.

Fuselier. Fuseli, Henry (Johann Heinrich Fussli) (*b.*Zurich, 1741;*d.*London, 1825), son of a painter, he was ordained priest (1761). He studied art in Berlin 1763, came to England as hack translator (1764) and was encouraged by Reynolds to become a painter: 1770 went to Rome for 8 years. R.A. 1790, Professor of Painting at the Academy 1799.99, 131, 132.

Gabrieli. Gabrielli, Catterina (1730–96), Roman, one of the most accomplished, capricious and beautiful singers of the 18th century. Daughter of Prince Gabrielli's cook (known therefore as Cochettina) she made her debut in 1747. She sang throughout Italy, in Vienna, in Russia. Her arrival in London was 'the most memorable musical event of the season of 1775 and 1776' (B).193.

Gafori, Franchino (Franchinus, Gaforius) (1451–1522), Italian priest and writer on music. He wrote a number of books the best known of which was *Practica Musicae*, Milan, 1496.58.

Galilei. Galileo, Galilei (1564–1642), Italian experimental philosopher and astronomer, a native of Pisa.118.

Galuppi, Baldassare (*b.*Island of Burano near Venice, 1706; *d.*Venice, 1785), known as Buranello from his birthplace, writer of comic operas. Maestro di cappella at St. Mark's, Venice (1762), director of the Conservatorio degli Incurabili (1762). His music, popular in England, was played throughout Europe including Russia.64, 75, 77, 80, 82, 83, 176, 223.

Garrick, David (1716–79) foremost English actor and theatre manager of his day; friend of all the Burneys.15, 22.

Gassman, Florian Leopold (*b.*Brüx, 1729; *d.*Vienna, 1774), Bohemian composer. Ran away from home, pupil of Father Martini at Bologna, best known as a composer of Italian operas (23). The Emperor Joseph II appointed him court Kapellmeister in 1772.45.

Geminiani, Francesco (*b.*Lucca, 1667; *d.*Dublin, 1762), renowned violinist and composer. Came to England in 1714, made a great reputation and went to Ireland (1733–40), giving concerts and teaching. In London until 1749, Paris until 1755 when he returned to London; and to Ireland in 1759. His compositions extended the technique of violin playing; his *Art of Playing the Violin* was his greatest legacy.177.

Giardini, Felice de (*b.*Turin, 1716; *d.*Moscow, 1796), eminent violinist, composer of chamber music for strings. He toured Germany 1748, appeared in London 1750, where he remained as performer, teacher, opera impresario until 1784, when he retired to Italy. He returned to London in 1790, but his ventures failed and he left for Russia.19. 47, 161, 194, 196, 197.

Giordano, Luca (1632–1705) a Neapolitan painter. He worked in Rome, Florence and Spain: the ceilings in the Escorial are probably his best works.68, 182.

Giotto, Ambrogio di Bondone (1266/7–1337), Florentine painter who in his naturalism and humanity laid down many of the guide lines for the subsequent development of painting.10, 210.

Glareanus, Henricus (1488–1563), a famo teacher of music, so called after Glarus birthplace, his real name being Loris (Loritu Friend of Erasmus and of many others of t leading scholars of the day. The *ΔΩΔEK. XOPΔON Dodecachordon*, treating of Gre and church modes also preserved examples 15th and 16th century music; it was publish in Basle (1547).68.

Godimel. Goudimel, Claude (*c.*1510–72) Fren composer, first of Roman Catholic chur music and later on his becoming a Protesta (*c.*1557, 1558) of psalm tunes. He also wro secular songs.140.

Goldoni, Carlo (1707–93), Italian dramati *b.*Venice, trained in the law (1731), his first pl was put on in Verona in 1734. He develop comedy of manners to high art. He went Paris in 1761, where he died.114, 222.

Grettry. Grétry, André Ernest Modeste (*b.*Lièg 1741; *d.*Montmorency, 1813), eminent compos of operas, the son of a violinist. He trained Liège, where he started to compose, and Ita before he went to Paris, produced a brillia opera-comique, *Le Huron*, in 1768 and thenc forward enjoyed a career of distinction.22, 2 220, 221.

Greville, Richard Fulke, son of the Hon. Algern Greville and grandson of Fulke Greville, fi Lord Brooke (1554–1628) friend of Sir Phi Sidney.159.

Grimm, Friedrich Melchior, Baron von (172 1807) German writer, through Rousseau (174 associated with the Encyclopédists, a brillia controversialist in literature, music and phi sophy.222.

Guadagni, La Signora, 'a most pleasing singer a elegant actress' (B). She was the sister Gaetano Guadagni, a famous male contralt *b.*Lodi, *c.*1725; *d.*1792.46.

Guarducci, Tommasso (*b.*Montefiascone, *c.*1720) castrato singer of the first class. He sang London in 1766 and stayed until 1769, when returned to his birthplace.88, 106, 113, 12 128, 131, 162, 201.

Guercini. Guercino, Il ('squint-eyed'), nickname Giovanni Francesco Barbieri (*b.*Cento, Ferra *c.*1591; *d.*Bologna, 1666), one of the leadi Baroque masters.60, 91, 100, 101, 131, 14 152, 153.

Guglielmo, della Porta (*b.*Porlezza; *d.*Rome, 157 sculptor, restorer of antique statues, a architect.134.

Guido, d'Arezzo (Guido Aretinus) (*b.*Arezz *c.*990), a great teacher and innovator in music theory and practice. His most important work *Micrologus* was written in about 1025. He is best known as the inventor of the stave.54, 220.

ido. Reni, Guido (1575–1642), Italian painter of the Bolognese school, and much influenced by Raphael.40, 60, 69, 91, 92, 100, 101, 111, 131, 134, 141, 142, 144, 148, 151, 153, 182, 184, 206.

alley, Edmund (1656–1742), English astronomer. Savilian Professor of Geometry, Oxford, 1703, Astronomer Royal 1720. Gave his name to the best known of the periodic comets.95.

amilton, Mrs. Catherine, wife of William Hamilton. She was a member of a substantial Welsh family, married Hamilton in 1758 and died in 1782. A woman of sympathetic personality she was also one of the best harpsichord players of the day.22, 176, 177, 183, 193, 195, 204.

amilton, William (1730–1803), diplomatist and archaeologist, the son of Lord Archibald Hamilton. From 1747 to 1758 in the Army, he was an M.P. (1761) and then appointed plenipotentiary at Naples (1764–1800), where he practised diplomacy, studied volcanoes and acquired a remarkable collection of antiquities. He was created a Knight of the Bath in 1772, F.R.S. 1766.159, 168, 170, 175, 176, 178, 179, 180, 181, 182, 183, 187, 192, 193, 195, 198, 199.

andel, George Frederick, composer (b.Halle, Lower Saxony, 1685; d.London, 1759). First visited England 1710 (*Rinaldo* 1711) and again in 1712, when he settled to exert lasting influence on English music and musical life.150, 175, 177, 201.

anway, Jonas (1712–86), traveller and philanthropist. In 1743–5 travelled down the Volga and the Caspian Sea to Persia. He published an account of his travels in 1753.57.

arpe, Jean-François de la (1739–1803), celebrated French critic, native of Paris.225.

arris, James (later Earl of Malmesbury), 1746–1820, statesman. He was the son of James ('Hermes') Harris: represented his country in Madrid (1769 chargé d'affaires, minister 1771), Berlin 1772–6, and elsewhere.119.

asse, Faustina Bordoni (1693–1783), native of Venice. A famous soprano singer, she came of a noble Venetian family, made her debut in 1716. She won a great reputation in Europe, and first sang in London in 1726 in Handel's *Alessandro*. She married the German composer Johann Adolph Hasse in Venice in 1730.v.

asse, Johann Adolph (b.Bergedorf, Hamburg, 1699 :d.Venice, 1783), one of the most prolific and successful composers of opera in the 18th century. He was a fine singer and was highly

proficient on the keyboard. In addition to opera he wrote oratorios, cantatas, masses, symphonies and other instrumental music.77, 84, 176, 203.

Heideggar. Heidegger, John James (b.c.1659/60; d.1749), a Swiss(?) by birth, arrived in England in 1707. Managed the Opera House 1708–34 and was in an operatic partnership with Handel 1729–34, at the Haymarket Theatre.193.

Hobart, George (1732–1804), third Earl of Buckinghamshire, succeeded 1793. Member of Parliament, and for a time manager of the opera in London.161.

Holbach, Baron Paul Henri Thyry d' (1723–89), philosopher, born in the Palatinate. A man of great wealth, he kept open house in Paris for the liberal thinkers of the day. He wrote on philosophy: on chemistry and mineralogy. He contributed to the *Encyclopédie*. In his own life he was 'simply simple'.20, 221, 222, 224, 226.

Hudson, Robert (b.London, 1732;d.Eton, 1815), organist and composer. In his younger days he sang at Ranelagh and Marylebone Gardens.127.

Hume, David (1711–76), Scottish philosopher and historian. He wrote a number of important books before 1763 when he accompanied Lord Hertford to Paris: he was secretary to the embassy (1765) and was for a time chargé d'affaires. He spent the last years of his life in Edinburgh.59.

Immola. Imola, Francucci, Innocenzo da (1494–1550), Italian painter who worked principally in Bologna. His work had much of the quality of Raphael, and his landscape and perspective had affinity with that of Leonardo da Vinci.95, 100.

Jenkins, Thomas, a native of Devonshire, died at Great Yarmouth in 1798. He accompanied Richard Wilson to Rome where he was in 1763. He turned banker and dealer in antiquities and fled to England in 1798 when the French occupied Rome and confiscated his property. 131, 132, 133, 139, 148, 152, 171, 205, 209.

Johnes, Mr., probably Thomas Johnes of Haford (1748–1816).204.

Jommelli, Niccolò (b.Aversa, 1714;d.Naples, 1774) Italian composer who excelled both in opera and in music for the church.47, 130, 164, 172, 175, 176, 177, 183, 185, 192, 196, 202, 223, 224.

Keeble (Keable), William, a painter known to have been at the St. Martin's Lane Academy, London, in 1754.99.

Keen, Sir Benjamin (1697–1757), diplomatist, consul 1724, ambassador 1727–39, 1748–57 at Madrid, where he died.92.

Keppler (or Kepler), Johannes (1571–1630), German astronomer, one of the founders of modern astronomical mathematics.68.

Kircher, Athanasius (*b*.Geisa, near Fulda, 1602;*d*. Rome, 1680), German polymath who spent most of his life in Rome: best known for his *Musurgia universalis* . . . (Rome 1650), a mixture of rubbish and valuable information on musical sound, composition etc, with extracts from the music of the 17th century.95, 212.

Kohaut, Joseph (*b*.Bohemia, 1736;*d*.Paris, 1793) and Charles (dates not known) were both excellent players on the lute. Joseph was also a successful composer of operas-comiques. Charles visited Paris and made a great impression with his playing.224.

Lacombe, Jacques (1724–1811), Parisian bookseller. He had trained and practised as an *avocat* before turning to book-selling. He was also an author, and a compiler and editor of dictionaries and encyclopaedias.16.

Lalande, Joseph-Jerome Le Français de (*b*.Bourg, Ain, 1732;*d*.Paris, 1807), celebrated astronomer. As well as publishing a great deal on his own subject he wrote *Voyage d'un français en Italie en 1762–66* (Venice and Paris 1769) to which all subsequent travellers in Italy and writers on Italian travel were much indebted.86, 92, 104, 105, 124, 194, 198, 205.

Lampugnani, Giovanni Battista (*b*.Milan, *c*.1706) composer of operas and concocter of pasticcios. He came to London in 1743 as director of the Italian opera and was later in Milan, 1779–89. 53, 60.

Lambertazzi, members of a Bolognese family and head of the Ghibelline Faction in the 13th century.93.

Lanfranc. Lanfranco, Giovanni (*b*.Parma, 1582; *d*.Rome, 1647), pupil of the Carracci. He excelled as a decorator of the interior surfaces of church domes.148, 153, 182.

Lasso, Orlando (Orlande de Lassus, *b*.Mons, Belgium, 1530 or 1532;*d*.Munich, 1594). He was a prolific writer of music for two or more voices of a quality shared only by that of Palestrina.117.

Latilla, Gaetano (*b*.Bari, *c*.1713;*d*.Naples, 1789), writer of operas, church music and string quartettes.75, 77, 80, 82, 128.

Legros, Joseph (*b*.Monampteuil, Laon, 1730;*d*. Rochelle, 1793), an operatic tenor. In 1777 he became managing director of the Concert Spirituel (Paris) until its dissolution (1791).220.

Leo, Leonardo [Lionardo Oronzo Salvatore de Leo] (*b*.S. Vito degli Sclavi, 1694;*d*.Naples, 1744), distinguished Italian composer famed for his sacred music and comic operas. His counterpoint much influenced subsequent developments: his comic operas were full of wit and sparkling music.130, 172.

Leonardo da Vinci (1452–1519), musician, painter, sculptor, engineer and architect, a man of universal intellect.46, 57, 58, 60, 61, 105, 153.

Leopold, The Emperor Leopold I (1640–1705) Holy Roman Emperor.145.

Lidarti, Christiano Giuseppe, a well-known violoncellist and composer of chamber music some catches and glees, and a musical drama 172, 215, 218.

Lincoln, Lord (1720–94), Henry Fiennes Clinton afterwards Pelham-Clinton, Duke of Newcastle under Lyme, Earl of Lincoln.202 204.

Linley, Thomas II (*b*.Bath, 1756;*d*.Lincolnshire 1778), a violinist and composer, son of Thomas Linley I. He was trained by his father and Boyce, and by Nardini in Florence as a violinist He met Mozart in Italy and the two boy became greatly attached: Mozart later wrote of Linley as a musician of genius cut off before his prime.114, 116, 117, 118, 128.

Liotard, Jean Etienne (1702–89). Swiss painter renowned for his portraits, enamels and pastels 22.

Lonardino. Ferrari, Leonardo, called Lonardino a Bolognese artist, painter of drolleries and carnival festivals. He also painted historical subjects and works for churches.100.

Lotti, Antonio (*c*.1667–1740), Venetian organist composer. He enjoyed the highest reputation as a composer of music for the church. He also wrote successfully for the stage. He was organist (1704) and maestro di cappella (1736) at St Mark's, Venice. He had a number of pupils who in their turn were illustrious musicians.77.

Lotti. Loth (Lotto, Carlotto), Johann Carl, painter (*b*.Munich, 1632;*d*.Venice, 1698), worked in many cities, notably on church altar pieces and mythologies.68.

Lully, Jean Baptiste [originally Giovanni Battista Lulli] (*b*.Florence, 1639;*d*.Paris, 1687), naturalised French 1661; violinist, brilliant composer of dances, ballets, church music and particularly opera: he was the first composer of legitimate French opera. A great favourite with Louis XIV he acquired musical supremacy at court and amassed a fortune.150, 221.

Lumisden (or Lumsden), Andrew (1720–1801), a staunch Jacobite who escaped to France after the Battle of Culloden. He was in Rome in 1757, was secretary to both the Old and Young Pretender. He was allowed to return home in 1773. In 1797 he published *Remarks on the Antiquities of Rome*.15, 19, 22, 130.

Macer, Aemilius (*d*.16 B.C.) of Verona, author of Latin didactic poems, which have not survived. He was a friend of Virgil and of Ovid.66.

was an artist known for water colours which he did of scenery and life along the St. Lawrence River, Canada, in the late 18th century. He was active in Canada between 1781 and 1795, as an army officer attached to the office of the Director of Surveys for British North America, and later as Deputy Surveyor General.120.

rgolese. Pergolesi, Giovanni Battista (*b*.Jesi, Ancona, 1710;*d*.Pozzuoli, 1736), Italian composer, violinist and church organist. He excelled in comic opera and his *La Serva Padrona* ('The maid as Mistress') had enormous success throughout Europe and was the immediate cause of the quarrel between the supporters of French and Italian opera in Paris.192.

rti, Giacomo Antonio (1661–1756), Bolognese, one of the most distinguished church composers of the period. He also wrote operas.98, 121.

rugino, Pietro (*c*.1445/50–1523), Italian painter, one of the masters of the Umbrian School. Worked in Florence (probably with Verrocchio). and Rome (Sistine Chapel frescoes 1481). From *c*.1500 to *c*.1504 Raphael was a pupil in his shop. 92, 105, 124, 147, 185, 202.

saro, Domenico, a Venetian instrument maker, active in the mid-16th century. He made a harpsichord for Gioseffe Zarlino based on a new theory of tuning formulated by Zarlino himself. 119.

trarch, Francesco Petrarca (1304–74), one of the greatest Italian lyric poets whose work had wide influence throughout Europe: he advocated the study of the ancient literatures of Greece and Rome and was one of the progenitors of the revival of learning.57, 192.

ilidar. Philidor, François André Danican (*b*.Dreux, 1726 ; *d*.London, 1795), the most accomplished of a family of French musicians and a brilliant chess player. He wrote highly original comic operas performed in Paris, and spent long periods in England where he was greatly esteemed as a chess player and as a writer on chess.222.

c. Carlo Le Picq, a dancer celebrated throughout Europe.68.

ccinni, Nicola (*b*.Bari, 1728;*d*.Passy, 1800), one of the most popular of Italian opera composers. His greatest success was *La buona figliola* ('The good girl') based upon Richardson's *Pamela* which was performed throughout Italy and Europe with acclaim. In 1776 he went to Paris, where his supporters clashed with those of Gluck and a war of pamphlets was sustained between them for years.47, 107, 159, 161, 164, 171, 172, 174, 176, 177, 179, 180, 192, 196, 203, 223.

nturicchio (Pintoricchio), Bernardino (*b*.Perugia

c.1454;*d*.Siena, 1513), Italian painter of the Umbrian School, active in Perugia (1481) and Rome (Sistine Chapel 1481/2) where he assisted Perugino.124.

Pirenese. Piranesi, Giovanni Battista (1720–78), Venetian architect who went to Rome in 1740 and recorded the city, ancient and contemporary, in hundreds of etchings. His most creative work lay in a series of plates representing imaginary prisons (*Carceri d'Invenzione*, begun *c*.1745).132, 204, 205, 211.

Pisari, Pasquale (1725–78), a Roman composer eminent as a writer of church music. He also had a fine bass voice.206, 211.

Piscetti, Giovanni Battista (1704–66), Italian composer for the theatre and church, harpsichordist and sometime organist of St. Mark's, Venice. From 1737 to 1740? he was in London, at Covent Garden and the King's Theatre.118.

Pordenone, Giovanni Antonio (1483/4–1539), a north Italian painter, whose work was influenced by the Venetians, particularly Titian: whom he rivalled.81.

Potenza, Pascall (*b*.Naples, *c*.1735), a distinguished castrato soprano. He sang in London in 1761 and subsequently had great success as an opera singer particularly in Padua (1770). He was singing at St. Mark's, Venice, as late as 1797 but the date of his death is unknown.68.

Poussin, Gaspard (1615–75), a painter who was born Dughet. He was brother-in-law to Nicolas Poussin whose name he adopted, and whose pupil he was (*c*.1630–3). He was very popular in the 18th century.

Poussin, Nicolas (*b*.Villers, 1594;*d*.Rome, 1665), French painter. After some training in Paris he went to Rome in 1624 where he lived for the rest of his life apart from two years (1640–2) when he returned to France to undertake a commission for Louis XIII. Called the Raphael of France he excelled in landscape and historical subjects.148, 153.

Prenestine, the Latin form of Palestrina.139.

Préville, Pierre Louis Dubus (1721–99), French actor who excelled in comedy. He joined the Comédie Française in 1753 and retired in 1786. 21, 22.

Priestley, Joseph (1733–1804), theologian and man of science, principally remembered for his work on oxygen and other gases, the 'father of modern chemistry who never would acknowledge his daughter'.41.

Pugnani, Gaetano (1731–98), a native of Turin, celebrated violinist, composer and teacher. He went to Paris in 1754, stayed a year, travelled Europe, made a long visit to London but was in Turin in 1770. In his teaching he transmitted

[241]

Pugnani—*contd*
the pure grand style of Corelli, Tartini and Vivaldi which was perpetuated in the art of his most celebrated pupils.205, 207.

Pythagoras (*c*.570–*c*.504 B.C.), Greek philosopher who is said to have discovered the numerical ratios which determine the principal musical intervals.225.

Racine, Jean (1639–99), great French dramatist, and historiographer to Louis XIV.225.

Rameau, Jean Phillipe (*b*.Dijon, 1683 ; *d*.Paris, 1764) eminent composer and writer on the theory of music, organist and harpsichord player. He held various appointments as organist as a young man, worked out revolutionary ideas on harmony (*Nouveau système* . . . 1726) and at 50 turned to writing for the stage (*Hippolyte et Aricie* 1733) where he excelled (*Castor and Pollux*, his masterpiece, was written in 1737).76.

Raphael, Raffaello Sanzio (*b*.Urbino, 1483; *d*.Rome, 1520) one of the greatest painters of all time, great in achievement and great in his abiding influence.40, 91, 92, 98, 101, 105, 111, 124, 131, 133, 136, 146, 147, 151, 152, 183, 184, 202, 206, 210.

Reiffenstein, Johann Friedrich (*b*.1719), artist and critic of painting, friend of Mengs.207.

Ricci, Sebastiano (*b*.Belluno, 1660 ; *d*.Venice, 1734). He studied at Venice and Bologna, and worked in many Italian cities and Vienna. He was in England (1712–16). ('The Resurrection', Chelsea Hospital Chapel.)68, 184.

Rinaldo di Capua, born early 1700/1710, an amateur musician who later turned professional. His harmony was less than strong, but his operas have dramatic power and melodic beauty.150, 154.

Robertson, George (*b*.London, *c*.1742 ; *d*.1788) English artist: studied drawing in London; went to Italy with W. Beckford and worked at landscape painting. He travelled to Jamaica and produced a collection of paintings and drawings which he exhibited in London (1775) without success. He fared better as a drawing master. 111, 181, 188.

Robertson, Alderman Robert, Mayor of Lynn in 1747 and 1761.69, 91.

Romanelli, Giovanni Francesco (1610?–62), a painter from Viterbo, in Italy, trained in Rome by P. da Cortona, some of whose work he finished. He also worked in France.128.

Romano, Giulio (Giulio Pippi de Giannuzzi) (*b*.Rome, 1492;*d*.Mantua, 1546), Italian painter and architect, favourite pupil and chief assistant to Raphael.65, 92, 147, 152, 153, 183, 184.

Rosa, Salvator (*b*.nr. Naples, 1615;*d*.Rome, 1673),

Italian poet, painter, etcher, actor, satirist and musician. As a painter he produced dramatic landscapes and battle scenes, as a musician, airs and cantatas.60, 100, 105, 141, 145, 148, 15 152, 211.

Rousseau, Jean Jacques (1712–78), born in Geneva writer and philosopher, in the 18th century be known as a composer, a music copyist an writer of musical polemics.16, 17, 27, 59, 22 222, 223.

Roussier, Pierre Joseph (1716–90), Frenc writer concerned with the problems and theo of harmony and with the music of the ancient He also studied Chinese music.18, 22, 88.

Rubens, Sir Peter Paul (*b*.Siegen, 1577;*d*. An werp, 1640), 'Prince of painters', the suprem artist in northern Europe of his age.40, 60, 9 105, 111, 153, 184.

Russell, Alexander, Dr. (1715?–68), physician an naturalist. In 1740 he went to Aleppo a physician to the English factory: returned t London in 1755 and in 1756 published *Natur History of Aleppo*. F.R.S. 1756.68.

Sacchi, Andrea (1599–1661), Roman artist, pup of Albani and the Carracci. Based on the wor of Raphael his painting exhibits the class strain of the baroque.151, 152, 153.

Sacchi, Barnebite Giovenale (*b*.Milan, 1726 *d*.Milan, 1789), a learned writer on music subjects, and biographer of Carlo Brosch (Farinelli) and Benedetto Marcello.58, 60.

Sacchini, Antonio Maria Gaspere (*b*.Pozzuol 1734;*d*.Paris, 1786), Italian composer of opera oratorios, motets. Trained as a singer an violinist, he produced his first opera in 1762 i Rome and later travelled. He arrived in Londc in 1772 where he had some success. He settle in Paris (1782?/4?). A graceful and elegan composer.68, 76, 83, 127, 176, 223.

St. Amant. Saint-Amans, Louis Joseph (*d* Marseilles, 1749;*d*.Paris, *c*.1820), French com poser, best known for his operas, but also teacher, and writer of church music, cantata and music for the piano. The work Burne heard was *Alvar et Mincia*.12.

Salviate, Francesco (1510–63), a Florentin mannerist artist, pupil of Andrea del Sart Painter of portraits and allegories.108.

San Martini. Sammartini, Giovanni Battist (*b*.1700/1;*d*.1775), a Milanese composer prolif in works for instruments and voices.

His elder brother, Giuseppe (Gioseff (*b*.Milan, *c*.1693;*d.c*.1750), was a virtuoso obc player. He composed for flutes and violin a well as for concerted instruments. He was i London in 1723? and was active there as late a 1744.47, 56.

Sansovino, Andrea, born Contucci (1460–1529), a Florentine sculptor who developed under the influence of Raphael and the antique. Worked in Florence, Portugal and Rome.69, 77.

Santarelli, Giuseppe (1710–90), Italian musician. He sang in the Sistine Chapel, composed a certain amount of music and wrote a history of the music of the church in two volumes, only one of which was published (Rome, 1764). It is thought that the second volume, advocating certain reforms, aroused displeasure in high places and was not published on this account. 136, 139, 140, 141, 144, 145, 149, 152, 203, 206, 211.

Sarto, Andrea del (1486–1530), Italian painter of the Florentine School, born as Andrea d'Agnolo, son of a tailor. Famed for the correctness of his drawing, he painted in the fully developed Renaissance style.105, 106, 148, 192.

Scamozzi, Vincenzo (1550–1616), Italian architect born at Vicenza. After study in Venice, Rome and Naples, he settled in Venice where, Palladio being dead, he became chief architect. He also wrote on architectural subjects.77.

Scarlatti, Alessandro (b.Palermo, 1659;d.Naples, 1725), Italian composer, one of the great figures of operatic history. He worked principally in Naples, but he had success too in Rome and Florence. He also wrote cantatas, oratorios, masses, madrigals and chamber music. Cavaliere (knight) 1716.150, 172, 176, 192, 201, 202.

Scarlatti, Giuseppe Domenico (1685–1757), Neapolitan musician, son of Cavaliere Alessandro Scarlatti: a composer of operas on the pattern of his father, but outstanding as a keyboard player, and composer for the harpsichord. His playing technique underlay much of the subsequent development of keyboard method. 93, 192.

Schidone. Schidoni (or Schedone) Bartolomeo (1560–1616), born at Modena, a painter who studied with the Carracci, but worked under the influence of Corregio. He was active in Parma and Modena: left works in fresco, easel portraits and paintings of religious subjects.184.

Serre, Jean-Adam, painter, chemist and musician, born at Geneva in 1704. He went to Paris in 1751 and wrote (1752) a critique of Blainville's third mode. He wrote other theoretical works on harmony in Paris and later in Geneva.29.

Shepherd, the Rev. Antony (1721–96), Plumian professor of astronomy at Cambridge 1760, F.R.S. 1763, master of mechanics to George III, 1768.50.

Short, James (1710–68), optician, trained in classics and divinity in Edinburgh, turned to mathematics and (1732) to the manufacture of reflecting mirrors in glass and metal for telescopes. F.R.S. 1737.49.

Smith, Father, the name usually given to Bernard Schmidt (b.Germany, c.1630;d.1708), an organ builder who came to England in 1660 with two nephews as his assistants. His organs were very fine and he was appointed Organ maker in Ordinary to the King.209.

Smith (Mr.), John Christopher (1712–95), musician, was the son of J. C. Schmidt of Anspach, who came to England to become Handel's treasurer. He was 13 when he became a pupil of Handel: he later had lessons from Dr. Pepusch and T. Roseingrave. He wrote operas and oratorios and when Handel became blind Smith acted as his amanuensis, taking down music at the composer's dictation.154.

Snetzler, John (b.Passau, c.1710;d.London, end of 18th century/beginning of the 19th century), organ builder. His instruments were of very high quality: among the best was the one he built for Lynn Regis (Burney's Norfolk home) in 1754.209.

Sodoma, Il (Giovanni Antonio Bazzi) (b. Vercelli, 1477 ; d.Siena, 1549), Italian painter of the Milanese school. He settled in Siena and worked in Rome and many other cities on frescoes in churches and palaces.125.

Soffi, Pasquale (b.Lucca, c.1732;d.Lucca, 1810), composer of religious music and an organist.114.

Sole, Giovanni Gioseppo (Giuseppe) dal (1654–1719), a Bolognese painter, of the Venetian school.148.

Spagnoletto. Lo Spagnoletto was the name by which Jusepe de Ribera, a Spanish painter (b.Jativa, Valencia, 1591;d.Naples, 1652) was known. He settled in Naples in 1616. He painted religious subjects and mythologies in strong light and shade.60, 64, 92, 100, 182.

Spinello, Aretino (b.Arezzo, active 1373–1410), Italian painter in the tradition of Giotto. He worked in fresco in Arezzo, Florence, Pisa and Siena.118.

Squarcialupi, Antonio (d.Florence, c.1475), a famous Florentine organist and composer, an esteemed contemporary of Dufay.104, 120.

Stradella, Allesandro (c.1645–82), Italian composer, probably born in Naples, died in Genoa. He wrote operas and cantatas (religious and secular), motets, madrigals and string concertos. He was a fine violinist and sang beautifully.139.

Strange, Robert (1721–92), Scottish engraver. Under the influence of Isabella Lumisden (whom he later married) Strange joined the Jacobite cause and engraved a bank note for the 'coming dynasty'. He studied in Paris (1749), was back in London in 1750, an artist of the

an unrivalled source book, has been translated into most languages.118.

Veini, Franchino (b.Como, 1738;d.Milan, 1820), a mathematician and musical theorist: his *Dissertazione sui principii dell' armonia musicale e poetica* ... was published in Paris (by Molini) in 1784.59.

Veronese, Paolo Caliari or Cagliari (b.Verona, 1528;d.Venice, 1588), Italian painter of the Venetian School, renowned for huge decorative compositions, crowded with people in dramatic architectural settings.60, 65, 66, 67, 68, 74, 77, 81, 82, 92, 105, 148, 183, 184.

Vignola (Giacomo Barozzi or Barocchi) (1507–73), Italian architect. He succeeded Michelangelo as the architect of St. Peter's, Rome, and designed the Escorial in Spain.40.

Vinci, Leonardo (b.Strongoli, 1690; d.Naples, 1730), composer of operas, serious and comic; he also wrote church music as pro-vice-maestro of the royal chapel, Naples, 1725 to his death. 192.

Vitruvius, Pollio, saw military service (c.50–26 B.C.) under Julius Caesar and Augustus, best known for his treatise on architecture: important as having influenced the principles of building at the Renaissance.66.

Vivaldi, Antonio, Italian violinist, b.Venice in the later half of the 17th century. Appointed maestro de' concerti at the Ospedale della Pieta in 1713 and remained there until his death in 1743. Best known as a virtuoso performer, he also composed for the violin and his concertos were much studied, not least by J. S. Bach who arranged sixteen for various combinations of instruments.177.

Voltaire, Jean François Marie de Arouet (1694–1778), French philosopher, dramatist and historian.23, 30, 221, 225.

Volterra, Daniele de (Daniele Ricciarelli) (b. Volterra, 1509;d.Rome, 1566), Italian painter, sculptor and architect, a follower of Michel-angelo.150, 151.

Walpole, the hon. Robert, second son of Horatio or Horace, first Baron Walpole of Wolterton (1678–1757); younger brother of Sir Robert Walpole, first Earl of Orford.15, 17.

Weymouth, Lord, Thomas, 3rd Viscount and 1st Marquess of Bath (1734–96).199.

Winckelmann, Johann Joachim Winckelmann (1717–68), the first of the great German art historians. He was the leading authority of his time on the arts of the ancients, particularly of the Greeks. He published his *On the Imitation of Greek Works* in 1755 and his history of ancient art, an epoch-making book, in 1764.148, 171.

Wren, Sir Christopher (1632–1723) astronomer, investigator of medical, anatomical and other scientific problems, prominent member of the circle which was incorporated as the Royal Society, architect (c.1663) prepared a scheme for rebuilding London after the Great Fire (1666) and was appointed surveyor general and principal architect for rebuilding the whole city.6.

York, Cardinal, Henry Benedict Maria Clement, Cardinal York (1725–1807), grandson of James II of England, styled by the Jacobites Henry IX. Took orders at an early age, obtained rapid preferment in the Church (Cardinal 1747) assembled a fine collection of works of art and books, but suffered cruelly at the hands of the French in 1799. Almost destitute and living on the proceeds of the sale of his silver plate, he was succoured by George III who made funds available to him.209.

Young, Dorothy, a friend of the Burneys at Lynn, author of a volume of *Translations from the French* (Lynn, 1770). Burney subscribed for six copies.225.

Zanotti, Giancalisto (1734–1817), a Bolognese musician. He was a pupil of Father Martini and wrote much music for the church. He also wrote for the stage. His uncle, Francesco Maria Zanotti (1692–1777), a Bolognese savant, professor of philosophy and geometer, also wrote on musical problems.88, 99.

Zarlino, Gioseffe (b.Chioggia, 1517; d. Venice, 1590), one of the most learned musical theorists of the 16th century. Deeply versed in languages, mathematics, theology and science, he made music his principal study. In 1565 he was elected first maestro di cappella at St. Mark's, Venice, and composed services for the church and other music. His lasting fame rests on three treatises *Institutioni armoniche* (1558), *Dimonstrationi armoniche* (1571) and *Sopplimenti musicali* (1588), all published in Venice in which he investigated the nature and theoretical structure of music.118, 119, 172.

Zink. Zincke was the name of a family of celebrated miniature painters and painters in enamel of whom the best known was C. F. Zincke who came to England in 1706 (d.1767) and who enjoyed European fame. The man referred to by Burney may have been Paul Francis Zincke who died in 1830 at a great age. He was a copyist and sometimes sold his copies as originals–hence his label 'wicked old Zincke'.152.

Zuccari. Zuccaro (Zuccari, Zuccheri). Taddeo Zuccaro (1529–66), and Federico (c.1540/3–1609) were Italians, brothers, who worked as painters together and separately on many considerable schemes of decoration in churches and palaces. 136.